Industrial Adjustment in Sub-Saharan Africa

EDI Series in Economic Development

EDI Series in Economic Development

Maxwell L. Brown, *Farm Budgets: From Farm Income Analysis to Agricultural Project Analysis.* Johns Hopkins University Press, 1979.

James E. Austin, *Agricultural Project Analysis.* Johns Hopkins University Press, 1981.

William Diamond and V. S. Raghavan, editors, *Aspects of Development Bank Management.* Johns Hopkins University Press, 1982.

J. Price Gittinger, *Economic Analysis of Agricultural Projects.* 2d ed. Johns Hopkins University Press, 1982.

Gerald M. Meier, editor, *Pricing Policy for Development Management.* Johns Hopkins University Press, 1983.

J. D. Von Pischke, Dale W. Adams, and Gordon Donald, editors. *Rural Financial Markets in Developing Countries.* Johns Hopkins University Press, 1983.

J. Price Gittinger, *Compounding and Discounting Tables for Project Analysis.* 2d ed. Johns Hopkins University Press, 1984.

K. C. Sivaramakrishnan and Leslie Green, *Metropolitan Management: The Asian Experience.* Oxford University Press, 1986.

Hans A. Adler, *Economic Appraisal of Transport Projects: A Manual with Case Studies.* Revised and expanded edition. Johns Hopkins University Press, 1987.

Philip H. Coombs and Jacques Hallak, *Cost Analysis in Education: A Tool for Policy and Planning.* Johns Hopkins University Press, 1987.

J. Price Gittinger, Joanne Leslie, and Caroline Hoisington, editors, *Food Policy: Integrating Supply, Distribution, and Consumption.* Johns Hopkins University Press, 1987.

Gabriel J. Roth, *The Private Provision of Public Services.* Oxford University Press, 1987.

Rudiger Dornbush and F. Leslie C. H. Helmers, editors, *The Open Economy: Tools for Policymakers in Developing Countries.* Oxford University Press, 1988.

Industrial Adjustment in Sub-Saharan Africa

edited by
Gerald M. Meier and William F. Steel
with the assistance of Richard J. Carroll

Published for The World Bank
Oxford University Press

Oxford University Press

NEW YORK OXFORD LONDON GLASGOW
TORONTO MELBOURNE WELLINGTON HONG KONG
TOKYO KUALA LUMPUR SINGAPORE JAKARTA
DELHI BOMBAY CALCUTTA MADRAS KARACHI
NAIROBI DAR ES SALAAM CAPE TOWN

Manufactured in the United States of America
First printing February 1989

Library of Congress Cataloging-in-Publication Data

Industrial adjustment in sub-Saharan Africa / edited by Gerald M.
Meier and William F. Steel with the assistance of Richard J. Carroll.
   p.   cm.—(EDI series in economic development)
''Published for the World Bank.''
Bibliography: p.
Includes index.
ISBN 0-19-520784-X
   1. Industry and state—Africa, Sub-Saharan.   I. Meier, Gerald M.
II. Steel, William F.   III. Carroll, Richard J.   IV. World Bank.
V. Series.
HD3616.A357153   1989
338.967—dc 19   88-38386

Contents

Preface

The articles in this book express a variety of viewpoints on industrial development and adjustment in Sub-Saharan Africa. Previously unpublished as well as published material from the World Bank analyze the Bank's experience with a wide range of countries. Other sources are also represented, particularly on strategic and theoretical issues. Although social and political factors are important constraints on industrial adjustment, the book is primarily concerned with economic strategies, experiences, and reforms. It focuses on policies that governments can control, regardless of external circumstances, rather than on the unfavorable international economic trends and other events that necessitate industrial adjustment.

The articles are grouped according to the central issues that policymakers need to address in designing industrial strategy. These issues are highlighted in the overview (chapter 1) and in the introductory section to each part. The purpose is to guide the reader in analyzing the impact of key policies and institutions. The selections have been substantially condensed (without the use of ellipses to signal omissions) and in some cases edited to emphasize the main themes of policy change and institutional responsiveness. Also included are technical notes on key concepts, a glossary intended to make the material more accessible to noneconomists, two summaries of relevant economic and industrial data on individual countries, and a selected bibliography. Country names are retained as originally cited in the articles, even though the names may have changed subsequently. (Ivory Coast is now Côte d'Ivoire and Upper Volta is now Burkina Faso.) "Africa" is used throughout the text to refer to Sub-Saharan Africa.

The idea for this book grew out of a series of seminars in 1984 on industrial policy in Sub-Saharan Africa. High-level officials from African countries met with representatives of the international development community at seminars in Annapolis, Berlin, and Dakar. These seminars were sponsored by the Economic Development Institute and the Industry Department of the World Bank and the German Foundation for International Development. They provided an illuminating interchange of experiences with industrial development and approaches to future industrial policy in Africa. Many participants urged that the seminars' papers and presentations be followed up with further work to bring together information on different countries' experiences, and this book is the result. The hope is that greater understanding of common problems will help individual countries to adapt future industrial policies to their particular conditions and objectives.

The editors are grateful to Barbara de Boinville and Phillip Sawicki for editing the text and to Leslie Helmers, Harinder Kohli, and Kemal Dervis for guiding the work in its early stages. The work has benefited greatly from comments provided by outside reviewers and by Paul Ballard, M'Hamed Cherif, Francis Colaço, David Davies, Christian Duvigneau, Ravi Gulhati, Tariq Husain, Michel Wormser, and other World Bank Staff. Special thanks are also due to the word-processing unit of the Industry Development Division and to Carmen Peri and other staff of the Economic Development Institute for prompt and excellent word-processing service.

Gerald M. Meier
William F. Steel
Richard J. Carroll

June 1988

Abbreviations

ACP	African, Caribbean, and Pacific countries (associated with the European Economic Community under the Lomé Convention)
ADB	African Development Bank
Africa	Refers to Sub-Saharan Africa
APPER	Africa's Priority Program for Economic Recovery 1986–90
CEAO	West African Economic Community (Communauté Economique de l'Afrique de l'Ouest)
CFA(F)	Communauté financière africaine (franc)
CGE	computable general equilibrium (model)
c.i.f.	cost, insurance, freight (import price)
CPD	Country Policy Department (World Bank)
CPI	consumer price index
DFC/DFI	development finance corporation/institution
DRC	domestic resource cost
EACM	East African Common Market
ECA	Economic Commission for Africa
ECOWAS	Economic Community of West African States (same as CEDEAO, Communauté des Etats de l'Afrique de l'Ouest)
EEC	European Economic Community
EER	effective exchange rate
EPC	effective protection coefficient
EPD	Economic Projections and Analysis Department (World Bank)
EPR or **ERP**	effective protection rate
EPZ	export processing zone
f.o.b.	free on board (export price)
GATT	General Agreement on Tariffs and Trade
GDP	gross domestic product
GNP	gross national product
IBRD	International Bank for Reconstruction and Development (the World Bank)

ICOR	incremental capital-output ratio
IDA	International Development Association (affiliate of the World Bank)
ILO	International Labour Organisation
IMF	International Monetary Fund
ISIC	International Standard Industrial Classification
LDCs	less developed countries
LPA	Lagos Plan of Action
MNC	multinational corporation
NGO	nongovernmental organization
OAU	Organization of Africa Unity
OECD	Organisation for Economic Co-operation and Development
PEs	public enterprises
PPP	purchasing power parity
PTA	Preferential Trade Area for East and Southern Africa
QRs	quantitative restrictions
R&D	research and development
RBI	resource-based industries
REER	real effective exchange rate
SAL	structural adjustment loan
SDR	Special drawing rights (a monetary unit valued on the basis of the weighted relative values of a number of major currencies)
SFA	Special Facility for Africa
SITC	Standard International Trade Classification
SMEs	small- and medium-scale enterprises
SOEs	state-owned enterprises
SSA	Sub-Saharan Africa
SSEs	small-scale enterprises
TFP	total factor productivity
TNC	transnational corporation
UDEAC	Central African Customs and Economic Union (Union Douanière et Economique de l'Afrique Centrale)
UMOA	West African Monetary Union (Union Monètaire de l'Afrique de l'Ouest)
US$** or **$	United States dollars
VAWP	value added at world prices
WPI	wholesale price index

Glossary

absolute advantage The ability of a country to produce a tradable commodity at an absolutely lower real cost than another country (see technical note A).

absorptive capacity The ability of an economy to use additional resources (such as investment or aid) efficiently without their productivity falling below a minimum level.

Africanization Replacing expatriate staff with African personnel, especially at the management level. Also used with the country name, for example, Zambianization.

agroindustry An industry that is based on processing an agricultural raw material. Occasionally used to refer also to an industry that produces inputs into agriculture, for example, tools.

balance of payments A record of a country's credit and debit transactions with foreign countries. The current account includes exports, imports, and transfers for "invisibles" (tourism, remittances, interest payments, services such as insurance and shipping); it provides a common measure of surplus or deficit. The capital account consists of inflows and outflows of money, including the source of finance for any deficit incurred on the current account.

black, or parallel, market The exchange of domestic for foreign currency outside the officially sanctioned system, with the buyer of foreign exchange paying a premium above the official exchange rate. The black market rate indicates the scarcity value of foreign exchange under prevailing constraints, which may be above the equilibrium rate necessary to clear demand and supply for foreign exchange if there were no constraints.

border price The unit value of a good at a country's border, used to measure the true economic value of tradable goods used in production. For importable goods (whether or not actually imported), it is the c.i.f. price; for exportables, the f.o.b. price.

capital goods Goods such as equipment and buildings that are used over time in the production of other goods (as distinct from inputs that are directly consumed in production).

capital-intensive   A production method is capital-intensive if it uses relatively more capital per unit of output, or per unit of another input such as labor, than other methods to which it is being compared (for the same good or an industrywide average).

comparative advantage   Country A possesses a comparative advantage over country B in the production of a tradable commodity if the ratio of the cost of that commodity relative to the cost of other tradable commodities is lower in A than in B (see technical note A).

computable general equilibrium (CGE) model   A model that simulates the implications of policy changes on the functioning of an economy by representing the behavior of the various economic agents, institutions, and the market-clearing process.

direct controls   Administrative allocation of resource, goods, and services; restrictions on their movement or prices (see technical note G).

domestic resource cost   The opportunity cost in terms of domestic resources of generating a net unit of foreign exchange through either exporting or import substitution (see technical note C).

dualistic economy   An economy characterized by two sectors using widely different production techniques (for example, capital-intensive, "modern" industry versus labor-intensive, "traditional" agriculture) with little direct linkages and interactions between them and, as a result, different factor productivities and wages.

economic rent   An amount paid or received that is over and above the cost of producing a good or service as a result of its scarcity or a distortion in the economy, such as import restrictions (see technical note G).

economies of scale   A more than proportional increase in output when inputs are increased; that is, a lowering of the unit cost of production when the scale of production is raised.

effective exchange rate   (a) The amount of local currency per unit of foreign exchange for a given type of foreign exchange transaction (for example, imports of a particular commodity or category of goods), which takes into account the impact of all measures that directly affect the domestic price of traded goods. (b) The average of a currency's bilateral nominal rates of exchange with other currencies, weighted by their importance in trade (see technical note F).

effective protection rate   The percentage increase in domestic value added in a given activity above value added at world prices that is permitted by the structure of protection, which is broadly defined to include all measures that directly affect the domestic prices of traded goods (see technical note C).

efficient production   Production at minimum cost in terms of the resources used, when the resources are valued at their opportunity cost. In other words, the resources involved would not yield a higher value of output if released to their best alternative use.

equilibrium exchange rate   The relative price of tradables to nontradables that is consistent with long-run sustainable external equilibrium and compatible with both internal equilibrium (full employment) and the long-run desired level of protection (see technical note E).

infant industry An industry in which average costs are expected to fall over time as it gains experience with production (see technical note B).

informal sector Economic activities (for example, petty trade, artisanal manufacturing) that take place outside the formal registration and tax system.

inputs, intermediate goods Goods that are directly used up in the production of other goods, whether or not they are physically transformed; they range from raw materials to components for assembly.

labor-intensive A production method is labor-intensive if it uses relatively more labor per unit of output, or per unit of another input such as capital, than other methods to which it is being compared (for the same good or an industrywide average).

nominal In current prices, without adjustment for inflation (or for price differentials between countries, in the case of the exchange rate).

nontradables Goods and services that are normally available (or can be sold) only on the domestic market because costs of external transport are prohibitive (as in the case of sand and water) or because they are tied to the location (as in the case of rent and repair services).

opportunity cost The additional output that would result from an additional unit of resource in its most productive use. The opportunity cost of the resources involved in one production process is the conceptual loss in the additional output those resources could have produced in their best alternative uses in other activities.

overvalued exchange rate Valuation of local currency above the equilibrium exchange rate; that is, an exchange rate that results in an unsustainable external deficit, internal disequilibrium, or excessive protective measures (see technical note E).

parallel market See ''black market.''

privatization Transfer of ownership from public to private hands, whether by outright sale of an enterprise or by sale of shares in it. Also refers to the process of increasing the share of privately owned production in a sector.

purchasing power parity The exchange rate that keeps the relative purchasing power of two currencies equal; that is, a base-year exchange rate adjusted for differential rates of inflation in the two countries (see technical note E).

quantitative restrictions (QRs) Regulations that set limits on the amount of goods that can be imported; for example, bans on certain goods, quotas, and import licensing. Restrictions on foreign exchange transactions may also serve to limit imports.

rationalization Combining, closing down, or expanding capacity in different plants or subsectors in order to achieve a structure of production that is consistent with current or expected demand and competitive conditions.

real Adjusted for the effects of price changes over time (or of price differentials between countries, in the case of the exchange rate).

real exchange rate A measure of the degree of competitiveness of domestically produced goods relative to goods produced in the rest of the world, such as the nominal exchange rate times the ratio of the foreign to the domestic price level. Also defined as the domestic relative price of tradable to nontradable goods (see technical notes E and F).

self-reliance   Maximum utilization of indigenous physical and human resources to reduce dependence on foreign resources, whereas self-sufficiency implies meeting needs *exclusively* through indigenous resources (see section 2.2).

terms of trade   The rate at which exports are traded for imports; for example, the ratio of the export price index to the import price index (see technical note E).

total factor productivity (TFP)   An index that sums up the partial productivities of all inputs in a production process. Changes in TFP measure changes in the efficiency with which all inputs are jointly utilized in production, for example because of technical change (see technical note D).

tradables   Goods and services that customarily enter into international trade, whether or not they are imported or exported in a particular case.

value added   The difference between the value of output and the cost of the inputs used to produce it. Depreciation and overhead are included in the input costs; labor is not (see technical note C).

Part I

Issues and Experience

Part I provides the context for the analysis of policy adjustment and institutional issues in parts II and III. Chapter 1 is a general overview of the principal themes, issues, and conclusions that emerge from the readings. It also explains the rationale for the selection of articles and cross-references the themes to the readings in which they are discussed. Chapter 2 introduces some of the basic strategic issues of industrial development in Africa, and chapter 3 relates them to typical experiences observed in a number of countries. A recurrent theme is the linkages between industry and other sectors, principally agriculture, both as an explanation for past failures and as orientation for future strategy (sections 2.1, 2.4, 3.3, and 3.6). Another important issue is the potential conflict between the objective of self-reliance (sections 2.2 and 2.4) and the negative impact on productivity and efficiency of policies that overprotect the domestic market (sections 2.3, 3.3, 3.4, and 3.6).

In reading the discussions of strategy in chapter 2, it is useful to distinguish between *objectives*, the *strategy* that defines areas of emphasis in pursuing those objectives, and the *policies* that are the means of implementing strategy and achieving the desired ends. For example, the objective of self-reliance may lead countries to adopt a strategic orientation toward import substitution and processing of domestic resources. But the readings suggest that policies, such as high protection of domestic industry and public investment in intermediate goods industries, may work counter to goals, such as decreasing dependence and raising export earnings (sections 2.4, 3.3, 3.5, and 3.6). Part II will take up further the question of adjusting policies so that the incentives they create are consistent with objectives.

Significant industrialization has taken place in Sub-Saharan Africa since 1960, and there is considerable scope for renewed growth in the future (sections 2.1, 3.1, and 3.2). But the general pattern has been one of stagnation or decline in output after an initial period of growth and diversification—even though the reasons for decline vary from country to country. The persistent lack of sufficient foreign exchange to meet the input requirements of the industrial sector points to trade and exchange rate policies as an important area for industrial development and highlights the issue of whether manufactured exports can be increased significantly through such reforms (sections 2.1, 3.2, 3.3, and 3.5).

1

Overview

The readings in this book reflect a shift in the focus of industrial policy in Sub-Saharan Africa from stimulating the creation of capacity in the 1960s to encouraging the effective use of resources in the 1980s. Growth and structural transformation were the objectives of policies in the early postindependence period that promoted the rapid expansion of investment in industry. Recently the attention of African leaders has turned to achieving a more efficient pattern of industrial development (section 4.4).

The shift in industrial policy derives from five important and interrelated themes that recur through the reviews of experience in chapters 3 and 4. First, despite initial rapid expansion, industry has gone from a leading to a lagging sector. Second, a substantial share of capacity created under "infant industry" policies exceeds the demand in local markets and appears unlikely to be competitive in international markets. Third, the growing gap between industry's imported input requirements and the availability of foreign exchange has further contributed to the underutilization of capacity. Fourth, unfavorable international economic trends and slowness in adjusting the macroeconomic policies associated with import-substitution industrialization strategies have caused export earnings and domestic production to stagnate. And fifth, inefficiencies in resource use and continuing subsidies in public industries have been a budgetary drain in a period when resources have become increasingly tight.

These problems have been exacerbated by external shocks and deteriorating export earnings, and they cannot be solved simply through additional resources (section 4.3). Most countries cannot readily mobilize substantial new resources at present, either internally or from international assistance. How, then, can industry be encouraged to play the dynamic role that African leaders continue to emphasize (section 2.2)?

The importance of policy reform was recognized in Africa's Priority Programme for Economic Recovery 1986–90, presented by the Organization of African Unity (OAU) to the United Nations Special Session on the Critical Economic Situation in Africa. The program urged improved incentives for

3

producers and higher productivity in public enterprises as part of the "radical change in development priorities" needed to revive growth. The premise underlying the current emphasis on industrial restructuring is that more effective use of existing resources can both raise production quickly in the short term and lay a stronger foundation for industry to sustain growth in output, employment, and productivity over the long term.

This book addresses an adjustment strategy for Africa from the viewpoint of industry, although not in isolation from economywide issues.[1] Indeed, Africa's experience demonstrates that industrialization cannot succeed when the policies that promote it conflict with the complementary development of agriculture and exports. Industrial development must be based on a sound strategy of agricultural development to take advantage of dynamic linkages on both the supply and demand sides, as the readings in part I and chapter 5 emphasize. The adjustment experiences of several countries (chapter 6) indicate that industrial restructuring can best be approached through prior macroeconomic adjustments in the exchange rate, trade policy, and monetary and fiscal policies. The selections concentrate on medium-term restructuring through policy changes and measures to stimulate a supply response. Space limitations preclude in-depth coverage of some important elements of long-run industrialization strategy—such as human resources, infrastructure, technology, and financial intermediation—except as possible constraints on the adjustment process. Although an improved international environment for economic and other types of assistance would greatly enhance the chances for success, the book focuses on domestic policies. It stresses the importance of establishing a suitable policy and institutional climate regardless of external conditions.

A key issue raised in the readings is the appropriate degree of intervention in the allocation of resources as opposed to reliance on market forces. Although the selections in chapter 4 represent different viewpoints, they conclude that government interventions to promote industrialization in Africa have often been counterproductive and excessive. Without denying the importance of market imperfections, Michael Roemer (section 5.3) makes the case that industrial efficiency and responsiveness can be enhanced by moving from direct intervention and regulation to a more decentralized economic management based on market signals, even in a socialist context. Because the public share of industrial ownership in many countries is large— as a result of direct investment and nationalization—the state needs to define clearly its role in the future development of productive sectors in order to improve its effectiveness (chapter 10).

The process of adjustment in industry, as in the economy as a whole, raises the question of how to promote equity and manage change for maximum economic impact and minimum adverse political consequences (section 5.6). Elements of industrial adjustment with highly visible short-run costs include eliminating price controls and laying off workers in overstaffed or inefficient industries (often in the public sector). Even though these actions may lead to

---

1. Throughout the text "Africa" refers to Sub-Saharan Africa.

increased supplies and employment in the long run, the negative political impact may prevent the government from sustaining reform (section 6.6). The cases of Côte d'Ivoire (section 6.5) and Ghana (section 6.6) suggest that a phased approach to lowering protection can help cushion the shock to producers. Experience is lacking, however, with programs to ensure that the poor do not bear the burden of adjustment and to provide alternatives for dislocated workers.

This chapter provides the context for analyzing the issues that arise in renewing industrial development in Africa. The analysis is based on, but not limited to, the selections presented in this book; the bibliography contains other readings that can throw further light on relevant experiences with industrialization and reform. An effort is made to draw generally applicable conclusions, but it is recognized that industrial adjustment strategy must be adapted to each country's situation, needs, and objectives. Developing a strategy for industrial adjustment and recovery involves three main steps, which are reflected in the three parts of this collection: first, analyzing experience to understand the reasons for past industrial performance and policy; second, adjusting policies to provide positive incentives for efficient resource use; and, third, making sure that a strong supply response is supported by the business environment, infrastructure, and institutions.

1.1 The African Experience with Industrialization

Appropriate strategies for industrial adjustment are as diverse as the African economies themselves. Although many countries have common problems, generalizing remains a difficult and hazardous undertaking. As background to the readings, this section reviews some of the features of African economies that affect their industrialization potential and patterns (see also sections 2.1, 3.2, and 4.1).

The Context

The more than forty Sub-Saharan countries contrast widely in resources and size (see appendix table A), ranging in population from more than 90 million people (Nigeria) to 0.1 million (São Tomé and Principe); in area from 2.5 million square kilometers (Sudan) to 1,000 square kilometers (São Tomé and Principe); and in gross national product (GNP) per capita (1986 data) from $3,080 (Gabon) to $120 (Ethiopia). Although the region is richly endowed, its resources are distributed extremely unevenly among countries. The contrast between the richness of Africa's resources and the poverty of much of its population presents a striking challenge both to its still relatively young governments and to the international development assistance community.

The diversity of African countries is reflected in the relative sizes of their industrial sectors (see appendix table B). When defined to include mining, petroleum, construction, utilities, and manufacturing, *industry* ranges from 63 percent of gross domestic product (GDP) in Gabon to 4 percent in Uganda, with a regional average of 29 percent.[2] *Manufacturing,* when defined narrowly to avoid the uneven distribution of mineral resources, reflects more commonality, ranging between 21 percent (Zimbabwe) and 2 percent (Guinea), with most countries falling into a narrow range around the average of 8 percent. This average is well below the manufacturing share of 14 percent for all low-income countries and 20 percent for all middle-income countries worldwide.

Sub-Saharan African economies generally have limited scope for benefiting from economies of scale through industrialization for domestic consumption because of the small economic size and isolation of their markets (Nigeria being the principal exception). Small market size is a function of low income per capita and of the large number of countries with small populations. Total Sub-Saharan GDP (about $200 billion) is comparable with that of Spain, although its population (380 million) is about ten times as large. Total manufacturing output (about $16 billion in 1980–81) is only a quarter that of Brazil or General Motors and two-thirds that of India. High transport costs are the result of the geographic isolation of landlocked and island countries, the lack of well-developed transport infrastructure between and even within countries, and low population density. Although these costs provide natural protection for domestic industries, they also raise the cost of obtaining spare parts and services and inhibit specialization to serve a wider market beyond national boundaries.

African economies tend to be more vulnerable than those of other developing regions because they rely heavily on primary production and trade. Agriculture commonly accounts for over 70 percent of the labor force and 30 to 60 percent of GDP, except in the mineral-exporting countries, which typically have 15 to 25 percent of GDP in mining and oil extraction.[3] Exports account for 21 percent of GDP in Sub-Saharan Africa compared with 14 percent in low-income countries as a whole (excluding India and China), although few African countries have achieved significant manufactured exports. One or two primary commodities commonly account for as much as two-thirds of export earnings. In the absence of effective buffer arrangements, fluctuations in international commodity prices have a direct impact on these relatively inflexible economies. Incomes are therefore strongly affected by fluctuations in climate and prices; droughts have been particularly devastating to many already fragile economies over the past twelve years.[4]

Colonialism has profoundly influenced culture and economic structure in the countries of Sub-Saharan Africa (except Ethiopia and Liberia). The partition of Africa into small, often ethnically diverse states and the lack of infra-

2. World Bank, *Financing Adjustment with Growth in Sub-Saharan Africa, 1986–90* (Washington, D.C., 1986), annex table 3 (1983 data); and Industry Development Division data base. The discussion of industry in this chapter (and in most of the readings) relates primarily to manufacturing, although the policies and conclusions generally are relevant to industry broadly defined. The term ''manufacturing'' is used when it is important to distinguish it from other industrial subsectors.

3. World Bank, *World Development Report 1987* (New York: Oxford University Press, 1986), annex tables 3, 5, and 32 (1985 data); Industry Development Division data base.

4. For further analysis, see World Bank, *Accelerated Development in Sub-Saharan Africa: An Agenda for Action* (Washington, D.C., 1981).

structure linking those states make achieving economies of scale through industrialization particularly difficult. Colonial policy, except in some settler colonies, was directed more at the growth of export and import trade than at developing the domestic economy (sections 2.2 and 4.1).

Objectives and Strategies of Industrialization

When most Sub-Saharan countries attained independence in the early 1960s, they saw industrial development as the way to move from the colonial pattern of heavy dependence on imported manufactures and primary exports and to achieve rapid growth and modernization. Greater self-reliance through the substitution of domestic for imported manufactures and the increased processing of local materials has consistently been the goal of African leaders' industrialization efforts.[5] Furthermore, industry offered the possibility of a relatively rapid growth of output both through rising productivity with the introduction of modern technology and methods and through the replacement of imports and the proportionately greater increase in demand for manufactures than for primary products as incomes rise. Hopes were also high that industry would absorb a substantial share of growing urban labor supplies.

In line with these objectives, the basic strategy for African industrialization during the 1960s and 1970s was to give incentives and protection for investment in industrial capacity, especially for products previously being imported. This strategy was consistent with economic development thinking at that time, which emphasized capital accumulation and import substitution on the Latin American model. (Various strategic orientations are discussed in chapter 2.) Replacing imports was a logical way to achieve rapid growth, because import suppliers were willing to invest in local production to protect their markets and because proven demand already existed. Marketing locally made goods was also a source of pride to countries that previously had depended on Europe for all their manufactures. But the illusion of reduced dependence on imports was subsequently dispelled by the inability to maintain production when exports fell and imported inputs became scarce (sections 2.3, 3.1, and 3.3).

Direct public investment in industry was another common element of most African industrialization strategies after independence (sections 3.3, 4.2, and 4.3). State ownership—a central feature of countries, such as Ghana, Tanzania, and Zambia, that emphasized a socialist approach to development—was present to at least some degree virtually everywhere. Public investment was considered to be the most direct way to increase capacity while reducing

5. See Kwame Nkrumah, *Africa Must Unite* (New York: International Publishers, 1970); Organization of African Unity (OAU), *Lagos Plan of Action for the Economic Development of Africa, 1980–2000* (Geneva: International Institute for Labour Studies, 1981); and Economic Commission for Africa (ECA), OAU, and the United Nations Industrial Development Organization (UNIDO), *A Programme for the Industrial Development Decade for Africa* (New York: United Nations, 1982).

6. The Ivory Coast is now called Côte d'Ivoire in English as well as in French. The previous name is retained in articles written before 1986.

reliance on foreign companies and nonindigenous residents, given the perceived lack of domestic private entrepreneurship and capital in most countries. Even governments following market-oriented strategies—as in Côte d'Ivoire (section 6.5),[6] Malawi (section 7.6), Nigeria (section 6.3), and Senegal (section 3.5)—have intervened strongly through various trade, financial, and other incentive policies and through public sector investments.

Since most of the population is still in smallholder agriculture and administrative capacity is limited, however, even the more socialist-oriented regimes have been unable to centralize the allocation of resources successfully on a wide scale (Ethiopia is an exception; section 10.3). Interventionism in the more market-oriented countries and decentralized markets in the more statist economies show that labels can be superficial and misleading. African economic strategies should be judged by the content of the policies rather than by the political orientation of the leaders. These policies are influenced by the wide range of African cultural and political traditions. Governments respond to different interest groups, and decisions tend to be made more on pragmatic than ideological grounds.

Trends and Results

Chapter 3 describes typical experiences with industrialization. Industrial capacity and production generally grew rapidly in the postindependence period, led by foreign trading companies trying to circumvent protective barriers and by large-scale public investments in many countries. Industry grew at 14.6 percent a year from 1965 to 1973 in Sub-Saharan Africa, more than twice as fast as total GDP at 6.6 percent,[7] and it became more diversified (section 3.4). But declining growth and declining utilization of capacity in the late 1970s and early 1980s indicated that this growth was not sustainable and did not represent a real transformation in the ability of African economies to adapt to changing conditions and external shocks. Industrial production grew at only 1.4 percent a year from 1973 to 1983, one-tenth the rate from 1965 to 1973 and well below the reduced GDP growth rate of 2.1 percent.[8] Countries such as Cameroon and Côte d'Ivoire that managed to sustain higher industrial growth in the 1970s were less successful in the 1980s as their terms of trade worsened.

This stagnation reflected less a decline in investment than a decline in productivity of new investment and underutilization because of constraints on input supply (sections 3.3, 3.4, and 4.3). Industry's performance was often compromised by public policies that favored employment and large investments at the expense of productivity. For example, in Senegal (section 3.5) the manufacturing wage bill rose by 60 percent and the capital intensity of new investments doubled while industrial production fell in the 1970s.

7. World Bank, *Financing Adjustment*, annex table 3. For low-income economies, industry grew at 5.7 percent a year and GDP at 3.7 percent.
8. Ibid. For low-income economies, industry grew at 1.6 percent a year and GDP at 2.1 percent. Services was the fastest-growing sector, at 3.5 percent a year overall and 2.4 percent for low-income countries.

Contrary to the intention of the import-substitution strategy, dependence on imports increased rather than decreased (sections 3.3, 3.4, 3.6, 4.1, and 4.3) for two main reasons: the import-substitution industries tended to be highly dependent on imported capital and inputs, and food imports became increasingly necessary because of the inability of agriculture to keep pace with population growth. The bias of policies toward industrialization discouraged agricultural investment and production. For example, despite Tanzania's emphasis on self-reliance and rapid growth of industry in the late 1960s, net import substitution was negligible because of increased reliance on imports of food, capital goods, inputs, and certain consumer goods.

Analysis of African countries' experiences with industrialization (chapters 3 and 4) reveals five frequent shortcomings of the structure of production, especially in the context of food scarcity, foreign exchange shortages, and declining investment ratios:

- Overexpansion of industrial capacity relative to agricultural production and to the ability of the economy to sustain that capacity, but low share of industrial output in GDP relative to services
- Overextension of public ownership relative to the economic justification for direct public investment and to the government's financial and managerial capacity to operate industries efficiently (see also sections 10.1 and 10.2)
- Overinvestment in import-substitution industries relative to domestic demand and to the export industries needed to generate more foreign exchange earnings
- Overinvestment in final-stage consumer goods relative to investment in the processing of raw materials and in intermediate and capital goods industries needed to increase linkages with the rest of the economy
- Excessively high import and capital components in production costs relative to the economy's generation of foreign exchange and savings and to the comparative advantage of using local resources and labor (see also sections 9.2 and 9.3).

These trends and the accompanying economic stagnation in Africa are partly the result of external factors such as drought and worsening terms of trade (sections 3.4, 4.2, 4.4, and 6.4). Reversing these trends, therefore, depends partly on the willingness of the more advanced countries to expand aid and trade opportunities. Tariff and nontariff barriers in the industrial countries limit the ability of African countries to compensate for their small domestic markets by manufacturing for export. Although not addressed explicitly in this book, efforts to improve the international economic environment are an important part of a strategy to improve the conditions for long-term industrial development in Africa.

The persistence of weak performance and high costs in many of Africa's industries suggests that the policies used to implement import substitution have poorly served the objectives of growth and transformation (section 2.1 and chapter 4). The impetus for import substitution was generally provided through very high protection—determined not by an evaluation of which infant industries were desirable but by tariff policies designed to raise revenues and penalize luxury consumption and by import restrictions needed to defend exchange rates aimed at keeping import prices low (see section 2.3 and technical note B). The resulting pattern of effective protection permitted high profits in industries (such as assembly of automobiles or appliances) that used domestic resources inefficiently and yielded little net savings of foreign exchange.[9]

At the same time, production for export was discouraged by the low return on export sales because of exchange rate policies and the absence of export subsidies that would offset the high protection of domestic sales (sections 2.3, 3.2, 3.6, 4.2, and 5.5). Maintenance of fixed exchange rates to hold down import prices in the face of rapid domestic inflation led to overvalued currencies and lowered the real return to exporters in terms of the purchasing power of their local currency earnings. Low import prices also discouraged the local production of industrial and agricultural goods that could be imported and helped promote the relatively rapid expansion of retail trade, public and personal services, and similar nontraded activities that did not face import competition. Agriculture was further discouraged by the bias of protection and investment incentives toward manufacturing for the domestic market. These policies shifted the structure of production away from dependence on agriculture and exports, but stagnation in these sectors ultimately constrained industrial expansion by slowing the growth of demand and input supply.

Direct public investment helped expand industrial capacity in the intermediate and capital goods industries that the private sector neglected under an incentive structure biased toward consumer goods (for example, in Zambia, section 3.4). But strongly interventionist strategies negatively affected private industrial investment, especially in Benin, Ghana, Somalia, Tanzania, Zambia, and Zaire, countries where nationalization was a primary tool of public industrial expansion (sections 3.3 and 10.1). Furthermore, public industries were often diverted from serving the growth objective when political and social considerations, not financial and economic performance, became paramount. When politics rather than the market determined the location and size of public firms, high operating costs could result, as in Ghana's oversized mango-processing factory and its glass and shoe plants located far from materials and markets (section 3.6).

1.2 Strategy for Industrial Restructuring

African leaders continue to emphasize industrial development as the route to economic transformation and self-reliance, objectives set forth in the Lagos Plan of Action and the Industrial Development Decade for Africa (section 2.2). The problem is that a realistic strategy for implementing these objectives has not been well articulated. The desirability of increased regional cooperation is apparent (sections 2.2 and 4.4), but the prospects for achieving significant economies of scale through industrialization on an integrated regional basis remain weak (sections 2.1, 3.3, 5.4, and 5.5). Although existing policies

---

9. These were industries with low or negative value added at world prices (see technical note C).

have been biased against domestic resource use, resource-based industrialization has limited scope as a strategy for efficient development because efficiency in processing is not necessarily related to comparative advantage in producing raw materials (sections 2.4, 3.3, and 5.5). Many observers advocate making policies more favorable to exports (sections 5.1, 5.4, 5.6, and 6.4), but there is considerable doubt that industrial exports can expand to significant levels in the near future (sections 2.1 and 3.3).

Notwithstanding the discouraging performance in the past decade, the industrial sector in Africa has the potential to resume rapid growth because it is still relatively small, and existing capacity is substantially underutilized (section 2.1). Manufacturing accounts for only 10 percent of GDP in Sub-Saharan Africa compared with 26 percent in low-income countries as a whole (12 percent excluding China and India) and 17 percent in lower-middle-income countries.[10] In all but a few oil- and mineral-exporting countries, industry remains considerably smaller than agriculture.[11] Two strategic themes dominate arguments that industry can return to a more dynamic role in Africa: the importance of agriculture and the need to establish a more efficient industrial base.

The relatively large size of agriculture, and the evident failure of past policies biased against it, have led to a new consensus that recurs throughout the readings: agricultural development is an essential foundation for industrial development in Africa. Improved agricultural incentives can stimulate industry by increasing supplies of domestic raw materials and raising rural incomes. Côte d'Ivoire's strong agricultural performance in the 1960s and 1970s helped sustain industrial growth through increased supplies of domestic raw materials and higher rural demand (section 6.5). Such a stimulus, together with rising productivity, can provide the basis for sustained industrial growth, although most likely not at the rapid rates fueled by import substitution in the 1960s. Conversely, in the 1970s countries with seemingly strong industrial growth such as Ghana, Kenya, and Senegal showed that lagging agricultural development eventually deprives industry of both resources and domestic demand. Increased agricultural production, however, can soften the impact of adjustment by making food and foreign exchange more available. A sound industrialization strategy thus must be founded on complementary agricultural development.

The success of an industrial restructuring strategy also depends heavily on the performance of the financial sector. The availability of finance—working capital and investments to shift or streamline capacity—will determine firms' ability to meet transitional costs. Although this book does not address in detail the reforms that may be needed in agricultural and financial policies,

10. World Bank, *World Development Report 1987*, annex table 3. ''Low income'' is defined as less than $400 per capita in 1985.

11. Ibid. Industry's contribution to GDP exceeds agriculture's in Botswana, Cameroon, Gabon, Mauritius, People's Republic of the Congo, Senegal, Zaire, Zambia, and Zimbabwe. The shift from primary to tertiary activities, however, has been greater in Africa than in other developing areas: services account for the largest share of GDP in most African countries, with a regional average of 43 percent compared with 29 percent in all low-income countries.

their importance for industrial adjustment should not be neglected in designing a strategy.

Renewed industrial growth also will greatly depend on improving the use and allocation of resources within the sector and on increasing competitiveness in international markets. Past policies have protected inefficient as well as efficient capacity and allocated scarce foreign exchange in a way that preserves existing industrial structure. For industrial productivity and value added to grow rapidly, however, the more viable industries will need access to additional resources; often these resources will be redirected away from high-cost, uncompetitive activities, which will be allowed to die. Prospects are limited in the near future for substantial inflows of new foreign investment, which has been discouraged by economic stagnation, regulatory controls, and the inability to repatriate profits. Foreign assistance to Africa is more readily available to support reform and rehabilitation than new industrial capacity (except in exports), and in any case it has not kept pace with needs. The question, therefore, is how to alter industrial structure and improve performance without excessive dependence on inflows of additional external resources.

A strategy of industrial restructuring involves shifting resources to achieve a more productive and dynamic pattern of industrial production. Industrial structure and efficiency can be improved by redressing imbalances at three levels (section 5.2): sectoral, subsectoral, and firm.

At the *sectoral level*, a more neutral incentive structure induces resources to shift from less directly productive nontradable sectors (such as retailing and public administration) to agriculture and exports (section 5.3). In Ghana (section 6.6), the export-oriented timber and wood products sector was an early beneficiary of an economic recovery program to restore production incentives, particularly through devaluation and export incentives, and food production responded quickly to better (and less controlled) prices. For the public sector (section 10.4), redressing sectoral imbalances implies liquidating some industrial holdings to reduce the amount of public financial and managerial resources devoted to them, with a correspondingly greater role for private investors and managers. It also implies a shift toward developing infrastructure and human resources to provide a sound foundation for long-term growth.

A *subsectoral shift* toward industries with a comparative advantage in using the country's resources, and away from those whose high costs make them inefficient, requires reducing the level and variation of protection and encouraging competitive behavior (section 5.4). With reductions in imported inputs and in production for the domestic market, industrial structure is likely to shift toward exports, intermediates, and the processing of local resources, to the extent that these activities are competitive and respond to removal of negative effective protection. In Nigeria (section 6.3), exchange rate depreciation and reduced protection from quantitative restrictions led to production cutbacks in vehicle assembly and other import-based consumer durables. Agroprocessing and other industries based on domestic inputs expanded, and exports to neighboring countries diversified. Because of substantial excess capacity in many industries, resources can be shifted without necessarily reducing value added if the retained labor and capital are made more productive. For example, private manufacturing raised capacity utilization from under 40 to over 50 percent in the first year of Zambia's industrial adjustment program and reversed the declining trend in total factor productivity (section 6.6). To facilitate supply responses, however, institutional reforms may be needed so that decisions to expand, contract, enter, or exit industries are free from restrictive regulation.

In the public sector (sections 10.4 and 10.5), even when market forces play a large role in determining profitability, administrative decisions will be needed on whether to rehabilitate, retain, or liquidate firms in order to shift the structure of holdings. Government interference in day-to-day management decisions is being reduced in Ethiopia, Ghana, Senegal, and Zambia through improved systems for signaling the performance of firms and subsectors. The emphasis on objective criteria (such as profitability, existence of competitive private sector capacity, and comparative advantage) has increased. In Zambia (section 6.6), for instance, a comprehensive study of economic as well as financial profitability in both existing and prospective public industrial investments strengthened resource allocation decisions within public sector holdings. To the extent that the government administers the allocation of foreign exchange and credit for the industrial sector as a whole, a similar strategy would be needed to establish intersectoral priorities for resources. But calculating each sector's comparative advantage is a difficult task when prices remain significantly distorted. Ghana, Madagascar, Nigeria, Senegal, and Zambia are working to identify high-cost, uncompetitive facilities that can be closed down to release resources to those with greater growth potential. Nevertheless, such policy decisions have proven difficult to implement when they involve laying off workers from large public enterprises.

Firm-level restructuring is needed to make firms more competitive in a changing policy environment by lowering product cost, raising quality, improving marketing, and strengthening the capital base (sections 5.2 and 10.5). This may involve changes in production techniques, equipment, personnel, organization, management, and financial structure. Additional incentives and funding may be needed to replace outmoded equipment and to train management and staff—as, for example, in Ghana and Mauritius. To improve competitiveness in the public sector, financial and economic performance must be used as a basis for managers' firm-level decisions and for the evaluation of managers' own performance.

Restructuring on the sectoral, subsectoral, and firm levels requires both reform of the general policy environment, to provide the appropriate incentives, and complementary improvements in the regulatory and institutional framework, to facilitate the desired supply response (section 5.1). Policies that determine profit and investment incentives need to be changed so that entry and exit decisions reflect comparative advantage and efficiency of resource use. The most critical broad policy objectives are a realistic exchange rate, control over fiscal deficits, and monetary stability. Regulatory and administrative obstacles that inhibit responsiveness to change incentives should be removed, and the infrastructure and services needed to support increased production should be strengthened. Institutional reforms include orienting the internal signaling system of public firms more toward performance and making organization and management more responsive to these signals.

1.3 Policy Adjustment

Industrial performance could be improved significantly through reform and coordination of policies that affect the allocation of resources in the economy as a whole (chapter 4). Trade policies (for example, exchange rates, tariffs, quantitative restrictions, export subsidies) in particular affect the incentives to invest in industry relative to other sectors, to seek foreign or domestic markets, and to be internationally competitive (section 5.4). Price controls prevent firms from perceiving the correct production incentives (sections 7.1 and 7.5), while direct allocation of imports and other inputs lock in the existing pattern of production. Liberalization of such policies is an essential precondition for sectoral and subsectoral shifts in structure (sections 5.3 and 6.2).

Thus, complementary corrections in policy biases are needed at three levels to promote the most efficient use of resources in industry. At the *sectoral level*, past pricing, protection, and exchange rate policies have held back agriculture and export production relative to manufacturing. (Whether overall investment in manufacturing has been excessively favored depends on whether the protective effect of tariffs and special incentives has more than offset low import prices because of currency overvaluation in each case.) Adjustment of exchange rates and flexibility in response to each country's changing balance of payments position need to be complemented by export incentives and by stabilization policies to reduce the inflationary pressures that led to overvaluation in the first place. Ghana, Guinea, Nigeria, Sierra Leone, Zaire, and Zambia, as a keystone of recent reform programs, have used foreign exchange auctions to make their exchange rates responsive to market forces (sections 6.1, 6.2, and 6.6).

Among *subsectors*, distortions in the pattern of protection have encouraged overinvestment in some activities that use resources inefficiently or even lose foreign exchange, and they have discouraged activities based on local resources or export. Greater exposure of domestic industry to international competition requires easing quantitative restrictions on imports (replacing them with a combination of devaluation, tariffs, and taxes) and equalizing protection across subsectors.

At the *firm level*, incentives have favored inappropriate imported techniques rather than the adaptation of technology to local resources and conditions (sections 9.2 and 9.3). Positive real interest rates and the removal of investment incentives and exemptions for imported capital and raw materials (other than for export production) are needed to complement the impact of trade policy reforms. Interest rates have been raised and inflation lowered in Ghana and Zaire, and investment codes have been revised in Ghana, Guinea, Togo, and Zambia.

Little controversy exists on the importance of encouraging greater agricultural and export production and more efficient industrial production; the direction of adjustment is clear. The central issues are, rather, the *extent* to which resources are to be allocated through market and competitive forces—

in contrast to protection and direct controls—and the *speed* of adjustment. These issues are the focus of chapters 5 and 6.

Outward Orientation

To what extent should African economies be protected from the vagaries of international markets? Current economic difficulties are partly the result of vulnerability to external forces such as oil price rises, drought, and weak commodity prices. But analysis of Africa's experience with industrialization has demonstrated the long-term adverse effects of exchange rate and protection policies that insulate domestic economies from changing international conditions and from competitive forces (chapters 2 to 4). Structural and industrial adjustment programs adopted by Côte d'Ivoire, Ghana, Kenya, Nigeria, Senegal, and Zaire, (chapter 6) have reduced the bias against exports (or actively promoted them), lessened protection of industry at the expense of agriculture, and generally aligned domestic prices more closely with world prices. Mauritius (section 6.4) has achieved rapid growth of manufactured exports through devaluation of the rupee and complementary policy reforms to stimulate competition. Evidence from a wide range of countries suggests that growth is better sustained under policies that minimize price distortions and are "outward oriented" in the sense of exposing producers to international prices and competition.[12]

Outward-oriented policies may conflict with the objective of decreasing dependence on trade and on industrialized countries (sections 2.2, 4.1, and 4.4). The term "outward orientation," however, is usually used to indicate *neutrality* of incentives and does not necessarily mean an export-led strategy of development or increased dependence on foreign investment. The policy reform may improve allocative efficiency and promote growth in import-substitution as well as export industries, without necessarily generating export-led growth. Outward-oriented policies may not be inconsistent with a socialist approach to development (section 5.3).

Protection

For manufacturing, the negative impact of an overvalued currency on investment in the production of tradable goods has generally been offset by protection in the form of high tariffs and restricted imports of manufactures. This protection, however, was more the by-product of measures introduced for balance of payments reasons than a conscious attempt to foster specific infant industries. The resulting haphazard structure of protection has distorted incentives among industrial subsectors and further discouraged agricultural and export production. In addition, the bias toward import-using, capital-intensive subsectors and techniques of production has been reinforced by

12. Ramgopal Agarwala, *Price Distortions and Growth in Developing Countries*, World Bank Staff Working Paper 575 (Washington, D.C., 1983); Anne O. Krueger, *Liberalization: Attempts and Consequences* (Cambridge, Mass.: National Bureau of Economic Research, 1978).

conscious policies to increase industrial investment by keeping down the cost of inputs and capital (for example, through tariff exemptions, low interest rates, and investment code benefits).

Many selections emphasize reducing excessive protection to stimulate competitive behavior and making the pattern of protection more uniform to reduce biases (sections 3.6 and 5.4 and chapter 6). How to determine the appropriate level of protection is not so clear. Many of the industrial countries strongly protected their industries in the initial stages. The Republic of Korea has combined incentives for export rivalry to induce cost-reducing behavior in internationally competitive industries with restrictions to protect industries that are in their infancy. Although helping infant industries offset high start-up costs may be justified, protection tends to insulate them from the competitive forces needed to prod them to maturity (technical note B). This argues for encouraging domestic competition (section 7.2), but most African countries (except Nigeria) have markets so small that competition is limited, especially in industries characterized by economies of scale. Strong export incentives can help raise productivity over the long term, but African industrial exports are still a small share of production. Competition from imports is therefore especially critical as an incentive for firms to lower costs and raise productivity and argues for generally low levels of protection.

How low a level of protection is practicable, however, depends partly on other policies and partly on political realities. Reduced protection must be offset by exchange rate adjustment to avoid excess demand for imports (section 5.4). This poses a problem for countries in the Communauté financière africaine (CFA) franc zone, whose exchange rate is fixed to the French franc as part of the system's emphasis on monetary and fiscal stability (sections 3.5 and 6.5). Côte d'Ivoire has embarked on a five-year program of tariff adjustment to equalize effective protection around 40 percent and provide a corresponding subsidy to export industries. Domestic tax collection may need to be increased so that consumption taxes can substitute for lower tariffs (section 7.3), although tariff revenues may actually increase if the policy reforms reduce evasion and smuggling.

On the political side, two principal considerations must be weighed: on the one hand, firms may close as a result of reduced protection (sections 6.1 and 10.4); on the other hand, higher consumer prices, lower quality, and budgetary subsidies may result from efforts to maintain inefficient industries (section 7.2). Over time, the economic advantages of more efficient production and lower prices from reduced variability and level of protection are likely to outweigh the costs of adjustment. The short-term employment costs of trade liberalization may be less than is often feared, especially compared with the benefits of more dynamic growth.[13] The challenge for governments, then, is to find ways to minimize the short-term adjustment costs while convincing the public of the long-term benefits.

13. Demetrios Papageorgiou, Michael Michaely, and Armeane M. Choksi, "The Phasing of a Trade Liberalization Policy: Preliminary Evidence," World Bank Country Policy Department Discussion Paper 1986–92, 1986.

Allocation of Resources

Controlled allocation of resources—especially foreign exchange—is an issue because they are so acutely scarce. For both ideological and pragmatic reasons, African governments have tended to intervene strongly in the allocation of resources to industry (chapter 4 and section 5.4). The ideological reasons arise from the high value accruing to scarce resources and the socialist ideal of using productive resources for the common good rather than for individual gain. The pragmatic reasons include indigenous entrepreneurs' lack of access to resources through the market because of weak financial intermediation and the dominance of nonindigenous businesses.

Nevertheless, the direct allocation of imports, domestic inputs, and credit has been very costly in Africa and has not brought the efficient use of those resources or even low consumer prices (chapter 3 and sections 7.1 and 7.2). In most cases of sustained administrative allocation of foreign exchange, substantial black markets have arisen for both foreign exchange and price-controlled commodities, and the gap between official and market prices has become a major source of income for those who can exploit it. In such circumstances, devaluation of the currency is virtually unavoidable if incentives to produce tradable goods are to be restored and the pursuit of windfall gains is to be discouraged.

Ironically, the direct allocation systems that were initially introduced in response to economic difficulties are increasingly being liberalized as crises deepen, especially in the balance of payments (sections 6.1, 6.2, and 6.6). The reasons are several: these systems are very costly; they often become ineffective, as when the value of import licenses issued greatly exceeds the foreign exchange available (for example, in Zambia in the early 1980s); and reform may provide the only access to additional resources from the international community (for example, the major devaluation in Ghana in 1983). These reforms are based more on pragmatism than on a fundamental commitment to a purely market-determined system, and they are likely to be sustained only to the extent that they produce positive economic and political benefits.

Greater reliance on market forces to determine the exchange rate and domestic prices has several advantages discussed in chapters 5 to 7 and technical note G: reduced incentives for black markets, smuggling, corruption, and rent-seeking behavior; shift of high-level government personnel from detailed administrative decisions to policymaking; increased incentives for production of exports and other tradable goods and services; and profit signals that reflect shifts in demand and supply. Specific policy reforms to make resource use more responsive to market forces include shifting from quantitative restrictions to more uniform, price-determined protection through tariffs; eliminating controlled pricing and resource allocation; and allowing greater play of competition through less restrictive regulation of domestic firms as well as liberalized imports.

Bearing the Burden

If market-oriented reforms are to have an effect, firms that cannot meet increased foreign and domestic competition must be allowed to decline so that resources can shift to more efficient uses (section 5.1). The prospect of laying workers off as some firms close, however, gives governments pause, even though the dynamic effect of higher growth may increase employment over time (sections 6.1 and 10.4). Some countries, such as Ghana, Guinea, and Senegal, have tried to reduce serious overstaffing of specific public enterprises. Further experimentation is needed with positive measures to facilitate labor shifts rather than restrictive measures that prevent them.

Since liberalization measures tend to have the greatest negative impact on those who previously had access to imports and domestic products below market prices, the initial political backing of powerful (usually urban) interests is needed. Ghana tried to gain support from civil servants and other workers through large wage increases. Such strategies, however, tend to offset the real effect of devaluation and to aggravate fiscal deficits.

Although the negative effect of adjustment policies may be relatively less on low-income groups (especially farmers) than on higher-income consumers, the absolute impact cannot be ignored. Policy reforms need to be widely perceived as equitable, especially to the low-income population. In a situation of unequal economic power, market allocation of resources may have politically unacceptable implications for income distribution (section 5.6). Those with the financial resources to obtain high-cost foreign exchange may simply have been the most successful at exploiting the previous controlled regime or may represent a politically sensitive minority. Problems of both perception and economic interest may arise. Zambia's foreign exchange auction was incorrectly seen as financing luxury imports, and price liberalization was suspended following riots over the removal of subsidies from refined corn meal and the ensuing shortage of the less-processed, price-controlled roller meal (section 6.6). To ease the short-run burden of major policy changes, phased adjustment and targeted measures to alleviate poverty may be needed.

Scale and Speed of Adjustment

The costs of adjusting to a more efficient industrial structure make the speed of adjustment an important issue for policy reform (section 5.6). On the one hand, a rapid and full change in incentives is desirable to give strong signals for resource reallocation. The political will to sustain gradual reform may weaken over time if benefits are diffuse and opposition gathers momentum. On the other hand, sudden, large changes in prices may themselves hinder adjustment, as in Ghana where industrial firms had severe difficulty financing the working capital requirements of a tenfold devaluation of the currency in 1983 (section 6.6). Volatile prices also raise the political stakes by creating major shifts in income distribution.

The appropriate speed and size of policy changes in each situation depend on how readily suppliers can respond to the changes, the extent to which the opposition from losers can be muted or compensated, and the availability of internal and external financial resources. Nevertheless, four general conclusions can be drawn from the readings (sections 4.2 and 5.6 and chapter 6).[14]

14. Ibid.

First, a reform program that begins with both a clear statement of objectives and measured, sustainable actions demonstrates a commitment to reform more effectively than do sweeping changes that are likely to be reversed. Creating the perception of a change in policy direction may be more important than the size of the change. Second, phasing in the changes gives producers sufficient time to adjust and to make adjustment costs less onerous and more avoidable by spreading them over time. Third, systematic implementation of reasonable, preannounced steps helps to build confidence that reform will be sustained. Fourth, successful trade liberalization depends on complementary exchange rate, fiscal, and monetary management policies on the one hand and reduced regulatory constraints (especially on prices, investment, and imported inputs) on the other. The former are needed to provide correct economic incentives to producers and the latter to enable investors to respond quickly.

1.4 Institutional Constraints on Response to Reform

Regulatory policies can inhibit the response to new incentives if they divert entrepreneurs into less productive unregulated activities, reward rent-seeking behavior, prevent prices from reflecting relative scarcities, and constrain resources from shifting where they are needed (chapter 7). The business environment established by these policies, together with taxation policies and the general attitude of the government toward private profit, strongly influence the willingness of investors (especially foreign) to take the long-term risks necessary for industrial development.

The limited experience with reform programs (chapter 6) suggests that responsiveness to changed incentives may also be inhibited by such constraints as controlled access to or limited availability of credit and foreign exchange, inadequate physical infrastructure, scarcity of entrepreneurial and managerial ability, weak financial intermediation, and absence of adapted technology or technological know-how. The importance of these factors needs to be assessed in each situation to design a comprehensive reform package that removes institutional constraints and provides support in areas such as financial structure, infrastructure, technology, and human resources. For effective institutional reform in most African countries, it is particularly important to rethink the objectives of public industries and evaluate whether existing firms and policies are meeting them.

Business Environment

The emphasis on the direct allocation of resources, present to varying degrees in African countries' industrial policies, has resulted in an extensive system of controls on prices and imports, entry and exit barriers, and bureaucratic management of public industry (sections 7.1, 7.2, and 10.1). These regulations entrench the existing industrial structure, and opposition to removing them can be strong. But reducing the government's direct intervention may be necessary, not just to lower the administrative and economic costs of regulation, but also to restructure the economy through shifts in resources and investment.

The policy reform process described earlier is intended to provide appropriate price and profit signals. But this incentive structure may be negated or enhanced by taxes, subsidies, special incentives or exemptions, protection, regulation, and the general attitude of the government toward business activity and profits (chapter 7). Where the government has taken over private firms, as in Zaire, private investors tend to be reluctant to come forward when the government subsequently takes measures to encourage them.

Even when controls on prices and foreign exchange are eliminated, firms in Africa still face extensive regulation of investment, production, and employment decisions (section 7.1). Some degree of regulation may be justified by the opportunities for exercising monopoly power in small African markets; Malawi has tempered its capitalist orientation with extensive discretionary regulation (section 7.6). But the objectives of such regulations must be clear and their implementation nonarbitrary to minimize the negative impact on investor response. Ghana, Malawi, and Zambia have tried to improve the business environment through industrial policy statements that emphasize the role of the private sector, reform of the investment code to simplify investment procedures, and ex post monitoring instead of ex ante control of pricing and other decisions.

Besides reducing the scope and clarifying the objectives of regulatory policies, the business environment can be improved by making government interventions more transparent and automatic (sections 2.1, 7.4, and 10.5). First, the objective and the cost or benefit of taxes and regulations should be clearly stated and easy to calculate. This is particularly important when providing investment incentives (for example, by relating tax reductions to objectives such as encouraging employment and phasing them out over a specified period). Second, these costs and benefits should be automatic rather than discretionary, so that they are directly linked to desirable outcomes (not just stated intentions) and decisions. African investment codes often work against their stated objectives of promoting employment and small-scale industries because their benefits favor capital-intensive investments or are provided on a discretionary basis to influential investors. Removing discretion can reduce administrators' ability to profit by manipulating the decisionmaking process.

Producers' access to labor, capital, and material inputs depends not only on price incentives, but also on how well markets function (sections 2.1, 4.1, 5.3, and 8.3). The development of factor and interindustry markets in Africa has been constrained in three principal ways. First, the growth and integration of markets have been hindered by the low density of rural populations, high transport costs, underdeveloped financial and administrative institutions, and low levels of income. Second, colonial governments had concentrated on export-import trade, to the neglect of domestic markets and (in West Africa) of transport linkages between countries, while commercial activity by Africans was often restricted (especially in East Africa). The colonial legacy was dualistic economies with fragmented capital and labor markets. Third, postindependence policies impeded the operation of markets by emphasizing direct intervention and controls—partly to overcome the shortcomings of fragmented markets. For example, wage and labor regulations that were intended to protect workers (especially from foreign owners) have discouraged labor-intensive techniques and prevented firms from cutting labor costs when production falls. Despite layoffs by some public enterprises, African countries have done little to make labor markets more responsive through greater wage flexibility and freedom in hiring and firing. Nevertheless, some evidence indicates that wages may adjust at the margin (section 8.4).

Small-Scale Entrepreneurs

The impact of extensive regulation and direct allocation of resources on the small-scale sector has been a particular concern in recent years (chapter 8). Small-scale firms have an important role in African industrial development because they employ more workers at a lower cost per job than do large firms, they provide an outlet and training ground for entrepreneurial and managerial skills, and they complement strategies that emphasize rural development (sections 5.1 and 8.1). The evidence is less clear on whether small firms use total factors more productively than do large firms in the same industry, but they have a clear advantage in many activities that involve processing local materials and serving small, low-density markets.[15] Past policies, however, have tended to channel financial and foreign exchange resources to large investments, and small enterprises have had to operate outside formal markets and institutions. Reforms that remove policy biases and reduce regulation of small enterprise are therefore likely to speed the growth of small-scale industries (section 5.1).

Institutions and programs to promote faster growth of small-scale enterprises—especially by increasing their access to finance—have had relatively little impact. This is partly because they have not addressed the fundamental problems of segmented markets and restrictive policies and partly because small-scale investors normally obtain their funds from family savings and retained earnings rather than from formal institutions (sections 8.1, 8.2, and 9.1) Furthermore, there has been little success in finding ways to develop entrepreneurs and deliver assistance to them (sections 8.5 and 8.6).

One interpretation (section 5.3) is that there is no shortage of entrepreneurs today, but that they are more often found in commerce and informal activities than in industry. These entrepreneurs may shift to small-scale manufacturing if incentives are improved, markets are opened up, and administrative restrictions removed (sections 8.2 and 8.6). In this view, a general policy of deregulation and nondiscrimination will do more to stimulate entrepreneurial activity in the short term than will the establishment of public institutions and specialized programs directed at the small-scale sector. But small-scale entrepreneurs may lack the appropriate experience and skills to respond to new incentives by shifting to industry (sections 8.5 and 8.6). Therefore, industrial extension services that help solve problems and develop accounting and man-

15. See also John M. Page, Jr., and William F. Steel, *Small Enterprise Development: Economic Issues from African Experience*, World Bank Technical Paper 26 (Washington, D.C., 1984).

agement skills are likely to be useful in raising industrial production and productivity.

Public Sector Restructuring

The public industrial sector is significant because of its size and tendency to be insulated from the effects of price and incentive changes (sections 4.3, 5.3, 10.1, and 10.2). But in many countries public firms are draining limited budgetary resources, while the indigenous private sector is becoming better established. Governments are therefore increasingly facing difficult decisions about the size of their holdings, the distribution of resources among industries, and the management of those resources (sections 9.1 and 10.4). The extent of government control over resources will remain substantial for the near future, even in Côte d'Ivoire, Ghana, and Senegal, which are deemphasizing direct public investment in industry. Ethiopia and Madagascar retain a strong ideological commitment to public ownership as a tool of economic transformation and income redistribution; in these countries, efficient operation is all the more crucial to the economic success of public enterprises.

Public sector investment and takeovers have been justified as generating revenues, providing nationally owned competition for foreign firms, and initiating key industries in the absence of private interest (sections 3.3, 4.3, 7.6, and 10.1). But the overriding motivation behind expansion of the public industrial sector in Africa has been to replace foreign capitalists (section 4.1). Economic and financial objectives for state investments were rarely specified clearly, and political considerations often conflicted with the stated objectives of making profits and saving foreign exchange. Sierra Leone's public enterprises (section 10.2) exemplify weak performance under conflicting objectives, with centrally imposed decisions and without performance criteria and information systems related to clear goals. Well-designed policy and management conditions, however, can produce well-run, productive state enterprises, for example in Ethiopia (section 10.3).

Restructuring the public industrial sector involves changes at two levels (sections 5.2 and 10.4): first, shifts in the extent and pattern of public sector holdings; and second, improvements in the financial structure, management, and organization of firms. Reevaluation of what is appropriate and feasible for the public sector is likely to result in both a reduction in capacity under public ownership, whether through sale to private investors or through outright closure, and a rationalization of public holdings by shifting resources to industries in which public investment is most justified and successful. This process has been going on throughout the 1980s, largely imposed by the inability of governments to carry loss-making enterprises. A survey of fifteen countries found approximately one hundred public firms (in all sectors) closed, sold, or liquidated between 1979 and 1984.[16] To shift resources toward more efficient uses, however, such decisions need to be made in the context of

16. Gérard Egnell, "The Rehabilitation of Malfunctioning Industrial Units in the ACP States." Report VIII/568(85)-EN of the Commission of the European Communities (Paris: Centre Nord-Sud of the Institut de l'Entreprise, 1985).

policy reforms that make profits a reliable indicator of efficiency. Both a reform of incentives and a review of public sector holdings are needed; they complement each other, as was recognized in the design of industrial adjustment programs in Zambia and Ghana (section 6.6).

At the firm level, public industries may find their profitability and ability to command resources threatened by policy reforms and liberalization. Several types of measures are being used to improve the public sector's competitive behavior and ability to manage resources efficiently (section 10.5). Conversion of debt to equity is one tool to put firms on a sound financial footing so that budgetary transfers can be eliminated. Decentralization of operating decisions helps to remove them from political influence. To orient decisions toward financial and economic performance, clear firm-level objectives and evaluation criteria for managers are needed. In addition, professional management training can make public sector managers better able to respond to more performance-oriented incentives. Indeed, measures such as these can help improve public sector performance regardless of what is done about policy reform and divestiture.

1.5 Other Issues

The adjustment measures featured in this book emphasize increasing production through more efficient use of existing resources. This section highlights three additional issues that are critical for successful industrial development over the long run: the availability of finance; the transfer, adaptation, and development of technology; and the need for adequate human resources and infrastructure.

Availability of Finance

Access to credit is a thorny issue of industrial adjustment programs. Devaluation suddenly increases the need of most industries for working capital since additional finance for imported inputs is required just to maintain production, let alone to increase it. But general financial expansion may conflict with stabilization policies. At the micro level, one objective of incentive reform is to squeeze out inefficient firms with poor long-term prospects. Some of these firms may be highly liquid as a result of past protection policies, whereas potentially viable firms (especially exporters) are often financially weak because of price controls and an overvalued currency. Special criteria and funding may be appropriate to facilitate the initial expansion of the latter, although directed credit to industry is generally incompatible with deregulating and improving the efficiency of financial markets (section 9.1). Financial intermediation is too large a subject for detailed discussion in this book, but improving the financial sector's ability to finance potentially viable firms is an essential complement to an industrial adjustment program.

At the same time, foreign borrowing can boost the acceptability and sustainability of reforms by financing a larger supply of imported consumer goods while domestic production (especially of exports) is adjusting. (The terms must be such that rising debt burdens do not compromise recovery in the medium term.) Loans for additional inputs enabled industry in Ghana and Nigeria to increase supplies of key products by using excess capacity, thus minimizing the inflationary effects of price decontrol (section 6.6). Conversely, continued shrinkage of foreign exchange and budgetary resources in Zambia in 1987 contributed to suspension of the reform process.

Technology

Both large and small entrepreneurs need technologies that are appropriate to Africa's comparative advantage (sections 9.1 and 9.3). As latecomers, African countries theoretically can benefit from technological advances already available, but the lack of competition in Africa's small, highly protected markets has yielded relatively little success in effectively transferring or adapting modern industrial techniques. At present, large-scale technology in Africa tends to be relatively capital-intensive and dependent on imports, while small-scale technology offers limited scope for raising productivity.

Policy reform can stimulate greater competitiveness and redress some of the bias toward capital- and import-intensive techniques. The means by which technology can be adapted and transferred, however, are less clear. Greater use of local resources is feasible, but can this be done without lowering the quality and consumers' acceptance of the product? Will more labor-intensive techniques necessarily lower the cost of production, given relatively high wages and low skills compared with Asian exporters of manufactures? Will foreign companies transfer technology through management or technical contracts even when they are reluctant to invest directly? Evidence on these issues is scanty in Africa. Although not covered in depth in this volume, new initiatives for the transfer, adaptation, and development of technology are needed if African industry is to become increasingly productive and competitive over time.

Human Resources

Shifting resources in response to policy changes requires trained personnel able to make and implement appropriate decisions. The success of an adjustment program will depend on the availability of entrepreneurial, managerial, and technical skills both to the reform process and to ensure the responsiveness of supply to changed incentives (sections 4.4, 7.6, 8.5, and 8.6). Broader investment in education and training (both formal and on-the-job) is essential to build up industrial capabilities as part of a strategy emphasizing greater self-reliance and exports (section 5.1). Although not lacking in entrepreneurs, Africa is critically short of managerial experience in industry and the technical skills needed for technological innovation. These are two important areas for experimentation and development of effective policy and institutional approaches.

Infrastructure

Inadequate infrastructure imposes high costs and risks that deter industrialization in Africa (sections 2.2, 4.1, and 4.3). Public expenditure on industrialization needs to shift from direct investment in production to supporting investment in reliable, low-cost energy, transport, communications, and other services.

Sustainability

Industrial adjustment is part of the larger problem of shifting resources to more efficient and dynamic uses through improved incentives and institutions. Industrial growth alone cannot sustain growth in African economies. Successful industrialization requires complementary growth in agricultural and export production. For industrial restructuring to reach its potential in raising productivity, stimulating growth, and diversifying the economy, it is necessary to remove policy distortions that favor nontradable sectors and discourage use of local inputs; restore fiscal and monetary stability; stimulate greater domestic and international competitiveness; reduce extensive direct public intervention and controls and establish a positive business environment; make taxation, regulations, and special incentives transparent and automatic; and reassess the objectives, size, distribution, and management of public industrial holdings.

The prospects for successful restructuring in Africa must be tempered by economic and political realities. Where markets function imperfectly, they may not transmit improved incentives and additional resources. Some degree of regulation and intervention is unavoidable, especially during transition periods when access to scarce resources can yield substantial rents, and economically disadvantaged groups may otherwise bear an excessive burden. Growth is not the only objective of African countries, and industrial strategy may have to be moderated by considerations of income distribution, national ownership, and self-reliance. Many of the adjustments discussed in this chapter represent corrections to excessive intervention in the past. Cases such as Zambia show, however, that there are limits to how rapidly and completely controls can be replaced by markets.

For countries hampered by rising debt and falling export prices, reform programs may only slow the decline, not reverse it. Even when the benefits of reform are clear, the short-term costs make it difficult to design a strategy that is politically manageable. Nevertheless, many African governments have launched ambitious reform programs in the mid-1980s. Some countries have opted for sudden, drastic change, while others have taken a more phased approach. The following chapters review the rationale and initial impact of these ongoing efforts to design and sustain effective strategies for industrial development in Africa.

2

Strategic Orientations

2.1 Constraints and Options
World Bank Staff

Industrialization has a crucial role in long-term development: it is one of the best training grounds for skill development; it is an important source of structural change and diversification; and it can increase the flexibility of the economy and reduce dependence on external forces. Industrialization also provides employment, foreign exchange, and domestic savings. Although these developmental benefits justify incurring some additional cost to promote industry, they do not justify the promotion of industry at any cost. Manufacturing is only a small sector in Africa and can make only a modest, though growing, contribution to development during the next decade. Excessive investment in industry can starve other sectors of capital, foreign exchange, and high-level manpower, while expensive manufactured products can raise costs in other sectors and limit their growth.

Industrialization has failed to provide many of the benefits expected of it in Africa during the past decade. Respectable rates of growth of manufacturing production were achieved for several years after independence, but large savings of foreign exchange upon which much industrial investment was based have not materialized.

There are reasons for optimism about the future, however. Some countries have built up an industrial base, which will permit increased growth if an appropriate policy framework is established. Several efficient processing industries have been established (in Cameroon and Zambia, for example) and some (such as Mauritius) have expanded manufactured exports to Europe. There are also some promising experiments with regional industrial cooperation in West Africa. The central issue is how to build on these promising aspects to promote long-term industrial development.

Excerpted and edited from World Bank, *Accelerated Development in Sub-Saharan Africa: An Agenda for Action* (Washington, D.C., 1981).

Constraints

Five main considerations bear on industrial strategy: market size, population density, wages and productivity, management costs, and capital and infrastructure costs.

MARKET SIZE. The small population and low per capita incomes of most African countries severely constrain their choice of industries because most industries require markets larger than those existing in most African countries. Only eight African countries have populations greater than 10 million. Only one African country (Nigeria, with a population of over 80 million) has a GDP greater than that of Hong Kong (population 5.0 million). The whole of Sub-Saharan Africa, including Nigeria, has a GDP that is only a third greater than that of the Netherlands, with a population of 14 million.

POPULATION DENSITY. Many African countries are very sparsely populated. This raises the cost of infrastructural development and limits the market for some industries—a cement plant, for example, usually serves only a 200- to 300-mile radius. High transport costs give natural protection to some industries but limit the achievements of economies of scale. At the same time, the difficulty of policing extensive frontiers leads to smuggling, which can undermine attempts to establish high-cost import-substitution industries.

WAGES AND PRODUCTIVITY. African wages are high compared with those in Asia. An International Labour Organisation (ILO) survey in 1949 showed that the median wage for textile workers in ten African countries was 50 percent higher than in Pakistan and more than twice as high as in Bangladesh. Higher African wages reflect both government wage policy, which in many countries sets industrial wages above the level they would otherwise be, and better opportunities for agricultural employment. African labor productivity also tends to compare unfavorably with many other parts of the world. A comparison of six African and four South American textile mills showed that the average number of spinners per 1,000 spindle shifts and the average number of weavers per equivalent loom shifts was more than twice as high in Africa. This lower productivity of labor is primarily a reflection of Africa's early stage of industrial development and should improve; meanwhile, it continues to slow development.

MANAGEMENT COSTS. African industry relies much more heavily than other parts of the developing world on expatriate management and technicians. In manufacturing firms in the Ivory Coast, for example, expatriate salaries account for one-quarter of value added. European managers and technicians usually cost two to three times as much in Africa as in Europe.

CAPITAL AND INFRASTRUCTURE COSTS. Industrial projects in Africa typically require investment costs that are 25 percent higher than in developed countries, and for some industries the margin may be as high as 60 percent. This extra expense is associated with transport costs and construction delays. Although there is no evidence that the extra cost of investment is systematically higher in Africa than in other developing areas, supporting infrastructure, such as roads, ports, utilities, and financial institutions, is less available than in most parts of Asia and Latin America.

Strategy Options

These factors obviously have a profound impact on the industrial strategy open to many African countries. Not all countries are equally affected, of course. Nigeria, by virtue of its market size and density of population, has broader options than most other Sub-Saharan nations. The potential varies considerably over the rest of the continent, however, in countries as disparate as Niger and Zimbabwe. In spite of this diversity, it is possible to make some generalizations about desirable forms of industrial development.

IMPORT SUBSTITUTION. Import substitution can be a sound policy, and most industrialization has started on that basis. But in many African countries it has been badly implemented. There also is always the risk that the protection afforded in the early stages may be maintained for excessive periods. The challenge is to establish an incentive and institutional structure that directs investment toward industries that are productive and can be competitive in the future. This means that attention must be paid to costs and to growth in productivity from the beginning. Because of the importance of economies of scale, it also means that many import-substitution industries should be set up with a view to becoming exporters.

For countries that have nearly completed the first stages of import substitution, such as Kenya, Ivory Coast, and Tanzania, few new import-substitution opportunities exist based on the internal market. The next step in import substitution usually involves going into intermediate goods production in which economies of scale are more important. Such import substitution in a small domestic market cannot sustain industrial growth. This is because even if high-cost intermediate industries are started, they will curtail the growth of other industries.

REGIONAL INTEGRATION. Economic integration, which allows production for a larger regional market, is one way in which small African countries can expand the scope for efficient industrialization. But there are four obstacles to such integration in the near future. First, transport and other links among African countries are poorly developed. Second, the distribution of industries is likely to be unequal in a union between countries at different levels of development or with different locational advantages. Unless counteracting measures are taken, industry will tend to concentrate in the more industrially advanced countries, at coastal locations, and in the larger countries. Third, inefficient industries may be unable to withstand competition from partner states following integration. Although a pruning of the industrial deadwood is an important benefit of integration, it naturally provokes resistance from the industry or country affected. Finally, political disputes, actual or potential, hamper prospects for integration since they increase the risk of investing in an industry that depends on an integrated market.

Two conclusions can be drawn. First, it will probably be easier to approach integration through the least formal channel possible, such as a regional project, rather than through a formal customs union. This is the thrust of most of the integration efforts in West Africa at present. Second, regional integration is far more likely to succeed if costs of production are fairly close to world levels. Governments resent the foreign exchange and tariff revenue forgone when purchasing from a high-cost plant in a partner state. Full economic integration in the future will be much more difficult if governments establish high-cost industries that will be unprofitable or perhaps not even survive in an integrated market. Consequently, only those national strategies of development that emphasize efficient production for the domestic or world markets are likely to be compatible with the process of economic integration.

PROCESSING RAW MATERIALS FOR EXPORT. African exports are dominated by primary products, and although processed products were the fastest-growing category of African exports between 1963 and 1975, two-thirds of the increase in value of processed products came from refined copper. There is much scope for increasing local processing. But the determinants of the location of processing (capital costs, structure of the market, tariffs, infrastructure availability) are so diverse that it hardly makes sense to speak of processing as a general industrial strategy as opposed to prospects for particular processing activities. Careful project analysis is necessary because of variations in local conditions, such as the quality of raw materials and other input costs.

MANUFACTURING FOR EXPORT. Neither the past record nor newly uncovered special advantages suggests that concentration on exports of labor-intensive manufactures is a promising strategy for most of Africa. Africa's share of world manufactured exports is low (0.2 percent in 1977), and its growth rate of manufactured exports is the lowest of any developing region. Many of Africa's manufactured exports under the conventional definitions are in fact slightly processed resources: 30 percent are diamonds and precious stones. Labor costs and productivity plus high management costs place Africa at a severe disadvantage compared with Asia.

Nonetheless, important potential for manufactured exports does exist. African manufactured exports (excluding diamonds and special transactions) to industrialized countries grew at an average annual rate of 8.5 percent between 1970 and 1979. This was from a very small base and was partially offset by a decline in exports to other developing countries, but it is an encouraging sign of the potential for growth. In any case, past performance is no guide to future prospects because of the policy bias against exports and the low protectivity of early-stage industrialization. Overvalued exchange rates and productive wage policy have contributed to a high wage level. Replacement of high-cost expatriate managers and technicians with personnel from other developing countries or local managers could lower these personnel costs. Improved incentives at the macro and plant levels should stimulate growth of productivity. Moreover, preferential access to the European market offers an opportunity to expand some labor-intensive exports; Ivory Coast and Mauritius already export some clothing to the European Economic Community (EEC). Finally, excess capacity in many countries could be turned to advantage if incentives were restructured to encourage exports.

This does not imply that any African country is yet in a position to follow the path of Korea or Taiwan. But there is no reason why some of the relatively more advanced countries, such as the Ivory Coast, Kenya, Mauritius, and Zimbabwe, should not be able to increase the volume of manufactured exports by at least 10 percent per year. This might come more from resource-based than labor-intensive industries. It might also come from new import-substitution industries built with an eye to the export market as well. Breaking into export markets is not easy and considerable marketing and other support will be needed, but for many African countries export production will have to play a more important role in overall economic growth.

Increasing Industry's Contribution

No single industrial strategy will fit the diverse conditions, prospects, and goals of all African countries. There are, however, a few generally applicable principles. To begin with, a conscious effort should be made to seek out profitable industrial export opportunities. Even though the bulk of investment opportunities will be in production for the domestic market, sooner or later most countries will also have to increase manufactured exports to maintain industrial growth, expand employment opportunities, and diversify exports.

Moreover, the pace of industrialization should not be forced. In many cases the choice is not between having or not having an industry, but between having a small-scale, high-cost industry now or an optimum-scale efficient industry a few years from now. Proper sequencing is vital. Rapid growth of metal engineering, for example, depends on competitive supplies, and this growth may, in time, provide demand for basic metal plants. But setting up a basic metal industry will retard the expansion of metal-using industries, for it is these that are the really important agents of development.

An agriculture-oriented development strategy with industry in a supporting role does not mean that Africa would forgo industrial development. Long-term industrial growth might, in fact, be higher with this approach. Although agriculture would be the driving force, industry would still grow faster than agriculture. In fact, higher agricultural incomes will stimulate demand for products from a number of industries—textiles, metal manufactures, building materials, and light consumer goods—that could be produced relatively efficiently in most African economies. Efficient industries generate their own momentum. And then export possibilities are opened up and the local market for intermediate goods widens.

Promotion of Indigenous Entrepreneurship

Promotion of indigeneous industry is a basic objective. It is important, therefore, to review how development of African entrepreneurship would be affected by policy or reorientation of industrial strategy.

Many African countries emphasize direct controls to promote large-scale import substitution, a policy that discriminates heavily against local small enterprises. Small indigenous firms typically lack the administrative resources to deal with import and industrial licensing regulations or to obtain special concessions, such as duty drawbacks. The policy of keeping interest rates on loans and deposits artificially low also discriminates against local small business. Banks respond to low interest rates by rationing credit and favoring traditional large customers with low risk of default and low administrative costs. Any policy reform in this area would clearly benefit local small businesses.

An agriculture-oriented development strategy would also benefit many of the subsectors with the greatest potential for small-scale development: food processing; manufacture of footwear, clothing, furniture, and small implements; and production of local construction materials. The metal engineering sector is another in which opportunities for small-scale business are exceptionally promising. Many of these industries can also be decentralized in small towns or rural areas, thus providing an alternative source of income for the rural population. World Bank research in Kenya suggests that off-farm income, in turn, can be a major source of finance for agricultural innovation. In this way, agricultural and industrial expansion interact to boost the growth of income and output in both sectors.

Changes in Policies and Institutions

The first and major change needed to improve industrial performance and lay a sounder base for long-term development is a reform of the incentive structure for industry. The essential requirements are to increase the incentives for industrial exports, to reduce protection for import substitution, to reduce the extreme variation in protection among industries, and to phase out direct controls. The methods and pace of reform will be different for each country, but the direction of change needed is clear enough.

Second, procedures for selecting projects should be strengthened. The most important measure that can be taken here, too, is a change in the incentive system. The amount and duration of incentives available for new investment in each sector should be spelled out. Some promotional devices—lengthy exclusive production rights, bans on competing imports, and tariff waivers on inputs—should be ruled out. Discriminatory concessions among firms should be eliminated. Above all, the investment decision must be separated from the decisions concerning appropriate investment incentives. Guidelines for infant industry protection and tax incentives should be laid down in advance and not tailor-made for each new investment. In much of Africa at present, investors actively seek government participation in joint ventures because they realize that this is the most certain way to obtain protection and concessions and thus ensure financial success of their project, regardless of its economic desirability.

A third area of reform should be in policies concerning public industrial enterprises. The problems that parastatals typically encounter do not stem from their public ownership, but rather come from their not being treated as commercial enterprises. They should not be burdened by requirements to hire more people than they need, to provide services without payment, or to hold down the prices of the goods and services they sell. Governments must still pursue social objectives, of course, but to the extent possible parastatals should be maintained as commercial enterprises and compensated for any social services they are required to perform. At the same time, parastatals should be subject to the same tax requirements as other private industrial enterprises. Parastatals should pay taxes on profits and on imported inputs, and they should receive only reasonable protection from outside competition.

Fourth, and finally, governments can use tax incentives more effectively to promote industrial investment. Tax credits can be limited to an amount that is some share of the investment, say 100 percent, although, in general, they should not be extended solely for equipment and fixed capital investment. Many countries have sought to avoid such fiscal waste and economic distortions by requiring substantial local value added before granting tax benefits. Mexico, for example, has required that imported parts of assembly-type industries be less than 40 percent of direct costs. Some countries—Pakistan and the Philippines, for example—have simply excluded packaging and assembly-type operations from tax benefits.

The effectiveness of fiscal incentives to foreign investors should not be overestimated. Investors are attracted more by political stability; a low probability of confiscation; a stable, predictable, and reasonable tax regimen; and the ability to repatriate profits. The evidence is overwhelming that where the investment climate is favorable—including measures to avoid double taxation with the home country—most foreign investment will occur without a need for tax concessions.

2.2 *Self-Reliant Industrial Development*
The United Nations Industrial Development Decade for Africa

The majority of African countries still suffer from underdevelopment and have little manufacturing activity. Industrial activities initiated by foreign investors have failed to meet the basic needs of the population: they have not made for an integrated economy nor have they contributed to the modernization of African society. The legacy of colonialism has perpetuated at best an economic structure featuring a comparatively small modern sector and a large backward agricultural sector; in fact, in many countries the industrial sector hardly exists.

Excerpted by permission from *A Programme for the Industrial Development Decade for Africa,* prepared jointly by the Economic Commission for Africa, the Organization of African Unity, and the United Nations Industrial Development Organization, New York, 1982.

Import substitution has been confined to the manufacture of products suited to the demands of a relatively small affluent group and its application has failed to integrate the agricultural sector into the growth process. Furthermore, the capital-intensive manufacture of sophisticated products has heightened the region's dependence on foreign manpower, capital and technology.

Self-Reliance

The principle of self-reliance involves the use of indigenous raw materials, indigenous labour and management, domestic and regional markets, etc. Self-sustainment relies on internal as opposed to external requirements and stimuli. Ever since political independence, foreign (private) enterprises have done most of the exploring for natural resources and they have exported raw materials in an unprocessed form—much to the detriment of the development of domestic industries.

Self-reliance calls for the maximum utilization of indigenous resources—physical and human—before resorting to foreign resources. The peoples of Africa have to rely mainly on their own efforts and make external assistance subservient to their development strategy. In pursuing this policy, Africa does not intend to isolate itself from the world of foreign science and technology. While striving to increase its scientific and technological links with the technologically advanced countries, Africa must develop its own scientific and technological capabilities. It must also be selective in seeking out international techno-scientific exchanges and co-operation, and develop both governmental and non-governmental contacts in all fields on the principle of equality and equal benefit. The attainment of self-reliance presupposes the institutionalization and intensification of integration and co-operation schemes among countries of the same subregion.

Self-reliance, therefore, implies a will to reduce the extent of dependence on former metropolitan powers in particular and on developed countries in general. No claim to self-reliance can be made by a country whose industrial structure is dominated by foreign investment, where the bulk of industrial output is produced by affiliates of foreign corporations, transnationals or entities owned by non-residents, and where no scientific and technological capability exists.

The extent of external dependence in terms of equipment can be assessed by visualizing the region being cut off from its developed country suppliers of equipment of all kinds, including spare parts, simple tools and implements. Of significance is the extent to which equipment imports relate to general purposes rather than to industrial and agricultural production and the needs of the people. Furthermore, present economic co-operation arrangements still reflect geographical patterns inherited from the colonial era and are less concerned with the central issues (of restructuring the natural resource and raw material base, promoting raw materials complementarities through intra-African trade in industrial raw materials, developing indigenous factor inputs and establishing institutions) then with either Africanizing (or effecting minor repairs to) inherited structures and formulating a common position on demands to be made of developed countries.

Implementing Self-Reliant Development

Self-reliant industrial development presupposes indigenous industrialization whereby industrial production is adjusted to the needs of the population. This contrasts sharply with the existing international division of labour which has led to the promotion of (a) the production of raw materials for export; and (b) light assembly industry oriented towards consumption patterns in the developed countries.

Self-reliance implies the introduction of a mechanism for income equalization commensurate with the needs of both the urban and rural population. The production of basic consumer goods takes priority over the manufacture of luxury goods. In this respect, industry should modernize agriculture and accord priority to the needs of society. The role of planning, including the decentralization of economic activities, is fundamental since structural change in rural areas is a prime objective of the Industrial Development Decade for Africa.

A strategy of self-reliance also entails the joint planning, financing and location of major educational institutions in countries in the same economic grouping so as to provide for the education and training of engineers, scientists, technologists and other skilled workers. Self-reliance in technology means developing indigenous capacity to evaluate various industrial techniques and to select the technology most appropriate to local demands. It also covers the adaptation and improvement of imported technology and the creation of indigenous technology.

Indigenous entrepreneurs, both public and private, should be fully involved in the industrialization of Africa. To this end, governments should enhance the participation of public and private entrepreneurs as well as other indigenous economic agents in this process by assisting them in the identification of relevant projects, the preparation of market and feasibility studies, the mobilization of investment funds, and the training of skilled labour for the production and commercialization of industrial products.

The attainment of self-reliant and self-sustaining industrialization hinges upon the securement of the requisite finance. Experience has shown that industrial investment in Africa has too often given rise to benefits which have been unequally distributed between the host country and various external suppliers and partners as a result of weakness in negotiations; all too frequently, industrial investment benefits the supplier far more than the African buyer. The high import content of investment includes: importation of capital goods and equipment; preference of foreign enterprises for imported raw materials and intermediate inputs; payment of royalties; transfer pricing; technical fees for project design and feasibility studies; spare parts; management fees; technical fees associated with the selection and purchase of equipment; and repatriation of profits by foreign agents of production and distribution. This system is self-perpetuating.

The process of developing an integrated industrial structure in Africa calls for far-reaching and complex changes. The trading structure inherited from the former colonial powers will have to be dismantled and an African trading sector created which controls the large African multi-national trading companies. In the context of self-reliance, commerce also determines the distribution of industrial products, the growth of national income, domestic capital formation and the volume of investment. Import substitution should be abandoned since it perpetuates colonial consumption patterns and restricts benefits. Key industrial sectors will have to be developed and controlled by African countries through the establishment of African multinational enterprises, thus creating viable industrial structures at the country level.

The national objective will be to create an integrated industrial structure with strong linkages between various industrial branches and with close ties between industry and other sectors, especially the agricultural sector. Production at the subregional level must provide the goods needed in domestic markets.

Apart from being an important element in collective self-reliance for industrialization, the establishment of complementary industrial production structures offers a large potential for growth in trade among member countries in the same economic community on account of the heterogeneity of resource endowments, while trade preferences encourage inter-industry and intra-industry specialization.

As stipulated in the Final Act of Lagos, the African countries agreed to strengthen existing regional economic communities and establish other economic groupings with the ultimate objective of creating an African Common Market and an African Economic Community by the year 2000. These economic communities would accelerate economic integration among countries and economic groupings in the same subregion.

Need for Industrial Planning

The implementation of a well-defined self-reliant industrial development strategy requires the elaboration of a coherent industrial development plan. While a number of African countries have made efforts to elaborate such a plan, the continent as a whole still suffers from a lack of clear and methodical planning. The planning and implementation of national industrial programmes and projects involves, inter alia: the preparation of industrial studies, the development of natural resources, the identification of priority industries, the diagnosis of existing industrial structures, the development of indigenous industrial capabilities, the development and transfer of technology, the development of an adequate industrial institutional infrastructure, the mobilization of financial resources, the provision of energy, and the development of negotiating capabilities.

The selection of key industries must be governed by the objectives of self-reliant industrial development. Industrial activities upstream and downstream of agriculture are of crucial significance. This is especially true of the iron and steel, copper and aluminum industries, on which mechanical industries can be based, leading to the production of agricultural machinery and implements as well as to the production and maintenance of agricultural processing equipment. Industrial plants producing fertilizers, pesticides, insecticides, irrigation equipment and packaging materials are essential, as are plants manufacturing inputs to the transportation sector.

2.3 Inward-Looking Import Substitution
Bela Balassa

Industrial development generally begins in response to domestic demand generated in the primary sector that also provides investable funds for manufacturing industries. Demand for industrial products and investable savings represents possible uses of the surplus generated in agriculture often associated with export expansion. Where family-size farms predominate, demand is generated for the necessities of life as well as for education. Such demand propels the development of domestic industry that enjoys "natural" protection from imports because of transportation costs. The process of industrial development may be accelerated if natural protection is complemented by tariff or quota protection.

First-Stage Import Substitution

With the exception of Britain at the time of the Industrial Revolution and today's Hong Kong, all present-day industrial and developing countries protected fledgling manufacturing industries producing for domestic markets. While the industrial countries relied on low tariffs, however, developing countries applied high tariffs or quantitative restrictions that limited or excluded competition from imports.

High protection discriminates against exports through explicit or implicit taxation of export activities. Explicit taxation may take the form of export taxes, while implicit taxation occurs as a result of the effects of protection on the exchange rate. The higher the rate of protection, the lower will be the exchange rate necessary to ensure equilibrium in the balance of payments, and the lower the amount of domestic currency that exporters will receive per unit of foreign exchange earned.

The adverse effects of high protection are exemplified in the case of Ghana, where import prohibitions encouraged inefficient, high-cost production in manufacturing industries. Taxes on the main export crop, cocoa, discouraged its production, and other crops were adversely affected by the unfavorable exchange rate. Ghana's neighbor, the Ivory Coast, followed a policy of encouraging both primary and manufacturing activities. As a result, it increased its share of cocoa exports, developed new primary exports, and expanded manufacturing industries. These differences may explain why per capita incomes fell from $430 to $390 in Ghana between 1960 and 1978 (in 1978 prices), compared with an increase from $540 to $840 in the Ivory Coast.

Excerpted and edited from Bela Balassa, *The Process of Industrial Development and Alternative Development Strategies*, World Bank Staff Working Paper 438 (Washington, D.C., October 1980).

There is no need for high protection at the first stage of import substitution, which entails the replacement of imports of nondurable consumer goods (clothing, shoes, household goods) and of their inputs (such as textile fabrics, leather, and wood) by domestic production. The goods in question are intensive in unskilled labor, the efficient scale of output is low, and costs do not rise substantially at lower output levels. Production does not involve the use of sophisticated technology, and a network of suppliers of parts, components, and accessories is not required.

Second-Stage Import Substitution

In the course of first-stage import substitution, domestic production will rise more rapidly than domestic consumption because it not only provides for increases in consumption but also replaces imports. But the rate of growth of output will decline to that of consumption once the first stage of import substitution has been completed. Maintaining high industrial growth rates then necessitates turning to the exportation of manufactured goods or moving to second-stage import substitution.

Second-stage import substitution was undertaken in the postwar period in several Latin American countries, following the ideas of Raúl Prebisch, in whose view adverse foreign market conditions for primary (agricultural and mineral) exports and lack of competitiveness in manufactured exports would not permit developing countries to attain high rates of economic growth by relying on export production.

Second-stage import substitution involves the replacement of imports of intermediate goods and producer and consumer durables by domestic production. Intermediate goods, such as petrochemicals and steel, tend to be highly capital-intensive. They are also subject to important economies of scale, with efficient plant size being large compared with the domestic needs of most developing countries and costs rising rapidly at lower output levels. Moreover, the margin of processing is relatively small, and organizational and technical inefficiencies may contribute to high costs.

Given their relative scarcity of physical and human capital, developing countries that complete the first stage of import substitution are at a disadvantage in the manufacture of intermediate goods and producer and consumer durables. By limiting the scope of economies of scale, the relatively small size of their national markets also contributes to high domestic costs. At the same time, foreign exchange savings tend to be small because of the need to import materials and machinery.

Countries applying inward-oriented industrial development strategies are characterized by the prevalence of sellers' markets. In capitalist countries in Latin America and South Asia, the size of national markets limited the possibilities of domestic competition at the second stage of import substitution, while import competition was virtually excluded by high protection. In socialist countries in Central and Eastern Europe, central planning did not permit competition among domestic firms or from imports. Given the sellers' markets, firms had little incentive to improve productivity.

Effects on Exports and on Economic Growth

Discrimination in favor of import substitution and against exports did not permit the development of manufactured exports in countries engaging in second-stage import substitution behind high protection. There were also adverse developments in primary exports as low prices for producers and for consumers reduced the exportable surplus by discouraging production and encouraging consumption.

In fact, rather than improvements in the external terms of trade that were supposed to result, the shift in internal terms of trade against primary goods led to a decline in export market shares. Decreases in market shares were especially pronounced in cereals, meat, oilseeds, and nonferrous metals, thus benefiting developed countries, particularly the United States, Canada, and Australia.

The slowdown in the growth of primary exports, in combination with the lack of emergence of manufactured exports, made it impossible to obtain the foreign exchange necessary for rapid economic growth in countries pursuing inward-oriented industrial development strategies. The situation was aggravated as net import savings declined because of the increased need for foreign materials, machinery, and technological know-how.

The cost of protection is estimated to have reached 6 to 7 percent of gross national product in several developing countries. At the same time, there is evidence that the rate of growth of total factor productivity was lower in countries engaging in second-stage import substitution than in the industrial countries. Rather than reducing the economic distance vis-à-vis the industrial countries that infant industry protection was supposed to promote, there was a tendency for this distance to increase over time.

2.4 Resource-Based Industrialization
Michael Roemer

Two industrial strategies that are primarily based on utilization of natural resources have been receiving emphasis in the third world: (i) more complete processing of raw materials for export, and (ii) utilization of domestic resources principally for domestic consumption. Although there is substantial refining of non-ferrous metals in the exporting countries, the bulk of other resource commodities is exported in unprocessed form and there is considerable scope for further processing or fabricating of all these products for export or home use. However, it is not obvious that resource-based industrialization (RBI) is better suited to achieve national development goals than other potential strategies. This paper surveys the development literature to shed light on the potential contribution of RBI to efficient growth, employment creation, greater equity and economic independence.

The two resource-based strategies, primary export processing and basic industries, contrast with import substitution, which first concentrates on con-

Excerpted by permission from Michael Roemer, ''Resource-Based Industrialization in the Developing Countries,'' *Journal of Development Economics* 6 (1979): 163–202.

sumer goods and sets up inherent barriers to the complete integration back to domestic raw materials; and with export substitution, which emphasizes labor-intensive, rather than material-intensive, industries.

RBI needs to be subjected to a systematic critique of its ability to satisfy some of the goals commonly held for industrialization, conducted along the following lines:

- Economic advantage. The most commonly given reason for processing resource exports is that the increase in value added means additional benefits for the country. Yet this depends on the nature of the resource, the processing technology and its complementary inputs, relative factor costs, and world market structure.
- Employment creation. The mineral processing industries are likely to be capital-intensive and employ very few, but wood and perhaps other tree crops may lead to quite labor-intensive industries.
- Distribution. The mineral-based industries are, in the absence of determined government intervention to the contrary, likely to further entrench the dual economy so typical of mining and to worsen inter-family income distribution. However, wood processing industries have very different characteristics and may help to improve income distribution among regions.
- Barriers to entry. Technological, locational or market barriers to entry may either contradict the notion that a country has comparative advantage in processing its own resources or may distort markets sufficiently to prevent a country from realizing that advantage.
- National dependence. Reduced dependence on world markets is a central aim of basic goods industrialization and may be an important component of strategies to process primary exports. However, there are different aspects of dependence and in this respect the two resource-based strategies differ as much from each other as from other strategies.

Economic Advantage

The potential economic benefits to a country processing its natural resources can be discussed in terms of general propositions about comparative advantage, such as labor intensity, weight reduction and transport costs; or all factors can be combined and weighted in an appropriate way to yield a single-dimensional indicator of efficiency, such as the internal rate of return or the domestic resource cost.

Comparative advantage deals with production functions and factor availabilities. The neoclassical (Heckscher-Ohlin) model predicts that developing countries should have a comparative advantage in exporting goods with technologies most intensive in labor.[1] Pulp and paper, chemicals, fertilizer, petroleum products, steel, wrought copper and wrought aluminum all have capital stock to labor ratios above, and mostly substantially above, the average for most industrial sectors. Only sawmill and board products are below average.

---

1. See technical note A.

However, all downstream industries using basic metals have low capital-labor ratios, indicating potential comparative advantage for LDCs if they can integrate beyond the basic metal stage.

Empirical testing of the Heckscher-Ohlin model has suggested several desirable modifications, among them the inclusion of human skills as a third factor of production. Third world countries are poorly endowed with trained manpower and would presumably have a comparative disadvantage in industries that require skilled workers most intensively. Moreover, of the 35 metal-using industries with below-average physical capital intensities, 14 have human capital ratios above the average, partially or completely cancelling the likelihood of LDC comparative advantage in these branches of metal fabrication.

Cost information on resource-based industries does not entirely support the conclusion based on factor intensities. Published costs are spotty at best and inconsistent, but table 2.4.1 summarizes the available data, giving approxi-

Table 2.4.1 *Approximate Cost Structures for Resource-Based Industries*

Output (with raw material input and stages of processing in parentheses)	Approximate share (percentage) of total cost due to		
	Raw materials	Value added	
		Labor	Capital[a]
Copper refined (ore inputs)	60	n.a.	n.a.
Aluminum, United States			
Alumina (bauxite; beneficiation)	24	10	40
Aluminum ingots			
(alumina; smelting only)	28	13	30
(bauxite; smelting and beneficiation)	7	16	41
Semi-fabricated products			
(aluminum; fabrication only)	43	21	15
(bauxite; all stages)	3	28	32
Steel, Latin America[b]			
Pig iron (ore, coal)	55–74	2–4	19–30
Crude steel			
(pig iron; steel-making only)	65–74	2–5	10–13
(ore, coal; iron- steel-making)	36–58	3–7; 11–22	24–34; 11–33
Rolled steel			
(crude steel; rolling only)	55–74	1–4	17–38
(ore, coal; all stages)	21–30	3–8	40–50
Ammonia (natural gas)	22–43	2–6	41–46
Wood products (timber), LDCs			
Sawmills	32	18	12
Plywood	31	10–16	12–23
Pulp/paper	25–40	3–6	25–50

n.a. Not available.

a. For aluminum, sawmills, and plywood, capital shares are a residual of revenues over all identified costs; for other commodities, capital shares are based on depreciation and a notional interest charge, but the rate is not uniform among studies.

b. Second set of figures for integrated crude steel production refers to OECD countries.

mate shares in total production costs for three factors: labor, capital and raw materials. Comparative advantage based on cheap labor can only be dismissed as insignificant if the wage share is also low in the industrial countries, as appears to be true for ammonia (and other petrochemicals). For steel, aluminum and wood products, however, the data in table 2.4.1 indicate that low labor costs might be a source of comparative advantage.

There is little data on the importance of skilled manpower costs, which are included in the labor shares in table 2.4.1. The only explicit cost reference is for sawmills and plywood: Page found that only about 2 percent of total costs in Ghanaian sawmills were due to skilled workers, though in plywood he attributes about 10 percent to skilled workers.[2] However, the critical impact of technical and managerial skills is not likely to be seen in their direct costs, but rather in the achievement of more efficient production and high quality output. It is generally accepted that most LDCs lack these skills and need to import them.

Capital costs are a high fraction for all industries in table 2.4.1, except aluminum fabrication (U.S. data) and some wood products. When capital costs are so high a fraction of the total, savings in capital charges are important. Cheaper sources of finance in the industrial countries may thus tip the balance of comparative advantage in their favor for many processing industries.

Balassa provides some approximate calculations to indicate that all of the six resource-based sectors in his sample (wood pulp, paper, organic chemicals, inorganic chemicals, petroleum products and carbon black) would have factor costs from 15 to 32 percent higher if produced in LDCs than if produced in the United States.[3]

It is generally held that, since processing reduces the weight and raises the value of the commodity, *transport costs* must favor the comparative advantage of the producing countries in processing their exports. However, the situation is more complex and depends on the commodity. For copper, which is probably typical of most non-ferrous metals except aluminum, there is considerable weight saving from smelting near the mine, since about two-thirds of the ore concentrates are waste material. However, there is a negligible weight saving in going from blister to refined copper, so no transport advantage [exists] for LDC location of refineries. For aluminum, also, there is a substantial weight saving in both beneficiation (producing alumina from bauxite cuts the weight in half) and smelting (producing aluminum ingots from alumina reduces the weight by half again or more). The weight loss in beneficiation gives a clear cost advantage to processing near the mine, which Radetzki estimates at 30 percent of total processing cost.[4] But shipping costs are much lower for bulk cargoes like alumina (a powder) than for metal ingots, which are more costly

2. John M. Page, Jr., "The Timber Industry and Ghanaian Development," in Scott R. Pearson and John Carnie, eds., *Commodity Exports and African Economic Development* (Lexington, Mass.: Heath, 1974), p. 107.

3. Bela Balassa, *A Stages Approach to Comparative Advantage*, World Bank Staff Working Paper 256 (Washington, D.C., May 1977), p. 25a.

4. Marian Radetzki, "Where Should Developing Countries' Minerals Be Processed? The Company View versus the Multinational Company View," *World Development* 5, no. 4 (1977): 327.

to handle, and [are] substantially higher per ton for fabricated metal than for ingots so that in general these work against LDC integration into semi-fabricating.

Substantial weight reduction is also a feature of timber processing, since up to half the wood is waste and logs take up more volume than sawnwood or boards. However, shipping conference freight rates are higher on processed wood than logs and cancel part of this advantage. Here, as in many instances of escalating rates, it is not clear how much is due to higher shipping costs and how much to price discrimination by conferences.

Food crops present some interesting contrasts. Cocoa beans lose 12 percent of their weight in processing into cocoa butter, and the butter is also easier to ship, since the chances of contamination are reduced. Chocolate, however, is both more dense and more susceptible to contamination, so costs more to ship than paste or butter. The quality problem also faces coffee roasters in exporting countries, since freshness is essential and can only be maintained for about a month. Vacuum packing in cans to protect freshness would increase transport costs. Soluble (instant) coffee faces neither of these disadvantages. Palm oil, like cocoa, is favored by a weight reduction to 5 to 10 percent in refining, but refined oil also faces deterioration in transit.

Almost all the industries based on natural resources are subject to *economies of scale*. The larger LDC exporters produce volumes of raw materials well in excess of minimum efficient levels. Except [for] wood products, the limitations are imposed by the ability of exporters to market the refined output from a plant achieving scale economies.

The situation is different for industries typically catering to the home market, such as steel, pulp and paper, and petrochemicals. For these industries, plants of efficient size are likely to exceed the consumption of all but the largest LDCs.

Despite the emphasis in the literature on scale economies, inability to achieve full-scale economies is not necessarily a bar to establishing an industry, especially one substituting for imports. A plant producing less than the output required to achieve minimum average cost may nevertheless be a socially profitable investment if the opportunity cost of the domestic factors used in production [is] below the opportunity cost of the foreign exchange needed to purchase competing imports.

External Economies

External economies are generally considered to confer comparative advantage on the industrial countries. The aluminum companies built alumina plants in Louisiana in the 1950s, despite the economies of location near the Jamaican bauxite mines, in part to gain economies of producing chemical inputs such as aluminum fluoride. Producing basic chemicals from salts, sulphur and hydrocarbons benefits from locations near user industries in the industrial centers, since each chemical has many end uses and many of these are subject to economies of scale. One of the important reasons for low productivity in wood processing in the developing countries is their inability to utilize residues from sawmilling and board manufacture.

The externality argument can be turned around and, in its familiar form of linkages, be used to justify processing in the exporting countries to stimulate related industry. This becomes an argument for dynamic comparative advantage, in contrast to the static approach used so far, and is one of the most often cited arguments for LDC processing. The linkage from ore mining through smelting and refining to fabrication of metal products and, finally, into capital goods is central to the basic industries approach. The strategic role of steel in industrial development since the industrial revolution is based on this series of linkages. The linkage argument for RBI finds support in a study by Yotopoulos and Nugent, who developed an index of total linkages, backward and forward, for 18 sectors.[5] In developing countries, basic metals has the second highest index, 2.36, compared with a median of 2.05 and a low of 1.41; paper, chemicals and petroleum refining, metal products and machinery, and wood and furniture are above the median; only rubber ranks below it, thirteenth, with an index of 1.93.

Only if home production can supply the resource-based input more cheaply (or with reduced risk of supply interruptions) can it be argued that the resource-based industry makes it more advantageous to invest in forward-linked industries. The cost factor reverts back to arguments of static comparative advantage. The case is stronger for backward-linked industries, since these typically require a domestic market for their output before being established. The exceptions—products in which the country has substantial cost advantages—might be developed as export industries in any case.

Employment Creation

Resource-based strategies do not seem to be good instruments for generating employment, at least directly. Indirect effects through linkages to other sectors do little to change the low ranking of resource-based industries other than wood products.

What scope is there for factor substitution to increase employment coefficients in these industries? The consensus is, not much, particularly in the basic metal and paper industries. Given the high fraction of raw material costs and the low share of labor costs, it seems unlikely that managers would focus much on substitution between labor and capital. Wood processing, with its higher labor shares in the tropical countries and considerably more potential for manual materials handling than in basic metal industries, should have more potential for labor-capital substitution. An estimated CES [constant elasticity of substitution] production function for sawmilling in Ghana, with pooled cross-section and time-series data and allowance for technological change, yielded a statistically significant elasticity estimate of 1.1.

Distribution of Income

With relatively few employees receiving high wages and a large share going to capital, most resource-processing industries can only increase the income

5. Pan A. Yotopoulos and Jeffrey Nugent, "A Balanced-Growth Version of the Linkage Hypothesis: A Test," *Quarterly Journal of Economics* 87, no. 2 (1973): 157–71.

concentration typical of dual economies. Exports of scale-intensive, capital-intensive commodities such as minerals and plantation crops have long been recognized as the genesis of the enclave-dominated, dualistic economy, with its characteristically skewed income distribution. Resource-based industries are thus introduced into an economy already characterized by entrenched dualism and cannot be blamed for it. However, with the possible exception of wood-based industries, resource processing has production characteristics consistent with dualism and is unlikely to break the existing pattern.

Resource-processing industries may help improve the regional distribution of development projects. Industries such as copper smelting, bauxite benefi-ciation, iron and steel, wood products and pulp and paper gain transporta-tion economies if located near the natural resources. Frequently the regions with these resources are among the least developed in a country. This is likely to be true especially for forest industries, since forests preclude extensive agriculture.

Barriers to Entry

The dominance of multinational firms in the metals industries presents a formidable barrier to LDC entry into processing for export. Multinationals may enjoy lower costs due to economies of marketing, management and diversifi-cation. Ease of market access varies with both the product and the stage of processing and may be easiest for refined copper and most difficult for alumi-num and petroleum. Ocean freight rates, set by shipping conferences, may discriminate against processed commodities, though evidence is scanty. More seriously, importing countries have established escalating tariff structures that provide substantial effective protection against LDC exports of fabricated copper products, many wood products and refined vegetable oils. Domestic-oriented RBI faces fewer barriers to entry. Small markets in the face of large-scale economies is the more serious problem, one that can be relieved by regional integration.

National Dependence

Lessening a country's dependence, either on the outside world in general or on particular countries, has long been a goal of economic development, from mercantilism through militarism to post-war nationalism. In recent years, "dependency theorists" have evolved an explanation for underdevelopment based largely on the dependence of third world countries (the periphery) upon the capitalist economies of the industrial countries (the center).

The two variants of RBI have different impacts on these problems of depen-dence. A strategy based on processing raw materials before export may well help improve the balance of payments, but it will intensify the lopsided structure of the economy, increasing dependence on export earnings to finance producer goods, especially capital equipment. The only way that export-oriented RBI might lead to structural transformation is if it includes linkages to stimulate a domestic producer goods industry, as might happen if metals are processed into fabricated products or basic chemicals are produced.

Because most resource-based processing for export is large scale and capital-intensive, the immediate impact is to deepen financial dependence. This could be reversed if, as some proponents expect, processing captures substantial oligopoly rents formerly enjoyed by multinational firms and thus increases national saving. Technological dependence will almost certainly deepen, as will managerial dependence. In copper, aluminum, petroleum, natural gas and steel, processing techniques and management must be obtained from multinational companies that control them.

Thus, export-oriented RBI does not seem to be a particularly useful instrument for reducing dependence, and the dependency theorists reject it as a strategy. The dependency school is more favorably disposed towards the home-oriented variant of RBI. Two prerequisites for development—a break with the world market and internal structural changes—also underlie the basic strategy. The central theme of that strategy is to break the colonial and import substitution trade structures and achieve a convergence of domestic resources, productive capacity and needs. A capital goods industry is essential to achieve this convergence and to provide a vehicle, as well as a stimulus, for technical innovation.

But the performance of home-oriented RBI in reducing other aspects of dependency is not so clear. It is a classic balanced growth strategy, likely to generate heavy demand for investment and to require outside finance for some time, especially for countries beginning with rudimentary industrial structures. Moreover, if resource-based industries do not represent the most efficient allocation of resources, it may be more difficult than with other strategies to generate surpluses for investment. Many of its industries will also have to borrow technology from overseas. And, although local managers, insulated from world markets, have time to learn to run these new plants, there must be some initial period when expatriates are brought in to manage each new industry.

3

Country Experiences

3.1 *Growth Trends in Manufacturing*
William F. Steel and Jonathan W. Evans

Manufacturing in Sub-Saharan Africa was a leading sector in the 1960s, with an average growth rate substantially higher than the growth rate of total GDP (table 3.1.1). Although manufacturing continued to play a leading role in the region's middle-income oil-exporting and oil-importing countries during the 1970s, albeit at a lower ratio to GDP growth, it became a lagging sector in the low-income Sub-Saharan countries during the period 1975–80. This suggests that the weaker resource position of the low-income countries made their industrial sector more vulnerable to the unfavorable external environment. The success of industrialization evidently depends at least partly on the generation of surplus resources elsewhere in the economy.

All in all, however, Sub-Saharan Africa has raised the contribution of manufacturing to its GDP. Manufacturing accounted for less than 7 percent of GDP in Sub-Saharan Africa in 1960 (table 3.1.2). This ratio had risen to nearly 10 percent by 1980, equal to that in all low-income countries (excluding China and India). Middle-income Sub-Saharan oil importers increased the manufacturing share of GDP from 10 to 14 percent during this period, whereas the share of middle-income oil importers as a group remained at 23 percent. Sub-Saharan oil exporters and North Africa had slightly declining shares (because of the impact of higher oil prices on GDP), whereas the share for all middle-income oil exporters rose somewhat.

Most of the increase in the manufacturing share of GDP took place during the 1960s. Although low-income countries apparently experienced a further increase during the 1970s in terms of current prices, the constant-price figures show a decline to 8 percent (table 3.1.2).

Sub-Saharan countries also raised the share of their total work force in the

Excerpted and edited from William F. Steel and Jonathan W. Evans, *Industrialization in Sub-Saharan Africa,* World Bank Technical Paper 25 (Washington, D.C., 1984).

Table 3.1.1 *African Manufacturing Output Growth and Ratio to GDP Growth, Five-Year Periods, 1960–80*
(annual percentage at constant 1970 prices)

Country group	Manufacturing output growth				Ratio of manufacturing growth to GDP growth			
	1960–65	1965–70	1970–75	1975–80	1960–65	1965–70	1970–75	1975–80
Low-income Sub-Saharan								
Semiarid	4.8	9.7	1.8	0.4	1.5	4.0	1.1	0.1
Other	9.3	8.2	2.4	–0.2	2.7	2.2	1.4	neg.
Middle-income Sub-Saharan								
Oil imports	7.5	7.6	7.7	4.2	1.6	1.7	1.5	1.2
Oil exporters	3.7	15.9	6.6	11.5	0.8	3.1	0.8	2.3
Sub-Saharan Africa, total	7.3	9.3	5.3	4.4	1.7	2.1	1.0	1.2
North Africa	6.2	5.6	5.6	11.7	1.8	0.9	1.4	1.6

Table 3.1.2 *Manufacturing Share of GDP, Sub-Saharan Africa
and Other Country Groups, 1960, 1970, and 1980*
(percentage of group GDP)

Country group	Current prices			1980 in constant 1970 prices
	1960	1970	1980	
Low-income Sub-Saharan Africa	6.3	9.0	9.6	8.3
Middle-income Sub-Saharan Africa				
Oil importers	10.0	13.1	14.0	15.3
Oil exporters	5.0	4.8	4.9	5.9
Sub-Saharan Africa, total	6.8	8.6	8.2	9.0
North Africa	15.0	14.2	13.4	19.2
All low-income economies	12	n.a.	15	n.a.
(excluding China and India)	(8)	n.a.	(10)	n.a.
All middle-income oil importers	23	n.a.	23	n.a.
All middle-income oil exporters	13	n.a.	16	n.a.
Industrial market economies	30	n.a.	27	n.a.

n.a. Not available.

industrial sector between 1960 and 1980, but did not fully close the gap between them and other developing countries. Industry's share of the total work force in all African country classifications reached nearly 10 percent in 1980 (as against 11 percent in all low-income countries except China and India), and 19 percent in Sub-Saharan oil exporters (as against 21 percent in all middle-income oil exporters). Industry's share of the work force in the middle-income Sub-Saharan oil importers, however, reached only 9 percent in 1980, which was less than the average for comparable countries.

Despite declining rates of growth in GDP and industrial output, the industrial labor force in African countries grew in the 1970s, or at least did not decline (with the exception of middle-income oil exporters). Annual growth in the industrial labor force of the semiarid countries during 1970–80 was projected to be 8 percent, a surprising figure in view of their weak economic performance. One possibility is that increased employment in industry became a paramount objective in the 1970s and that a combination of government pressure on existing firms and continued new investments caused employment in the sector to grow even though output did not.

Although the pace of industrial growth in Africa before 1975 was impressive, it lagged behind that in other developing regions. From 1960 to 1975, Africa's share of world manufacturing value added rose only from 0.7 to 0.8 percent, whereas the share of value added in Asian countries grew from 2.2 to 3.0 percent and that of Latin America rose from 4.1 to 4.8 percent.

African countries did not take advantage of the growing world market for manufactured exports from developing countries during the 1970s. Their share of the world's manufactured exports fell from 1.1 percent in 1970–71 to 0.6 percent in 1975–76, whereas the share of world exports supplied by other developing regions (especially South Asia) grew. This suggests that African manufactures were not competitive on world markets.

At the same time, African countries lagged behind other developing countries in exporting raw materials and in exporting processed commodities

Table 3.1.3 *Growth in Value of Exports of Selected Commodities from Africa
and All Developing Countries, 1961–77 and 1977–80*
(annual percentage)

	1961–77[a]		1977–80[a]	
Products	*Africa*	*Developing countries*	*Africa*	*Developing countries*
Raw materials				
Palm oil	0.2	15.9	6.7	21.3
Copra	0.3	−0.2	−12.7	−13.8
Groundnuts	−1.8	0.7	−19.6	−5.3
Cocoa beans	9.5	10.2	6.4	1.9
Roundwood	9.9	14.1	8.4	16.6
Processed commodities				
Palm kernel oil	10.2	18.3	45.8	32.2
Copra oil	0.4	11.5	52.5	14.0
Groundnut oil	6.9	8.1	−25.2	−12.7
Cocoa paste	31.1	31.8	−29.4	6.5
Cocoa butter	24.8	19.0	−1.9	11.2
Sawnwood	8.1	15.2	−0.2	24.5
Veneers	13.7	16.3	3.9	2.8
Plywood	5.7	23.3	1.2	16.7

a. Fitted growth rates for 1961–77; compound annual rates for 1977–80.

Source: W. F. Steel and B. A. Sarr, "Agro-Industrial Development in Africa" (Abidjan: African
Development Bank, 1983), research memorandum 2, table 3.3.

based on raw materials. Exports of palm oil, copra, and groundnuts stagnated
between 1961 and 1977 as African countries shifted into processing them (and
as domestic markets consumed larger shares of the marketed surplus), but
growth in these processed exports fell below that for developing countries as
a whole (table 3.1.3). Relatively high rates of growth were achieved at all
stages of timber exports, processed and unprocessed, but the growth rates
were below those for other developing areas. Only in cocoa products was
Africa's expansion equal to or greater than that of other regions. In the period
1977–80, however, the value of Africa's processed cocoa products fell, while it
rose in other developing areas. The value of groundnut and groundnut oil
exports collapsed during this period, but at a much faster rate in Africa than
in developing countries as a whole. On the other hand, Africa's exports of
palm kernel oil and copra oil performed relatively very well. Generally, however, exports of processed raw materials did not grow much, as African countries failed to encourage rapid growth in raw materials production and
domestic demand for these materials increased.

3.2 *Industrial Structure and Exports*
Sanjaya Lall

As countries develop, the shares of intermediate and capital goods in industrial output usually increase, bringing greater industrial balance and indepen-

Excerpted and edited from Sanjaya Lall with Gladson Kayira, "Long-Term Perspectives on Sub-
Saharan Africa: Industry," World Bank, Africa Region, Special Economic Office, 1987 (restricted
circulation).

Table 3.2.1 Composition of Manufacturing Value Added by Income Group in Africa and Asia, 1973 and 1984
(percent)

	Low-income Africa		Low-income Asia		Middle-income Africa		Middle-income Asia		World	
Subsector	1973	1984	1973	1984	1973	1984	1973	1984	1973	1984
1. Food, beverages, tobacco	37.7	35.0	12.5	12.7	32.8	27.5	20.3	12.3	12.4	11.2
2. Textiles, apparel, leather	22.3	15.9	24.2	14.7	13.2	9.9	22.6	28.0	10.2	8.4
3. Wood and wood products	5.9	3.4	2.2	2.0	3.7	6.1	4.1	1.4	4.1	3.2
4. Paper and paper products	4.9	5.0	4.4	3.5	4.8	6.5	5.0	4.6	6.3	0.1
5. Chemicals, petroleum, products	11.7	28.5	14.5	19.7	16.2	14.2	18.9	14.4	14.0	17.7
6. Nonmetallic mineral products	4.1	2.8	4.7	4.9	4.5	5.3	4.2	2.2	5.3	4.7
7. Basic metals	2.9	1.5	9.5	17.0	11.8	5.2	5.0	4.9	8.7	8.1
8. Metal products, machinery, equipment	9.8	7.5	24.8	22.8	12.5	21.7	18.3	29.9	37.1	38.9
9. Other manufactures	0.6	0.3	3.2	2.6	0.8	3.5	1.6	2.2	1.8	1.8
Industries										
Traditional (1–3)	65.9	54.3	38.9	29.4	49.5	43.5	47.0	41.7	26.7	22.8
Nontraditional (4–9)	34.1	45.7	61.1	70.6	50.5	56.5	53.0	58.3	73.3	77.2
Consumer goods (1, 2, 9)	60.6	51.2	39.9	30.0	46.6	40.9	44.5	42.5	24.4	21.4
Intermediate goods (3–7)	29.6	41.3	35.3	47.1	40.9	37.4	37.2	27.6	38.5	39.7
Capital goods (8)	9.8	7.5	24.8	22.8	12.5	21.7	18.3	29.9	37.1	38.9
Engineering intensity										
Low (1–4)	70.8	59.3	43.3	32.9	54.3	50.0	52.0	46.3	33.0	28.9
Medium (5, 6, 7)	18.7	32.8	28.7	41.6	32.5	24.7	28.1	21.5	28.0	30.5
High (8, 9)	10.4	7.8	28.0	25.4	13.3	25.2	19.9	32.1	38.9	40.7
Skill intensity										
Low (1–4, 9)	71.4	59.6	46.5	35.5	55.1	53.5	53.6	48.5	34.8	30.7
Medium (6, 8)	13.9	10.3	29.5	27.7	17.0	27.0	22.5	32.1	42.4	43.6
High (5, 7)	14.6	30.0	24.0	36.7	28.0	19.4	23.9	19.3	22.7	25.8

Note: Engineering and skill intensity are based on U.S. data for ratio of engineers and technicians to total employment and for relative wages and salaries.
Source: World Bank, industry data base.

dence. This "deepening" is associated with greater economies of scale, more advanced skills, and increased interindustry linkages. Econometric analysis of industrial structure across African countries confirms that the share of producer goods rises with per capita income. The pattern of industrialization differs, however, in several respects from that in other developing regions (table 3.2.1):

- Over time the food, beverage, and tobacco group has remained predominant and is far more important in Africa than elsewhere.
- Textiles, apparel, and leather in middle-income Africa are far below their share in middle-income Asia because the labor-intensive industries that led export growth in Asia never took off in Africa.
- In low-income Africa between 1973 and 1984, the increase in the share of chemicals and petroleum, and of intermediate goods industries generally, is attributable mainly to petroleum refining under high protection and does not reflect real industrial maturity.
- Metal products and machinery are well below the share in comparable Asian countries, especially in the low-income category.
- Despite some decline, traditional and consumer goods industries remain much more important in low-income Africa than elsewhere.
- Industries with low requirements for engineering and skills are relatively more important in low-income African countries, consistent with their presumed comparative advantage; this gap diminishes, however, for countries in the middle-income range.

Selected Countries

Consumer goods industries predominate for different reasons in different countries. Côte d'Ivoire, Ghana, Kenya, Mauritius, and Zimbabwe have large, partly export-based, food processing sectors. The share of food rose in Ghana during the 1970s because it declined less than did more import-dependent activities. Mauritius has diversified within consumer goods through a dramatic increase in textiles and clothing for export (from 5 percent of industrial output in 1960 to 37 percent in 1980). In Nigeria, however, the share of consumer goods fell sharply as expansion of petroleum raised the shares of intermediate and heavy industries and adversely affected agriculture and processing industries.

Zimbabwe has the most advanced capital goods industry and is one of the few African countries with a subcontracting and service network. Most countries have some relatively simple metalworking capabilities, especially countries such as Ghana where repairs and spare parts manufacture have flourished for lack of imported parts. In many countries capital goods production consists largely of automobile assembly plants of questionable economic value, given their poor prospects for achieving significant economies of scale.

Manufactured Exports

African countries account for a small and diminishing share of world trade in manufactures: from 0.5 percent of world exports of nonpetroleum manufac-

Table 3.2.2 *Distribution of Manufactured Exports by Subsector in Sub-Saharan Africa and Developing Countries, 1973 and 1983*
(percent)

Year and region	Processed food and agriculture	Textiles, leather, clothing	Machines and transport equipment	Chemicals	Other	Total, excluding petroleum	Petroleum and petroleum products	Total
1973								
Sub-Saharan Africa								
Low-income	23.1	49.9	2.3	4.1	20.6	100.0	8.4	100.0
Middle-income								
Oil importers	59.2	13.0	9.5	4.6	13.7	100.0	10.2	100.0
Oil exporters	24.4	22.8	2.7	4.6	45.4	100.0	89.9	100.0
Total	28.5	38.9	3.4	4.3	24.9	100.0	66.3	100.0
(Millions of dollars)[a]	(493)	(672)	(59)	(74)	(431)	(1,729)	(3,402)	(5,130)
All developing countries	18.4	29.7	22.4	6.3	23.1	100.0	46.3	100.0
(Millions of dollars)[a]	(8,162)	(13,161)	(9,916)	(2,784)	(10,233)	(44,256)	(38,228)	(82,484)
Sub-Saharan Africa as percentage of								
All developing countries	6.0	5.1	0.6	2.6	4.2	3.9	8.9	6.2
World	1.6	1.4	0.0	0.2	0.5	0.5	6.5	1.3
1983								
Sub-Saharan Africa								
Low-income	25.4	31.8	4.9	17.2	20.7	100.0	27.3	100.0
Middle-income								
Oil importers	39.6	26.9	5.7	4.7	23.1	100.0	18.8	100.0
Oil exporters	12.1	19.1	12.9	8.0	47.9	100.0	98.1	100.0
Total	28.9	28.8	6.0	12.0	24.3	100.0	84.7	100.0
(Millions of dollars)[a]	(918)	(914)	(190)	(381)	(771)	(3,174)	(17,520)	(20,694)
All developing countries	9.8	24.1	33.1	7.7	25.3	100.0	54.7	100.0
(Millions of dollars)[a]	(16,726)	(41,188)	(15,672)	(13,201)	(43,209)	(170,996)	(206,750)	(377,746)
Sub-Saharan Africa as percentage of								
All developing countries	5.5	2.2	0.3	2.9	1.8	1.9	8.5	5.5
World	1.3	0.8	0.0	0.3	0.2	0.3	7.0	1.5

a. Figures in parentheses are millions of current U.S. dollars.
Source: United Nations, trade data system.

tures in 1973 to 0.3 percent in 1983 (table 3.2.2). Their share of total exports of petroleum products rose from 6.5 percent to 7.0 percent in the same period, and petroleum products account for two-thirds of Africa's industrial exports. Compared with nonpetroleum exports in the rest of the developing world, Africa shows above average shares for the food and textiles groups and a below average share for engineering industries.[1] Consumer goods (including "other") account for 92 percent of total Sub-Saharan African exports of nonpetroleum manufactures, a far higher proportion than the weight of consumer goods in the structure of manufacturing.

Export performance varies by income group. Low-income African countries specialized in textiles (mainly yarn from cotton producers) in 1973, but the textile share fell sharply by 1983 as chemical and petrochemical exports rose. Middle-income countries showed faster growth of manufactured exports over the decade (283 percent versus 101 percent for low-income countries, in current dollars) and a rising rather than falling share of textiles. In the oil-exporting countries, nonpetroleum exports, especially food products, declined in current dollar terms.

The five largest African exporters of nonpetroleum industrial products in 1985 were Côte d'Ivoire, Mauritius, Niger, Sudan, and Zimbabwe. Côte d'Ivoire is the fastest-growing exporter among the major nonoil economies, and it is among the top three African exporters of equipment, textiles, chemicals, and food products. It has the most diversified export basket; Niger has the least, with phosphates accounting for 98 percent of its exports. Sudan and Mauritius obtain over 93 percent of manufactured export earnings from food and textile products, whereas Zimbabwe has a much more diversified structure.

3.3 Three Late Starters
Ravi Gulhati and Uday Sekhar

Countries in Sub-Saharan Africa were among the last of the colonies to achieve independence. Their attempts to industrialize have only just begun, and their industrial strategies are influenced by this late start. On the one hand, they can benefit from the world's accumulated production technology and experience regarding industrial organization; on the other hand, the established market positions of earlier industrializers pose special problems for the newcomers. Three of these late starters—Kenya, Tanzania and Zambia—made a promising beginning during the second half of the 1960s. These economies are similar in several respects, but they have pursued strategies which diverge in crucial areas.

The broad contours of industrial strategy in the wake of independence were remarkably similar in the three economies. All three countries opted for the

Excerpted by permission from Ravi Gulhati and Uday Sekhar, "Industrial Strategy for Late Starters: The Experience of Kenya, Tanzania and Zambia," *World Development* 10, no. 11 (1982): 949–72.
1. Econometric cross-section analysis reveals higher levels of engineering exports per capita in countries that are relatively open (higher ratio of trade to GDP), more industrialized (higher manufacturing value added per capita), and located on the coast.

Figure 3.3.1 *Real Value Added in Manufacturing: Kenya, Tanzania, and Zambia, 1964–78*
(value added at factor cost, in constant prices)

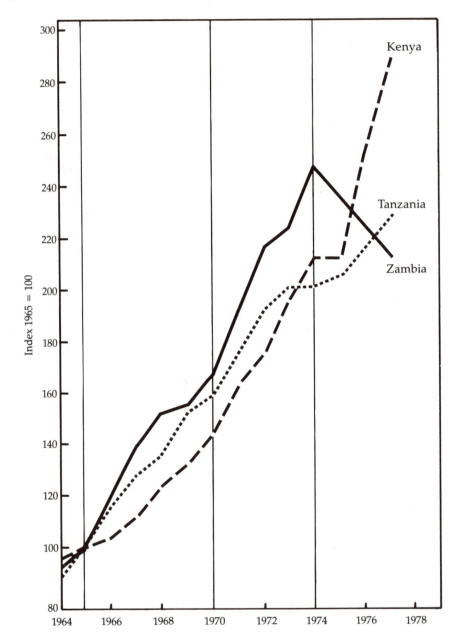

capitalistic road. All three recognized the dearth of indigenous entrepreneur-ship as the critical impediment and put heavy reliance on foreign private parties to supply not only capital but also technology and management. There was scarcely any break with the colonial period. The strategy was essentially to carry on as before. The emphasis was clearly on import substitution. Com-peting in world markets was considered to be beyond the range of feasibility but there was considerable interest in regional markets.

The similarity of industrial strategies in the three countries ended in 1967 with the Arusha Declaration. This was part of a major transformation in the overall Tanzanian strategy of socio-economic development. The capitalistic road based on foreign capital was abandoned in favour of socialism and self-reliance. In the industrial sphere, there was a significant shift in strategy. The Second Plan (1969–74) opted for a "basic goods" strategy and this was further elaborated in the next plan. By 1966, the share of intermediate and capital goods was to be raised to 60 percent. Emphasis was to be placed on meeting the essential needs of the Tanzanian people through domestic resources. Special attention was to be given to the processing of local raw materials.

The Arusha wind blew in Mulungushi in 1968, where Dr. Kaunda announced a series of nationalizations and other reforms to implement Zam-bia's humanist philosophy. Here too the capitalist solution was rejected and the goal of self-reliance proclaimed. The Second Zambia Plan (1972–76) visu-alized a rate of growth of value-added in manufacturing of 15 percent per annum. The Plan's main emphasis was on import substitution. Major expan-sion of meat processing, dairy products and textile capacity was visualized. In addition, there was the intention to produce sulphuric acid for the mining industry and fertilizer for farming. The aim of promoting small enterprises in rural areas was given considerable prominence, and it was believed that the opening up of the Tanzam railroad would generate many opportunities of this kind.

While Tanzania and Zambia opted for the socialist path, Kenya continued to rely on private initiative, including private foreign investment. The long-term goal was "localization of capitalism." The Second Plan talked about "an active and growing participation of Kenyan citizens in management and own-ership of industry." Localization was promoted through: (i) the refusal to give citizenship to alien minorities; (ii) the requirement that non-citizens obtain work permits; and (iii) the imposition of restrictions on foreign busi-ness in such areas as domestic trade. Nevertheless, the open-door policy for large foreign investors in manufacturing continued intact.

Growth and Import Substitution

The manufacturing sector expanded more rapidly in Kenya than in the other two countries over the period a a whole (figure 3.3.1). Up to the early 1970s, Zambia was leading the field but suffered a major setback; subsequently, output has been falling since 1974. The share of manufacturing in GDP climbed up from 6.8 percent in 1965 to 11.9 percent in 1973 but then dropped to 10.4 percent by 1977. In Tanzania, too, manufacturing output rose very rapidly in the initial period but slowed down after 1972. Kenya manufacturing output stagnated in 1975, then recovered briskly.

Import substitution was a major impetus behind Zambian industrialization; exports were unimportant and domestic demand rose at a much slower pace than in the other two countries. This is one of the conclusions of a statistical disaggregation of the sources of industrial growth we have carried out (table 3.3.1). Import substitution accounts for 55 percent of the overall rise in Zambia's manufacturing output during 1965–72. A sharp expansion in the textile, clothing and leather industry reduced the share of imports in total supply of these items from 77 to 46 percent during this period. Corresponding ratios for rubber, chemicals and petroleum products also declined very sharply. The import substitution drive was part of Zambia's search for self-reliance.

Import substitution was a considerably smaller source of industrial growth in Kenya, with domestic demand and exports playing a larger role than in Zambia. The share of imports in total supply of finished textiles, clothing, beverages, tobacco and non-metallic mineral products dropped in Kenya; but this was offset to some extent by a heavier reliance on imports of food products, semi-processed textiles, footwear, wood products.

The most surprising finding was that import substitution played no role whatever in overall expansion in Tanzanian manufacturing. This was so despite the emphasis on self-reliance in several strategy pronouncements. There was considerable import replacement of beverage, textiles, wearing apparel and non-metallic mineral products; but this was offset by increased reliance on imports of food products, wood products, furniture and fixtures, capital goods, metals and metal products. The import to supply ratio for capital goods, metals and metal products in 1965 was 80 percent, compared to 41 percent for consumer goods. The share of imported capital goods, metal and metal products in total supply rose by 0.7 percent during 1965–72. This

Table 3.3.1 *Sources of Growth of Manufacturing Output and Import Substitution*

Indicator	Kenya	Tanzania	Zambia
Sources of growth[a]			
Import substitution (%)	17	−1	55
Domestic demand (%)	70	96	44
Export demand (%)	13	5	1
Period (years)	1963–71	1965–72	1965–72
Manufactured imports as percentage of supply[b]			
1965	49[c]	56	66
1972	41[d]	57	47
Imported inputs as percentage of gross output			
1964	20[c]	16[e]	26
1970	30[d]	14	18[f]

a. For the methodology underlying this calculation, see P. Desai, "Alternative Measures of Import Substitution," *Oxford Economic Papers* (November 1969).

b. Imports plus gross output of manufactures.

c. 1963.

d. 1971.

e. 1965.

f. 1969.

seemingly small rise from a very high initial level was enough to swamp the impact of import substitution in several consumer products.

So far we have examined import substitution in the form of expansion in the share of locally produced manufactured goods in total supply of such goods. Now we will look at another dimension, i.e., the dependence of local manufacturing output on imported raw materials and semi-processed inputs. Again, Zambia scored the sharpest decline in such import dependence from 26 percent in 1964 to 18 percent in 1969. Import coefficients declined and therefore local value-added rose markedly as a proportion of gross output in beverages, tobacco, textiles, wood, non-metallic mineral products and fabricated metal industries.

By way of contrast, the import coefficient in Tanzanian manufacturing fell by only 2 percent during roughly the same period. There was a large drop in many branches producing consumer goods, e.g., food, beverages, tobacco and textiles; but the coefficient rose sharply in several industries producing intermediate and capital goods.

While the import coefficient fell sharply in Zambia and marginally in Tanzania, there was a large upsurge in the dependence on imports of Kenyan manufacturing. The coefficient of imported inputs rose by a full ten percentage points, and its absolute level at 30 percent in 1970 exceeded by far the corresponding proportion in neighbouring countries. Food, textile raw materials, wood, rubber, chemicals, and non-metallic minerals experienced large upward shifts in import dependence. Only beverages, tobacco, textile finishing, clothing, footwear and fabricated metal branches secured a reduction. Input dependence was high in Kenya partly because the output mix of the manufacturing sector there was much more diversified than in Tanzania and Zambia. The share of capital and intermediate goods in total Kenyan manufacturing output was higher, and these branches tend to have a larger import coefficient. If the Tanzanian manufacturing sector had Kenya's output mix, then its overall import coefficient would be 18 percent in 1970 instead of the actual 14 percent. Another factor which may be responsible for Kenya's high import dependence is the fact that a large part of its industry is controlled by transnational corporations. These firms frequently preferred foreign inputs to local ones on the grounds that the former were more compatible with the technological process in use and their supply was more dependable.

Exports were a significant part of manufacturing production in Kenya and Tanzania, and the regional East African Common Market (EACM) accounted for a substantial part of export sales. Unfortunately, the Common Market failed to expand rapidly and collapsed in 1977. Exports to international markets increased more rapidly—especially in the case of Kenya. But altogether, the export orientation of the manufacturing sector in these two countries diminished. Zambia's manufacturing continued to ignore export sales.

Parastatals

The role of parastatals had risen rapidly after 1967 in Zambia and Tanzania (table 3.3.2). They accounted for 40–50 percent of employment and output in the manufacturing sector. The question of how these parastatals have per-

Table 3.3.2 *Role of Parastatals in Manufacturing, Tanzania and Zambia*
(percent)

		Share of employment		Share in gross output	
	Year	Tanzania	Zambia	Tanzania	Zambia
	1966	7.7	n.a.	8.9	n.a.
	1967	17.0	n.a.	25.8	n.a.
	1968	23.1	14	30.4	10
	1969	28.5	12	35.1	17
	1970	32.0	17	37.8	27
	1971	46.4	36	42.9	46
	1972	40.9	37	47.1	45
	1973	47.6	n.a.	43.4	n.a.
	1974	49.7	n.a.	44.9	n.a.

n.a. Not available.

Sources: Tanzania, Ministry of Finance and Planning, Bureau of Statistics, *Survey of Industrial Production; Analysis of Accounts of Parastatals 1966–1974;* and *Economic Survey.* Zambia, Central Statistical Organization, *Census of Industrial Production,* 1968 to 1972, and *Indeco Ltd. Annual Reports,* 1968–69 to 1971–72.

formed has aroused some controversy. Official Tanzanian data suggest that while employment and the capital stock in parastatals rose by seven times during 1966–1967 to 1972–1973, value-added in these firms expanded by less than five times. Consequently, the incremental capital-output ratio rose from 2.5 in the late 1960s to about 5.6 in the mid-1970s, and output per worker fell by roughly 30 percent.

Some Strategic Issues

Three issues deserve consideration. First, what is the scope for expanding sales of manufactures in world markets? Secondly, what are the prospects for organizing import substitution on a sub-regional or regional basis so as to escape from the predicament of limited national markets for manufactures? Finally, what policy measures are necessary for strengthening linkages between industry and the rest of the national economy? These issues are not mutually exclusive; strengthening linkages within the national economy and promoting trade within Africa are worthwhile objectives even if there is plenty of scope for industry to serve global markets. But it is true that the third issue becomes crucial, if serving nearby and distant export markets is judged to be problematical.

It has been suggested that the comparative advantage of African economies lies in the processing of natural resource-based commodities. For example, Zambia exports its copper in refined form, thereby adding value to the mined ore. It does not convert refined copper into fabricated products (e.g., wires, tubes and pipes), however. Coffee from Kenya and Tanzania is exported in green or roasted form but not as essences or extracts. The economics of successive stages of processing varies greatly by commodity, and few generalizations are safe. Many resource-based activities are very demanding of skills, capital or energy. Many are subject to sizeable economies of scale. Some are subject to the monopolistic or oligopolistic control of transnational corporations. Tariff rates in OECD markets tend to rise with the extent of processing, and shipping freight rates are frequently biased in favour of primary commodities.

Many present-day LDC exporters of manufactures broke into global markets by exploiting their comparative advantage in labour-intensive items, given their relatively low level of wages. But African economies tend to have high rates of compensation for factory labour while worker productivity remains at a very low level. Zambian wages, for example, are much higher than in Kenya and Tanzania, and wages in all three Eastern African countries are substantially higher than in India or Philippines (see table 3.3.3). The level of African wages reflects the high reservation price of labour, the legacy of the colonial period, and the adoption of minimum wage legislation in some cases.

Altogether, our conclusion is that sales to world markets are not likely to become the engine of industrial growth in many African countries in the near-term future. These qualifications notwithstanding, the bias against exports that now pervades the incentive systems of African economies ought to be removed. In fact, governments should adopt a strong promotional posture, given the key role that manufactured exports play in assimilating technological change and in breaking the barrier imposed by small domestic markets.

A way out of the small-size dilemma for African economies is to pool their national markets together into a regional or sub-regional common market. The idea is not new, of course. The accent of the Lagos Plan is on collective self-reliance. The aim is to move towards an Africa-wide economic community by the year 2000. We have seen how this approach was tried in Eastern Africa, and how it led to an impasse in 1977. It would be wrong to conclude from this history that the idea of a regional approach is altogether bankrupt. We do not believe that difficulties in re-establishing and maintaining similar institutional arrangements are insurmountable. A key problem is that the net benefits of regional cooperation in the industrial sphere tend to accrue in large measure to countries which are relatively advanced. It follows that a customs union approach to regional cooperation by itself will not suffice, if participating countries are at different points on the development scale. Industrial planning on a regional level and some mechanism for the redistribution of benefits among member countries are essential.

Perhaps a more fruitful course of action at this stage of economic develop-

Table 3.3.3 *Index of Wages in Manufacturing Sector*
(Zambia mid-1970s = 100)

		Wages	
	Country	Mid-1960s	Mid-1970s
	Zambia	83	100
	Kenya	72	66
	Tanzania	49	58
	Republic of Korea	42	52
	Philippines	37	30
	India	26	30

ment would be to consider ways of strengthening linkages between industry and the rest of the national economy. Industrial strategy in Africa must be closely tied to the mainspring of rural development and agricultural growth. Although industry and agriculture compete for funds and scarce skilled manpower, the two sectors are complementary in large measure. Industry relies on farm production for local raw materials, food for its workers and foreign exchange to purchase capital goods or other imported inputs. Farmers are, or can become, the major market outlet for manufactured output of consumer goods, farm implements and other inputs. Given these close connections, it is virtually futile to aim at rapid industrialization in Africa except in the context of progressive rural development. Given its direct and indirect importance for the home market for manufactures, industrial strategy should eschew tax, tariff or exchange rate measures which undermine the profitability of agriculture.

3.4 *The Pattern of Industrial Development in Zambia*
World Bank Staff

Zambia's manufacturing sector is large compared with that of other Sub-Saharan countries, contributing over $600 million to gross domestic product (GDP) in 1982 and employing nearly 60,000 workers. The 18 percent share of manufacturing in Zambia's GDP is higher than any other country for which data are available except Zimbabwe, and only Zimbabwe and Ivory Coast have higher per capita GDP originating in manufacturing. Although Zambia ranks nineteenth among Sub-Saharan countries in population and twelfth in total GDP, its manufacturing output ranks sixth. This relatively high ranking many be attributed in part to demand generated by mining activity and to the natural protection afforded by its landlocked position.

The contribution of manufacturing to GDP has tripled in Zambia since independence in 1964, when it was about 6 percent. Manufacturing was the most dynamic component of GDP in the first decade of independence, although it was too small to offset stagnation in other sectors. From 1965 to 1970, manufacturing GDP grew at over 11 percent per year, but falling agricultural production together with negligible growth in mining resulted in a decline in real GDP per capita (table 3.4.1). Growth picked up in other sectors and in GDP per capita during 1970–74, with manufacturing continuing to lead, though at a slightly reduced rate of over 8 percent per year.

In 1975, the price of copper fell by 40 percent, copper production fell by 9 percent, and the contribution of the mining sector to GDP (in 1970 prices) fell by 10 percent (table 3.4.1). The impact was severe on the balance of payments, the economy in general, and particularly on manufacturing output, which fell by nearly 12 percent in 1975. This decrease can be attributed largely to a drop in demand, both in the aggregate and in the mining sector in particular.

Excerpted and edited from "Zambia: Industrial Policy and Performance," World Bank Industry Department and Eastern Africa Projects Department, August 1984 (restricted circulation).

Both mining and total GDP remained lower in 1979 than in 1975 (in constant prices), while manufacturing, agriculture, and services (excluding trade) were able to show only a slight increase over 1975–79. The supply of imported inputs was a problem during this period following the closure of the Rhodesian border and subsequent congestion in the Dar-es-Salaam Port. Imports were also cut back sharply in response to falling foreign exchange earnings, with a negative impact on industrial production.

Since 1980, Zambia has had some degree of recovery (or at least no further major decline) in the principal economic sectors and in total GDP, which had returned to its 1974 level by 1983. The independence of Zimbabwe in 1980 helped ease Zambia's transport problems, but foreign exchange availability remained constrained. Manufacturing output increased during the period 1979–83 at an annual average of 3 percent measured in value terms and 1 percent according to the physical index (table 3.4.1).

The Structure of Production

Industrial production in Zambia has become increasingly diversified over the years, moving from a predominance of consumer goods to a greater share of output in intermediate and capital goods and with increasing contributions from previously negligible branches of industry. Half of gross manufacturing output in 1965 was in food, beverages, and tobacco, with an additional 9 percent in textiles, wearing apparel, and leather. The heavier industries (International Standard Industrial Classification categories 35–38: chemicals, mineral products, metal industries and products, machinery and equipment) accounted for less than a third of gross output—still a reasonably large share relative to other Sub-Saharan countries in the early 1960s. Ten years later, in 1975, the share of food, beverages, tobacco, textiles, wearing apparel, and leather combined (ISIC categories 31–32) had fallen below 40 percent, while categories 35–38 had reached 49 percent of gross output.

The 1975 fall in mining prices and production and in aggregate demand had differential effects on different branches of industry, as did the subsequent cutbacks in foreign exchange available for imported inputs. The fall in output was most severe in wood products, basic metals, and metal products—the branches most closely allied with mining.

The shift in industrial production toward intermediate and capital goods reflects the pattern of investment. Whereas categories 35–38 accounted for only 38 percent of fixed capital formation in 1965, they exceeded 45 percent of new investment in all years except one from 1967 to 1980. This investment pattern is evidence of the government's emphasis on basic industries. The industry receiving the largest share of new fixed capital formation during these years was basic industrial chemicals.

Employment, Productivity, and Wages

Manufacturing employment grew at a relatively rapid annual rate of 11 percent during the 1960s, accounting for about 10 percent of total recorded employment in the mid-1960s and around 12 percent after 1972. The ''elastic-

Table 3.4.1 Zambia's Manufacturing Production and GDP at Constant Prices, Selected Years, 1965–83

Manufacturing production and GDP	1965[a]	1970	1974	1975	1979	1983
Index of industrial production (1973 = 100)	n.a.	81.8	110.6	105.5	96.2	99.3[b]
Manufacturing GDP at constant 1970 prices						
Value (millions of kwacha)	75.0	129.2	178.9	157.6	163.0	184.5
As percentage of GDP at market prices						
Constant 1970 prices	6.8	10.2	12.1	11.0	11.9	12.5
Current prices	6.8	10.2	12.6	15.8	17.0	18.6
Total GDP at constant 1970 prices						
Value (millions of kwacha)	1,103.0	1,268.5	1,473.9	1,438.1	1,370.1	1,479.1
Per capita (kwacha)	325.9	305.0	313.6	296.8	250.2	236.5

	Annual growth at constant prices (percent)[c]				
	1965–70	1970–74	1974–75	1975–79	1979–83
Industrial production index	n.a.	7.8	–4.6	–2.3	1.1
Manufacturing GDP	11.4	8.5	–11.9	0.8	3.1
Mining GDP	0.4	0.8	–9.8	–2.2	4.7
Agricultural GDP	–2.1	2.5	4.3	0.5	1.8
Total GDP	2.8	3.8	–2.4	–1.2	1.9
GDP per capita	–1.3	0.7	–5.4	–4.2	–1.4

n.a. Not available.
a. Former national accounting methodology.
b. For 1982.
c. Compound growth between end points.
Sources: Zambia, Central Statistical Organization, Monthly Digest of Statistics, and World Bank data.

ity" of employment growth with respect to growth of output was around 0.9, a relatively high ratio implying few gains in terms of economies of scale and labor productivity. Growth continued at a slower pace of under 6 percent per year during 1970–74, with an employment/production growth "elasticity" of 0.6 to 0.7—more nearly what would be expected for an African country in the early stages of industrialization. Employment continued to grow during 1975–80, albeit at only 1 percent per year. This trend was maintained through public and parastatal sector employment policies, with employment growing over 5 percent per year during 1975–80, more than twice as fast as the sector's contribution to GDP. In the private sector, however, both employment and real GDP fell at about 3 percent during this period.

As a result of efforts to maintain a high rate of employment growth, labor productivity in manufacturing has declined steadily since 1973. Value added per worker in constant 1970 prices rose at an annual average of 3.5 percent from 1965 to 1973, but dropped at an annual average of 11 percent over the next two years. From 1975 to 1980, value added per worker continued declining at an annual average of 1.5 percent, while employment grew at 1 percent.

In accordance with the government's policy of Zambianization, employment gains were entirely of Zambian workers, with the number of non-Zambian workers declining steadily to 1,900 in 1980, about half the 1965 figure. In 1965, Africans accounted for 87 percent of the manufacturing work force. By 1980, 96 percent of manufacturing employees were Zambian.

Real wages in manufacturing rose substantially during the postindependence boom period but have followed a declining trend since 1973. Real wages of Zambian workers grew over 1966–70 at an annual average of nearly 8 percent in manufacturing and in all recorded employment. Over the next five years, however, wage increases barely kept pace with price changes in manufacturing, and then showed a net decline over the period 1975–80 at an average annual rate of 2 percent.

Investment and Capacity Utilization

Investment in manufacturing rose rapidly in the late 1960s and early 1970s, doubling to 13 percent of investment in 1972. Over 45 percent of total manufacturing investment from 1965 to 1975 was in chemicals and nonmetallic mineral products. One consequence of the substantial public investment in larger, capital-intensive industries was a rise in the incremental capital-output ratio (ICOR) from 2 or less in 1966–67 to 3.5 in 1971–72. The industries that received the most investment between 1965 and 1975 also had the highest (or negative) ICORs: chemical and petroleum products, with an overall ICOR of 5.5; food products with 8.6; and nonmetallic mineral products, with a negative ratio.

High ICORs are attributable to underutilization of capacity as well as to capital-intensive investment. Underutilization occurred because of delays in bringing new investments into full production, especially in the early 1970s, and to scarcity of foreign exchange available for imported inputs and spare parts. In seven firms for which data are available, average capacity utilization rose from 46 percent in 1972–73 to 65 percent in 1974–75, but then fell to 60 percent in 1982–83.

Total Factor Productivity Change

Declining labor productivity accompanied by an increase in the capital-labor ratio is symptomatic of a deterioration in total factor productivity (TFP)—the level of output that is obtained from all factor inputs combined.[2] Since the industrial sector in Zambia can grow only as fast as the rate of expansion of its factor inputs, primarily labor and capital, plus the rate of productivity change of these inputs, total factor productivity change is an important component of industrial growth and development. Moreover, international competitiveness in industry requires rates of productivity change in Zambia to equal or exceed those of competing countries.

Table 3.4.2 presents rates of change in total factor productivity and other variables for the period 1965 to 1980 for major industrial sectors. The most striking feature of the table is the uniform deterioration in total factor productivity over the fifteen-year period. For manufacturing as a whole, TFP declined at an annual average rate of 3.8 percent. Fourteen of the seventeen individual sectors experienced rates of TFP decline ranging from -0.1 to -13.8 percent. Only three sectors—leather products and footwear, petroleum and coal products, and rubber—had positive rates of productivity change over the entire period. In five sectors—wearing apparel, basic industrial chemicals, plastic products, basic metals, and other manufacturing—the rates of productivity decline exceeded 5 percent per year.

Deterioration of this magnitude over so long a period is a reason for concern. Since TFP declines are equivalent to increases in unit costs, these results indicate a substantial increase in the average costs of production. The major source of the productivity decline was evidently a deterioration in capital productivity caused by rapidly growing investment coupled with relatively slower growth of output. Capital deepening, the rate of growth in the capital-labor ratio, occurred at a very rapid rate in virtually all sectors. Labor productivity did not increase in proportion, however, and actually declined in seven sectors.

In general, the pattern of productivity decline conforms closely to macroeconomic trends in aggregate demand and foreign exchange availability. Productivity rose in eight of thirteen sectors between 1965 and 1970, a period when both national income and foreign exchange availability were rising rapidly. The pattern then became strongly negative for the periods 1970–75 and 1975–80.

In several subsectors, both the magnitude and the pattern of productivity decline are striking. Food products had one of the most rapid overall rates of TFP decline and was the only subsector in which rising real output was accompanied by a productivity decline between 1975 and 1980. The productivity decline for basic industrial chemicals in 1975–80 far exceeded the decline in output and suggests rising inefficiency in the use of plant. The same applies to plastics manufacturing, in which rising output was accompanied by declining productivity throughout the period 1965–80.

---

2. See technical note D.

Table 3.4.2 *Growth of Total Factor Productivity, Value Added, and Inputs by Subsector, 1965–80*
(average annual percentage growth in constant 1970 prices)

Subsector	Total factor productivity	Value added	Capital input	Labor input	Capital-labor ratio	Output-capital ratio	Output-labor ratio
Food	−4.5	−4.9	10.5	8.5	1.9	−6.0	−4.0
Beverages and tobacco	−0.1	6.8	8.7	3.7	5.0	−1.9	3.1
Textiles	−1.2	15.2	21.0	12.5	8.5	−5.8	2.7
Wearing apparel	−7.4	8.8	25.9	6.1	19.8	−17.1	2.7
Leather products and footwear	8.4	21.8	13.1	13.6	−0.5	8.6	8.1
Wood and wood products	−0.6	3.8	13.6	−3.0	16.6	−9.8	6.8
Furniture	−1.8	3.8	7.3	3.3	4.0	−3.5	1.0
Paper, printing, and publishing	−2.7	5.7	15.4	5.3	10.1	−9.7	0.4
Basic industrial chemicals	−5.8	9.4	22.9	4.0	18.9	−13.5	5.4
Other chemical products	−2.7	3.7	7.4	4.7	2.7	−3.8	−1.1
Petroleum and coal products	4.0	15.9	8.1	22.4	−14.2	7.8	−6.4
Rubber products	1.0	10.1	7.5	11.1	−3.7	2.7	−1.6
Plastic products	−13.8	8.0	27.2	9.6	17.6	−19.2	−1.6
Nonmetallic mineral products	−3.8	2.3	9.4	0.7	8.8	−7.1	1.7
Basic metals	−9.2	−2.8	7.9	4.1	3.8	−10.7	−6.9
Metal products, machinery, and equipment	−1.7	13.4	14.3	4.9	−0.6	−1.0	−1.5
Other manufacturing industries	−5.7	6.0	16.7	3.8	12.9	−10.7	2.1
Total manufacturing	−3.8	7.2	14.0	6.3	7.7	−6.8	0.9

Import Intensity and Export Performance

Capacity utilization in Zambian manufacturing was affected by the shortage of foreign exchange because it is highly dependent on imported inputs and spare parts (though not necessarily more so than other comparable African countries). Only the food, textile, and footwear industries import less than half their intermediate goods. Metal products is the most import-intensive activity (of the branches sampled), with imports accounting for 81 percent of all intermediates and 40 percent of the value of gross output.

Although Zambia's industrial sector is relatively large and advanced compared with that of other African countries, its manufactured exports are exceptionally small. The largest amount of exported manufactures achieved by Zambia was US$3.3 million in 1974, which was more than only eight out of thirty-four African countries for which data are available. The six principal products that have been exported consistently in recent years are cement, sugar and molasses, copper cable, menswear, crushed stone and lime, and explosives; these account for about two-thirds of total manufactured exports. Including sugar, molasses, crushed stone, and lime, manufactured goods made up only 1.3 percent of Zambia exports in 1977 and 0.7 percent in 1980, and they represented only 0.6 percent of gross manufacturing output in 1980.

Conclusions

The pattern of industrialization in Zambia has many positive aspects: relatively large size, reasonable diversity in both structure of production and location, and development of technologically advanced industries, particularly engineering. Nevertheless, a number of issues arise from the preceding analysis.

The overriding issues are growth and capacity utilization. The basic causes are macroeconomic: on the demand side, falling income per capita and declining production in mining and construction; on the supply side, lack of growth in the foreign exchange earnings needed for imported inputs and weak incentives to domestic producers of raw materials.

Specific policy aspects relate to obtaining maximum performance from the industrial sector under whatever macroeconomic conditions may prevail and to adjusting to an anticipated long-term slowdown in mining production and export earnings. This means providing the incentives for firms to make the most efficient use of scarce foreign exchange. The issues of adjustment and efficiency apply in particular to the public and parastatal sector, which dominates several of the most important branches of industry.

The question of the future role of the public and parastatal sector must also be raised. This sector has played a leading role in building Zambian industry, but declining productivity, together with constraints on public finance, raise the question of whether this role can be sustained. Domestic entrepreneurial capacity and managerial skills may have improved to the extent that a greater role for the private sector can be permitted without sacrificing the objective of keeping industry under the control of Zambians. An infusion of foreign investment may also be needed to stimulate new growth. The question is how to achieve this in a way consistent with national objectives and resource availability.

3.5 *Industrial Structure and Incentives in Senegal*
World Bank Staff

Although the Senegalese industrial sector is one of the most diversified and mature in Sub-Saharan Africa and has enjoyed sustained levels of both foreign and domestic investment, annual real growth of industrial output (manufacturing and construction) declined from an average rate of over 4 percent

Excerpted, edited, and updated from "Senegal: Country Economic Memorandum," 1984, and "Senegal: An Economy under Adjustment," 1987, World Bank Western Africa Regional Office (restricted circulation).

per annum in the 1960s to less than 3 percent per annum in the 1970s. Manufacturing alone grew more slowly, averaging only 0.8 percent per year between 1970 and 1982, well below the performance of several other African countries over the same period: Ivory Coast, 5.4 percent; Sudan, 6.0 percent; Cameroon, 8.4 percent; Kenya, 9.0 percent; and Tunisia, 11.6 percent.

There has been almost no employment growth in the Senegalese economy since the mid-1970s except in the informal sector, public administration, and public enterprises. Employment in modern enterprises in the secondary sector actually fell between 1976 and 1980 (table 3.5.1). At the same time, however, total wages and salaries paid by these enterprises increased an astounding 60 percent although Senegal's index of industrial production showed a decline in output. In addition, the capital intensity of new investments in Senegal increased from roughly CFAF 3.5 million per job in the early 1970s to roughly CFAF 12.5 million per job by the early 1980s. In real terms, this was an approximate doubling of the capital intensity of new investments.

The Structure of Industry

Three export-oriented industries (groundnut processing, phosphate mining, and fish processing) and a range of import-substituting light industries make up Senegal's industrial sector, which (including construction) accounts for about 25 percent of GDP. The sector has three basic characteristics: limited competition, limited export prospects, and a low degree of integration.

The largest 140 of some 600 modern industrial enterprises account for over 94 percent of total business turnover. About half are under French-majority ownership, while the government holds majority interests in seventeen of the most important industrial companies. There is high concentration, with virtually all branches of industry dominated by two or three companies, usually either government-controlled or foreign-owned.

Manufacturing in Senegal is oriented toward the domestic market, with exports (other than groundnuts, phosphates, and fish) representing less than 30 percent of industrial sector sales. Processed primary products are exported mainly to Europe, especially France, and light manufactured goods (princi-

Table 3.5.1 *Industrial Output, Employment, and Labor Costs, 1976 and 1980*

Indicator	1976	1980
Index of industrial production	100	90.9
Number of workers[a]	42,576	40,976
Industrial sector wages and salaries[b]	26.26	41.62
Index of industrial wages	100	158

a. Modern industrial sector only; excludes construction, artisanal production, and unclassified industry.
b. In current CFAF billions.
Source: Senegal Finance Ministry, Statistical Department.

pally textiles, chemicals, tobacco, and paper products) are traded almost exclusively to CEAO (West African Economic Community) trade zone neighbors.[3]

Despite preferential tariff arrangements in both the European Economic Community (EEC) and CEAO markets, exports have neither diversified nor significantly expanded. Exports (excluding groundnuts) declined by almost 20 percent between 1977 and 1984, and only fish exports demonstrated consistent real growth. In 1983, processed primary products still constituted two-thirds of Senegal's total exports, and 90 percent of its exports to developed country markets.

Outside of groundnuts, phosphates, fish, sugar, phosphate fertilizer, and textiles production, most enterprises in Senegal process imported materials. Protection has given manufacturers little incentive to procure intermediate goods locally. Strikingly little backward integration of the industrial sector was visible between 1960 and 1980. Trade statistics since 1960 show considerable substitution of food and consumer goods imports, but no appreciable displacement of imports of intermediate goods and capital equipment.

Policies and Incentives

The Senegalese government has made extensive use of incentives to promote industry. These include an attractive investment code, an innovative export subsidy scheme, and West Africa's only export free zone. The impact of these schemes has been limited, for three reasons: (1) macroeconomic distortions (notably, low labor productivity and exchange rate inflexibility); (2) inconsistencies in policy implementation and a climate of longer-term policy uncertainties (notably, recent proposed minimum staffing levels for all large-scale enterprises and talk of reserving certain activities for Senegalese entrepreneurs); and (3) excessive public sector deficits.

The trade regime in Senegal is a prime example of overlapping policies with contradictory effects. Nominal tariffs are high (ranging from 25 percent to 90 percent) and escalate sharply for finished goods as opposed to intermediate products and raw materials, with effective protection over 100 percent for many of the more capital-intensive enterprises. On the other hand, extensive exemptions and waivers have vitiated tariff protection for some industries. Actual duty collection averages only 20 percent of the value of imports, which is even less than the minimum legal tariff level. The government has thus been pressed by domestic producers and assemblers to adopt quantitative import restrictions, which have significant effects on domestic market prices for over 160 commodities in several subsectors.

Senegal's poor export performance arises from two fundamental problems. High trade protection in the domestic market (which to a large extent guarantees profits) has made exporting relatively unattractive and has led entrepreneurs to concentrate their efforts on import substitution. In addition, factor costs are high because of wage and employment policies, and they have been

3. The CEAO comprises Senegal, the Ivory Coast, Mauritania, Mali, Niger, and Burkina Faso. Togo and Benin have observer status.

exacerbated by differentials in inflation rates compared with those of France and Senegal's other trading partners. Because Senegal, like other members of the UMOA (West African Monetary Union), is not able to adjust its exchange rate, the government in recent years has attempted to simulate some of the effects of devaluation by means of tariff increases (to make imports less cheap) and an export subsidy (to make exports more competitive). A combined 5 percent across-the-board tariff increase and the introduction of a 10 percent export subsidy in 1981 was not, it appears, a sufficient adjustment. Part of the problem is that the 5 percent increase in tariffs did not result in a 5 percent increase in duties collected.

In theory, an export subsidy increases exports in the short term by inducing firms to shift resources away from production for the domestic market and into export production because exporting is made more profitable, and by enabling firms to lower their prices in overseas markets and thereby expand the demand for Senegalese products. Yet the limited evidence suggests that the 15 percent f.o.b. (free on board) subsidy was not sufficient to make exporting as attractive as the domestic market after consumer demand rebounded in 1982. For subsectors oriented to export markets (fishing, cotton, fruit, and vegetables), the export subsidy was accompanied by export expansion that was no faster than growth before the sudsidy was introduced. The subsidy largely failed to stimulate incremental exports in other subsectors, either because the premium was insufficient to bring production costs into line with world costs or because protection in the domestic market remained a stronger incentive.

An export processing zone was established in 1976. The zone offers total exemption from import duties, taxes on profits, and all other direct and indirect taxes to exporters that locate there, and it provides fully developed land and subsidized electricity at a modest rent. Local goods used in production are purchased free of sales taxes, and Senegalese firms that sell to the zone can consider these as exports and obtain temporary admission for their own raw materials. Development of the zone has been slow. By 1980, only four companies had invested, two of which promptly failed. By 1983, only seven firms were operating in the zone, utilizing less than half of the area developed since 1976.[4]

New investment codes were adopted in 1981 to reduce the long-term fiscal costs of investment incentives, to extend incentives to small- and medium-

---

4. The zone's impact on Senegal's trade balance and industrial employment is likely to remain marginal. The country hosting a free zone can reap only two benefits—employment of its nationals and some procurement of locally produced goods. Employment gains are usually significant only if the zone attracts large-scale, employment-intensive production designed for overseas markets that would not otherwise be accessible. Almost none of the investments in the zone fits this description. As far as multinational investors are concerned, the fundamental problem is that the export free zone is not competitive with other zones in terms of labor productivity, transport costs, or utilities costs. Firms must still contend with burdensome bureaucratic and labor regulations. For producers interested in the West African market, location in the zone has the additional disadvantage of excluding them from selling in Senegal, one of the largest and most sophisticated markets in the region. Finally, for a range of industries, the producers' margin created by trade protection in Senegal, even after taxes, is probably greater than that available to zone exporters, who must match world market prices.

scale industries (including agricultural, tourism, and energy investments) as well as to promoters of large projects, and to improve administrative efficiency. A cash subsidy equal to 20 percent of incremental wages and salaries paid by the enterprise (for up to nine years) as a result of the new investment was substituted for long-term duty exemptions on raw materials imports. The proportion of smaller-scale projects went up by 20 percent. The value-added subsidy made Senegal the first country in the region to attempt to reduce the bias toward capital intensity inherent in most investment incentives. But the impact of the new code has been limited because of unclear eligibility criteria, complex bureaucratic requirements and delays, price controls, and burdensome internal trade regulations.

Adjustment Program

A structural adjustment effort launched at the end of 1980 attempted to stabilize the financial situation, increase investment in the productive sectors, raise public savings, reduce state participation in the economy, and streamline the parastatal sector. A 3.4 percent annual growth in the index of industrial production over 1984–85 indicates a positive impact on manufacturing. The extent of reform was limited, however, by the inability to use the exchange rate as a policy instrument and by the difficulty of implementing certain measures, such as reform of the subsidized central seed and fertilizer distribution system. Drought inhibited the macroeconomic impact, and GDP grew at only 2.3 percent per annum during 1980–84, while exports stagnated. The political events surrounding the change in president diverted attention away from the reform process, and commitment to the program lapsed.

Reform efforts were renewed in 1986. The macroeconomic adjustment program succeeded in stabilizing the balance of payments and public finance, approximately halving the trade deficit (to 6 percent of GDP in 1986) and the rate of inflation (to 7.5 percent in 1986). Several industrial policy reforms were introduced in 1986 and 1987 to create a more growth-oriented incentive environment. *Export incentives* were improved by basing the subsidy scheme on value added, streamlining the duty drawback system, and restructuring the export promotion and credit agencies. The dispersion of *protection* was reduced by narrowing the range of tariffs, lowering the average nominal level to about 40 percent, and eliminating product-specific exemptions. To stimulate *competitive behavior*, quantitative restrictions were phased out over eighteen months, and the use of reference prices was curtailed. The *Investment Code* was revised to make eligibility clear and automatic, remove the bias toward capital intensity, reduce benefits over a specified time period, and discontinue enterprise-specific conventions. *Business regulation* was eased by amending the labor law to give firms greater autonomy and by relaxing price and distribution controls.

The more competitive environment created immediate pressure to shut down firms in industries that are sensitive to economies of scale and low-cost Asian imports, such as paper products, vehicle assembly, and shoes. An initial loss of over 4,000 jobs was expected, although the majority were in agroindustries, which are expected to grow through increased export demand once their cost structures are streamlined. The total cost of restructuring potentially viable firms to compete with imports and take advantage of new export opportunities was estimated at over $40 million, most of it in agroindustries and textiles. Nevertheless, the responsiveness of exports to these reforms has been limited by the difficulty of expanding output, by weak international prices for most of Senegal's traditional exports, such as groundnuts and phosphates, and by declining competitiveness because the weakening dollar has appreciated the real effective exchange rate.

3.6 *Industrialization Policies in Ghana*
Tony Killick

Industrialization [in Ghana] was accompanied by slower growth, partly because the supply of foodstuffs failed to keep pace with demand, leading to inflation and pressures for large quantities of imported foods. Industrialization was expected to reduce unemployment, but despite industrial expansion, total recorded employment in "large-scale" manufacturing in 1970 was only about 1.6 percent of the total labour force, while it contributed about 10.0 percent of GDP, indicating the capital-intensive nature of the developments which occurred. Strengthening the balance of payments was another objective, but, despite import substitution, this was not achieved either. Ghana's experience was typical of other countries in discovering that import substitution worsened rather than improved shortages of foreign exchange, at least for some years. Steel found that in 1967–68 about a quarter of manufacturing output was undertaken at a net loss of foreign exchange—i.e., foreign exchange costs exceeded the amount of foreign exchange saved.[5]

Explaining the Inefficiency of Industrial Expansion

Large investments in the creation of manufacturing plants resulted in an industrial structure which was inefficient in static terms and also apparently failed to generate longer-run dynamic effects on the rest of the economy to compensate for the short-term inefficiency. How may we explain this?

At the end of 1966 the government estimated actual manufacturing output to be only a fifth of single-shift production capacity. Steel's 1967–68 survey of manufacturing found firms still operating at an average of only 35 percent of what they nominated as their "maximum theoretical output." What is surprising about the Ghanaian experience is the extent of underutilization (table 3.6.1).

The explanation usually given for below-capacity use of Ghana's manufacturing plant is that foreign exchange shortages and the resulting import controls kept factories short of materials, components and spare parts. There are,

Excerpted by permission from Tony Killick, *Development Economics in Action: A Study of Economic Policies in Ghana* (New York: St. Martin's Press, 1978).

5. William F. Steel, "Import Substitution and Excess Capacity in Ghana," *Oxford Economic Papers* 24, no. 2 (July 1972): 212–40.

Table 3.6.1 *Comparative Manufacturing Capacity Utilization:*
Ghana and Other Developing Countries

Country	Year	Utilization as percentage of capacity
Argentina[a]	1964	64.6
India[b]	1964	65.4
West Pakistan[a]	1965	73.8
Taiwan[a,c]	1965	62.3
Ghana	1967–68	34.8

a. Capacity in the cases of Argentina, West Pakistan, and Taiwan was defined as "full utilization at the customary number of shifts." The figure shown for Argentina is an unweighted mean of all industries shown by Little, Scitovsky, and Scott.

b. The standard used in this case was "estimated productive capacity." The figure shown is an unweighted mean of all industries recorded in the lower half of Little, Scitovsky, and Scott's table 3.5.

c. A calculation of an unweighted mean estimated from grouped data in Little, Scitovsky, and Scott's table 3.7. This figure can be regarded as no more than a rough order of magnitude.

Sources: Ghana: William F. Steel, "Import Substitution and Excess Capacity in Ghana," *Oxford Economic Papers* 24, no. 2 (July 1972): 212–40. Other countries: Ian Little, Tibor Scitovsky, and Maurice Scott, *Industry and Trade in Some Developing Countries* (London: Oxford University Press, 1970), tables 3.4–3.7.

however, strong reasons for believing that much underutilization stemmed from more fundamental causes.

Ghana's industrial statistics show that between 1966 and 1970, when the quantity of imports of industrial raw materials went up by nearly half, gross output per manufacturing establishment actually declined in real terms by 9 percent, and that constant-price value-added per establishment went down by a remarkable 24 percent over the same period. These figures are truly surprising, for improved capacity utilization would imply greater output per establishment. The evidence runs strongly counter to a belief that underutilization resulted largely from import shortages and could, therefore, easily be reduced by improved foreign exchange allocations.

This conclusion is reinforced by the results of an official survey conducted in 1968 of a sample of manufacturing firms. Only 24 percent of them thought that the market was big enough to absorb the full capacity output of their industry at ruling prices, and 63 percent believed that industrial capacity exceeded the market size at any feasible price. No less striking, 37 percent of the respondents thought their own capacity exceeded the market. Why should so many plants have been built with capacities in excess of reasonable expectations of demand and market shares? Whatever the answer, the evidence of this paragraph points far more to market size as a constraint than to supply factors.

Ghana's economy had been quite a fast-growing one until the beginning of the sixties. It was only later that people began to realize that stagnation was not just a passing phase, and it is likely that factories were built in expectation of a faster growth of consumer demand than actually materialized. The expansion of the past, and the optimism induced by Nkrumah's big push and

Table 3.6.2 *Linkages of Ghana's Manufacturing Sector with Rest of Economy,*
1960 and 1968

Linkage	1960	1968
Purchases from other sectors as percentage of total material inputs	65	46
Sales to other sectors as percentage of total sales	25	14

the Seven-year Plan, may provide some explanation of the apparent over-investment.

Associated with this was a deteriorating flow of economic information upon which to base investment decisions. As the government intervened more and more in the economy and as relative prices departed further and further from equilibrium, information provided by the interaction of supply and demand became increasingly misleading. A decline in the quality of investment decisions was probably inevitable. [There was] a factory for processing mangoes with a capacity said to be several times the size of total world trade in canned mango products, sheet glass capacity far in excess of the domestic market, and so on. The rapid expansion of state involvement in industry by a government which placed little weight on efficiency considerations and whose decision-making processes became increasingly chaotic did nothing to rationalize industry.

Other causes of the inefficacy of Ghana's industrialization [include] the tendency toward capital-intensity. A variety of conditions were shown to have resulted in a capital-intensive path of development, diminishing the impact of investment on the overall growth of the economy. Given that factor prices, import licensing policies, wage legislation and the government's own predilection for technologically advanced processes all operated in favour of the use of capital, we may conjecture that one of the reasons for the short-run inefficiency of Ghana's manufacturing sector and its limited spillover effects on the remainder of the domestic economy was its capital-intensity, and we may recall that manufacturing contributed proportionately about six times as much to GDP as it did to total employment.

One of the main theoretical advantages advanced in favour of an industry-led strategy of economic development is that manufacturing is supposed to have greater linkages with other sectors and may thus be expected to induce investments and expansion elsewhere in the economy. In Ghana's case, however, the linkages did not develop, which helps to explain why industrialization failed to galvanize the rest of the economy into more rapid growth. Comparison of figures in a 1968 input:output table with one prepared by Szereszewski for 1960 is most revealing in this respect (table 3.6.2).[6]

Both backwards and forwards, the linkages weakened quite markedly in

6. Robert Szereszewski, "The Sectoral Structure of the Economy," in Walter Birmingham, I. Neustadt, and E. N. Omaboe, eds., *A Study of Contemporary Ghana*, vol. 1: *The Economy of Ghana* (Evanston, Ill.: Northwestern University Press, 1966), p. 72.

relative terms. The implication of these *averages* is that the linkages of the factories set up *during the sixties* must have been appreciably weaker even than the proportions shown for 1968. Many industrial enclaves were created, and it is therefore not surprising that Ghana's industry tended to have high costs and few dynamic effects.

No survey of the causes of industrial inefficiency in Ghana would be complete without discussion of industrial protection, which the government was very willing to provide to investors. Typically, protection was granted on an ad hoc basis or as a by-product of revenue-raising measures, and the results were irrational and arbitrary. Abban and Leith investigated the protection of Ghanaian manufacturing for 1968 and found nominal rates of between zero and 128 percent, with no readily apparent rationale.[7] Leith also made calculations of effective protection and showed rates between -246 percent and 116,993 percent.[8] Both in the enormous variations in the effective rates and in their lack of any system, effective protection was even more irrational than nominal protection. The general prevalence of protection and the lack of system about it helped to produce the inefficiencies noted earlier; this was a cost of Nkrumah's rejection of comparative advantage.

While there was little system in the structure of industrial protection, it did nevertheless have consistent biases; tariffs expressed as percentages of the value of imports were highest on consumer goods and lowest on intermediate and capital goods. The effect, of course, was a strong incentive towards "finishing touches" industries, since the largest protection was for producers of finished consumer goods, with much less for producers of materials and capital goods. Relief from import duties provided under the Capital Investments Act had similar effects, and the low taxation of capital goods also had the effect of encouraging capital-intensity.

In sum, a wide-ranging set of conditions conspired to limit the efficacy of the industrialization drive. Over-optimism about the future growth of the economy and a search for economies of scale produced an underutilized and high-cost structure of industry. The unselective and arbitrary protection, a variety of biases favouring capital-intensity and processes with few linkages with other sectors, a deteriorating quality of investment decisions, and substandard performance on the part of state enterprises, when taken together, provide a fairly powerful explanation of the failure of industrialization. There are, however, limitations to the approach, so far adopted, of treating agricultural and industrial performance as independent of each other, and the next paragraphs explore the ways in which they interacted.

The Consequences of Unbalanced Growth

The well-known three-sector model of balanced growth developed by Professor Lewis is useful at this point.[9] Taking agricultural production for the home

---

7. J. B. Abban and J. Clark Leith, "Protection of Ghanaian Manufacturing Due to Tariffs and Indirect Taxes," (Accra, n.d. [ca. 1971]); processed.

8. See W. M. Corden, *The Theory of Protection* (London: Oxford University Press, 1971), chap. 3, for an explanation of the concept of effective protection. (See also technical note C).

9. W. Arthur Lewis, *The Theory of Economic Growth* (London: Allen and Unwin, 1955), pp. 277–78.

market, manufacturing production for the home market, and production for export, he argues that stagnation of any one of these sectors will tend to retard the growth of the others. The most successful development path is one which achieves a balance in the expansion of each of these sectors. It was a balance which Ghana failed to achieve in the sixties.

This lack of balance was inimical to the success of the development effort. The neglect of exports contributed in a major way to the constant shortages of foreign exchange. These, in turn, led to shortages of imported inputs for industry and even for agriculture, and so held back both sectors. Similarly, the failure of agriculture affected industry in a number of negative ways. Since Ghana remained an essentially agricultural economy, most domestic demand for the products of the country's manufactures would have had to emanate from the rural economy, but this source of demand remained largely static. Lagging output raised food prices relative to other prices and, on the reasonable assumption that the price elasticity of demand for local food was less than unity, this means that an increasing proportion of total disposable incomes was being devoted to the purchase of foodstuffs, with correspondingly less for manufactures. With per capita private consumption declining and expenditure elasticities for food items less than unity, the combined effect of these forces was to subtract in a serious way from the demand for Ghana's manufactures—which may help to explain the large underutilization of industrial capacity discussed earlier.

Agricultural stagnation hit industry in the supply side too. Industries processing local agricultural products, such as sugar, fruit and vegetable oils, encountered great difficulties in obtaining adequate and reliable supplies; other industries which could have been based upon local agriculture, like textiles, fibre bags, meat canning and cigarettes, relied upon imported supplies—to the detriment of their production costs, their contribution to the balance of payments, and their spillover effects on the rest of the economy. The incapacity of agriculture to keep pace with domestic demand for food maintained constant pressure for large allocations of foreign exchange for food, and such imports competed directly with the needs of industry for foreign exchange. Lastly, the inflation of food prices and its impact on the general price level helped to raise manufacturing production costs. This trend, coupled with the overvalued cedi (the Ghanaian currency) and the inelasticity of supplies of agricultural raw materials, effectively foreclosed the possibility of profitable exporting for most industries and kept them to the narrow confines of the domestic market.

Some Conclusions

The foregoing serves to draw attention to the pervasive importance of government policies and the importance, therefore, of getting them right. The failings of both agriculture and industry were due essentially to policy mistakes. Moreover, these interacted upon each other to produce circumstances in one sector which undermined the possibilities of success in the other. Though Ghana's economic structure remained a relatively simple one, the web of inter-relationships between its various parts was becoming sufficiently complex for policy measures directed at one part to have subtle but real consequences elsewhere in the system. Specifically, the failure to maintain some reasonable balance in sectoral expansion proved self-defeating. The priority placed on industry combined with stagnation elsewhere in the economy to undermine the industrialization itself.

Part II

Policy Adjustment

Part II relates the problems encountered in African industrialization to the need for new industrial strategies (chapter 4). It discusses how different policies affect incentives and addresses issues that arise in making policy adjustments (chapter 5). The experiences of several countries in adjusting their policies are reviewed (chapter 6).

The readings in chapter 4 analyze policy deficiencies that must be resolved to improve industrial growth, productivity, and efficiency. Domestic policies are emphasized because they are the instrument most susceptible to control by African governments. Furthermore, without policies that establish incentives consistent with objectives, other measures—such as foreign investment, external borrowing and assistance, deregulation, and an improved business environment—may be to no avail or may perpetuate existing structural problems. Long-term industrial development in Africa is constrained by other basic factors as well: economic dualism generated by colonial policies (section 4.1), fragile political frameworks (section 4.2), inadequate infrastructure (section 4.3), and insufficient human resources and technical capability (section 4.4).

Policies adopted for different reasons have often contradicted each other by establishing incentives that conflicted with basic objectives. Achieving a more appropriate industrial structure will require, therefore, a strategy that makes policies consistent with objectives at the sectoral, subsectoral, and firm levels (section 5.1 and 5.2). The experiences—both positive and negative—of a number of countries demonstrate the importance of consistency among macroeconomic reforms, policies affecting subsectoral resource allocation, and microeconomic responses (sections 6.1, 6.2, 6.3, and 6.6).

Sections 5.3 and 5.4 discuss the policy implications of the strategic debate between import substitution and outward orientation. Similarly, policies relevant to strategies of self-reliance and resource-based industrialization are analyzed in sections 5.3 and 5.5. In this connection a central issue is the degree to which domestic industry is to be sheltered from, exposed to, or stimulated by international markets. The role of trade policy reform in improving industrial performance raises critical questions concerning the appropriate speed, size, and sequencing of such reform (section 5.6).

It is difficult to separate the problems of industrial adjustment from the process of overall macroeconomic and exchange rate management (sections 6.1, 6.2, 6.3, and 6.5). Nigeria's fiscal and monetary restraints enabled exchange rate liberalization to favor increased industrial exports and value added without substantial inflationary impact (section 6.3). In Mauritius, the process of overall adjustment led to an explicit focus on stimulating industrial exports (section 6.4; see also section 3.5). In the CFA franc zone, the fixed exchange rate means that other measures must be used to shift industrial incentives (section 6.5). The phasing and political acceptability of reforms critically determine whether adjustment can be sustained, especially in periods of economic stagnation (section 6.6).

4

The Need for Reform

4.1 *Features of the African Industrial Economy*
Ojetunji Aboyade

The typical African country has a relatively small population, is fairly well endowed with natural resources, has long international borders, does not yet experience heavy population pressure on the land, is afflicted by enormous problems of governance, and is dominated in its nontraditional sectors by the industrialized countries. The consuming desire of the typical African country to industrialize is matched only by its failure so far to create an enduring basis for rational and sustained economic development.

The industrial sector in the typical African country has grown tremendously over the past three decades but still remains very small in comparison with the industrial sectors of the developed countries. This growth has been propelled much more by protective tariffs than by tax incentives. The ensuing import-substitution activities can be explained more by the desires of multinational corporations to protect their export markets in the African countries than by any desires of the countries themselves to utilize their domestic resource endowments. A preponderant share of the growth in manufacturing output is attributable to this kind of direct import substitution; only a minor portion is the result of a real expansion of the domestic resource base.

The countries of Sub-Saharan Africa are still in the early stages of industrial development. By world standards, production processes are rather elementary. Output structure and demand profile are heavily biased in favor of simple consumer goods, and industrial plants are small. Linkages with the rest of the domestic economy are very weak, while leakages to the rest of the world remain significant.

The African industrial economy is also characterized by very low domestic

Excerpted and edited by permission from Ojetunji Aboyade, "African Industrialization: The International and Regional Context," paper prepared for the Economic Development Institute High-Level Industrial Policy Seminar for Africa, Annapolis, Md., April 1984.

value added; a preponderance of depreciation (on imported equipment) and expatriate labor incomes in "domestic" value added; a concentration of industrial investments on simple consumer goods; a lack of competition that virtually guarantees a sellers' market; unrealistic prices for labor, capital, and foreign exchange; little interaction between port or capital cities and the hinterland; and few backward or forward linkages with the rest of the economy.

The expectation that industrialization would foster increases in national productivity and promote the development of natural and human resources has not been met. In particular, the hope that an expanding industrial economy would mean less dependence on external sources of product supplies, if not of critical inputs, has proved to be an illusion.

The structural distortion in the industrial development of Sub-Saharan Africa has its roots in the region's colonial history, but even more so in consumption habits promoted and sustained by international imitations. This has resulted in a faulty alignment between domestic production and domestic resource endowment.

In Asia and Latin America, policymakers and industrialists have been able to exploit changing international market-factor opportunities to move successfully from import substitution to domestic competitiveness with imports and then to sales of exports. Investment funds from multinational corporations have sometimes been involved, especially in manufacturing by their wholly owned subsidiaries. But even more important have been the entrepreneurial initiative and managerial skill unleashed in those countries over the past three decades. Government policies have been designed to maintain high national productivity and low domestic costs.

In Sub-Saharan Africa, on the other hand, there has been little autonomous industrial growth, technological adaption, or managerial self-fulfillment, perhaps because its economy is structurally different from the typical Asian or Latin American economy. The gap between gross *domestic* and *national* product is wide and growing in most African countries. Their typically large resource endowments relative to small populations have favored reliance on primary exports and delayed development of competitive industrial processing for both domestic and export markets. Problems in consolidating the powers of the nation are more intractable in Africa and often consume a large portion of national energy.

The tendency in Africa has been to rely on a strategy of embracing the subsidiaries of multinational corporations under heavy protective tariffs. The result has been a self-defeating process of perpetual industrial infancy as these foreign-owned companies have demanded and secured more and more protection to ward off cheaper and better imports.

The international division of labor since the Korean War has meant that, compared with the labor-surplus economies of Asia, Sub-Saharan Africa has suffered from two disadvantages. One is its high-cost, high-real-wage, and overprotected industrial sector. The second is the stagnant or at best slow-growth agricultural sector, which has seen a loss in labor supply without a compensatory increase in labor productivity. The sectors that have suffered the most have thus been nontraded food and food importables. The underlying policy explanations are a combination of overvalued exchange rates and development policies biased toward urban areas.

Manifestations of these can be discerned in the ease with which industries are established (turnkey projects, standard equipment, easier financing, and attractive commissions for both vendors and political agents), and in the pressure for urban social services and infrastructure. Manufacturers expect very high rates of investment profitability, and they do everything necessary to ensure that they get them. The policymakers find it convenient to accommodate these manufacturers.

Indeed, the pattern of industrialization in Sub-Saharan Africa has tended to squeeze the domestic food and agricultural sector through:

- Underpricing of foreign exchange and overpricing of labor
- Underpricing of domestic financial capital
- Underpricing of public services and utilities
- Underinvestment in the resource-based, export-oriented industrial processing sector and overspending on inefficient public sector enterprises and administrative infrastructures
- Weak technological linkages within and among industries
- High private industrial profits side by side with high social costs
- High urbanization rates combined with high real wages and high urban unemployment.

We conclude that import substitution and high rural-urban migration in Sub-Saharan Africa have resulted in greater dependence on external trade, not less. The character of urban demand, the capital intensity of domestic industries, and the motivation of both private and public management have combined to ensure that the urban economy cannot survive without imported capital goods, intermediate products, raw materials, and management. It is ironic that the industrialization strategy adopted years ago has become a major obstacle to further industrialization. The obstacle is composed not simply of comparatively high industrial costs relative to international prices but also the much higher costs of producing food and agricultural products. The outcome has been detrimental to the rural sector (worsening internal terms of trade) and has compounded the problems of balance of payments, exchange rate management, external debt, domestic inflation, and income distribution.

4.2 *Manufacturing in East Africa*
Donald B. Keesing

Attempts in recent years to stimulate industrial growth in East Africa have not been very successful. Seven of the eleven East African countries with the largest populations, which are also the most industrially developed, experienced declines in output that left them with less gross domestic product (GDP) from manufacturing in the last year for which data are available (1981, 1982, or 1983) than in 1973 or earlier years. The smaller countries of the region have done better; six of the seven increased their GDP from manufacturing after 1973. In Botswana and Rwanda the 1973–81 growth rate averaged a little less

Excerpted and edited from Donald B. Keesing, "Industrial Policy Issues in Eastern Africa," World Bank Eastern and Southern Africa Projects Department, September 1984 (restricted circulation).

Table 4.2.1 *Evidence of Trade Problems Based on Index Numbers for East African Countries, 1973–82*

Country	Percentage change in terms of trade, 1973–82	Exports			Imports		
		Year of all-time high quantum	Percentage change from all-time high to 1982	Percentage change, 1973–82	Year of all-time high quantum	Percentage change from all-time high to 1982	Percentage change, 1978–82
Ethiopia	−49	1982	0	0	1978	−13	−13
Kenya	−16	1973	−47	−47	1978	−53	−53
Madagascar	−27	1978	−39	−37	1971	−45	−34
Malawi	−17	1980	−10	36	1978	−34	−34
Mozambique	−21	1968, 1973	−76	−76	1970	−80	−57
Sudan	−15	1962	−44	−42	1975	−21	−16
Tanzania	−25	1972	−54	−45	1978	−34	−34
Uganda	−7	1970	−54	−50	1971	−63	13[b]
Zaire[a]	−51	1972	−61	−57	1972	−81	−45
Zambia	−68	1969	−6	5	1971	−53	−19
Zimbabwe	−15	1974	−15	−11	1982	0	n.a.

n.a. Not available.

a. Underlying trade data for Zaire are particularly unreliable.

b. Uganda was disrupted by war in 1978–79 so this is from a low base.

Sources: For all countries except Zimbabwe, UNCTAD Trade Indices from Economic Projections and Analysis Department, World Bank. For Zimbabwe, that country's Central Statistical Office, *Quarterly Digest of Statistics* (December 1983), table 10.2, p. 15.

than 10 percent a year; in Burundi the rate was more than 6 percent, if available data are to be trusted. These favorable results occurred in tiny manufacturing sectors, however, and do not outweigh the setbacks in the larger countries.

Trade Woes

Intimately related to lagging industrialization was the poor trade performance of most of these countries over the same period. A shrinking—or, at best, slow-growing—volume of exports contributed to diminishing or barely growing imports in almost all of the eleven largest countries. This inability to pay for imports, of course, held back industrial growth. As table 4.2.1 shows, eight of the eleven suffered declines in the volume of exports from 1973 to 1982, while two registered small gains. Only one, Malawi, made a sizable gain. During the same period, all eleven countries suffered a decline in their terms of trade. That is not a fair comparison, however, since 1973 was a boom year internationally, whereas 1982 was a year of severe recession. Moreover, in between those dates every country except Zaire and Zambia had at least three years (and several had five years) when the terms of trade were even better than in 1973. The overall result was a sharp decline in the purchasing power of exports from 1973 to 1982 in ten of the eleven countries. The exception was Malawi, where the purchasing power of exports rose by 12 percent.

These declines were offset temporarily, in countries such as Sudan and Tanzania, by bigger inflows of development assistance from abroad, but export troubles helped cause balance of payments pressures as that aid leveled off. Table 4.2.1 shows changes in the volume of imports from 1978–the end of the coffee boom–to 1982. Imports sagged in nine of the countries and were already very low in another. A generally negative shift in imports also took place in relation to earlier years. Only Malawi, Sudan, and Zimbabwe achieved a net growth in import volume from 1970 to either 1981 or 1982, and only Sudan and Zimbabwe expanded imports on balance from 1971 to 1982.

Economywide Policy Problems

Explanations for the poor industrial growth and the trade setbacks are many, including everything from the expulsion or withdrawal of skilled and commercially adept Europeans and Asians to the breakdown of civil order, not to speak of economic policy mistakes. Four of the most common explanations are discussed below.

FRAGILE POLITICAL FRAMEWORKS. Highly visible turmoil in several countries during the period under study generally had high costs to the economies involved, although two of the countries affected, Ethiopia and Zimbabwe, managed to rank third and fourth out of eleven in industrial growth. Probably in no case was turmoil or the costs of war more than half the explanation for a country's economic troubles. Nevertheless, the costs in lost growth were significant in Ethiopia and Zimbabwe as well as in Angola, Somalia, Tanzania, Zaire, and elsewhere. Kenya and Sudan increased their military spending, and Zambia was shaken by a threat of foreign-supported insurgency.

Political stability, and the confidence of the people (including business people) that the economic system will prove durable, are prerequisites for vigorous industrial development. These conditions were missing in varying degrees in at least half of the larger countries. In a few cases the troubles were many-sided, prolonged, and very serious, as in Uganda or Mozambique. In some other cases the political regime has endured, but the economic situation has become unstable, as in Zaire, Sudan, and Tanzania. Less frequently, a political regime and its economic policy commitments have shifted drastically, as in Ethiopia in 1974 and Zimbabwe in 1980.

NATIONALIZATION OF PRIVATE MANUFACTURING ENTERPRISES. Whatever their nationality, private business people are quick to withdraw or reduce their operations when they see a shift from government involvement in industry, which they can easily accept, to forcible takeovers of existing private enterprises.

Out of the eleven most populous countries in East Africa (excluding Angola), no fewer than eight have gone through dramatic sequences of nationalizing many, most, or all of the larger private firms in manufacturing, finance, and other sectors. In a few countries these takeovers included outright confiscation of assets. Where compensation was promised it often remained inadequate. In each of the eight countries the leaders still in power today carried out (or were closely associated with) nationalization. Zambia's leadership may be closest to regaining a measure of trust from foreign businesses, but nowhere has this relationship been fully mended.

Most of these countries are trying to run their public enterprises as part of a mixed economy that includes many sizable private manufacturing enterprises. Ethiopia has gone furthest, taking over all but the smallest firms and organizing the state firms along centrally planned lines, with official output targets. Madagascar and Mozambique appear to be next in terms of state controls, but their controls have not been nearly as effective as Ethiopia's.

It does not seem to be an accident that the three countries (Kenya, Malawi, Zimbabwe) that have avoided forcible takeovers of private assets ranked at or near the top in industrial growth performance from 1973 to 1982. Most of the other countries cannot do without private (and foreign) industrial enterprises, but they have aroused the mistrust of business people to the point where almost no private industrialist is investing (except for profits that cannot be taken out of the country).

Seven of the larger countries have shown negative industrial growth since nationalization. In four of them—Mozambique, Sudan, Uganda, and Zaire—a severe decline in output took place simultaneously with or immediately after the nationalization-confiscation sequence. To a varying extent the slide was also brought about by the departure of skilled minorities, precipitated in part by the new policies. These economies have never fully recovered, although Sudan is apparently not far from doing so. In the others—Madagascar, Tanzania, and Zambia—growth was achieved for some years by sheer weight of investment but could not be sustained amidst foreign exchange shortages. Among the other countries, only Angola and Somalia have gone through nationalization, which in both cases was followed by negative growth. Thus, only one country has attained positive industrial growth following nationalization.

INCENTIVES FOR INDUSTRY. Economywide troubles in most countries of East Africa can be traced in large measure to excessive incentives for industry relative to exports and agriculture. Nearly all the countries in the region have furnished powerful protection to their industries, thus turning their internal terms of trade against primary agricultural and mineral producers. The latter have also been subjected to overvalued exchange rates, marketing board arrangements, low prices, export taxes, nationalization of large enterprises followed by poor management (especially in mining), competition from imported grain sold at low prices, and deterioration in the quality and variety of manufactured goods sold in rural areas.

Meanwhile, artificial efforts to push up the industrial growth rate by such measures as stronger protection and larger public investment have led in some cases to premature development. Typically, the industries have been both capital-intensive and import-intensive from the start. This reflects such things as the artificially low costs of investment funds and of foreign exchange, cheap suppliers' credits, the high costs of local labor, and the difficulties of producing inputs locally. Excessive import requirements in connection with manufacturing have contributed to setbacks in industrial growth.

Industry has hardly gained from being overemphasized because, except where it can export, its growth is limited by the size of the domestic market. To be sure, industrial growth took place within this market in most of the larger countries in earlier eras. "Easy" import substitution often allowed rapid expansion of simple industries serving local markets. But this stage is long since past. At this point, the growth of industry depends on the health of the rest of the economy. It is also strongly dependent on foreign exchange rates.

If the rest of the economy and its international transactions are growing in a healthy way, industrial output for the domestic market can grow somewhat faster, first because of the high income elasticity of demand for many of its products and second because of possibilities of foreign exchange savings through increased efficiency and further import substitution. Sustainable industrial growth rates will, as a rule, be a little less than double those of GDP growth—for example, 7 percent in manufacturing compared with 4 percent in the economy as a whole. What counts most, however, is continued growth over several decades. Industrial success cannot be achieved quickly.

Among the East African countries with sizable populations, Malawi has probably put the most emphasis on agriculture and exports while maintaining prices that are relatively close to world prices. Protection for industry was based for a long time mainly on moderate tariffs, and only a moderate number of imports required licenses. Kenya has probably made the most vigorous attempts to strengthen agriculture and exports over the past ten or fifteen years while giving strong protection to industry. Zimbabwe may be ahead of Kenya in holding to a moderate range the price distortions resulting from its protectionist policies, and thus perhaps the price bias against agriculture and primary exports. In both these countries and also in Malawi, the functioning of the commercial market economy has not been disrupted in rural areas, although there may have been scarcities of important goods. Ethiopia too has tried to rely on private distribution channels in rural areas while allowing private traders their profits, and it has given high priority to goods for mass consumption.

MACROECONOMIC BALANCE. Most of the major East African countries are under pressure today to adopt austerity programs, and it is possible that austerity is needed to compensate for lax controls and overspending in the past.

Some correlation can be discerned, in fact, between average annual rates of inflation from 1970 to 1982 in the eleven largest countries of East Africa and their industrial growth performance over the same period. The lowest inflation rates for 1970–82 were those of Ethiopia (4.0 percent), Zimbabwe (8.4 percent), Zambia (8.7 percent), Malawi (9.5 percent), and Kenya (10.1 percent). To some extent these rates reflect fiscal and financial discipline and conservative macroeconomic policies, although Ethiopia's low figure also reflects the power of the state to hold the line on all but the lowest wages and salaries and on many product prices. The same five countries had the best growth performances from 1970 or 1973 on, if Sudan's growth is discounted as an incomplete recovery. By contrast, overspending and financial indiscipline can be seen in the inflation rates for Uganda (47.4 percent), Zaire (35.3 percent), and even Sudan (15.2 percent). Tanzania held its rate to 11.9 percent only by postponing much needed devaluation. Madagascar recorded 11.5 percent, and no figure is available for Mozambique. Some of these countries, including Madagascar, have used price controls and the command powers of the state to hold down inflation, and none has devalued except under strong pressure. Thus, there can be little doubt that macroeconomic imbalance has gone hand in hand with unsatisfactory industrial output performance.

4.3 Excess Capacity
William F. Steel and Jonathan W. Evans

Industrial growth in Sub-Saharan African has fallen short of expectations. This unsatisfactory performance has in part been the result of the distorted incentives established by exchange rate, protection, pricing, and other policies, and their impact on capacity utilization, productivity, factor intensity, unit costs, and efficiency. The public sector has had particular problems stemming from its excessively rapid growth.

Excerpted and edited from William F. Steel and Jonathan W. Evans, *Industrialization in Sub-Saharan Africa*, World Bank Technical Paper 25 (Washington, D.C., 1984).

Capacity Utilization

The dependence of Sub-Saharan Africa's import-substitution industries on imported inputs has made capacity utilization vulnerable to fluctuations in the availability of foreign exchange. Underutilization of capacity due to inability to import materials and spare parts is a recurrent problem. The data available show considerable variation, ranging from an average utilization rate of 26 percent in Ghana in 1980 to 70 percent in Zambia in 1974–75. The variation between subsectors within a country, and between firms within a subsector, is even larger. The average figures are low in comparison with those for other developing areas. Capacity utilization trends worsened during the second half of the 1970s, when mounting economic and balance of payments difficulties reduced the amount of foreign exchange available to pay for imported inputs.

The persistence of capacity underutilization suggests that a temporary shortage of foreign exchange is not the fundamental problem. The fundamental problems are dependence on imported rather than domestically produced inputs and excessive growth of production capacity relative to the growth of import capacity—and in many cases relative to the size of the market. In other words, industrial expansion has tended to outstrip both the supply of inputs and the demand for industrial output.

Processing industries often suffered extremely low utilization rates because of the inadequate planning of supplies, controls on the prices they could offer to farmers, crop failures, and other problems. Although the Sub-Saharan countries have tried to add value to their exports through more extensive processing, poor agricultural performance has resulted in declining agricultural exports without any increase in processed exports.[1]

Even if sufficient inputs were available, however, domestic markets would be insufficient for full utilization of capacity in some subsectors, at least in some countries. In Ghana, for example, a 1968 survey showed that 63 percent of firms thought that their subsector's capacity exceeded the market and 37 percent that demand was insufficient to absorb their own firm's maximum output. Excessive expansion of capacity may have resulted from overoptimistic projections based on high growth rates in the early import-substitution period. In some countries the demand problem has been accentuated by falling real income. Despite capacity underutilization, new investment has been encouraged by high effective protection (which makes it possible to earn profits even at low utilization rates) and by the availability of financing for

1. "Although developing countries are exporting an increasing portion of their commodities in processed form, regional disparities still exist. The performance of African countries matched that of other developing countries only in cocoa and wood products during 1961–77 and fell behind even in these two categories during 1977–80. Sluggish growth in production and increased absorption by domestic demand have led to a decline in export volume of many raw commodities. This decline has not been compensated, however, by increased exports of processed products. For some commodities, it is apparent that domestic demand has absorbed an increasing share of exportable materials and their products." William F. Steel and Bassirou A. Sarr, "Agro-Industrial Development in Africa" (Abidjan: African Development Bank, June 1983), research memorandum 2, pp. 30–31.

new projects but not for factory inputs. Some degree of underutilization may, however, be desirable if it represents the entry of new firms whose competition brings prices down. And in some cases, overbuilding of capacity may be justified if the minimum efficient size of plant is big and market expansion is expected in the near future.

Capacity underutilization may also be partly caused by the infrastructural problems of operating in low-income countries. Inadequate or uncertain availability of transport and power must be addressed through long-term investment. Short-term problems also arise, such as the cutoff of southern rail routes to Zambia in the late 1960s and 1970s and the lack of hydroelectric power because of drought in the Ivory Coast and Ghana in 1983–84. Another problem is the lack of local repair and maintenance services and spare parts supplies, which has resulted in deterioration of equipment.

Productivity and Factor Intensity

Capacity underutilization, combined with pressure to sustain employment growth even when output is falling, has made it difficult for Sub-Saharan countries to maintain rising industrial productivity. Labor productivity rose in the early phases of industrialization, partly because of the relatively high capital intensity of new investments. Subsequently, however, declining output growth has made falling productivity—both labor productivity and total factor productivity—a common problem.[2] In Tanzania, for example, value added per worker grew at over 10 percent per year from 1965 to 1971, but then declined so that by 1977 it was lower in real terms than it was in 1964. The parastatal sector suffered an especially severe decline, with labor productivity falling by nearly 25 percent even though capital per worker rose by 22 percent. In Zambia, valued added per worker at constant prices grew at 3.5 percent per year from 1965 to 1973, but then dropped (along with capacity utilization) at 11 percent per year over the next two years and continued falling at an annual rate of 1.5 percent.

Excessively high capital intensity is a commonly cited problem in studies of large scale import-substitution industries in Sub-Saharan Africa. The principal explanations are the existence of a structure of incentives that is highly biased toward capital and a pattern of decisionmaking that favors large investments in the most up-to-date equipment. Incentives favoring capital include exchange rates that keep the price of imported goods artificially low, low or zero tariffs on capital goods, accelerated depreciation allowances and other benefits based on amount of investment, the availability of low-interest loans, and profit repatriation guarantees that depend on the size of investment. Furthermore, multinational corporations prefer the modern techniques used in their home countries, where labor is relatively scarce and capital is abundant. Public sector decisionmakers in Africa are said to give inadequate attention to economic and factor-intensity criteria. They also are subject to the influence of equipment sales people, whose interest is in maximizing the amount of equipment sold rather than ensuring the viability of the plant.

2. See technical note D.

Public Sector Expansion and Performance

Public sector investment has played an important role in the expansion of the industrial sector throughout Sub-Saharan Africa. For example, even though the Ivory Coast and Nigeria were relatively open to foreign investment, the share of their public sectors in industrial equity capital rose from 10 to 22 percent in the 1960s to 24 and 38 percent, respectively, in 1975. In Tanzania, the share of parastatals in total industrial investment rose from 13 percent in 1966 to 39 percent in 1972.

The public sector share in manufacturing output has risen steadily in most Sub-Saharan countries, and the pace has generally been gradual except when particular countries have nationalized foreign-owned firms. Zambia, for example, achieved a relatively high public sector share of production (56 percent of value added in 1980, as shown in table 4.3.1) largely through acquisition of foreign-owned companies, although thirteen out of twenty-nine parastatal firms were jointly owned by foreigners as of 1982. The breakdown is clearer in the figures for Ghana, with 27 percent of value added originating from wholly owned state firms in 1979 (double the 1964 share) and 26 percent from joint state-private firms. In Kenya, however, production in publicly owned industry has expanded only slightly faster overall than that in private hands.

The evidence suggests that it is difficult to divide the industrial strategies of Sub-Saharan African countries into state versus private investment. Each

Table 4.3.1 *Public and Private Sector Shares of Manufacturing Value Added in Selected Countries*
(percent)

Country, years, and sector	Early to mid-1960s	1969	1972–73	1979–80
Ghana (1964, 1969, 1973, 1979)				
State-owned	13.3	16.0	17.2	27.1
Joint state-private	7.9	19.7	18.0	25.6
Private	78.9	64.5	64.8	47.3[a]
Zambia (1972, 1980)				
Public-parastatal	n.a.	n.a.	53.2	56.4
Private	n.a.	n.a.	46.8	43.6
Tanzania (1966, 1969, 1972, 1979)				
Parastatal	5.0	22.5	33.2	31.0
Private	95.0	77.5	66.8	69.0
Kenya (1964, 1969, 1972)				
Public	15.5	13.2	18.0	n.a.
Private	84.5	86.8	82.0	n.a.

Note: May not add to 100 percent because of rounding.

n.a. Not available.

a. Consists of 25.7 percent private Ghanaian, 12.7 percent private foreign, and 12.7 percent private mixed.

Sources: John Burrows, *Kenya: Into the Second Decade* (Baltimore, Md.: Johns Hopkins University Press, 1975), p. 333; and World Bank data.

country has generally adopted a pragmatic approach to maintaining some degree of balance between the public and private sectors. Ghana is an example of a country that has apparently swung between "socialist" and "capitalist" extremes but whose fundamental industrial policies and ownership patterns have changed relatively little. Other countries, such as Zaire, have had to moderate major shifts in strategy.

Countries that adopted a policy of nationalization often did so partly to gain control over high-profit industries so that the surplus could be used for investment in the national interest rather than repatriated. On the whole, however, the nationalized firms have proved disappointing in their ability to generate investment funds and even to earn a profit. Some parastatal firms, if not the parastatal sector as a whole, have represented a net drain on public finances in Ghana, Mali, Senegal, and Tanzania. In Zambia, direct subsidies have sometimes been necessary to cover large losses due to price control policies. Undercapitalization and lack of working capital are common problems of parastatal firms. Although many parastatal firms do operate profitably (especially those producing nonbasic consumer goods under high protection), their contribution is often offset by those that chronically run at a loss.

Public sector investments have consistently been found to be more capital-intensive than those in the private sector, but this has not necessarily resulted in higher productivity. In Tanzania, for example, the more capital-intensive public sector had slightly lower output per worker during the period 1970–75 and significantly lower productivity of capital. Labor productivity in state enterprises in Ghana was only 55 percent that in the private sector in 1969–70. At the same time, public sector firms are often overstaffed as a result of governments' desire to increase employment. Thus parastatal firms appear to have a tendency to use both more capital and more labor than private sector firms (especially small ones) to achieve the same amount of output. In other words, they are less efficient.

The principal problems of management have not been the qualifications of managers but the limitations imposed on parastatal firms by governments. Political interference is a common concern, not only in investment decisions but also in day-to-day operations. Parastatals are often used to carry out political objectives, such as maximizing employment or holding down prices, to the detriment of their ability to operate profitably. The ability of parastatal managers to establish incentives and to hold staff accountable is limited by the imposition of fixed wage structures and by lack of autonomy in hiring and firing. Accounting systems and operating procedures—as well as the wage structure and the managers themselves—often are taken from the civil service and tend to be bureaucratic rather than businesslike.

4.4 Background to the Lagos Plan of Action
African Development Bank

A review of industrial development in Africa since independence shows that the African continent registered the lowest rate of industrialization in compar-

Excerpted by permission from *Policy and Operational Guidelines for the Industrial Sector* (Abidjan: African Development Bank, 1984).

ison with other continents as measured by aggregate production over the period and by its present contribution to world industrial output. However, some industrial development, of course, has taken place over the period featuring the implementation of some large-scale industrial projects that were expected to meet local demand for consumer goods and generate an export market as well. Such projects were also being counted upon to create jobs for an increasingly educated and urbanized population, train them in new skills, and integrate them into a modern money economy. With only a few exceptions, the large-scale projects have failed to achieve their original objectives, and in many cases continue to be operated under conditions that are burdensome to taxpayers. But perhaps of far more concern is the fact that this industrial effort has failed to give birth to an entrepreneurial class that can be relied upon to conceive and launch new viable industries tomorrow.

The result of this record is that many African states are saddled now with industrial excess capacity and little production, but still have to meet debt service payments in foreign exchange on loans contracted for the projects (as most of these projects were financed with foreign borrowings). Generally the industrial plants are operating at a loss and at reduced capacity (with government subsidy) because the government view is that industrial plant closures cannot be decided on the basis of economic considerations alone. The price of this alternative, of course, has been high taxes for taxpayers and higher prices for all consumers.

Reasons for Unsatisfactory Performance

The primary reason for the unsatisfactory results in industrial development has been the unfavourable investment climate and policy environment in most African states. This climate, which has been characterized by political instability, social unrest, inadequate investment incentives, and very high business risks, has been responsible for discouraging not only foreign investors from capital surplus countries but also indigenous investors from these states.

Some of the specific reasons why industrial projects have not lived up to expectations include the following: (1) The nationals of African states were unable to master the complex technology involved in these projects. (2) Lacking in most African states were the experienced management skills required to plan, coordinate, and execute the technical, financial marketing, and administrative functions of a complex industrial enterprise. (3) Government influence has been pervasive and not always positive. (4) Labour costs in African industries have been generally high because the wage bill has been high in relation to the productivity of labour. (5) The fall in the prices of commodities during the 1970s led to declining terms of trade and sent the balance of payments position of most African countries into deficit. (6) The lack of capital in most African states meant that most industrial enterprises tended to be under-capitalized and hence financed by funded debt in proportions that were higher than prudent. (7) Many countries have built industrial plants that were far too big for their needs, hoping to become exporters to neighboring markets. (8) The absence or inadequacy of existing transport and communications infrastructure has necessitated [adding] rather high incremental investments in infrastructural facilities to the basic investment costs of new industries.

The Lagos Plan of Action

It was against the background of this rather gloomy picture that reflection on future options led to a series of consultations between development experts and ministers of various African states. In April of 1980, the Heads of State and Government of the Organization of African Unity (OAU) met in Lagos and adopted the plan of action for economic development in Africa for the twenty-year period from 1980 to 2000. The Lagos Plan of Action, or LPA, covers all sectors including agriculture, industry, transport, energy, mining, telecommunications, and so on. The LPA gives top priority to agriculture and sets the target of food self-sufficiency by the year 2000.

The LPA [also] advocates an industrialization strategy based on the concept of national and regional self-reliance. That means that the axis of trade flows will have to shift substantially from its present vertical position characterized by the flow of raw materials and manufactured goods between African states and the industrialized countries to more horizontal trade in complementary goods between African states. This will not only require more cooperation between African states in lowering trade barriers with one another but also necessitate greater intragovernmental consultation in national economic planning and the formulation of subregional strategies by groups of countries whose economies offer opportunities for complementarity.

The LPA does represent a new approach, and its significance lies in the fact that it has been accepted by the political leadership of the region. However, since the concept of regional self-reliance is one of its cardinal principles, this means that regional integration is an important prerequisite for the implementation of the LPA.

But even before such regional integration becomes a reality it is necessary for African states to start formulating strategies that transcend national borders. This implies that more consultation and even coordination among states within a given region is required in formulating national economic planning. Trade barriers should be lowered, and each state should concentrate on producing those goods for which it has obvious comparative advantage.

5

Policy Perspectives

5.1 *Achieving a More Ideal Structure*
Sanjaya Lall

To gain a long-term perspective on policy requirements for industrialization in Sub-Saharan Africa, it is helpful to compare an ideal view of what African industry should look like with the existing structure. Given exogenous economic and political conditions and the current debt crisis, the ideal structure for most African countries is determined by four main factors: the small size of most domestic markets; constrained, often falling, import capacities; limited industrial capabilities; and the possibility of drawing on non-African sources.

The small size of the domestic market means that sustained industrial development, especially of scale-intensive industries, requires increased export orientation. This conclusion is strengthened by poor prospects for expanding foreign exchange earnings from traditional exports and for receiving increased foreign aid for industrial investment. Industry must become capable of financing a larger portion of its own foreign exchange needs.

On the other hand, production for export requires higher levels of industrial capabilities than most African countries have achieved in their production for sheltered domestic markets. Considerable upgrading of both embodied technology and operational know-how are needed to reach higher levels of competitiveness. The gradual process of indigenous learning-by-doing can be enhanced, and to some extent supplanted, by imported "tutors." But overoptimism about the ability to reach high levels of productivity with imported modern technology should be avoided.

Excerpted and edited from Sanjaya Lall with Gladson Kayira, "Long-term Perspectives on Sub-Saharan Africa," and Thelma Triche, "Small-Scale Industry in Sub-Saharan Africa: Policy Issues"; both papers prepared for the World Bank Africa Region, Special Economic Office, 1987 (restricted circulation).

The comparative advantage of most African countries lies in products that use relatively simple production technologies, enjoy natural protection because of transport costs, and rely largely on domestic materials. Much of the industry in Africa conforms to this pattern. Some African countries, however, have gone beyond their potential for economic industrialization by setting up intrinsically unviable activities and building capacity that exceeds domestic market needs, export prospects, and management capabilities. Although a few countries have drawn on nonindigenous expertise to reach moderate levels of efficiency, much of African industry is characterized by inadequate technological competence and insufficient productivity improvements over time.

Strategy

The structural needs and characteristics of most African countries suggest the following ideal industrial configuration.

The small-scale and informal sectors should remain areas of strength and should be encouraged to grow, upgrade productivity, and enter export markets. Past policies to promote the small-scale sector have not been particularly successful. They should be reformulated to focus on upgrading industrial capabilities. Policy biases against small enterprises should be removed and incentives introduced so that the enterprises grow larger, attract people with modern skills (including non-Africans), establish linkages with large-scale industry, and export. Measures that protect small units from competition with large ones and discourage growth should be avoided. Market forces should determine which activities are viable, and small enterprises should be allowed to exploit competitive advantages where there are economies of small-scale production. Metalworking and engineering are particularly promising areas for small-scale industry to build vital industrial skills and reduce dependence on imported spare parts, components, and services.

In medium- and large-scale industry, two kinds of inefficient capacity need to be eliminated to reduce the drain on national resources: unviable white elephants and activities that are too difficult for the country to manage competitively. Industrial capabilities should be concentrated in subsectors where technical requirements are low and change slowly; adequate technical and managerial skills exist and can be readily transmitted; productivity can be raised rapidly with a minimal infusion of capital and know-how; local resources provide an advantage in exporting; scale economies are' fully exploited within the limits of the domestic market; production for the domestic market can survive with only moderate protection; and import dependence is low.

These considerations imply a trimmer industrial sector, specialized in resource-based activities and those where transport costs give local processing a comparative advantage. Obvious examples of such industries with low or moderate engineering and skill requirements are agro-based industries, textiles, paper, wood, cement, simple metal products, and perhaps some chemicals.

Exceptions to this ideal include Nigeria, whose large, resource-endowed economy could take on many heavier industries (although the availability of industrial capabilities remains a pertinent constraint), and Zimbabwe, whose advanced capabilities could handle more skill-intensive, complex technologies. At the other extreme, remote, resource-poor countries such as Chad and Burkina Faso are unlikely to establish viable industries outside a few basic food-processing activities.

Policies at two levels are needed to support this strategy. First, macroeconomic and trade policies should provide the incentive framework for healthy industrial development. Second, supply-side measures are needed to enable enterprises to respond effectively to macro signals. Positive policies can help rationalize the existing industrial structure and foster infant industries by supporting the acquisition of new technical capabilities, the creation of new linkages, and the search for export markets.

Macroeconomic and Trade Policies

The macroeconomic and trade policy reforms needed for industrial producers and investors to make decisions on the basis of relatively undistorted prices are well known. The critical instruments are internationally realistic exchange and interest rates, noninflationary monetary policies, removal of price controls and labor market rigidities, elimination of artificial restraints to internal investment and competition, and fair economic prices for agricultural commodities and infrastructural services. Also well established are the adverse effects of wrong price signals and excessive controls in these areas on investment decisions, technology choice, skill acquisition, and international competitiveness.

Some reforms produce immediate effects. Shifting to a market-determined system of allocating foreign exchange, for example, can enable efficient industries to raise capacity utilization and productivity quickly (if they can obtain the necessary finance). Other reforms operate over the medium term. For example, small-scale producers can expand as prices improve, uneconomic enterprises close, and former export markets are regained. Still other responses—raising technical efficiency, improving factor allocation, accelerating technological learning, and establishing new export markets—take much longer.

Small-scale producers should benefit relative to large-scale firms as policy reforms remove biases that favor the latter (for example, through import restrictions or low interest rates). But inadequate demand may constrain growth, especially under contractionary macroeconomic policies. Since most small enterprises are located in rural areas where the expenditure elasticity of demand for their products is high, policies that promote broad-based agricultural development help stimulate small-scale growth.

Since the success of policy reforms depends on an efficient supply response from industry, different elements may have to be implemented at different rates. For instance, if the shift in resources between product lines and industries depends on industrial capabilities that must be built up over time, then the pace at which potentially viable industries are exposed to international competition must also be gradual. A problem of balance may arise between providing the competitive spur by changing the incentive structure and ensuring that economic agents are able to respond appropriately.

Supply-Side Policies for Small-Scale Enterprises

The expansion of small-scale enterprises is inhibited in most Sub-Saharan African countries by overregulation of the private formal sector and by their lack of access to resources and services.

REGULATION. Successful entrepreneurs in the informal sector often prefer to diversify into other small-scale activities rather than be subjected to the myriad taxes, licenses, labor regulations, and procurement rules that apply to formally registered firms. Their informal status, however, prevents them from taking advantage of public services and developing links with the formal sector. Reduced regulation of the formal sector and a simplified legal status for small firms would help these entrepreneurs play a more dynamic and integrated role in industrialization.

FINANCE. Lack of working capital is a pervasive problem of small enterprises; it lowers capacity utilization and prevents bulk purchases of inputs. Successful working capital schemes generally provide small initial loans with short maturity. Subsequent loans are conditioned on repayment of previous ones. Interest rates need to be high enough to cover all costs, including bad debts. Channeling loans through peer groups that approve borrowers on the basis of personal familiarity offers good potential for both broad applicability and adaptation to local circumstances.

TRAINING AND TECHNOLOGY TRANSFER. Programs that strengthen existing entrepreneurs and institutions (such as apprenticeship) are likely to have greater impact than those oriented toward creating new businesses. Improving linkages with the modern sector is a particularly effective way to transfer technology. This can be accomplished through subcontracting, on-site training programs, or giving small entrepreneurs experience in a modern industry.

Restructuring Policies for the Large-Scale Modern Sector

Restructuring policies are needed to complement macroeconomic policy reforms that provide appropriate incentives for competitive firms and rationalization measures that release the resources tied up in white elephants.

OWNERSHIP. To increase access to investment resources and industrial capabilities, African countries will have to remove biases against ownership by foreigners and local non-Africans. Although many governments have recently made their investment regimes more welcoming, Africa remains unattractive relative to other developing areas for foreign investors. Restrictions in the larger economies of Kenya, Nigeria, and Zimbabwe still create an unfavorable climate, while some countries, such as Ethiopia, remain ideologically averse to foreign investment.

Most African countries no longer offer the two principal attractions for past foreign investment: exportable natural resources are not as cheaply exploited or highly priced as previously, and domestic markets are less highly protected as countries move toward more competitive policies. In this situation two types of investors offer special advantages over multinationals from developed countries. Investors from other developing countries are more amenable to joint ventures with local partners and can provide cheaper skilled personnel and more appropriate, small-scale technologies. Many of Mauritius's export processing industries came from Hong Kong, and India has provided some of Kenya's most successful enterprises. Investors from non-African communities in African countries can play a leading role in developing industries with strong local linkages. Although governments worry that the latter group may inhibit the growth of African industrial capabilities, the African entrepreneurs in Kenya Industrial Estates who subsequently entered into partnerships with non-Africans fared best. Skills and know-how can be transferred by non-African enterprises to Africans under the right conditions, which include an adequate supply of capable African technicians.

SCALE AND SPECIALIZATION. Where small domestic markets have resulted in plants smaller than minimum economic size, increasing the scale of operation will also require improving the technology and production engineering capabilities to permit entering export markets. In addition, lack of specialization leads to high costs in many African industries because production runs are too short. Reducing diversity involves giving up well-entrenched strategies and managerial practices, and it may require intervention by the government or industry associations to allocate specific products to particular manufacturers.

INFRASTRUCTURE. Investment in infrastructure will be needed to facilitate structural change in African industry. Services should be priced at economic levels so as to provide users with correct market signals.

EQUIPMENT UPGRADING AND REHABILITATION. The evidence suggests that much of the equipment in place needs to be replaced, upgraded, or rehabilitated to introduce more productive technology and repair the damages of inadequate maintenance. Such investment, however, must be undertaken with caution. Some activities may not be economically viable even with rehabilitation. Others may not achieve their potential for viable operation if the requisite design, procurement, and operational capabilities are lacking. Upgrading technological capabilities is a prerequisite for rehabilitating equipment.

UPGRADING INDUSTRIAL CAPABILITIES. Acquisition of industrial capabilities is a slow learning process. While the correct strategy depends on the country in question, it will involve some combination of the following elements: formal education and training, especially literacy, scientific disciplines, and managerial skills; specialized training facilities; on-the-job training; scientific, academic, and research centers oriented toward adapting imported technologies to local production requirements; incentives for productivity-enhancing innovations within firms; and consultancy services able to provide practical solutions to technical problems.

Conclusion

The limitations of African industrial capabilities have been exacerbated by exogenous shocks and misguided policies. A benign, if not favorable, external environment is important for governments to be able to sustain the commitment needed for major reform of trade and industry policy. The course of industrial adjustment may prove difficult in countries that are constrained by heavy debt burdens, uncertain prospects for primary exports, and internal or external political stresses (especially in southern Africa).

Although there are no quick fixes to the structural problems of African industry, macroeconomic and trade policy reforms can be implemented relatively quickly to ensure that future industrial development is healthier than it has been in the past. But neither "getting the prices right" nor additional physical investment is sufficient in itself, and the process of industrial restructuring and development will be slow in most countries. Building up industrial capabilities is a gradual learning process that cannot be bypassed, although it can be speeded up by filling gaps from abroad, providing appropriate education and training, exposing enterprises to competitive stimuli, increasing access to know-how, and permitting entrepreneurial groups to grow freely. The cumulative nature of learning implies that the better-off countries are likely to continue industrializing more rapidly and efficiently than others.

5.2 Strategies for Restructuring
Anil Sood and Harinder Kohli

There is nothing fundamentally new about industrial restructuring. It is a natural phenomenon associated with economic growth and change and can proceed with or without the involvement of government. What is new is the magnitude, suddenness, rapidity, and complexity of the industrial restructuring necessitated by a much changed global economic environment over the past decade. The intensified pressure for change and its economic and social implications have increasingly led governments of all economic persuasions to play a more active role in inducing and facilitating effective restructuring so that international competitiveness can be improved or regained.

Restructuring embraces all dimensions of structural change, including modifications in the efficiency and relative size of industries; the start-up, closing, growth, or shrinkage of enterprises; and alterations in product mix and technology. It calls for the movement of resources—labor, capital, and technology—from one part of the economy to another, and sometimes across countries.

Restructuring can occur on an enterprise, individual industry, or industrial sector-wide level. It can likewise take place for different reasons. It may be "defensive," that is, in response to a threat already present, or it may be

Excerpted and edited by permission from Anil Sood and Harinder Kohli, "Industrial Restructuring in Developing Countries," *Finance & Development* 22, no. 4 (December 1985): 46–49.

"positive," if change is pursued to build a stronger competitive position for the future. The dominant type of restructuring used by advanced European countries to assist declining industries such as steel or shipbuilding is a defensive nature. Efforts by a number of countries, for example, France, Germany, and Japan, to accelerate the development of emerging industries, such as electronics and information technology, provide examples of positive restructuring.

This article notes some of the key factors that have recently increased the need to restructure; it looks specifically, however, at circumstances in developing countries and the policy and institutional reforms that can form the basis of effective restructuring programs there. Particular attention is paid to the roles of government and industry in the various levels and types of restructuring. For its recommendations, which are primarily of a general nature, this paper draws heavily on the World Bank's analysis of past restructuring efforts and its own research, policy, and operational work in this field.

Pressures to Restructure

The increasing need to restructure has a number of complex and interacting causes. Some are specific to developing countries, but four developments stand out as fundamental explanations. First, changing consumer tastes, market saturation in many products, and changes in technology and in the relative costs of factors of production have dramatically reduced demand worldwide for the major industrial products, such as steel, that traditionally fueled growth and development.

Second, the world economy has been unable to sustain the very high growth rates of the 1950s and 1960s. While growth rates are expected to recover somewhat from the depressed levels of the past decade, most economists expect them to reach only moderate levels in the immediate future. This increases prospects for continued excess capacities, intense international competition, and poor profitability in many industries. Third, the pace of change in technology, design, and production processes has quickened tremendously; increasingly, product life cycles are shorter and, because of increased efficiency, manufacturing costs are dropping. Fast-changing consumer tastes and the emerging technological revolution are likely to accelerate this trend, making the competitive environment even more dynamic and uncertain.

Fourth, as a result of these changes, technological development, product design, marketing, and distribution—rather than manufacturing itself—account for an increasing proportion of a product's value. For more than a decade now, the service sector has been the leading sector of the world economy, not only in OECD countries, where the bulk of world GDP originates, but also in some major developing countries, such as India.

Restructuring in Developing Countries

Although much discussion of industrial restructuring has focused on developed countries, restructuring is equally relevant for developing countries, and arguably more urgent. The fundamental pressures to restructure industry in LDCs stem from the same causes but have been exacerbated by additional external and internal factors. The debt crisis and declining terms of trade for major commodities, combined with slower domestic growth and limited potential for further import substitution, have put tremendous pressure on developing countries to increase their manufactured exports. For most, this will mean restructuring their industries to make them more internationally competitive.

Various internal factors in developing countries compound these pressures. Market distortions and constraints caused by past government policies have often promoted inefficient investments, while reducing and sometimes eliminating internal and external competition and providing little incentive to improve productivity. Trade protection measures, including tariffs and unrealistic exchange rates, have led to high and fluctuating inflation and interest rates, restrictive labor and wage policies, state monopolies, regulatory restrictions on private investment, price controls, and subsidies. Not only inefficient, these policies are also increasingly untenable; governments have been unable to sustain the large subsidies required to continue them.

The significant—often virtually monopolistic—role assigned to public enterprise in key industrial sectors also requires special attention. In many countries poor management and disappointing operating performance have placed a heavy financial burden on already strained government resources. Inefficiencies in the heavy capital-intensive industries—for example, steel, capital goods, and chemicals—that supply inputs to other industries also seriously undermine the competitiveness and performance of the entire industrial sector.

Other key factors relate to the stage of a country's development. The most significant is a lack of adequate institutions and infrastructure, which can hinder efficient operations and timely movement of capital, labor, and technology from inefficient to efficient parts of the economy. The absence of efficient financial markets is a serious obstacle to the normal market-based restructuring that takes place through decline or bankruptcy of inefficient firms and the movement of capital to profitable ventures. Inadequate infrastructures—and here infrastructure includes "software" elements such as management, marketing know-how, distribution networks, and so on—is also a constraint.

Strategies for Restructuring

Given the urgent need to restructure and the additional obstacles developing countries face, what strategies offer the most effective means of restructuring? And what can be the most effective roles of government and industry in this process?

Past restructuring efforts and the findings of recent World Bank work yield some useful lessons for developing countries. First, there is no universally applicable model. Industrial restructuring strategies and programs must be based on an in-depth understanding of the fundamental causes and nature of the particular restructuring efforts. Second, restructuring requires complementary, rather than contradictory, actions on the part of government, industry, labor unions, the financial system, and individual enterprises. Third, a mix of self-reinforcing policy reforms, institutional changes, and direct measures at the individual industry and enterprise level is needed to facilitate sustainable industrial restructuring. Effective restructuring requires improvements not only in the physical plant facilities but also changes in the behavior and motivations of enterprises, managers, and workers. The exact mix of such measures depends very much on the nature of the restructuring, the economic and social system of the country, and the ability of individual enterprises to respond in a timely manner to the changed policy environment.

The role of government must be one of fostering an appropriate policy and business environment that facilitates restructuring. Rather than intervening in the decisionmaking process at the enterprise level, governments must concentrate on eliminating policy distortions, promoting efficient institutions, and strengthening market mechanisms. Direct restructuring measures should normally be determined and implemented by individual enterprises—public and private. Governments may, however, have an important role in working with industry to develop and support the implementation of desirable restructuring strategies.

Policy and Institutional Reforms

Policy reforms are a necessary, and often the most crucial, condition for sustained restructuring in most developing countries. The basic objective of these reforms, akin to those of the overall structural adjustment of economies, should be to increase competition, improve market discipline, and facilitate movement of capital, labor, and technology. Such reforms normally include measures to remove distortions in trade, pricing, interest rate, taxation, labor, and wage policies. It is also important to examine the respective roles of the public and private sectors in industry, degree of competition, constraints on direct foreign investment, corporate legal framework, and regulation and supervision of industrial and financial institutions. The specific measures needed will depend on the nature of existing distortions and sociopolitical and institutional settings in different countries.

The development of efficient financial markets—banking systems and capital markets—and institutions promoting the accumulation and dissemination of technology, management, and marketing know-how is a critical supplement to policy reform, particularly for less developed countries, where efficient markets and institutions are not yet available. In addition, specific institutional measures, including the dismantling or reorienting of regulatory agencies and the strengthening of legal and accounting systems, are usually necessary to strengthen market mechanisms.

When are policy reforms sufficient, and when are direct measures, aimed at individual enterprises and institutions, whether supported by governments or other outside agencies, justified? Much depends on the urgency and the magnitude of the restructuring, the financial and social costs, and ability and willingness of the sectors of enterprises to move on their own, and, in general, the extent of constraints on the movement of resources that must be overcome through direct intervention.

Industry-wide policy actions may often need to be supplemented by parallel efforts in major enterprises and institutions to ensure expeditious response to changing circumstances. In defensively motivated restructuring, selective direct government support may be justified at the subsector and enterprise levels, particularly where sharp cutbacks in capacity and jobs are likely to result in high social costs and meet substantial resistance. Government support in these instances should include steps to ameliorate short-term social costs, such as temporary unemployment. Government intervention to eliminate uncompetitive capacity is also necessary in industries dominated by public enterprises.

An industrial sector dominated by large monopolistic public enterprises, as is the case in many African and centrally planned countries, requires much more direct intervention than one composed of numerous profit-oriented companies operating in an open, competitive environment. Experience in developed countries with positive restructuring suggests, however, that industry-wide incentives and temporary market-support measures are generally preferable to providing public financial support to specific products or enterprises over extended periods.

Enterprise Restructuring

Ultimately all industrial restructuring programs rely on actions at the enterprise level. These actions include "hardware" elements relating to plant and equipment, improvement of existing products, and the introduction of new varieties, as well as "software" such as corporate strategy, organizational structure, improvement of management and labor skills, financial systems and controls, and marketing and distribution. The software elements are particularly critical to building the organizational and management capability needed to maintain and enhance competitiveness. In the restructuring program for Gecamines, the major copper producer in Zaire, which operates in a fiercely competitive international market, such software elements are the most crucial part of the package and took some three years to develop.

The design of enterprise restructuring programs should start with the formulation by management of a well-defined strategy for the business based on a thorough analysis of competitive position and the specific measures required to increase the overall organizational ability to operate in a changing and competitive environment. Financial restructuring is often essential when enterprises face liquidity problems that result from sudden increases in inflation, very high nominal or real interest rates, and large devaluations that increase debt-service obligations in local currency terms. In these instances conversion of foreign exchange debts into local currencies, rescheduling of debts, provision of guarantees, and infusion of equity through different mechanisms may be justified. However, a critical assessment of the underlying viability and competitiveness of the enterprise is vital before proceeding with any major financial restructuring.

A solution to the interrelated problems of restructuring and mounting fiscal burdens of public enterprises increasingly being considered by many developing countries—ranging from Turkey to Togo and Uganda—is that of "privatization." Privatization includes not only a transfer of equity ownership but also other means of enhancing private sector involvement in management and operations, such as leasing and management contracts. These latter arrangements may be of particular relevance to developing countries where it seems impracticable to attract significant amounts of private capital at this time.

Restructuring Specific Industries

Restructuring at the level of a subsector, industry, or segment of industry best takes place in the context of a well-defined strategy based on a rigorous analysis of its current and potential international competitiveness in different markets and product groups. In most instances, governments need to take the initiative to work with private and public enterprises to carry out the required analyses of industries; industry associations can also play a leading role.

Industries producing bulk commodities frequently comprise few enterprises; these are large and—particularly in developing countries—often state-owned. Capacities and the manufacturing and distribution costs of competitors can generally be estimated with reasonable accuracy so that international competitiveness can rather readily be determined. Relatively deterministic restructuring strategies can thus be designed; measures such as plant closures, production linkages and rationalization between producers, and investments to reduce costs can be readily identified. Specific policies, where appropriate, and implementation assistance can be directed toward the few key enterprises.

Industries involving a large number of segments, by contrast, are marked by differences in products, markets, geographical location, and consumer base, and in most cases a much larger number of plants and enterprises. The requirements for competitiveness and success vary substantially in different segments. The analytical work to formulate a restructuring strategy must differentiate between these segments, and is thus more complex than for commodity industries. Government efforts are best concentrated on developing an overall industry strategy, general policy actions, and provision of infrastructure. Development of appropriate technology and marketing infrastructure is critical to support the restructuring efforts of the small- and medium-sized enterprises in such industries. But actual investment and other business decisions are best taken and implemented by individual enterprises in response to market signals and the new policy and institutional environment. Some direct support at the enterprise level, however, may be necessary where a few large enterprises play a dominant role and are unlikely to restructure on their own.

Conclusion

In considering the strategy and role of developing country governments in industrial restructuring, it is important to recognize the constraints imposed by the current scarcity of resources and the limits of effective state intervention. The emphasis should be on low-cost investments with high returns to improve the utilization and efficiency of existing assets rather than on the creation of much new capacity, which characterized past structural change in an environment of high economic growth and expanding resource availability. While hardware investments, such as for equipment upgrading, will inevitably be required, the returns from software investments are expected to be far more significant.

Though restructuring strategies will need to be tailored to specific circumstances, past experiences nonetheless highlight some important general lessons. Industrial restructuring is a complex process with significant, sustainable results likely only over the medium term. It can entail substantial social costs and is likely to meet with opposition from many sources. Firm commitment on the part of government, private sector, and enterprises is a prerequisite for success. Appropriate phasing of actions, early successes that provide a valuable demonstration effect, and specific attention to meeting transitional social and financial costs are essential to sustaining commitment and enhancing prospects for success.

5.3 *Making Use of Market Signals*
Michael Roemer

This essay argues for the adoption of an outward-looking market-oriented strategy, one that will correct the defects of the import-substitution strategy now widely in vogue in Africa and depend less on skilled government mangers to propel development. I will concentrate on three goals: rapid income growth, self-reliance, and the equitable distribution of income. I will argue that the conflict between these goals is not necessarily severe. Modernization is really a subsidiary goal, one that follows eventually from growth. Although employment creation is often treated as a separate goal, and does carry with it the important aim of participation in the development process, in fact it is really an instrumental variable; it forms an important link between growth and equity and helps to moderate the conflict between those two goals.

Role of Markets

Human skills are a pivotal constraint on the nature of African development strategies. Strategies depending heavily on government intervention and administration are likely to fail. If government cannot effectively direct and control development, the only alternative is to rely increasingly on market mechanisms to guide economic decisionmaking, and on private activity to implement development goals. Two distinctions are involved in this argument. First, market mechanisms, in which prices provide incentives for the actions of economic units, are preferable to administrative controls over individuals and enterprises. This dictum holds for both capitalist (really, mixed)

Excerpted and edited by permission from Michael Roemer, "Economic Development in Africa: Performance since Independence, and a Strategy for the Future," *Daedalus* 3, no. 2 (Spring 1982): 134–46.

and socialist economies. Second, private individuals and enterprises, directed by the market, can be harnessed more effectively to achieve national development goals than can government officials and agencies, even if the latter are guided by market considerations. Baldly put, in Africa, capitalist economies can probably achieve growth, equality, and self-reliance more readily than socialist ones. But socialist countries will also do better using market mechanisms instead of administrative controls.

The market is no panacea. Certain pervasive features, which economists call "market imperfections," require government intervention: control of monopoly when it cannot be avoided; implementation of large investments that have substantial benefits external to the project itself, such as transportation systems or power dams with potential for irrigation or flood control; regulation of activities that create external costs, such as pollution or the wasting of common, but limited, resources like forests and fisheries; promotion of infant industries. Other interventions may be justified by national development goals that markets typically cannot achieve: helping disadvantaged groups or substantially equalizing income and asset distribution over short periods. The use of the market is not ideologically prescribed. It is, rather, one of the tools of public policy, and a very powerful one, that helps guide the economy to achieve national goals.

The market is alive and well in Africa and continues to spawn entrepreneurially gifted people. Most activity centers on trading, agriculture, and very small industry, and much of it is in the informal sector. This is simply a condition of underdevelopment: entrepreneurial activity was similarly concentrated in Europe before industrialization. African governments should foster African entrepreneurs on a large scale, rather than assume that government enterprise is an adequate substitute.

Outward Orientation

If the scarcity of managerial and other skills dictates a market-oriented approach, the shortages of capital and, especially, of foreign exchange suggest an outward-looking strategy for African development to build upon its resources by encouraging production of a diverse set of foods and raw materials grown by labor-intensive, smallholder agriculture, both for export and home consumption. At the same time, the strategy would move gradually toward labor-intensive manufactures for export and the domestic market.

The outward-looking strategy is based on comparative advantage.[1] This means that exchange rates need to be kept in line with domestic and world inflation, and devalued whenever necessary to stimulate production for export or efficient import substitution. Taxes on exports have to be modest to avoid discouraging producers. Protective tariffs should be moderate and decline gradually, forcing import-substituting manufacturers to increase productivity toward world standards, while quota restrictions should be avoided altogether. These policies place a high value on activities that save or earn foreign exchange and discourage those that use it.

1. See technical note A.

Over time, an outward-looking strategy should help to reestablish African smallholder, cash-crop agriculture as a dynamic sector in several countries. It should also establish manufacturing in fields in which African countries may have comparative advantage: labor-intensive manufacture of textiles, clothing, and wood products for export; processing of crops and raw materials for export; and manufacture of commodities like cement, glass, and eventually even steel and chemicals for the home market, as incomes grow and home demand rises to accommodate large plants in industries with economies of scale. The process of widening the domestic market can be accelerated dramatically if countries group together in common markets and cooperate in investment policies.

The Government's Role

Government's role in such a strategy is twofold. The more difficult part will be to liberalize the economy, that is, to reduce controls and establish, and then maintain, the market environment in which an outward-looking strategy might flourish. Realistic and frequently adjusted exchange rates; reduction of protective tariffs; elimination of quotas, wage restraint, and high interest rates; and the other elements of a market-based strategy are all controversial measures in economies that have grown used to inward-looking policies and administered prices. One should not underestimate the difficulty of navigating this passage, especially in countries that have been plagued by coups since independence.

The second aspect of government's role is a more familiar one in Africa: support, through government services or investment, for private activities that form the core of the strategy. Not only must government continue to provide agricultural extension service and credit to small farmers, but it must intensify its research on both food and export crops as well. Infrastructure must be provided and social services extended to the rural areas. What government need not—indeed, should not—do is run state farms, spend resources trying to control what farmers produce and market, or take over transport and distribution services from those parts of the private sector that can provide them most efficiently.

Similar prescriptions apply to urban activities, such as manufacturing or banking. To push manufacturers toward world markets, government will have to make clear that it supports exporting. The "right" price signals are necessary, but not sufficient. To the extent that government controls remain, exporters will have to see that these work for, not against, them; if political favors are done, as they inevitably are, they must favor exporters; embassies or trade offices have to provide market information and in other ways be responsive to exporters; infrastructure investments need to include facilities, like ports, designed to enhance export capacity.

Dependence

The outward-looking strategy will not appeal to dependency theorists, such as A. G. Frank and Samir Amin, who view continued involvement in the capitalist world economy and continued structural dependence on agricultural exports as barriers to be overcome, rather than as opportunities to be exploited.[2] Two writers who have prescribed strategies for reduced dependence in African countries, Clive Thomas and Justinian Rweyemamu, focus on the problem of dependence upon primary exports, a legacy of the colonial period.[3] To overcome this, they suggest fundamental structural change, in which countries develop a fully articulated set of industries, including heavy industries, that are capable of utilizing domestic resources to produce primarily for domestic needs. Although both Thomas and Rweyemamu allow for the exports of "surplus" manufactures, their strategy is essentially autarkic, a more complete version of import substitution than is commonly practiced. Such a reduction in trade dependence is, unfortunately, accompanied by an increase in dependence on foreign capital and foreign technical and managerial skills, because no African economy has the resources to implement such a strategy without outside help. For Thomas, the way out is to turn to socialist countries for these resources, avoiding deeper involvement in the capitalist world. Although some African countries could move toward self-sufficiency, very few of them can even contemplate a completely self-sufficient strategy because they are too small and lack many critical resources that must inevitably be imported.

But dependence is not merely being involved in international trade. It is, rather, being committed to trading only a few products, possibly in only a few markets, and being unable to switch among products as world market conditions change. Senegal and Zambia are extremely dependent countries in this sense. South Korea, on the other hand, exports a third of its GNP, but is in a fundamental sense self-reliant because it has developed a wide variety of potential export industries. No African country today is self-reliant in the sense that South Korea is. But several countries do have the potential to broaden their export base, gradually substitute efficiently for many imports, and generally move toward more flexible economies that can adjust readily to changes in world market conditions.

The bête noire of dependency theorists is foreign investment. Concern about the political and social influence of foreign investors, especially of multinationals, is legitimate. Indeed, the hard core of dependency theory may be the notion that national elites in developing countries have interests closely aligned with those of the capitalist countries, and foreign investors probably play a major role in bringing this alignment about. However, strong-willed leadership can control foreign investment so that it serves national development. The high, perhaps excessive profits earned by foreign-owned import-substituting firms are often due to the excessive protection granted by government, sometimes exacerbated by tax holidays or other inducements. The outward-looking policies suggested here would end such favorable treatment.

2. A. G. Frank, *Lumpenbourgeoisie: Lumpen Development* (New York: Monthly Review Press, 1972); and Samir Amin, *Accumulation on a World Scale* (New York: Monthly Review Press, 1974).

3. Justinian Rweyemamu, *Underdevelopment and Industrialization in Tanzania* (Nairobi: Oxford University Press, 1973); and Clive Y. Thomas, *Dependence and Transformation: The Economics of the Transition to Socialism* (New York: Monthly Review Press, 1974.)

A Socialist Variant to the Strategy

The market-oriented outward-looking strategy can be adapted in part to serve the needs of socialist countries, such as Tanzania, Mozambique, and Guinea, and to accommodate the public enterprises that abound even in Africa's mixed economies. In this section, we are concerned only with the distinction between the price incentives of the market and government control through administrative fiat; questions of private versus public activity are assumed to have been decided in favor of the latter. The role of central planners in this system is to set prices of all commodities and productive factors so that supply is equated with demand in each market and prices cover the full value of resources (the opportunity cost) to society. Prices may also be used to influence economic decisions in directions consistent with particular national goals and policies.

A full definition or description of socialism in Africa is beyond the scope of this article. Two characteristics are of particular interest: government owner-ship of productive enterprises, especially in industry, and promotion of rural equity. Public enterprises, often called "parastatals," have mushroomed in all African countries since independence. Governments, regardless of economic ideology, resort to parastatals for several reasons: (1) the pursuit of national goals, such as investment in undeveloped regions or provision of massive finance to industry, that would not be accomplished soon enough by market forces; (2) a desire to nationalize large foreign firms, such as the copper mines in Zambia, which local entrepreneurs and managers are incapable of running; (3) the need for a vehicle to accommodate foreign investment, technology, and expertise in joint enterprises, in the absence of local entrepreneurs and managers who would be effective partners and counterweights to foreign interests; and (4) an unwillingness to encourage entrepreneurs and managers from economically advantaged minority groups, such as the Asians in East Africa and the Lebanese in West Africa. In addition, socialist countries use parastatals because they do not want to encourage the growth of a national bourgeoisie.

Public enterprises in all economically productive sectors can be managed to fit within the outward-looking strategy. Each parastatal should be given a specific task—produce cement, manage an irrigation scheme, develop a hydroelectric facility—and then charged to maximize their profits, that is, to run the firm as efficiently as possible. To ensure this, managers and workers should be given incentives based strictly on profitability, and these should form a substantial part of their income. If nonefficiency goals—such as invest-ment in a disadvantaged region—are considered essential, the added costs of pursuing these objectives should be calculated and subsidized by government so that the firm's profits and employees' bonuses are not adversely affected and government knows the opportunity costs of such activities. Capital should be made available to firms only on market terms, at interest rates reflecting the scarcity of capital, and government should insist on dividends that reflect its own opportunity costs. Once government sets the generally defined tasks of the enterprise and establishes the rewards system, it must

refrain from interfering in the management of the enterprise, except to promote, demote, or fire managers based on their success in earning profits.

If profit-oriented public firms are set within a competitive market context,
they will behave substantially like private firms. The competitive environment can be established easily enough in mixed economies, in which private
firms are permitted to compete with government enterprises, or in socialist
countries, if several public firms are established in each sector. Where markets
are small and the economic size of the firm large, as is true for most African
countries and many industries, there are two alternatives. Either government
can permit the import of competing goods at close to world prices, forcing the
public enterprise to achieve efficiency on a world market standard if it is to
earn profits, or government planners can set prices at similar levels with
similar outcomes. The shortage of trained officials in Africa, together with the
tendency of political and bureaucratic processes to incorporate noneconomic
considerations, argues strongly against the latter approach.

The outward-looking strategy can also contribute to the goal of rural equity
stressed by socialist countries like Tanzania and Ethiopia. Small farmers in
both Taiwan and South Korea benefited from rapid outward-oriented growth,
first, because both countries imposed thoroughgoing land reforms a decade
before rapid growth began, and second, because their market-based strategies offered small farmers access to credit, farm inputs, and both domestic
and foreign markets. The question for socialist countries like Tanzania is how
far beyond land reform the country should go to ensure equitable relationships in rural areas, without sacrificing the pecuniary incentives to which
African farmers have responded historically.

This prescription may not sound much like socialism, especially to governments that have well-articulated socialist policies. But if the ultimate goal is
greater equity based on rural prosperity, some compromise with socialist
principles is probably inevitable in Africa. Rural capitalists there will have to
be, but small ones, who can pass the rigorous tests of competitive markets.

5.4 *Promoting Exports and Reducing Excessive Protection*
Donald B. Keesing

A few countries in East Africa produce significant amounts of manufactured
exports: Botswana, Kenya, Mauritius, and Zimbabwe. Most of these manufactured exports go to other countries in the region. The chief exceptions are
those from Mauritius, along with a few items from Zimbabwe—principally
steel (produced at a loss and usually exported to Japan) and ferro-chrome.
Industrial exports are held back by inefficiency and lack of know-how, by
high labor costs, and by transport costs to distant markets. Nearly as serious

Excerpted and edited from Donald B. Keesing, "Industrial Policy Issues in Eastern Africa,"
World Bank Eastern and Southern Africa Projects Department, September 1984; and "Trade
Policy for Sub-Saharan Africa: Where Next?" paper prepared for the High-Level Seminar on
Industrial Policy in Africa, Berlin, May 31, 1984, sponsored by the World Bank and the German
Foundation for International Development (restricted circulation).

are the obstacles posed by overvalued exchange rates in combination with protection and incentive structures biased against exports.

No other measure to help exports is as powerful as adjusting the exchange rate so that the adjustment remains real—that is, so that devaluation is not offset by inflation. Several other policy measures are also needed in practically all countries: (1) measures to give export industries virtually automatic duty-free access to imported inputs and to spare them other indirect taxes; (2) measures to ensure exporters easy access to credit, especially for working capital; (3) institutional means to allow exporting firms to notify the government of their problems and to get a response; (4) measures to improve transport and communications facilities crucial to exports, to ensure exporting enterprises of reliable infrastructure services, to provide plant sites in locations well suited for exports, and to ensure that the more efficient export enterprises receive allocations reliably; (5) measures to allow industrial firms that are heavily engaged in producing exports to lay off workers without being penalized. Export markets are volatile and risky, and industrial firms must be assured that they will not be burdened by unnecessary costs.

Duty-Free Access to Imports

Duty-free access to imported inputs can be ensured in various ways: export processing (free trade) zones; bonded manufacturing in which enterprises specializing in exports have their own bonded warehouses; and duty-free schemes offering initial tariff waivers validated by subsequent evidence of corresponding exports, or rapid drawbacks of duties and other indirect taxes (whether according to a fixed rate or taxes actually paid). In addition, rapid customs clearance needs to be ensured for imported inputs used in exports and for exports themselves. Exemptions from value-added taxes and from turnover, sales, and excise taxes are also important.

From a practical standpoint, duty-free treatment is especially difficult to implement for plants selling part of their output at home and part of it abroad. In such cases, rules are needed giving the firm drawbacks or prior waivers on the proportion of imports corresponding to the proportion exported, or the allowance can be based on assumed input-output ratios for the product. An alternative approach favored in Latin America is a system of tax rebates based on indirect taxes presumed paid. Neither approach compensates exporters for the costs of prohibitions or restrictions on imported inputs, and if tax rebates are paid, trading partners may see it as a way of subsidizing products to the extent required to sell them.

Another important step is to extend automatic access to credit for working capital and duty-free access to imported inputs to indirect exporters—that is, enterprises that supply inputs into exports or inputs for those inputs. This is hard to do unless banks identify indirect exporters by giving them domestic letters of credit.

In addition to permanent measures like these, others may be introduced temporarily:

(1) An entitlement scheme allowing exporters of qualifying manufactured goods to use part of the foreign exchange they earn for specified purposes

related to their businesses, or else to sell or trade privileges related to its use. Schemes of this kind have been used in Tanzania and Zambia, among other places.

(2) Subsidies. The most obvious is a direct subsidy to all qualifying manufactured exports. Payment should be immediate and automatic, not slow and uncertain. In Zimbabwe, export subsidies take the form of tax-free cash bonuses. Another method is to grant low interest rate loans only to exporters. In practice, many subsidies are obtained by firms, whether they are producing for export or for the domestic market. For example, firms may be given infrastructure, energy, and sites at reduced prices—or even direct financial assistance (as in Botswana, where subsidies vary according to the size of the enterprise, whether it is owner operated, the citizenship and sex of the owner-manager, and where it is located). Subsidies such as these have had the effect of promoting exports from Botswana because its home market is small and its membership in a customs union increases the feasibility of producing for nearby markets. But in a country with high protection and substantial exchange rate overvaluation, subsidies for exports must be pinpointed to be effective.

(3) Implicit cross-subsidies. Satisfactory export performance by a firm can be made a condition for access to finance for whatever purpose, for getting government contracts, for receiving high protection in the domestic market, for licenses to import goods in short supply that command high prices, for fiscal concessions on various taxes, for receiving imported inputs needed to produce for the domestic market, or for being allowed to operate as a foreign firm in good standing. Thus, the firm is induced to subsidize its exports out of the profits it receives from selling in the protected domestic market.

(4) Low-cost (and, if necessary, marginal cost) pricing of exports in industries with economies of scale, since domestic customers must pay the fixed costs in any case. This trick is well known in much of Africa. Kenya and Zambia, for example, sell exported cement at less than half the domestic price.

Some Policy Issues

The rules of international trade, as well as pressures from trade partners and from the International Monetary Fund (IMF), limit the incentives that can be given to exports. Yet manufactured exports may be the quintessence of a true infant industry. There seems to be much to gain through a learning process—learning how to penetrate foreign markets by finding buyers and outlets and by making products that meet foreign needs and tastes and standards. Buyers can help by supplying designs and by assisting with technology and management—for example, by organizing production and quality control. The lessons learned by one firm then spread to other firms. At the same time, foreign buyers learn that the country is a new source of goods.

Is it feasible in East Africa to make the rewards for manufactured exports as large or larger than those for products manufactured for the domestic market? On a different plane, is liberalization of imports desirable or essential as a way of helping manufactured exports? Or can exports be promoted side by side with quantitative restrictions (QRs) and substantial protection?

Perhaps the main answer is that some liberalization will almost certainly be needed, starting with inputs into exports. Some countries have liberalized many of their QRs at times with an eye to the effects on exports. But their experience shows that the possibility does exist of achieving an export break-through while using QRs and protection, if the underlying objectives of protection can be shifted to emphasize creating early exports, mastering technology, and enabling the country to manage the foreign exchange demands generated by an export-oriented strategy. In any case, for a country with payments problems and high protection, it is usually sensible to expand exports first and then liberalize imports as export growth continues.

Preferential Trade Areas

Economic integration arrangements among the countries in Africa have come to nought except for the South African Customs Union, where South Africa gives its less developed partners special advantages for reasons partly politi-cal. Recently, however, diplomacy has begun to create a much broader inte-gration scheme. A Preferential Trade Area (PTA) for East Africa and Southern Africa has been emerging since late 1982. In 1984, the PTA was declared to have reached its "operational" stage, at which trade liberalization measures would commence. Fourteen countries have agreed to join the PTA, while six other invited countries have sent observers but expressed reluctance about becoming members.

Most of the countries involved have inconvertible currencies, and all have at least some balance of payments difficulties. Preferential tariff concessions among members will mean little in countries where imports and foreign exchange are being rationed or where quantitative import restrictions prevail, since tariffs have little effect on trade in these circumstances. Governments in any case are used to intervening to assist domestic firms in trouble, and these interventions might well prevent competition with existing enterprises.

Other difficulties abound. For example, there is likely to be a demand for development assistance from less to more developed countries to compensate the smaller and more backward countries for importing manufactures from strong partners. More generally, a polarization of industrial growth may be experienced. Zimbabwe and Kenya, among others, are likely to be asked to supply credit to less developed partners.

If problems such as these can be overcome, a PTA or similar organization could have a positive effect on manufacturing industries by giving them opportunities to learn to export manufactures in a halfway competitive mar-ket and by subjecting them to not-too-fierce competition in their own local markets. But transport costs among the far-flung participants will tend to offset any scale economies. As a rule, countries will not agree to pay more than the usual import prices to foster their partners' industries. Efforts to spur exports within the PTA, however, could lead to desirable policy improve-ments at the national level. If the PTA could inject greater stability into the trade and payments situation without eliminating the trade opportunities that now exist, this would be a welcome result.

Protectionism

Protectionism used to be the main policy instrument for fostering industry in most of Africa. Its high tide has passed, however. Increasingly, protection has given way in importance to foreign exchange allocations, including import licensing. Industrial firms have been learning that there is not much value in high protection if they cannot get the imported inputs needed to make the product. Increasing government ownership in industry has also reduced the importance of protection. In some countries, price controls have also reduced protection's role.

Deliberate protection today takes two forms: (1) tariff protection, broadly defined to include all taxes on imports, including surcharges; and (2) QRS, including quotas, outright prohibitions, and case-by-case licensing decisions. Most developing countries use both QRS and tariffs. What are the advantages of each?

Tariffs make it possible to collect revenues from imports that actually enter the country. (Indeed, some tariffs are designed mainly for revenue, and protection is a side effect.) Another advantage is that the limits of the price effects can be known with certainty.

QRS, on the other hand, make it possible to pin down the quantity or value imported. This makes it possible to guarantee a large share of the domestic market to a local enterprise and is especially important in an industry with substantial economies of scale. QRS also make it possible to set limits on the value of imports, whether for the sake of protection or to defend the balance of payments. Unlike tariffs, QRS usually lead to windfall profits for importers (usually industrialists) who receive part or all of the allowed imports.

Price controls are sometimes used in conjunction with QRS to hold down the price-raising effects of the restrictions. If they are not, the price effect of a QR is much like that of a tariff. Except where domestic competition holds down the price, it rises, allowing firms to pay high costs, obtain high profits, or both. QRS are a more flexible instrument than tariffs in countries where legislative approval is needed to change tariffs. The flexible, discretionary character of QRS and the windfall gains they distribute lead fairly often to abuse, ranging from excessive or erratic intervention to blatant corruption.

Protection of either kind has effects on both sides of a protected industry or firm's operations: the input side (costs) and the output side (revenues). The combined effect of protection on the input and output sides is commonly measured by "effective protection."[4] More often than not, developing countries have many industries enjoying effective protection of several hundred percent. But there is almost always a great dispersion of rates, including quite a few activities with negative effective protection. Usually, there is negative

4. See technical note C.

effective protection for exports, most capital goods, and most agricultural products.

Exchange Rates

Some observers have pointed to overvalued exchange rates as the central problem of industry in Africa. To support and defend an official exchange rate (overvalued or not), a country must keep outflows of foreign exchange from exceeding inflows over a period of months and years or else the country must borrow abroad or use its revenues (if it has any) to make up each shortfall. Defending the rate as it becomes overvalued means rationing foreign exchange. It implies sharp cutbacks of imports along with economywide austerity measures, such as reduced public expenditures, reduced credit availability, and new taxes. A typical result of all these measures is low and falling GDP growth, combined with negative or zero industrial growth.

Since the exchange rate is out of line, speculative outflows of foreign exchange must be combated by repressive controls. Even so, people will find ways to take money out—for example, by falsifying invoices in authorized trade. A black market for foreign currencies can also be expected to emerge.

Overvaluation also shapes the way people in and out of the country regard its industry. Industry conveys the impression of being costly, inefficient, poorly managed, and dependent on government help. As a shorthand description, an overvalued rate can properly be called a low growth, high-cost, disequilibrium exchange rate. Such rates are typical in Africa today.

The solution may be devaluation. But devaluation has inflationary effects (pushing up the prices of tradable goods in the first instance). Thus, it can easily lead back into a new disequilibrium, with higher prices and more low or zero growth. For these reasons, it is indispensable to combine devaluation with deflationary fiscal and monetary policies. However, some deliberate credit expansion is needed following a devaluation to pay for working capital now that inputs are more expensive. Here as elsewhere, austerity measures should not be allowed to reduce output sharply and therefore the supply of goods available. Apart from special measures to keep output up, however, much austerity is required. Minimum wages, public sector wages, and union wages should not be allowed to rise by more than some small fraction of the devaluation. If investment is now already low, the country may also have to cut it back, despite the negative effects of the cutbacks on construction and employment.

A long-term problem lies at the root of the short-term problem of overvalued exchange rates. This is the trend toward overvalued exchange rates that occurs because real earnings from primary exports usually grow little while import needs keep growing. In most of Africa, the easy possibilities for natural-resource-based exports have been recognized for a long time and have been fairly thoroughly exploited. But every modernizing sector needs more imports as it grows. Thus, over a period of years the supply of foreign exchange tends to stay much the same but demand goes up. The value of foreign exchange then increases, and what started as a high-growth, low-cost exchange rate becomes a low-growth, high-cost rate that drags growth down.

This tendency toward foreign exchange scarcity will probably continue in most African countries for decades.

The exchange rate is also affected by policy performance in protection. If a country prefers high protection and direct controls, this in itself will push the exchange rate in a direction that discourages exports and natural, unassisted import substitution. Conversely, if the country avoids any but the mildest protection, the resulting exchange rate will be more favorable to exports and make strong protection less necessary. Getting rid of controls and protection requires an exchange rate adjustment or else an equivalent reduction in the price level through use of deflationary policies. Such an adjustment through devaluation, if it can be made real and lasting, can be a substitute or partial substitute for protection; protection can be decreased without a rise in imports at the same time.

One interpretation of economic history is that Japan, the Federal Republic of Germany, Italy, and some of the smaller European industrial countries systematically undervalued their currencies from the late 1940s to the late 1960s as a way of bringing about faster economic growth. Somewhat later the same thing was done by the star performers in East Asia. In all or most of these cases, manufactured exports served as the sector spearheading growth; other exports were also stimulated, along with efficient import substitution.

In Sub-Saharan Africa, by contrast, the trend has been toward overvaluation. At most, the devaluations of the past two or three years have only roughly compensated for rises in prices. Nothing has happened to make African prices and wages seem low compared with those elsewhere.

5.5 Agroprocessing
William F. Steel and Bassirou A. Sarr

Most African countries are basically producers of primary products and have an obvious potential for developing resource-based industries. Many countries produce a large number of crops suitable for processing. For some of the poorer landlocked countries, processing of agricultural products for local consumption appears to be the most likely ground for development of an industrial sector.

Nevertheless, neither theoretical reasoning nor empirical evidence argues convincingly that resource-based industrialization is likely to succeed in Africa unless it is developed under appropriate conditions. Comparative advantage in producing a raw material does not necessarily imply comparative advantage in processing the material. Processing is most likely to be efficient if it leads to substantial savings in transport costs and if it utilizes factors that are available at relatively low cost. The industrial processing of many commodities, however, requires large capital sums and large amounts of skilled labor, both of which are generally scarce in Africa. The processed products are therefore often more expensive per ton to transport to foreign markets, reducing the advantage originally obtained by reducing weight.

Excerpted by permission from William F. Steel and Bassirou A. Sarr, *"Agro-Industrial Development in Africa"* (Abidjan: African Development Bank, June 1983), research memorandum 2.

Lack of success in establishing an appropriate policy and institutional framework is one explanation for the limited growth of agroprocessing (as well as import-substitution) industries in many African countries. The decline in the volume of raw material exports resulting from increased domestic processing in Africa has not been compensated for by increased exports of processed products. Consequently, African countries have not been as successful as other developing countries in raising their foreign exchange earnings through increased processing.

Agricultural Raw Material Supplies

A prerequisite for agroindustrial development is a supply of raw materials that is growing faster than local demand. Farmers therefore need incentives both to produce the commodities and to sell them in regular markets (rather than parallel or black markets). African farmers are quite sensitive to relative prices, which help them to decide which crops to plant, whether to harvest the crops, and where to sell them.

African governments have customarily intervened in product markets to maintain producer prices below the free market level. Although this policy often began as a way of using surpluses built up during years of high commodity prices to subsidize prices during slumps, the surpluses have not become an important financial resource. Thus, government budgetary considerations may constrain countries that would otherwise like to bolster incentives for producers. Structural adjustment, backed by international technical assistance and program-type lending, would enable African countries to make a transition to more producer-oriented policies and more responsive institutional structures.

Essential components of agroindustrial development include a system of stocking and storing raw materials and providing processing firms with guaranteed supplies, either through a national marketing agency or some other mechanism.

When processing of nonfood crops is being promoted, care must be taken not to interfere with food self-sufficiency objectives. That is, the prices of both food and nonfood crops must be raised in a balanced manner that encourages the growth of both types, rather than expansion of nonfood crops at the expense of food crops.

Markets and Regional Cooperation

Processing crops for export is an apparently attractive means of adding value to a country's resources and earning additional foreign exchange. For several reasons, however, agroindustrial production in Africa for external markets may not generally be successful. First, industrial production costs in Africa tend to be high relative to those in other developing regions. Second, barriers to developing country manufactures persist in the industrialized countries. Third, large-scale, export-oriented industries often need capital-intensive techniques and considerable expatriate assistance in management and marketing to be internationally competitive, both of which minimize the beneficial impact of processing on domestic employment and value added.

Processing for the domestic market has the advantage that demand can be ensured through protection. Overprotection of resource-based industries, however, risks supporting inefficient, high-cost production, as has happened with many import-substitution industries in Africa. Protection is not generally suitable as a tool for stimulating investment, although it may be justified to enable an infant industry to get on its feet. Since locally consumed goods produced from domestic materials enjoy the double "protection" of avoiding both outward and inward transport costs, processing industries that cannot survive without additional protection are unlikely to be efficient users of domestic resources.

Resource-based industrialization for subregional markets (that is, two or more neighboring countries) offers the possibility of overcoming some of the problems associated with processing primarily for foreign markets. Subregional markets offer greater prospects for the operation of plants of sufficiently large scale to avoid the high unit cost of suboptimal plants geared to limited national markets. Subregional markets also offer some scope for protection through transport cost advantages if not through cooperative policy measures, while still requiring firms to remain internationally competitive. Regional cooperation can be both a cause and an effect of increased processing. Better intercountry linkages and coordinated policies can stimulate production for subregional trade; vice versa, increasing trade requires expansion of the infrastructure that links countries. Inadequate market information are commonly cited constraints on industrialization in Africa. Furthermore, better intercountry transport linkages would help to ensure that intra-African freight charges were structured to provide a competitive advantage over North-South trade.

Although many countries have established special development banks for the agricultural and industrial sectors, neither type of bank may regard agricultural processing as in its domain, since the other type of activity is also inevitably involved. In some cases, processing industries come under the jurisdiction of the marketing board responsible for raw materials, which helps to avoid the problems of supply uncertainty. In any case, each country should make clear which agency is responsible for agricultural processing activities and ensure that these activities are given due priority by the appropriate agencies.

Although it is probably unnecessary to establish a special agency to promote agroindustries, countries may wish to set up priorities or targets for lending to agroindustries. Such priorities, however, should be aimed only at overcoming biases against processing industries, not at giving them unrestricted advantages.

5.6 *Phasing of Trade Liberalization*
Michael Michaely

A trade liberalization policy is often seen as a measure of primary importance that can be expected to improve allocation of an economy's resources, lead to

Excerpted and edited by permission from Michael Michaely, "The Timing and Sequencing of a Trade Liberalization Policy," in Armeane Choksi and Demetrios Papageorgiou, eds., *Economic Liberalization in Developing Countries* (Oxford: Basil Blackwell, 1986).

greater efficiency, expand the economy's output, and accelerate its growth. The manner in which such a policy is introduced—the desirable path of policy implementation—should be inseparable from consideration of such a policy. Yet the problem of *phasing* or *sequencing* trade policy has not often been addressed.

A trade liberalization policy is defined in the actions leading to reduction of the level and variance of a system of trade protection. In an environment of import barriers, in which existing policies are biased in favor of import substitution, the introduction of new policies that provide incentives for the production of exportables will constitute such an act of liberalization. Their effect will be to reduce the variance of protection across sectors and move the economy toward a neutral trade regime. Complete liberalization would mean the elimination of all protection (save for a few exceptions) and near-zero variance in the system. The term *liberalization policy* will be used here to refer to actions concerned with the economy's international trade.

The question of sequencing has three components: (1) How fast should the process of liberalization be? In particular, is a once-and-for-all, one-stage liberalization superior or inferior to a multistage policy? (2) What would be the attributes of the stages of implementation? (3) What should be the relationship between liberalization of imports and other economic policies?

Speed of Implementation

If a postliberalization situation is assumed to be superior to a preliberalization situation, it would seem that the shift from one to the other would best be made swiftly to achieve immediate realization of the benefits yielded by the new, superior situation. This would thus call for a single-stage policy of liberalization—implementing it fully and at once. In addition, the response to a policy change would presumably be strongly dependent on the credibility assigned to the change by individual economic agents. As a stronger signal, the single-stage policy would be expected to evoke a stronger response, in terms of reallocation of resources, than a multistage implementation. This would have been unequivocally true in a world free of rigidities, in which all responses are immediate. In reality, however, other considerations must be taken into account.

In an activity from which protection is removed (partially or totally), production is likely to decline. Resources—labor as well as physical and human capital—will be partly unemployed, rather than transferred immediately to an expanding industry. This state of affairs will be more severe the shorter the time elapsed since the policy change.

Aside from the loss of production, unemployment would naturally tend to change income distribution in a manner likely to be considered undesirable. Furthermore, unemployment is likely to be regarded by the unemployed and by society at large as a situation whose cost is not limited to the loss of income. For all these reasons, unemployment is bound to be a consideration of crucial political importance when decisions are made regarding liberalization.

Income distribution is affected, of course, not just by unemployment. The change in relative prices resulting from liberalization leads to the reduction of quasi rents enjoyed by owners of physical and human capital in the contracting industries to the potential point of elimination of such rents. It leads, on the other had, to increases in the rents enjoyed by capital owners in newly encouraged industries.

An immediate and large liberalization of trade would thus have a relatively large impact on income distribution, whereas a gradual change would minimize it. It cannot be known whether the income distribution existing at the start would be superior or inferior to the one that would be established with a large and immediate change in relative prices. It can be assumed, however, that the status quo generally enjoys, in the eyes of the public and of policymakers, a particular esteem. This would therefore be an additional element working, in principle, against an immediate and large change in relative prices. Thus, a general presumption is established that gradual, multistage implementation of a liberalization policy would be superior to a once-and-for-all large change.

The preceding discussion also provides some indication of the appropriate speed of implementation. In general, the process should be shorter the fewer the rigidities in the labor market, the less specific the physical and human capital, the more flexible the responses of entrepreneurs, and the shorter the life span of the physical capital in the contracting activities. The process of implementation should thus be faster the higher the elasticities of substitution in production among various activities, and the faster the reaction of agents that are potential movers to expanding sectors. These attributes will obviously be different from case to case. No clear-cut rule can be offered on the relationship between the desired speed of implementation and the level of development in the economy undertaking liberalization.

A consideration that could presumable lead either way is the political feasibility of alternative paths. The one-stage policy, leading to larger unemployment and larger changes in income distribution, could be expected to generate more resistance and thus be less feasible politically. On the other hand, it can be assumed that a multistage process would generate a long political struggle. Such a struggle would be prevented by the one-stage alternative.

Path of Liberalization

What should policymakers infer on a priori grounds about the nature of the stages of liberalization? A few specific questions can be posed.

The first concerns shifts between forms of protection. Government interference in imports frequently takes the form of quantitative restrictions (QRs) rather than (or in addition to) tariffs. Indeed, the term *liberalization* is very often understood as a shift from QRs to protection through tariffs, rather than as the lowering of tariffs. Assuming that a country does indeed rely on quantitative restrictions, which is a quite common case, the first question would be: Is it desirable to start the process of liberalization by shifting from QRs to protection through tariffs without affecting much the levels of protection, or would it be better to dispense with this stage and perform the gradual lowering of protection by a gradual relaxation of quantitative restrictions?

Shifting protection to the price mechanism does have a few major advantages. It may contribute to eliminating any lack of uniformity in the system that is not intended (and probably, most often, unknown), but which is inevitably embodied in a system of QRs. Probably no less important is the preannouncement of future levels of protection. Multistage implementation makes sense only if the correct signals are given in advance; the future course of the process should be known at the start. This would be very difficult, if not impossible, to achieve with a system of QRs. Neither the government nor private economic agents can be expected to possess the knowledge required to transform a future (preannounced) level and structure of QRs into levels of prices and protection. The signals must be transmitted directly by announcing prices, and this, in turn, requires an initial shift to protection through prices.

The main argument against this initial shift is the time involved in the process. An unduly long time, during which no other liberalization steps are undertaken, may outweigh the advantages. Another possible argument, which could work either way, is the impact of the shift on income distribution. The quota profits enjoyed by the holders of import licenses under QRs (unless these licenses are auctioned in the market) are transferred, with the shift to tariffs, to recipients of government expenditures or to taxpayers.

A "uniform" path of liberalization is one in which no specific activity is mentioned. At least three alternative uniform paths are possible. One is an equi-proportional ("across the board") reduction in protection of various activities. This path has the advantage of leading to an increased convergence of protection rates and a gradual reduction in the variance of the protection system. Another possible path is the reduction of protection rates by equally large amounts. This has the defect of potentially leading, at least in the initial stages, to increased variance in the system of protection rates. It may have the advantage, on the other hand, of making the transitory impact on employment less severe by avoiding large reductions of relative prices in the highly protected activities. The slower the responsiveness of expanding activities, and the stronger the reduction of employment caused by changes in prices, the more does this advantage become relevant. The third alternative is what has been described as the *concertina method*. This works as follows. In the initial stage of the policy, all protection rates above a certain ceiling are lowered to that ceiling, with no changes in other rates. In the next stage, all rates are brought down to a lower ceiling, and so on. This rule not only would consistently lower the variance in the system but would have the advantage of reaping the highest possible net benefit from any change in production and consumption patterns.

Employment considerations appear to be a primary motivation for the adoption of a discriminatory, nonuniform path of liberalization. In general, activities whose contraction would result in relatively large unemployment should be candidates for a more prolonged process of liberalization. These may be activities that are relatively labor intensive; even more so, activities intensive in human capital.

A legitimate argument for the removal of quantitative restrictions on imports of intermediate inputs is that their existence leads to highly inefficient production processes. But the removal of QRs should be accompanied by the imposition of tariffs as long as final goods activities are protected.

Import Liberalization and Other Policies in the Sequence

It would seem that neither inflation nor unemployment is conducive to successful liberalization. Unaccompanied by accommodating changes in exchange rates, inflation is bound to lead to balance of payments deterioration, making the maintenance of a free market for imports a more difficult undertaking. Heavy unemployment, on the other hand, would again make free imports, with their associated transitory unemployment, more difficult to defend. In general, therefore, it would seem that liberalization is most likely to succeed if introduced under what can be described as domestic and external equilibrium.

Very often—perhaps on most occasions—liberalization would be considered not in the context of equilibrium but in economies suffering from inflation, perhaps in combination with acute balance of payments difficulties. In these circumstances, a liberalization policy would stand a chance of success only if undertaken in conjunction with a stabilization policy and an appropriate exchange rate policy—policies that would have to be undertaken for their own sake, regardless of the adoption of a liberalization policy.

Exchange Rate Policy and Export Promotion

It is assumed here that the economy's position before liberalization is that of a balance of payments "equilibrium" in a very narrow sense; that is, given all the price and quantity restrictions on imports and at the existing exchange rate, the "basic" payments account is balanced. Import liberalization, which raises the volume of imports, must thus be accompanied by exchange rate devaluation. The latter, in turn, may take a variety of forms, from a uniform, formal devaluation to a discriminatory system of export-promotion policies.

In this process, some import-competing activities decline, whereas other activities—primarily export, and presumably also some other import-competing sectors—expand. This involves not only, and usually not primarily, a shift of sales of existing production between the home and the foreign markets, but rather a structural change involving a shift of productive resources. It may be presumed that contracting activities will respond more quickly than potentially expanding activities.

Several alternative solutions may be considered. One is to have a relatively large price increase in the export sector in the initial stages. This would increase the extent of responsiveness and of export expansion, but it would still not relieve the balance of payments problem in the initial stages.

Another response might be the securing of foreign aid, if it is available, to bridge the initial gap between exports and imports. But even if the foreign exchange gap is closed in this way, the problem of initial disparities between expanding and contracting activities would not be solved by the extra availability of foreign exchange.

A third response is advancing export promotion (by a formal devaluation or through export-promotion measures) so that it precedes the first stage of import liberalization. By the time the latter starts, the process of expanding export activities would already be on its way.

Capital Market Liberalization

The existence of distortions in one market implies that the elimination of distortions in another market does not necessarily increase welfare. However, a simultaneous and complete liberalization of *all* markets must be beneficial. Similarly, in a world with two markets, a complete liberalization in one market would make a liberalization policy (whether complete or partial) in the other necessarily beneficial.

Restrictions in the capital market could either be of a nature that reinforces the distortions because of import restrictions or, to the contrary, one set may tend to offset the other. Thus, rationing of long- and short-term credit, capital grants, concessionary loans, investment licensing, and similar interference in the capital market may be applied to direct capital toward, or away from, the protected activities. If it is the former, removal of restrictions in one market while they remain intact in the other is most likely to be beneficial. If it is the latter alternative, on the other hand, liberalization in one market may lower the economy's welfare, leading to a larger degree of misallocation of resources than that found with the two offsetting schemes.

6

Adjustment Experiences

6.1 Recent Adjustment Programs
World Bank Staff

Africa's regional institutions have been leading a change in attitudes toward development policy. A 1985 report by the Economic Commission for Africa and the African Development Bank argued that mistaken policies have depressed agricultural output and industrial productivity, promoted inefficiency in state-owned enterprises, and damaged incentives for the domestic private sector. The Organization of African Unity's summit meeting in July 1985 echoed the theme by adopting ''Africa's Priority Programme for Economic Recovery, 1986–90.'' This strategy also stressed the importance of agriculture, the need for new industrial policies that give the private sector a larger economic role, and the desirability of more active population programs. This shift in African thinking toward a more pragmatic approach to development is important and encouraging.

Since 1984, more countries have started adjustment programs, and the changes go deeper than before. Ghana, Togo, and Zaire have reinforced the comprehensive economic and financial reforms that they introduced in 1983. In 1984–85, Guinea, Mauritania, Senegal, and Zambia adopted similar policies to improve broad macroeconomic performance as well as to assist individual economic sectors. Madagascar, Mali, and Niger continue to adopt important policy reforms, although more slowly. The reform movement seems likely to endure, and perhaps to gather speed, as more countries see the results in those that have led the way.

These reforms cover a wide range of measures. Their aim is to give prices, markets, and the private sector a greater role in promoting development in

Excerpted and edited from World Bank, *Financing Adjustment with Growth in Sub-Saharan Africa, 1986–90* (Washington, D.C., 1986); and *Proposals for Enhancing Assistance to Low-Income Countries That Face Exceptional Difficulties,* Development Committee Pamphlet 16 (Washington, D.C.: World Bank and International Monetary Fund, 1988).

Figure 6.1.1 *Real Effective Exchange Rate Indexes in Developing Countries, 1971-84*

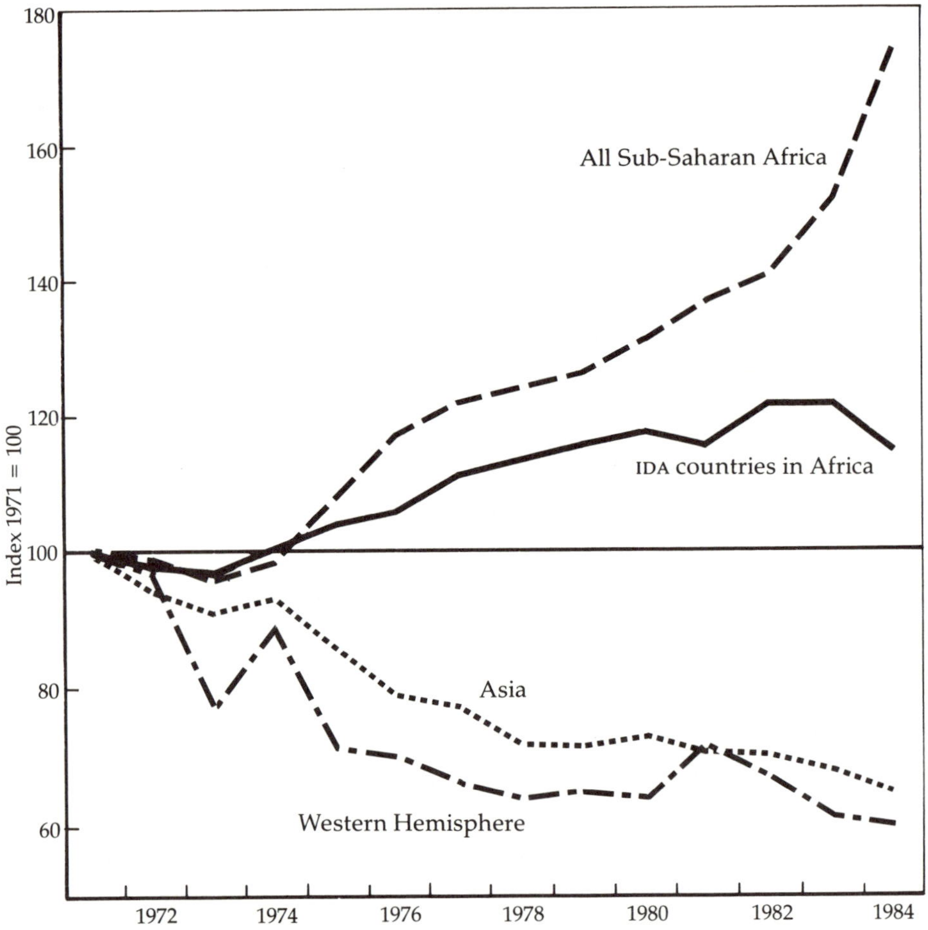

Note: See explanation of real effective exchange rates in technical note F. IDA countries are the poorest developing countries, which are eligible to receive interest-free loans from the International Development Association, an affiliate of the World Bank.

Africa. In particular, they reflect a desire to reduce administrative intervention in setting prices, to end monopolies on trade and marketing, and to lessen the government's role in allocating credit.

Correcting Overvalued Exchange Rates

For the low-income African countries as a group, unlike Asian and Latin American countries, the real effective exchange rate (REER) appreciated significantly in the 1970s and early 1980s (see figure 6.1.1).[1] By late 1985, the real effective exchange rate was about 15 percent above its 1970–72 level. More-

1. See technical notes E and F for measurement of changes in the exchange rate.

over, even the 1970–72 level was too high for some countries, especially those where terms of trade shifts had been large and negative. In Zaire and Zambia, for example, market-determined real effective exchange rates had fallen at the end of 1985 by over 40 percent from their level in 1970–72.

One reason that countries delay or minimize adjustments in the exchange rate is fear of the social and political consequences. Resistance to adjustment comes from groups, often in the urban sector, that benefit from the implicit subsidies of currency overvaluation. The distributional effects of devaluation differ according to the underlying structure of the economy, but they are likely to benefit lower-income groups in many African countries. Moreover, devaluation allows the removal of controls and trade restrictions that create artificial scarcities and bring "rents" to those with access to scarce resources. Rarely will the poor be the principal losers from devaluation.

Correcting overvaluation of currencies helps to reduce balance of payments deficits. It also shifts the internal terms of trade in favor of those who produce for export (mainly rural households) and away from those who consume imports (predominantly urban households). After more than a decade of creeping appreciation, the average REER for African countries that are eligible for funding from the International Development Association (IDA) began to depreciate in 1984. This trend apparently continued into 1985. A growing number of governments have adopted more flexible exchange rates that are determined by supply and demand in the foreign exchange market.

Following a huge devaluation, Zaire introduced a floating rate system in 1983, and by 1984 the exchange rate was freely determined in an interbank market. By the end of 1984, the real effective exchange rate had fallen by three-quarters, and the premium on the parallel market was no more than 10 percent, roughly in line with the cost of bank commissions. In 1985, Zambia

Figure 6.1.2. *Real Effective Exchange Rate Indexes in Sub-Saharan African Countries Eligible for IDA Funds, 1980–87*

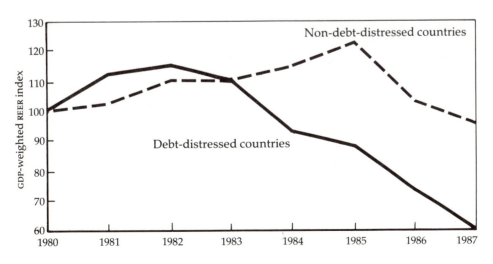

Table 6.1.1 *Key Indicators of Reform for Adjusting and Nonadjusting Countries, Selected Years, 1980–87*

Indicator of reform	Period	Adjusting countries	Nonadjusting countries
Real effective exchange rate index (1980–82=100)	1987	73	79
Fiscal deficit (percentage of GDP)	1980–82	7.9	6.7
	1987	3.6	6.7
Inflation rate (percentage a year)	1980–82	17	15
	1987	14	38
Commercial bank lending rates (real percentage a year)	1980–82	−2.8	−2.1
	1987	4.6	−11.6
Agricultural incentive indexes			
Export crop prices (real, 1980/81–82/83=100)	1986/87	148	114
Food crop prices (real, 1980/81–82/83=100)	1986/87	125	87

Note: As many as twenty adjusting countries and eleven nonadjusting countries have been included; the actual number varies by indicator. Averages are unweighted.

Source: World Bank, *World Development Report 1988* (New York: Oxford University Press, 1988), box 1.5.

introduced an auction system for most trade-related exchange transactions. Although the government and selected public enterprises continue to receive an administrative allocation of foreign exchange, the value of foreign exchange is determined by the auction. After the introduction of the new system, the nominal exchange rate fell by two-thirds in three weeks. Madagascar took a step toward more flexible exchange rates in March 1984 when it began to adjust the Malagasy franc every quarter in line with the change in the consumer price index during the previous quarter. By the third quarter of 1985, the REER had depreciated by about 15 percent. Ghana, Guinea, and Mauritania made substantial devaluations in 1983 and 1984 by combining vigorous nominal devaluations with effective measures to contain inflation.

By 1986, REERs in countries with ongoing reform programs had fallen by 30 to 50 percent from their peak in 1981–83. The debt-distressed countries in this group, whose exchange rates had become relatively more misaligned, started their adjustments two to three years earlier than the other countries, and adjustments have been more rapid and substantial (see figure 6.1.2 and table 6.1.1). In about three-fourths of these countries, the REER in 1987 was no higher and often lower than in the early 1970s. Exchange rates remain relatively high in Africa, however, compared with those in other low-income countries, especially in Asia.

Restoring Fiscal and Monetary Stability

Many governments have restored fiscal and financial discipline by restraining public expenditures and increasing revenues, by liquidating or privatizing inefficient parastatals, and by strengthening management. As a result, fiscal deficits have shrunk substantially. By 1986, fiscal deficits in adjusting countries averaged less than 4 percent of gross domestic product, only one-third of the high level of the early 1980s. Nonadjusting countries, in contrast, had not succeeded in reducing their deficits.

Tighter fiscal and monetary policy enabled adjusting countries to reduce the rate of inflation somewhat by 1987 and to achieve positive real interest rates. Inflation in the nonadjusting countries was more than double the average rate of the 1980–82 period, making interest rates increasingly negative in real terms.

Changing Urban-Rural Bias

There is a growing consensus in Africa to change policies that discriminate against agriculture and favor the urban sector. There are at least three links between farming and development. First, the largest part of the population and the majority of the poor depend on agriculture for a living. Second, production is still heavily agricultural; higher output will require incentives to improve productivity in farming. Third, exports will be mostly agricultural for the medium term, but they will rise only slowly as long as governments channel most of the profits to urban populations.

Figure 6.1.3 *Rural-Urban Terms of Trade Index for Low-Income Sub-Saharan African Countries, 1980–86*

(ratio of real food crop price to wage)

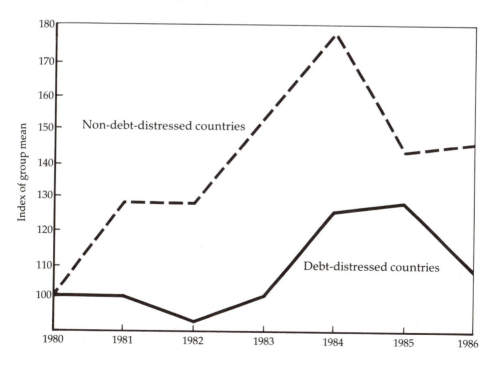

Many governments have improved agricultural incentives by increasing official prices in conjunction with currency devaluation. Some have done it by deregulating markets to give farmers access to higher prices on parallel markets. Others are introducing more flexible systems of official pricing as a step toward lifting controls on agricultural trade.

Since 1980, the real export prices of debt-distressed countries with adjustment programs have improved steadily at about 5 percent a year. Food prices improved in real terms through 1985, with some decline in 1986 following two successive years of good harvests. For both export and food crops, improvements were greater for adjusting than nonadjusting countries (table 6.1.1).

Urban wages have fallen substantially in real terms, largely because governments have restrained adjustments in minimum wages and public sector salaries, despite often rapid inflation. The purchasing power of minimum wage earnings in 1985 was only about half its 1970 average.

As a result of the movements in agricultural prices and urban wages, the internal terms of trade have moved in favor of the rural sector during the 1980s. For the debt-distressed countries, gross minimum wages fell from over twice average agricultural incomes in the early 1970s to only 30 percent higher by the mid-1980s. Adjustment programs in these countries helped farmers' terms of trade for export crops grow steadily at about 15 percent a year during 1980–85. The terms of trade for food crops rose sharply from 1980 to 1984 and then leveled off at 45 percent above the 1980 index (see figure 6.1.3). The non-debt-distressed countries showed little net improvement in the terms of trade for either export or food crops.

6.2 *World Bank Lending in Support of Adjustment in Sub-Saharan Africa, 1980–88*
Malathi Jayawickrama, Benoit Morin, and William F. Steel

In the early 1980s, the World Bank initiated fast-disbursing loans to assist countries in adjusting their policies and economic structures to changes in their economic conditions. Economic distress resulted from external circumstances, such as higher oil prices, lower export prices, and drought, and from domestic policies that proved unsustainable over time. The Bank has supported macroeconomic stabilization and policy change through structural adjustment loans (SALS) and more sector-specific reforms through sectoral adjustment loans (SECALS). These loans provide quick-disbursing funds for imports in support of agreed-upon reforms designed to improve economic performance. Other lending instruments with these characteristics provide supplemental support for adjustment. They include loans for economic recovery, export development, imports under a trade liberalization program, technical assistance, and reform of public enterprise management.

African countries gradually adopted adjustment programs in the early 1980s. By 1988 eighteen had initiated structural adjustment operations, and another fourteen had borrowed to support reforms at the sectoral level. This article describes the evolution and policy content of World Bank lending in support of adjustment in Sub-Saharan Africa. Differences among groups of countries and over time are analyzed. Technical assistance loans for public sector management are discussed separately from other adjustment-related lending.

Amount and Types of World Bank Lending

As the amount lent and the number of countries that were assisted grew, lending by the Bank in support of adjustment (excluding technical assistance) evolved from an initial emphasis on macroeconomic policies through SALs to a wider range of more narrrowly focused operations. From 1980 to 1982, African countries received a total of only $0.7 billion in twelve adjustment-related loans, five of them SALs and three of them general import financing (table 6.2.1). Between 1983 and 1985, the number and level of adjustment-related

Table 6.2.1 *Adjustment and Nonproject Loans from the World Bank to Sub-Saharan Africa by Category and Fiscal Year, 1980–88*
(number of new loans approved)

Category	1980	1981	1982	1983	1984	1985	1986	1987	1988	Total
Macro										
Structural adjustment	1	3	1	2	3	1	6	8	6	31
Economic recovery, rehabilitation	1	0	1	0	1	2	1	1	2	9
Public management										
Public enterprise sector	0	0	0	0	0	1	0	2	2	5
Technical assistance	3	10	8	4	9	10	7	6	9	66
Trade policy										
Import	1	2	0	1	0	2	1	1	0	8
Export	0	1	0	1	2	0	0	0	0	4
Sector adjustment										
Industry	0	0	0	0	0	1	4	2	2	9
Agriculture	1	0	0	3	2	2	3	0	2	13
Education	0	0	0	0	0	0	0	1	0	1
Financial	0	0	0	0	0	0	0	0	1	1
Total										
Number of loans	7	16	10	11	17	19	22	21	24	147
Number excluding technical assistance	4	6	2	7	8	9	15	15	15	81
Amount (millions of U.S. dollars)	243	384	277	439	899	318	1,089	1,307	1,159	6,122
Special Facility for Africa	—	—	—	—	—	—	466[a]	421[b]	103[c]	987
Excluding technical assistance	233	277	220	407	818	243	1,030	1,256	1,063	5,546

Note: Amounts include funds from the International Bank for Reconstruction and Development, the International Development Association, and the Special Facility for Africa (SFA).

— Not applicable.

a. Includes $72 million in supplements to adjustment loans approved in 1985; excludes $70 million for transport sector loans.

b. Includes a $10 million supplement to an adjustment loan approved in 1986.

c. Includes a $25 million supplement to an adjustment loan approved in 1987; excludes $10 million for a transport sector loan.

Table 6.2.2 Adjustment and Nonproject Loans from the World Bank to Sub-Saharan Africa by Country and Fiscal Year, 1980–88
(new loans approved)

Country	1980	1981	1982	1983	1984	1985	1986	1987	1988	Number of loans	Technical assistance loans
With structural adjustment operations											
Kenya	SA						AG		IND	4	4
Malawi		SA		AG	SA		SA		IND/IM	5	2
Mauritius		SA			SA		SA	IND		3	1
Senegal		SA					SA	SA		3	3
Côte d'Ivoire			SA		SA		SA			3	1
Togo				SA		SA			SA	3	2
Niger							SA	PE		2	2
Guinea							SA		SA	2	1
Burundi							SA		SA	2	2
Ghana				IM		IM	IND	SA;ED	FIN	7	3
Mauritania						PE	IND	SA		3	3
Guinea Bissau						IM		SA		2	2
Sao Tome						ER		SA		2	0
Zaire					EX		IND	SA		2	4
Central African Republic								SA	AG;SA	3	2
Gambia								SA		1	0
Congo									SA	1	3
Gabon									SA	1	0

With sectoral adjustment only	4	6	2	7	8	9	15	15	15	81	57
Uganda	ER		ER	AG	ER				ER	5	2
Sudan	AG;IM			AG						3	2
Tanzania		EX		EX				ER		2	3
Zimbabwe		IM(2)								3	0
Zambia					EX	AG	IND;ER			4	1
Nigeria					AG			IM/EX		2	3
Sierra Leone					AG					1	1
Madagascar						IND	AG	IND/IM	PE	4	4
Mozambique						AG				1	0
Burkina Faso						ER			ER	2	0
Somalia							AG			1	1
Equatorial Guinea							IM			1	1
Benin								PE		1	1
Mali									AG;PE	2	3
Number of loans	4	6	2	7	8	9	15	15	15	81	57

Note: Countries are listed by fiscal year of first structural (or sectoral) adjustment operation. A slash (/) indicates a hybrid loan. Categories of adjustment and nonproject loans include structural adjustment (SA), economic recovery or rehabilitation (ER), public enterprise sector (PE), import (IM), export (EX), industry (IND), agriculture (AG), education (ED) and financial (FIN). Technical assistance loans are not shown in the table, but totals are listed in the last column.

loans increased to an average of eight per year and a total of $1.5 billion. Although the level of adjustment support waned in 1985, that year the World Bank initiated the Special Facility for Africa (SFA) as a vehicle for other countries to increase their assistance directly to African countries that were undertaking major reforms. Adjustment-related lending rose sharply to $3.6 billion in the three-year period 1986–88 (including $1.0 billion from the SFA) and fifteen loans a year. This increase supported ongoing programs in sixteen of the twenty-eight countries involved.[2]

Of the twenty World Bank loans for technical assistance during 1980–82, only eight went to countries undertaking structural or sectoral adjustment loans in that period. Technical assistance loans continued at the rate of about seven per year during 1983–88, but were oriented more toward developing and implementing adjustment programs. Six countries received technical assistance loans without any adjustment operations.[3]

The large number of agricultural adjustment loans (ten) from 1983 to 1986 reflected a growing emphasis on stimulating production through improved incentives to food crop producers. Industrial production came to the fore with eight SECALs in 1986–88, often combined with trade policy loans that supported industrial efficiency and recovery. The typical sequencing of adjustment shifted from an initial SAL with no further adjustment support for two years (among the six countries that launched a full-fledged structural adjustment program between 1980 and 1983) to laying the groundwork with an initial series of sectoral and technical assistance operations (see table 6.2.2). Five of the twelve countries whose first SAL came after 1983 had a prior sectoral loan, and eight had prior technical assistance (not shown). Only two had neither. But the preparation process did not always lead to a full-fledged structural adjustment program; nine countries with their first sectoral, non-project, or technical assistance loan during 1984–86 failed to go on to a SAL.

Table 6.2.3 illustrates trends in the type of adjustment support and the effect on industrial lending. Although year-to-year fluctuations make generalization difficult, the introduction of industrial SECALs and public enterprise loans after 1984 made adjustment support less concentrated in SALs and agricultural SECALs, which accounted for 66 percent of the total from 1982 to 1984. Within industry, there was a strong shift away from lines of credit (which declined in absolute terms) and traditional industrial investment projects toward policy-based industrial SECALs. Industrial SECALs and trade policy loans affected industry directly through increased import competition or export incentives. They accounted for over a third of the support for adjustment from 1985 to 1987, double the share in the previous period.

2. Half of the $3.5 billion went to Nigeria, Ghana, Madagascar, Côte d'Ivoire, Zaire, and Kenya (in descending order). Half of the SFA funds went to Zaire, Ghana, Madagascar, and Tanzania (in descending order). SFA funds accounted for 43, 32, and 9 percent of total adjustment and nonproject lending in fiscal years 1986, 1987, and 1988, respectively.

3. Botswana, Cameroon, Chad, Djibouti, Ethiopia, and Rwanda (3). One technical assistance loan was also provided to the Banque Ouest-Africaine de Développement.

Table 6.2.3 *Amount and Distribution of Adjustment, Nonproject,
and Industry Loans from the World Bank to Sub-Saharan Africa,
Fiscal 1982–84 and 1985–87*

Category	Millions of dollars		Percentage change	Percentage distribution	
	1982–84	1985–87		1982–84	1985–87
Macro					
Structural adjustment	667	1,015	52.3	41.4	37.2
Recovery, rehabilitation	120	196	63.5	7.4	7.2
Public management					
Public enterprise sector	0	111	—	0.0	4.1
Technical assistance	166	197	18.3	10.3	7.2
Trade policy	262	564	115.4	16.2	20.7
Sector adjustment					
Industry	0	384	—	0.0	14.1
Agriculture, education	397	259	−34.7	24.6	9.5
Total adjustment support	1,611	2,726	69.2	100.0	100.0
Industrial adjustment	0	398	—	0.0	57.2
Industrial investment					
Lines of credit	585	107	−81.7	85.3	16.0
Industrial projects	101	180	78.2	14.7	26.9
Total industrial					
adjustment and investment	686	671	−2.2	100.0	100.0

— Not applicable; base period is nil.

Policy Content of Adjustment Lending

The World Bank's first adjustment operations in Sub-Saharan Africa focused
on macroeconomic policy, often in conjunction with stabilization programs
assisted by the International Monetary Fund, and on price adjustments in
agriculture. Côte d'Ivoire, Kenya, Malawi, Mauritius, and Senegal had economies and industrial sectors that were better developed than those of many
smaller, lower-income countries that began adjustment after 1984. But as a
whole, African countries initiated adjustment from a position of lower
income, greater policy distortions, and more severe economic distress than
most countries in other regions of the world.

A sample of thirty-two Bank loans for structural and industrial adjustment,
economic recovery, trade policy, and public enterprise management was
studied (out of the forty-nine made for those purposes from 1982 to 1987) and
compared with forty-five (out of fifty-four) similar Bank loans in other
regions.[4] Loan conditions were classified by twenty-five types of policy measures in eight areas, by timing (actions taken prior to loan appraisal, require-

4. Agriculture, energy, and education SECALs are not included. The results show policy measures for these sectors because they were often included in SALs. The sample for Africa covers
two-thirds of the value of adjustment-related lending from 1982 to 1987, excluding nonindustrial
SECALs and technical assistance.

ments of effectiveness or tranche release, and other proposed measures), and by specificity (whether or not objectively verifiable targets were specified). The following analysis examines both the share of loans that included at least one policy measure in a given area and the distribution of all measures by policy area.[5]

More than half of the Bank's adjustment support loans in Africa contained policy measures relating to public finance, public enterprises, agriculture, tax policy, and the exchange rate (table 6.2.4). In non-African countries, however, these policy areas were covered in no more than 36 percent of the loans. The only areas in which non-African countries had coverage higher than 37 percent (and higher than African countries) were trade policy (especially import duties, export incentives, and liberalization of quantitative restrictions), financial intermediation, and miscellaneous macroeconomic policies. In virtually all other areas, loans to Africa had a higher coverage rate. African countries averaged twenty-seven conditions per adjustment loan, compared with twenty-three for other regions. These results suggest that the problems in Africa were more systemic and adjustment reforms more comprehensive; in other regions, correction of distortions in relatively few areas was sufficient to initiate the adjustment process.

Differences in policy emphasis can be observed in the distribution of adjustment measures by policy area (figure 6.2.1). Lending to Africa concentrated much more heavily on public expenditures, other macro policies, and agricultural reforms; adjustment measures in the rest of the world were strongly oriented toward trade policies and, to a lesser extent, to financial sector reform. Loans outside Africa were less likely to treat multiple policies. Only in the trade policy area was the proportion of loans outside Africa consistently as high as or higher than in both CFA and non-CFA African groups (figure 6.2.2 and table 6.2.4). In addition, loans to Africa had a higher proportion of measures in the form of specific, verifiable, legally binding requirements of the loan (darkest shading in figure 6.2.1).

The focus of adjustment differed significantly between countries in the CFA franc zone and other African countries. Because the CFA franc exchange rate is fixed to the French franc and interest rates and money supply are closely controlled, only 10 to 20 percent of adjustment support loans to CFA countries included these policy measures, in contrast to 41 to 77 percent in the non-CFA countries (table 6.2.4). Loans to CFA countries focused more on the areas of agricultural policy, public enterprise management, and taxation (80 to 90 percent compared with 55 to 60 percent in non-CFA countries). Conditionality in loans to CFA countries was heavily concentrated in these few areas, whereas conditionality in non-CFA countries was spread out more evenly, with reforms of exchange rate, financial, and trade policies playing a more significant role

5. The first criterion is biased toward policy areas that are relatively aggregative, while the latter gives undue weight to policies that are divided into more detailed conditions. Neither necessarily reflects the importance of the economic objectives they are supporting, although taken together they indicate the principal areas of emphasis of a loan.

Table 6.2.4 *Coverage of Policy Areas in World Bank Loans for Adjustment
Support by Country Grouping, Fiscal 1982–87*
(percentage of all loans in group)

Policy area and measure	CFA[a]	Non-CFA	Africa	Other	All countries
Exchange rate	10.0	77.3	56.3	35.6	44.2
Public finance	80.0	72.7	75.0	35.6	51.9
Other macro					
Tax	80.0	54.5	62.5	35.6	46.8
Labor	40.0	13.6	21.9	20.0	20.8
Debt management	70.0	45.5	53.1	22.2	35.1
Public enterprises	90.0	59.1	68.8	24.4	42.9
Other	20.0	31.8	28.1	37.8	33.8
Financial					
Interest rate	10.0	50.0	37.5	28.9	32.5
Money supply	20.0	40.9	34.4	20.0	26.0
Financial intermediation	50.0	13.6	25.0	37.8	32.5
Other	0.0	0.0	0.0	17.8	10.4
Trade					
Quantitative restrictions	50.0	45.5	46.9	53.3	50.6
Import duties or subsidies	40.0	40.9	40.6	57.8	50.6
Export duties or subsidies	50.0	22.7	31.3	20.0	24.7
Financing	30.0	36.4	34.4	31.1	32.5
Export incentives	10.0	27.3	21.9	44.4	35.1
Export institutions	20.0	36.4	31.3	33.3	32.5
Other	30.0	22.7	25.0	28.9	27.3
Firm restructuring	50.0	18.2	28.1	26.7	27.3
Industrial policy					
Price regulations	40.0	50.0	46.9	20.0	31.2
Entry or exit regulation	30.0	4.5	12.5	11.1	11.7
Other regulation	20.0	13.6	15.6	8.9	11.7
Investment incentives	50.0	31.8	37.5	20.0	27.3
Technology	10.0	0.0	3.1	11.1	7.8
Other	20.0	9.1	12.5	8.9	10.4
Other sectors					
Agriculture	90.0	59.1	68.8	31.1	46.8
Other	30.0	9.1	15.6	0.0	6.5
Total	100.0	100.0	100.0	100.0	100.0
Number of loans	10	22	32	45	77

a. Communauté financière africaine.

(figure 6.2.3). These differences held in both 1982–84 and 1985–87 even though conditionality for CFA countries became somewhat less concentrated over time.

In CFA and non-CFA countries, emphasis on agricultural policy reforms decreased (figure 6.2.3). In the non-CFA countries, trade policy received a corresponding increase in relative emphasis, whereas in the CFA countries, the shift was spread fairly evenly over all nonagricultural categories.

Figure 6.2.1 *Distribution of Adjustment Measures by Policy Area in African and Non-African Countries, 1982–87*

a   African Countries

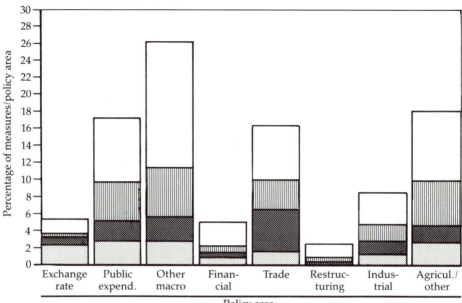

b   Non-African Countries

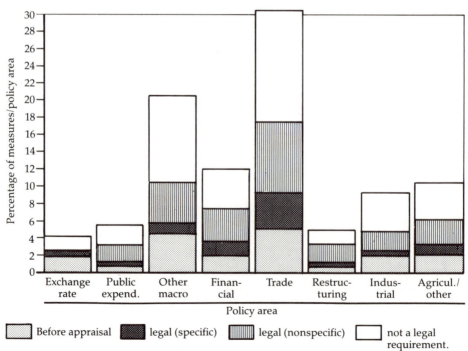

Figure 6.2.2 *Share of World Bank Loans Covering Policy Area in* CFA, *Non-*CFA, *and Non-African Countries, Fiscal Years 1982–87*

(percentage of all loans in grouping)

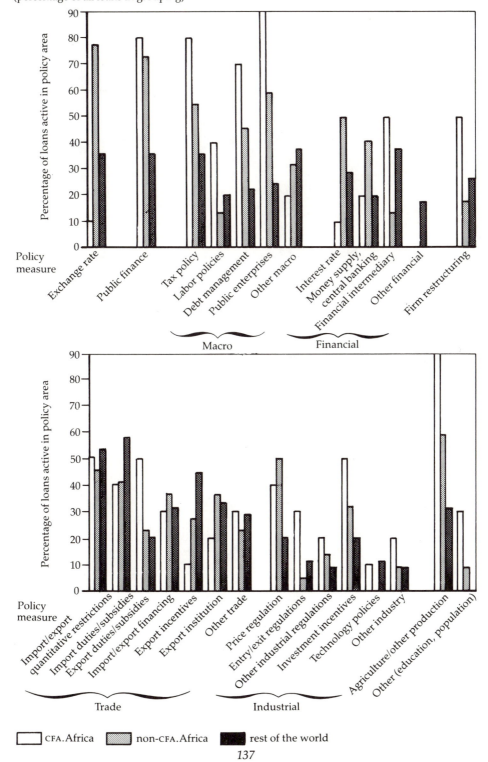

CFA.Africa   non-CFA.Africa   rest of the world

137

Figure 6.2.3 *Distribution of Adjustment Measures by Policy Area in* CFA *and Non-*CFA *Countries, Fiscal Years 1982–84 and 1985–87*

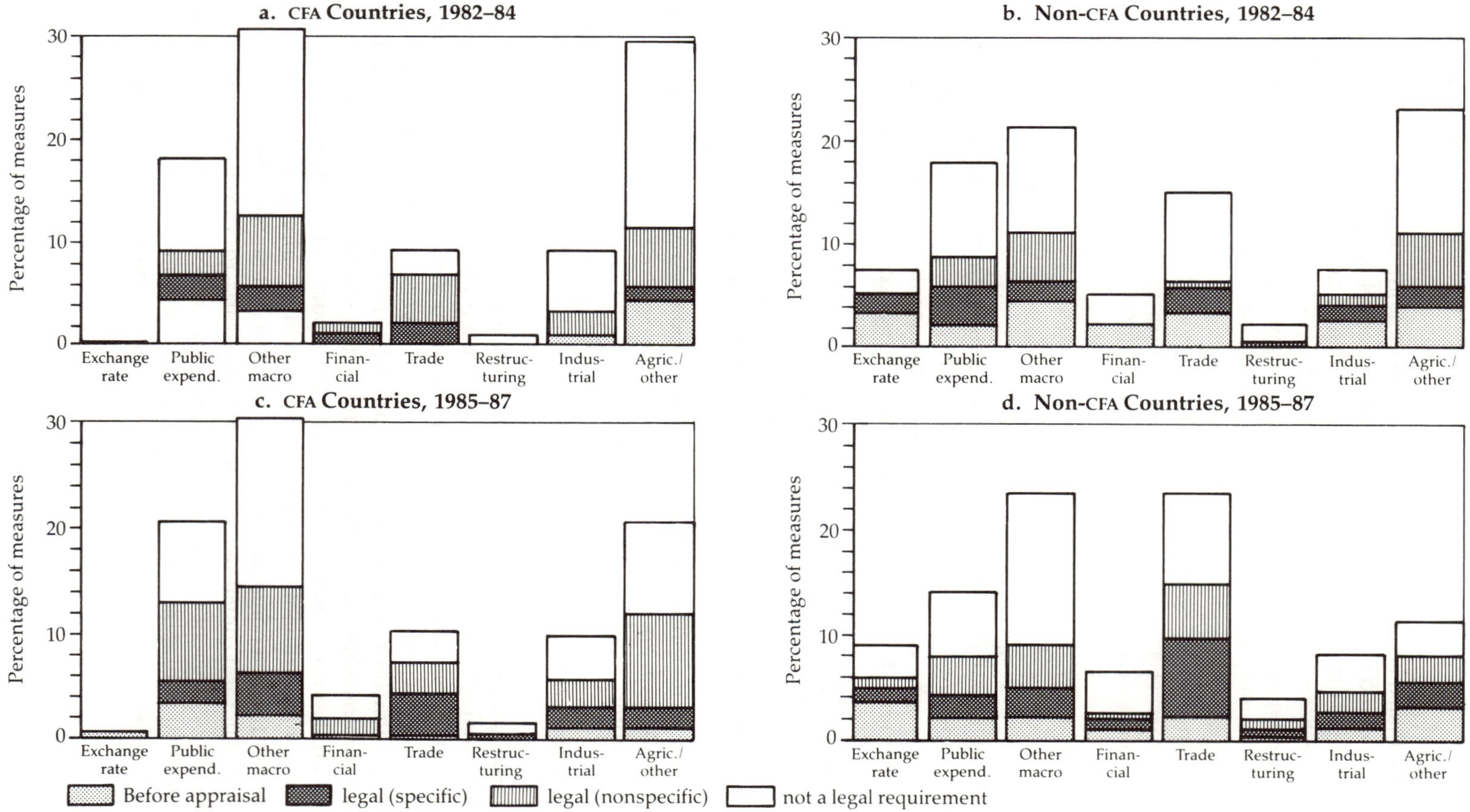

a. CFA Countries, 1982–84

b. Non-CFA Countries, 1982–84

c. CFA Countries, 1985–87

d. Non-CFA Countries, 1985–87

Before appraisal legal (specific) legal (nonspecific) not a legal requirement

6.3 *Impact of Adjustment Policies on Manufacturing in Nigeria*
World Bank Staff

Faced with a continuing weak market for oil, the Babangida government, which came to power in Nigeria in August 1985, declared its intention to move from "austerity alone to austerity with structural adjustment." Its Structural Adjustment Program for 1986–88 combined exchange rate and trade policy reforms with overall macroeconomic restraint. It attempted to shrink the size of the public sector and to improve its efficiency.

In September 1986, the government introduced a market-determined, second-tier foreign exchange market (SFEM) for trade transactions. The result was a 66 percent depreciation relative to the official first-tier naira rate of US$0.64, which was retained for debt service payments and other international obligations. Under the SFEM, authorized dealers (essentially the commercial and merchant banks) could bid for foreign exchange auctioned weekly (subsequently, biweekly) by the central bank and buy and sell foreign exchange on an interbank market. The interbank market enabled dealers to acquire about one-fourth of their foreign exchange from non-oil-export earnings, remittances, invisibles, and capital transfers. The banks were eventually allowed to charge different rates for funds obtained on the interbank and auction markets, as long as the margin between buying and selling rates was within 1 percent. The naira regained some of its value on the auction during 1986 but depreciated again in 1987 as the amounts auctioned were decreased. The naira averaged US$0.24 for the second half of 1987, about 10 percent below the last quarter of 1986. The first and second tiers were merged in July 1987.

In conjunction with the opening of the second-tier foreign exchange market, the Nigerian government abolished the 30 percent import surcharge (introduced as an interim measure in January 1986) and the import licensing system. In addition, it reduced the import prohibition list from seventy-four to sixteen items.[6] Under the previous system, quantitative import controls had insulated relative prices in Nigeria from world prices and, together with the overvalued exchange rate, overshadowed tariffs, excise taxes, and export duties in shaping the incentive environment. Recognizing that abolition of import controls would make customs duties and excise taxes the key determinants of the incentive structure, the government implemented an interim revision of customs and excise tariffs in October 1986. This reduced the average trade-weighted tariff rate from 35 to 25 percent, with most rates falling between 10 and 30 percent. Nevertheless, a number of previously banned products retained much higher rates, and several industries (cotton, cotton yarn, synthetic yarn, paper packaging, light bulbs, motor vehicles, and margarine) won subsequent increases to protect them during the transition

---

Excerpted and edited from "Nigeria: Country Economic Memorandum," World Bank, Africa Region, 1988; and Gianni Zanini, "SFEM Impact on 32 Industrial Companies in Nigeria," World Bank, Western Africa Projects Department, June 1987 (restricted circulation).
    6. Nevertheless, the remaining bans protected about 40 percent of manufacturing value added, including vegetable oils, wood and furniture, plastic wares, textile fabrics, cigarettes, and beer.

period, at least until a more comprehensive tariff review could be completed.

Non-oil exporters were given unrestricted access to the SFEM for their export earnings and import requirements (in effect, 100 percent retention rights). Remaining export prohibitions were abolished, and export licensing requirements were significantly reduced. Schemes were devised for duty drawbacks and rediscounting short-term bills, although implementation proved difficult.

For stabilization purposes, monetary policy was tightened during the period of the Structural Adjustment Program (1986–88) to minimize excessive demand for foreign exchange, which could cause inflationary pressures through the SFEM. Interest rates were liberalized in 1987 to orient the financial system more toward market rates and enable it to mobilize and allocate financial savings more efficiently. Ceilings on expansion of commercial banks' loans and advances helped limit domestic credit expansion to 9 percent in 1986, but with a shift away from public sector credit (which contracted by 6 percent) toward private sector credit (which increased by 29 percent). The large fiscal deficits in the federal budget that resulted from the weakening of the oil market in the early 1980s were brought within 3 percent of the gross domestic product through across-the-board cuts in capital and recurrent expenditures.

Effect on Prices

Prior to the Structural Adjustment Program, Nigeria had an elaborate system of ex-factory price controls that required prior approval by the Prices, Productivity, and Incomes Board. In general, these controls did not work very well, and even when they worked at the ex-factory level, retail prices usually reflected market values, with the scarcity rents accruing to traders. This system was abolished with the introduction of the second-tier foreign exchange market.

Concerns that the SFEM would accelerate inflation proved unfounded. Indeed, introduction of the market ended short-term inflationary pressures from speculative stockpiling, and prices actually fell from September to December 1986 as speculators attempted to liquidate stocks. Exchange rate adjustment scarcely affected prices of most imports and import-dependent goods because consumers were already paying prices that reflected an exchange rate of about US$0.33 to the naira. The consumer price index averaged only 5 percent higher in 1986 than in 1985, aided considerably by favorable growth of agricultural output.

Removal of price controls also had no sustained overall effect on inflation at the retail level, and some prices that had initially been raised fell as supplies increased and demand weakened. Ex-factory prices were generally 25 to 100 percent higher in early 1987 than in early 1986, but retail prices of the same products had increased by less than 30 percent, implying a substantial decrease in scarcity rents to traders. Producers also absorbed some of the cost increases resulting from depreciation of the naira. Gross margins fell from as high as 50 percent of the sales price to 5 to 15 percent.

Effect on Manufacturing

About thirty manufacturing firms were surveyed in February and May 1987 and subsequently in March 1988. Average capacity utilization rose from 56.8 percent in May 1987 to 58.9 percent in March 1988. Employment, however, declined by 6.8 percent as firms adjusted and rationalized their production processes. Most of the reduction in employment took place in the larger firms.

Exchange rate depreciation made tariffs the operative instrument of protection and favored branches of industry with high domestic value added over assembly-type activities. The new tariff regime also reduced effective protection more drastically for low-value-added activities. Agroprocessing industries, textiles, wood furniture, tanneries, and food products performed relatively well in the post-SFEM environment, mainly because their import content was less than 50 percent of factory cost. Cement and cosmetics also did well despite their greater exposure to international competition. On the other hand, production fell in a number of assembly-type operations, largely in response to lower consumer demand. Temporary closures occurred in motor vehicle assembly, bicycles, detergents, and milk powder packaging, although most plants subsequently reopened at low rates of capacity utilization.

The more favorable exchange rate increased interest in exporting as confidence in the SFEM grew and internal demand weakened. Greater access to imported raw materials and spare parts facilitated growth of existing exports of cosmetic products and palm kernel cake to Europe. New exports—both official and unofficial—to neighboring countries were achieved in textiles, tires, industrial adhesives, tiles, carpets, perfumes, beer, and fiberglass boat shells.

Although most firms reported profits, only half would have been profitable if assets had been replaced at the new exchange rate. Firms were only gradually revaluing assets or taking replacement costs into account. Financing for new investment was not seen as a difficulty, but a number of firms experienced short-term liquidity problems. These problems were most pronounced for small firms with little access to credit facilities and for firms with a high import content.

Rehabilitation expenditures concentrated mainly on spare parts and maintenance to improve capacity utilization and efficiency. Previously, import license allocations had been used almost exclusively for raw materials. Most firms initially were reluctant to undertake major investments while tariffs were under review. More recently, they have firmed up investment plans, with emphasis on backward integration (for example, agroindustries, textiles, and vehicle assembly operations); diversification (for example, new consumer goods for lower levels of income and the development of new plastic packaging materials); and expansion (for example, tire and cement production).

The incentive to shift to domestic rather than imported inputs was muted by continuing protection for many products under the interim tariff structure and bans. Palm kernel oil, for example, remained twice as expensive in Nigeria as on the world market because imported vegetable oils were banned; a major soap producer was forced to use imported animal fats to remain com-petitive. Inadequate supplies and poor quality also hampered use of domesti-cally manufactured intermediate goods. Nevertheless, industries that could use domestic raw materials, such as beer, textiles, leather products, cement, and tires, shifted away from imported inputs. The firms surveyed reported a 31 percent increase in domestic input purchases in 1986 but only 7 percent in imported raw materials.

Firms generally became more cost conscious and more aggressive in mar-keting. Realizing that profits would depend on increasing sales volume at a lower margin, they took measures to reduce gross margins. Some firms put more emphasis on equipment maintenance; others tried to reduce packaging costs. Marketing efforts took the form of selling on credit and shifting to new product lines as demand for old products fell.

Conclusion

Even within the first year after foreign exchange, imports, and prices were liberalized, adjustments in industrial structure and behavior became evident. Production and capacity utilization (but not employment) rose in domestic resource-based and export industries, while those with low value added were squeezed between increased import costs and depressed domestic demand. This shift was passed through to increased use of domestic raw materials but not to manufactured intermediate goods, which remained highly protected. The binding constraints shifted from input supply to demand for production and from quantitative restrictions to tariffs for import prices.

6.4 Export-Led Growth in Mauritius
World Bank Staff

Mauritius began promoting industrial development in 1964 with an incentive scheme to encourage import substitution activities through tax holidays, pri-ority access to credit, duty-free entry of capital goods, and protection in the form of import tariffs and quotas. This approach had little immediate impact on industrial growth; only a few enterprises were set up to service the sugar industry or to provide simple goods for domestic consumption. At the time of independence in 1968, the Mauritian economy was characterized by low growth, conservative management, and high unemployment. GDP increased at an average rate of 1.1 percent per year, while the investment level remained virtually constant at about 16 percent of GDP.

In 1970 the government began trying to attract local and foreign private investors into export activities through the Export Processing Zones (EPZ) Act, which provided free repatriation of capital and dividends, duty-free entry of inputs, and greater flexibility for exporters in dismissing workers. Land and factory space were developed through the Development Bank of Mauritius. These export promotion policies attracted foreign investors and encouraged

Excerpted, edited, and updated from "Mauritius: From Austerity to Growth," World Bank, Eastern and Southern Africa Country Programs Department, March 1985 (restricted circulation).

many local entrepreneurs to invest sugar profits in manufacturing. Manufacturing value added grew at 17 percent per year from 1970 to 1977, and manufactured exports rose from practically nil to nearly 24 percent of total exports. Exceptional sugar prices and crops in 1973–74 also stimulated demand for import substitution industries. In the decade following independence, GNP per capita rose above $1,000, equivalent to the level of a middle-income developing country, and the adult literacy rate reached 80 percent.

Serious economic difficulties emerged in the late 1970s, however. A sharp turnaround in Mauritius's international terms of trade following the decline of sugar prices in 1976 and the second price increase in petroleum led to rapid deterioration in the balance of payments. Growing current account deficits of the balance of payments were financed largely by external borrowing on nonconcessionary terms. This resulted in a rapid increase in Mauritius's debt service obligations. From 1976 to 1979, the country's external debt more than tripled, and the debt service ratio rose from 1 percent in 1976 to nearly 10 percent in 1979. This period was also marked by a deceleration of GDP and export growth. The domestic inflation rate rose drastically, and the unemployment rate surpassed 25 percent.

Beginning in 1979, the government embarked on a series of stabilization and structural adjustment programs. Central to these programs were reductions in consumer subsidies, wage restraints, restrictive credit and monetary policies, reductions in the overall fiscal deficit, agricultural diversification, and the maintenance of a liberal system of trade and payments. The latter policy shifted incentives strongly toward production for export.

In 1979 the Mauritian rupee was devalued by 30 percent and in 1981 by 20 percent. In 1983 the government changed the peg of the Mauritian rupee from the SDR to a trade-weighted basket of currencies more representative of Mauritius's external trade pattern. Since then, Mauritius has pursued a flexible exchange rate policy that, together with a tight wage policy, has been highly effective in maintaining its export competitiveness. The real exchange rate has depreciated by 2.5 percent each year since 1981.

Additional policy measures were taken in the early 1980s to stimulate industrial exports. They included an export credit guarantee scheme, agreements to avoid double taxation, and intensified export promotion activities abroad. Exports from non-EPZ firms were encouraged by making them eligible for duty drawback on the import content of any exports and by reducing the corporate tax rate by 2 percentage points for each 10 percent of output exported.

Import liberalization shifted incentives away from production for the domestic market. The government stopped issuing new quantitative restrictions (QRs) in 1983 and abolished existing QRs in two stages in 1984 and 1985. Tariffs on newly liberalized commodities were raised in some cases, but not enough to provide equivalent protection. Imports of these commodities did not expand greatly in 1985.

The economy showed signs of a modest recovery, growing at 4.6 percent in 1984, 6.5 percent in 1985, and around 6.0 percent in 1986. The strongest area of recovery was the manufacturing sector, led by growth of real output in EPZ firms at 31.5 percent per year from 1983 to 1986. The EPZ's share in GDP increased from 5 to 9 percent during this period, accounting for the rise in the share of manufacturing from 16 to 20 percent. The number of EPZ firms rose from 146 to 408 and employment from 25,500 to 74,000.

The upsurge in investment, output, and employment in the export processing zone was attributable to a number of factors: expansion of economic activity abroad, a promotional campaign by the government, investment incentives for the private sector, tax reform, and the emergence of the "Hong Kong syndrome." The majority of applications to start new export enterprises, mainly in knitwear and textile industries, came from Hong Kong, spurred by political uncertainties and courted by government promotional efforts. Several incentives attracted new investors, such as the provision of tax holidays, import duty exemptions, and infrastructural facilities. Administrative procedures were centralized and simplified.

About 80 percent of Mauritius's manufactured goods exports go to EEC countries. The United Kingdom and France together take 50 percent of all exports. Some 70 percent of the manufactured goods exported to the EEC market are textiles. Because of the narrow range of its export products and markets, Mauritius is particularly vulnerable to changes in international economic conditions. Between 1979 and 1981, exports of manufactured goods increased in real terms by almost 17 percent per year. They slackened, however, in 1982 and 1983 because of recession in major export markets and protectionist measures (for example, imposition of quota restrictions by the United States on knitwear). Then they picked up, rising from 32 percent of total exports in 1983 to nearly 50 percent in 1985 (see table 6.4.1).

Export Promotion

Mauritius's primary objectives in industry are to maintain competitiveness in export-oriented manufacturing and to move toward an industrial incentive system that encourages all manufacturing industries to export.

Under the EPZ scheme, enterprises setting up factories to sell their entire output outside Mauritius are eligible for export enterprise certificates, by which they are granted a company tax holiday on retained earnings for ten years with a possible extension to twenty years, tax-free dividends in the first

Table 6.4.1 *Exports of Goods from Mauritius, 1979–84*

Goods	Average annual growth rate in constant prices (percent)				Percentage share, 1985
	1979–81	1982	1983	1984	
Sugar	−16.0	37.7	2.0	−9.0	40.9
Molasses	−3.0	8.9	−21.6	−2.0	1.0
Tea	2.5	7.3	11.3	8.0	2.5
Manufactured goods	3.8	−4.1	1.6	15.6	46.7
Clothing	(16.7)	(−7.4)	(−1.0)	(20.0)	(36.1)
Other	5.0	−2.6	−3.6	5.0	1.8
Total	−8.3	19.5	1.2	−1.0	100.0

Source: Mauritius Central Statistical Office.

five years, and exemption of duty for imports of machinery and equipment. Finally, in August 1981 the complementary Export Service Zones Act extended similar tax incentives to firms providing services. Other benefits offered include free repatriation of profits, liberal work permits for specialist expatriate staff, and export financing at preferential rates. Priority was initially given to labor-intensive industries and to those that introduced new technology and marketing skills. Local participation in equity was encouraged. As of mid-1986, the EPZ companies in operation employed some 68,000 people.

Beginning in 1981, the government also broadened fiscal incentives for export promotion and trading, improved export financing facilities, simplified and centralized export procedures, and strengthened institutions that promote exports and international trade. A double taxation arrangement was reached with Germany, France, and the United Kingdom to extend the benefits of the Mauritius tax-holiday provisions to German, French, and British investors on taxes they pay in their home countries. A tax rebate (duty drawback) system was introduced to encourage the growth of manufactured exports by nonexport enterprises. An export credit guarantee scheme was established to provide collateral support to commercial banks to stimulate liberal and flexible export credit.

In general, export-oriented firms specialize in textiles and garment production, are larger, and have grown faster. On the import side, production is more diversified and accounts for most of the output in food and beverages, chemicals, metals, and nonmetallic mineral products. Export processing industries provide more than 80 percent of all jobs in the manufacturing sector and about 50 percent of total export earnings. Although value added in the import-competing sector continues to grow, its share is diminishing. From 1976 to 1983, the export processing industries grew at about 14 percent per year compared with 5 percent per year for import-competing firms. The share of the export processing industries in manufacturing value added increased from 31 to 41 percent during the same period and to 55 percent by 1985.

Mauritius has been highly successful in promoting export processing industries and in maintaining the country's export competitiveness through appropriate exchange rate and wage policies and a vigorous promotional campaign. Macroeconomic policies have generally been adjusted to support the country's strategy. Inflation has been kept moderate, with a leveling off or decline in prices of some imported commodities and products. Annual wage adjustments in the industrial sector have been held considerably below the rise in the cost of living. Despite comprehensive labor legislation designed to protect workers, wage rates in the export manufacturing sector are at present lower than those of most of Mauritius's competitors. The government has been following a relatively liberal interest rate policy, and the exchange rate has been kept flexible.

Other Policy Reforms

TAXES. The corporate income tax rate was reduced from 65 to 35 percent in 1984. In 1985, the various concessional rates applying to EPZ and development certificate firms were consolidated to a single rate of 15 percent with dividends exempted from income tax for the first ten years of operation. These moderate taxation rates proved attractive to foreign investors.

TARIFFS. The tariff system in Mauritius is highly complex and is subject to frequent changes. It comprises five elements: fiscal, customs, and stamp duties; surcharges; and exemptions from payment of duty. Frequent changes in the tariff schedule have been prompted by balance of payments considerations, fiscal need, and the desire to protect local industry. Rationalization of the tariff structure would involve consolidating the fiscal, customs, and stamp duties and the surcharges into a unified ad valorem tariff and implementing a more uniform tariff structure to lower the existing effective protection and narrow the spread of effective rates. Average effective rates of protection for import-competing industries vary between −24 percent for food processing to 824 percent for electrical machinery. As the first step toward rationalization, the government lowered the maximum tariff rate to 110 percent (plus stamp duty of 17 percent) in 1987, except for petroleum, tobacco products, and alcoholic beverages.

PRICE CONTROLS. Regulation determines both maximum prices and maximum mark-ups. Price controls were imposed to maintain low prices for essential food and household items that are important to low-income groups and to curtail possible monopoly abuse by importers or local producers favored by the existing system of industrial protection. With the removal of QRS, the government has reduced the number of goods subject to price regulation. In 1984 controls were removed from about fifty commodities and subsequently on all but eight items. The number of commodities under maximum mark-up control was initially expanded to some forty items, but subsequently reduced to eighteen.

DEVELOPMENT CERTIFICATES. The Development Certificates (DC) scheme, introduced in 1964, provided selected import-substituting enterprises with significant tax and duty exemptions. More than 200 companies in food and beverages, textiles and garments, chemical products, iron and steel, and tourism have benefited from the scheme. In addition to duty-free import of capital goods, DC firms often obtained exemption from payment of duty on imported material inputs. These two privileges were disallowed in October 1983, which reduced the bias toward the domestic market. No new DCs have been issued since 1984.

6.5 A Phased Approach to Adjustment in Côte d'Ivoire
World Bank Staff

The development of Côte d'Ivoire in the 1960s to mid-1970s was characterized by rapid expansion of agriculture and import-substituting industries and by profound structural changes within a relatively stable external environment.

Excerpted, edited, and updated from "The Côte d'Ivoire in Transition," World Bank, Western Africa Region, March 1987 (restricted circulation).

The government encouraged the productive use of domestic and foreign factors in key areas of comparative advantage and reallocated the resulting surpluses to diversify the economy. With vigorous growth of export crops (especially coffee and cocoa) and an influx of foreign workers, GDP between 1975 and 1985 grew at 7.9 percent per year, nearly double the rate of population increase. Public investment grew almost twice as fast as did private investment, rising from 6.9 to 8.3 percent of GDP during this period. The overall share of investment in GDP remained at about 20 percent. Manufactured goods grew from 20 percent of exports to 25 percent.

Côte d'Ivoire's initial phase of industrialization was based on import substitution for the domestic market and other countries in the West African Economic Community (CEAO).[7] By the end of the 1960s, 30,000 workers were employed in the industrial sector, which generated about 15 percent of the country's GDP. This growth was fostered by a generous investment code and a tariff schedule that provided moderate and fairly uniform protection across subsectors without recourse to quantitative restrictions.

The two five-year development plans, covering the period 1970 to 1980, emphasized greater processing of domestic natural resources and export orientation as industrial development objectives. During the first half of the 1970s, however, constraints on the sustainability of the "Ivorian miracle" became apparent. Weak incentives for export crops and depletion of forestry reserves threatened to slow export growth. Import substitution had reached the limits of the market within the country and the protected CEAO. The 1976–80 five-year plan responded with an outward-oriented strategy to accelerate growth in areas of comparative advantage while strengthening neglected areas of human resource development. The textiles and agroprocessing (especially cocoa) subsectors were the main beneficiaries of these policies, with further diversification into new resource-based activities such as wood processing, tuna canning, and oil palm refining.

Overexpansion despite External Shocks

External shocks in the late 1970s undermined the country's economic and financial situation and necessitated changes in policy. Export prices boomed to extraordinary levels between 1975 and 1977. The government then used increased revenues from the Stabilization Fund for export crops to sharply raise public investment, much of it in large projects with high unit costs and low economic returns (for example, sugar complexes, transport, higher education, and administration). The government also raised public expenditures on social services. But a 30 percent decline in coffee and cocoa prices between 1977 and 1980, together with steep increases in import prices following the 1979 oil crisis, drastically worsened the terms of trade and depleted the Stabilization Fund.

The government responded by increasing foreign borrowing, thereby abandoning the prudent debt management policy pursued since independence. It also adopted macroeconomic and sectoral policies that weakened the growth

7. Communauté Economique de l'Afrique de l'Ouest.

potential of the productive sectors. Demands for higher protection to offset increasing domestic costs and to promote further import substitution were granted through a reform of the customs code in 1973. The acceleration of domestic inflation starting in 1975 further eroded the competitiveness of Ivorian firms. The purchasing power parity index was 27 percent overvalued in 1978 compared with the 1970–75 average.[8] Import restrictions, introduced to shield industry from increased import competition, biased incentives against agriculture and against export activities within both industry and agriculture.

Export growth slowed down, while imports rose dramatically to an average of 13 percent per year between 1975 and 1980. Manufactured exports declined by 10 percent in 1980. The trade surplus between 1965 and 1975 turned into a deficit exceeding 5 percent of GDP by 1980. Public savings fell sharply, while the public sector deficit rose from 2 percent of GDP in 1975 to 12 percent in 1980. Medium- to long-term debt increased from 24 percent of GDP to 47 percent over the same interval. By 1980, official foreign reserves were exhausted, and severe contraction of economic activity was imminent to correct for overexpansion of the public sector.

Stabilization Phase

In 1981, the government launched a far-reaching economic adjustment program aimed at stabilizing the economy while gradually laying the foundation for a resumption of sustainable growth. The program was supported by three World Bank structural adjustment loans in 1981, 1983, and 1986, and by agreements with the International Monetary Fund in 1981, 1984, and 1986. Monetary policy and credit were tightened through ceilings and subceilings. The government raised taxes and reduced public expenditures by freezing salaries and cutting back contract workers. Public enterprise reforms were introduced to attack three areas of weakness: unclear definition of purpose, ineffective supervision, and mediocre financial and economic performance. Measures to correct distorted economic incentives included higher producer prices for major crops and closer alignment of consumer prices with world prices for bread, rice, and palm oil.

Cutbacks in public spending, reduced losses in public enterprises, and a sharp recovery in Stabilization Fund revenues produced a budget surplus by 1985. Inflation fell steadily to 3 percent that year. The foreign exchange situation, however, remained constrained by the high debt-service ratio (over 30 percent of export from 1985 through 1988, following some relief in 1984 and 1985 because of rescheduling).

Furthermore, the policies that improved the macroeconomic situation adversely affected the productive sectors. Public investment contracted drastically from 14 percent of GDP in 1980 to 6 percent in 1985, and private investment in manufacturing sharply declined from an estimated CFAF 154 billion in 1980 to about CFAF 95 billion by 1984. The economy went into recession between 1981 and 1984; drought aggravated agricultural decline in 1983 and 1984. Yet the industrial sector responded to the unfavorable environment by

---

8. See technical note E for a discussion of purchasing power parity.

promoting exports and pursuing investments in agroindustries, textiles, wood processing, building materials, and petroleum processing.

Adjustment Phase

After 1981, Côte d'Ivoire experienced fundamental structural changes in the saving and investment behavior of key economic agents. Both the public sector and corporations increased their savings while reducing their investments. Households boosted their savings from less than 1 percent of their disposable income in 1981 to above 6 percent in 1985 while keeping their housing investment constant. These favorable financial developments led to reduced use of foreign savings, although at some cost in terms of expansion of productive capacity.

Stabilization measures were strictly pursued, despite slippages in 1982 and 1983 caused by external factors. In 1985, the economy as a whole began to recover. GDP and consumption rose by 5 percent, even though public expenditures continued to decline. Private investment grew by 6 percent—not enough to fully offset further reductions in public investment. Export growth of 10 percent per year in 1984–85 enabled imports to grow in 1985 for the first time in the 1980s. Higher producer prices and lower inflation restored rural-urban terms of trade to their 1980 level by 1985, and agriculture grew by 9 percent that year. Although industrial value added increased slightly in 1985, the dollar value of manufactured exports was 10 percent below the 1980 level, as was the terms of trade between tradables and nontradables.

Having brought variables under control by 1985, the government moved into an adjustment phase aimed at resuming growth through the following strategies: increased savings, investment, and exploitation of comparative advantage to raise exports and GDP growth; shift in incentives toward tradables to accelerate the reallocation of resources away from nontradables and toward exports; shift in the internal terms of trade to stimulate rural incomes and productivity; reduced debt-service ratio to restore international creditworthiness; and equilibrium in the public sector budget and the balance of payments to maintain macroeconomic stability.

Côte d'Ivoire's membership in the West African Monetary Union (UMOA)[9] limited the ways in which it could shift incentives. Membership promotes macroeconomic stability by providing full convertibility with the French franc and monetary and fiscal restraint, but it prevents exchange rate, monetary, and fiscal policies from being used as instruments to adjust relative prices. Since fixed parity with the French franc ruled out using devaluation to stimulate exports and liberalize imports, the government in 1985 used subsidies and duties to provide effective protection of 40 percent to both industrial exports and import substitutes.[10] Quota restrictions were replaced by nominal tariff surcharges that were reduced steadily over a five-year period. Since agriculture remained largely unprotected, industries using domestic agricul-

9. Union Monétaire de l'Afrique de l'Ouest.
10. See technical note C for a discussion of effective protection.

tural input were given nominal tariffs below 40 percent to yield effective protection of 40 percent. Manufacturing export value added was given a corresponding subsidy of 40 percent.

The structural adjustment program strengthened macroeconomic management, liberalized the trade regime, and increased the efficiency of domestic and foreign resources used by the public sector. Late in 1987, Côte d'Ivoire generalized the tariff-cum-subsidy scheme and extended it to nontraditional export crops.

The stabilization effort was helped by a significant improvement in the real effective exchange rate over the 1980–85 period and by the conclusion of multiyear reschedulings with external bilateral and commercial creditors in 1986. With GDP rising by 3.4 percent in 1986, the country appeared to have entered a growth phase compatible with public finance and balance of payments equilibria. But underlying weaknesses remained: high debt-service obligations; heavy dependence on world commodity prices; and the absence of flexible policy instruments to adapt the real price of traded goods to the evolving competitive position of Côte d'Ivoire. Those weaknesses led to a substantial setback in 1987 when export prices for cocoa and coffee plummeted, and the U.S. dollar depreciated sharply. As a result, GDP growth declined by about 2.5 percent in real terms in 1987, reversing the recovery in industrial output that had begun in 1985.

Effect of Subsidy-cum-Tariff

After the 1981–84 recession, industrial output recovered in 1985 and 1986, but its heavy dependence on the domestic market led to a decline in the volume of industrial output by about 5 percent in 1985. Import liberalization, although gradual, may have accelerated the decline in some industries, notably textiles and shoes. But several trends indicated that recovery and adjustment had begun. Manufactured exports grew strongly (15 percent in value in 1987), reaching 2.4 times the value of inputs imported by the sector. Imported raw materials became less important, partly because the 1984 investment code eliminated duty exemptions. Investment growth reached 10 percent in volume in 1987, and the number of recorded firms increased, preventing employment from falling despite overall stagnation in production. The financial health of firms improved significantly; profitability increased, and short-term debt declined, while medium- to long-term debt grew in line with the growth in investment. The rise in applications for priority agreements under the investment code reflected expectations that these trends would continue.

Subsectoral trends revealed a shift in structure away from assembly and certain import-substituting consumer goods toward export activities (table 6.5.1). Even within an industry such as wood products, production shifted from the domestic market (furniture) toward exports (plywood). Export growth was attributable to the increased profitability provided by the export subsidy, as depreciation of the dollar actually made exports less competitive in terms of the exchange rate fixed vis-à-vis the French franc. While these trends reflected the shift in incentives, the performance of some sectors was linked directly to other sectors: agricultural demand for fertilizer remained

Table 6.5.1 *Production Trends of Selected Manufacturers in Côte d'Ivoire,*
1985–87

Selected manufactures	Production trend		
	Declining	Stable	Growing
Food and beverages	Bakery products	*Coffee products Confectionery, sugar Yogurt Cooking oil Flour Beer, soft drinks	*Cocoa products
Other agro-based industries	Tobacco products Furniture	Soap, glycerine[a]	Animal feed *Plywood
Textiles, shoes, and leather	Shoes Leather goods Garments and fabrics		*Jeans Sacherie (made-up textile goods)
Chemicals, rubber, paper, plastics	Fertilizer	Paint, glue, ink[a] Industrial gases Matches Mattresses Cardboard Plastic products (except shoes)	
Construction materials	Cement[a]	Sawn wood	Metal products
Metal products, appliances	Vehicle assembly Refrigerator, air conditioner assembly	Aluminum products Metal containers for food products	

Note: Asterisks denote exports. Other products are for the domestic market.
a. Positive growth in 1987.

weak, whereas increased construction helped revive the manufacture of certain building materials.

Self-Sustained Growth Phase

Having carried out major reforms to stimulate productivity in the industrial sector, Côte d'Ivoire must address the remaining constraints on continued recovery in industrial economic activity. It should strengthen the linkages between agricultural and industrial incentive reforms to expand processing of domestic products along the lines of comparative advantage. Infrastructural investment is needed to reduce the production costs of water, electricity, and petroleum products.

Sustained growth of industrial exports and production will require investment in new capacity. Most investment during the stabilization phase was to rehabilitate and restructure existing plants. Despite the profits generated by the export subsidy, and a favorable industrial incentives system, exporters have been reluctant to invest in new capacity for fear that this policy could be abandoned if it becomes difficult to finance. Limited competitiveness of Ivorian industry without the subsidy, under the prevailing cost structure and the given exchange rate, may limit long-term export expansion despite short-term success. A related issue is whether the government will be able to sustain gradual reduction of temporary surcharges and rebates if the affected industries prove unable to adjust and survive. To thwart customs fraud through underinvoicing, it has reintroduced reference prices and extended the scope of import licencing and controls, including bans on certain used vehicles that compete with domestic vehicle assembly.

The tariff-cum-subsidy scheme provides neutral incentives between exports and import substitutes within industry, and it favors agricultural exports other than coffee and cocoa. It does not eliminate the overall bias against agriculture and other tradables, however. Higher producer prices would encourage agricultural growth, but would also worsen the deficits incurred by the Stabilization Fund. Savings from other sources would have to be increased to maintain fiscal balance. Therefore, the price incentives for renewed long-term growth of the productive sectors may involve tradeoffs with the objectives of fiscal, monetary, and exchange rate stability. Building on the relative success of its program to date, the government is likely to continue approaching these adjustment problems through gradual, phased modifications of policies rather than through drastic changes.

6.6. Recent Policy Reform and Industrial Adjustment in Zambia and Ghana
William F. Steel

This article compares recent efforts of Zambia and Ghana to move toward less interventionist policies. Both countries attempted to reverse their deteriorating economic performance by introducing major reform programs during the mid-1980s. Their different experiences illustrate the positive effects of liberalization when resource allocation has been constrained by extensive controls, as well as the difficulties of sustaining and financing reform.

Industry figures prominently both in the thinking that led to reform measures and in the recovery process because of its visibility and its sensitivity to policy incentives. Industry by itself neither caused economic deterioration in these countries nor can solve it. Inadequate incentives to agricultural producers and poor fiscal performance were more general causes. Worsening export prices and balance of payments deficits precipitated the crises. But industrial decline helped convince politicians to change policies that clearly were not stimulating rapid growth through industrialization.

Zambia and Ghana introduced similar measures to improve incentives for greater production and efficiency. Exchange rate adjustment, trade liberalization, and reorientation of the public sector's role in industry shifted price structures, opened access to foreign exchange and finance, and encouraged competitive behavior. This article evaluates the impact of these changes on

Excerpted and edited from William F. Steel, ''Recent Policy Reform and Industrial Adjustment in Zambia and Ghana,'' *Journal of Modern African Studies* 26 (1988): 157–64.

industrial incentives, performance, and supply response. It also investigates the importance of political will in sustaining reform long enough to generate an adequate supply response.

Supply responsiveness is a function of the size and speed of adjustment, public perceptions of the sustainability of reform, and the availability and flexibility of resources. The political will to sustain reform is influenced by the interaction of public perceptions and economic performance, and the latter in turn depends on supply response and on complementary measures to achieve fiscal and monetary stability. The experiences of Zambia and Ghana show how the ability to sustain reform may differ despite the seeming similarity of their economic problems and adjustment programs. Important determinants of their relative success include the size of debt, export response, and control over budget deficits and inflation.

Industrial Growth and Decline

Following political independence for Ghana in 1957 and for Zambia in 1964, both countries looked to industrialization to stimulate economic growth and freedom from imported manufactures. Increased protection (through tariffs and import restrictions in response to balance of payments deficits) and vigorous direct public investment spurred rapid growth of their industrial output at over 10 percent per year in the 1960s. The share of manufacturing rose from 4 and 7 percent of GDP at independence to 14 and 19 percent in the mid-to-late 1970s in Ghana and Zambia, respectively.[11]

The reversal of industrial growth was precipitated by foreign exchange difficulties. The drastic fall in the price of copper in 1975 cut back both demand and imported inputs for Zambia's manufacturing output, which fell at 5.6 percent per year from 1974 to 1980. Currency overvaluation, falling cocoa exports, and rising import costs contributed to the decline of output in Ghana at 12.8 percent per year between 1977 and 1982.

Worsening industrial performance prompted both countries to reassess their industrial strategies.[12] Exchange rate, tariff, interest rate, and investment promotion policies were found to have favored excessive investment in consumer-oriented, import-dependent, capital-intensive industries. Both countries created cumbersome import licensing and price control systems that protected and perpetuated existing industrial structures and provided little incentive for efficiency. Public sector firms, many seized from private owners, often drained the public coffers despite receiving priority in resource allocation. Takeovers and inability to repatriate profits discouraged new foreign investment.

---

11. Data throughout the article are taken from internal World Bank sources.

12. See sections 3.4 and 3.6 above. In Ghana economic deterioration contributed to political instability (several changes of government, including two brief attempts to return to civilian rule), although political factors were more proximate causes of coups. Successive governments tightened controls (especially on prices and distribution of imports) and later loosened restrictions when they proved unworkable. Zambia showed greater stability both in its political regime and in its attempts to control the economy from the center. But the stability of political forces may have worked against efforts to change direction in economic policy.

In both countries key economic policymakers decided that prices had to be shifted in favor of productive activities if the economy was to adjust to and improve under prevailing conditions. Although many of Ghana's leaders initially ruled out devaluation, they were eventually swayed by pragmatic arguments that farmers and exporters could not survive without substantial price adjustment. President Kenneth Kaunda was a principal proponent of reform in Zambia, where an entrenched system of centralized allocation had created many vested interests against liberalization. Alternative strategies were discussed at a series of public meetings in 1983 and at a party convention in 1984, but no national consensus was achieved that drastic reform was necessary.

Impending crises in foreign exchange gave the impetus to major reform programs, which were needed to gain access to external resources. By the end of 1982, Zambia's current account deficit had exceeded 17 percent of GDP for three years, external debt outstanding and disbursed had reached 61 percent of GNP, and debt repayments had to be suspended. Ghana, on the other hand, had been increasingly unable to borrow, with external debt falling from 15 percent of GDP in 1975 to less than 4 percent in 1982. Declining export receipts and the inability to finance current account deficits forced imports to fall by nearly half from 1980 to 1982. By implementing reforms, the leaders of both countries were able to mobilize the resources necessary to stave off even more drastic cutbacks in imports.[13]

Design of Reform Programs

Zambia and Ghana initiated reform through managed adjustments in the exchange rate. Faced with a parallel market rate of one-twentieth the official exchange rate, the Ghanaian authorities devalued the currency by a factor of ten during 1983. With a less distorted foreign exchange market, Zambia devalued its official rate by 35 percent in 1983 and established a flexible exchange rate policy (based on a formula, not market conditions). Both countries gave exporters extra incentives through partial retention of earnings. Zambia eliminated import licensing in 1985 by introducing a foreign exchange auction for all imports (except for the government and the mining company, which received allocations but paid the auction rate). Ghana partially liberalized imports through expanded licensing of those not requiring official foreign exchange; a surtax made this a source of new revenue. Liberalization expanded in 1986 when a limited foreign exchange auction for raw materials and intermediate goods was introduced.

Both countries narrowed the range of tariff protection, Ghana through an early reform to establish nearly uniform tariffs and Zambia through an increase in minimum rates and reduction in top rates. Tariff reforms, however, had little impact on effective protection to producers until liberalization of import restrictions reduced scarcity rents.

13. Purchases from the IMF in 1983 and 1984 corresponded closely to the current account deficits in both countries, and they accounted for 27 and 29 percent of imports in those years in Zambia and 48 and 31 percent in Ghana.

These measures raised the cost of industrial production closer to economic levels and increased competition from imports. The quid pro quo was successive elimination of most price controls, which enabled efficient producers to cover their increased costs. Agricultural prices likewise were raised or shifted from controlled to market-determined pricing, and most subsidies to farmers were to be phased out.

Both countries attempted to improve the investment climate by issuing new investment codes and public policy statements that specified an important role for private production. Programs were launched to make the public sector more efficient by reducing government holdings in unviable firms and improving public enterprise management and organization. Zambia's industrial holding company undertook economic evaluations of existing and proposed investments.

Changes in fiscal and monetary policies were important components of the reform programs. These included lowering the relative share of government borrowing in the economy, reducing budgetary subsidies, and achieving market-determined, positive real interest rates.

The reform programs attracted substantial new assistance (including rescheduling of debt in the case of Zambia) from the International Monetary Fund, the World Bank, and bilateral donors. This financing reduced the rate of accumulation of arrears. It also permitted a higher level of imports than would otherwise have been the case. Debt increased, but the economy's response to the policy reforms was expected to generate sufficient additional resources to service that debt. In 1987, however, the adverse political consequences of certain reforms and the rising debt burden led Zambia to suspend its program.

The Breakdown of Reform in Zambia

Liberalization of the import regime via the auction improved industrial performance and structure in Zambia. Manufacturing output grew at 7.8 percent in 1985, and capacity utilization in the private sector rose dramatically from an estimated 38 percent in 1985 to 54 percent in 1986, but fell in five notably inefficient parastatals from 56 to 26 percent. Although manufacturing continued to receive 18 percent of total imports before and after the auction, the private sector's share of imported inputs for manufacturing rose to 61 percent, from 50 percent before introduction of the auction. Liberalization shifted production toward more efficient private firms, away from the least efficient parastatals, and this boosted the growth of output.

Manufactured exports responded dramatically to improved incentives under the auction, with an estimated tenfold increase during 1986. Nevertheless, exports remained too insignificant to counter the continued decline in copper production and weakness in copper prices, which led to further sizable falls in export receipts (table 6.6.1). Poor export performance held merchandise import growth to only 1 percent in 1985 and 3 percent in 1986, despite substantial foreign financial assistance.

Rapid expansion of the money supply and credit to the government at over 20 percent during 1985 precluded monetary and fiscal stability. Continuing

Table 6.6.1 *Economic Indicators for Zambia and Ghana, 1983–86*

Indicator	Zambia				Ghana			
	1983	1984	1985	1986[a]	1983	1984	1985	1986[a]
Annual percentage growth rate								
GDP at market prices	-2.0	-0.4	1.5	0.5	-4.7	8.7	5.1	5.3
Industrial output[b]	-2.9	-2.4	0.8	-0.6	-11.9	8.9	18.0	6.4
Manufacturing output	-7.4	1.2	7.8	0.4	-11.1	12.8	22.2	6.9
Agricultural output	8.4	5.6	3.5	5.8	-7.0	9.7	0.8	5.3
Exports (f.o.b.)	-7.5	-11.0	-6.1	-13.6	-31.5	28.9	11.7	22.3
Imports (c.i.f.)	-27.5	-11.6	1.3	3.1	-14.6	26.3	6.8	7.3
Money supply	11.1	17.2	23.5	92.7	38.1	72.0	59.5	53.6
Credit to government	5.8	9.0	22.8	39.3	90.5	14.8	12.5	8.8
Consumer price index	19.6	20.0	37.4	51.7	122.8	39.7	10.3	24.6
GDP deflator	18.8	18.5	40.9	70.7	123.3	35.7	31.2	30.2
Real effective exchange rate	-7.3	-14.0	-7.6	n.a.	-76.6	-30.8	-17.5	-47.1
Ratios								
Parallel market to official rate	n.a.	n.a.	n.a.	n.a.	22.2	3.2	2.8	1.8
Debt service to exports								
Excluding arrears	0.11	0.12	0.13	n.a.	0.21	0.36	0.53	0.47
Including arrears	0.13	0.44[c]	0.46[c]	0.50[c]	0.28	0.46	0.62	0.47
Public debt outstanding and disbursed to GDP[d]	0.92	1.18	1.56	n.a.	0.19	0.21	0.19	0.25
Percentage of GDP								
Government budget deficit	-8.9	-9.3	19.0	n.a.	-2.7	-1.8	-2.0	0.1
Balance of payments	-7.7	-11.1	-8.1	-32.9	-1.4	-2.8	-3.9	-3.9
Index of export volume[e]								
Copper/Cocoa	81	78	70	68	63	60	68	78
Zinc/Timber	121	100	n.a.	n.a.	19	23	46	66

n.a. Not available.
a. Provisional.
b. Includes mining, manufacturing, construction, and utilities.
c. Scheduled.
d. Excluding IMF credits and arrears.
e. For Zambia, 1980=100; for Ghana, 1977=100. Copper and zinc are Zambia's exports; cocoa and timber are Ghana's.
Source: World Bank data.

rapid growth of the money supply and fiscal deficit in 1986 accelerated price inflation from 20 percent in 1983–84 to 37 percent in 1985 and 52 percent in 1986. The expansion of credit directly affected the market-determined exchange rate. Rapid depreciation of the kwacha aggravated political opposition, which stemmed from the inaccurate belief that the auction was financing luxury consumer goods and, more fundamentally, from the loss of scarcity rents that had accrued under the import licensing regime.

Liberalization of price controls had a positive impact on Zambian producers, especially in agriculture, which moved to a surplus position in maize by 1986. But the negative impact on consumers exploded at the end of 1986 when the removal of subsidies and price controls on refined breakfast maize meal was aborted following riots. Although subsidies were not removed from the less processed type of roller meal consumed by lower-income groups, shortages developed as producers shifted toward the now more profitable breakfast meal, and violent protests ensued. The incident crystallized opposition to the reform program by those who stood to lose from it and by political leaders who had never fully accepted it. With income per capita still declining under weak economic growth (1.5 percent in 1985 and 0.5 percent in 1986), consumers generally were losers, while the exporters and producers on whom gains were concentrated had relatively little political influence.

In May 1987, the Zambian government suspended the reform program, arguing that mounting debt threatened to consume all export earnings. Debt repayments were restricted, and the exchange rate was fixed at just over a third of the last auction rate. Prices were frozen and controls reinstituted for twelve major commodities. Interest rates were fixed at a maximum of 20 percent. The principle of reform was not renounced, but replaced by a new strategy of "growth from our own resources," with particular emphasis on public works to increase employment. The immediate impact, however, was that price-controlled commodities became available only on the black market, and several factories closed for lack of foreign exchange.

Ghana's Sustained Response

Unlike Zambia, Ghana achieved a significant turnaround in its imports, with 26 percent growth in 1984 and 7 percent in the two succeeding years (table 6.6.1). The increase in import supplies supplemented a major expansion of domestic food production, favored by good rains and liberalized prices. Consumer price inflation fell from 123 percent in 1983 to 40 percent in 1984 and 10 percent in 1985, despite continuing devaluations. These had little impact on inflation largely because market prices had already adjusted to international prices at black market rates; the increased availability of goods at the devalued exchange rate even caused prices to fall for some consumables, such as milk and beer. Tight control over credit to the government helped restrain inflation, even though the money supply expanded relatively rapidly.

The initial response of Ghanaian industry was constrained by inadequate infrastructure and lack of finance. The export-oriented timber and sawmilling industry benefited from the massive devaluations of 1983 and 1984, but the response was slowed by the need to replace worn-out and abandoned processing and transport equipment. The recovery of mining likewise required rehabilitation of the railway and mining equipment. Poor creditworthiness after years of low turnover at controlled prices made it difficult for most firms to obtain sufficient working capital for imports—now over ten times as much in local currency.

Nevertheless, manufacturing responded strongly, leading GDP growth from 1984 to 1986. The influx of imported inputs through foreign borrowing fueled rapid manufacturing growth in 1985 at 22 percent, offsetting a temporary sag in agricultural performance. The volume of timber exports doubled that year, and rising cocoa production in 1985 and 1986 enabled export earnings to continue growing despite weak prices. Export growth and concessional assistance permitted imports to rise faster than GDP—in contrast to Zambia, whose import capacity was constrained by the difficulty of increasing copper production and by prices below projections.

Ghana's foreign exchange auction gave industry greater access to imported inputs. Less efficient producers, however, were pinched by a narrowing of the gap between the auction rate they paid for imported inputs and the parallel rate that still determined the prices of consumer goods. At the same time, the existence of this gap gave potentially efficient producers more time to adjust than in Zambia, where all goods were eligible for the auction. Nevertheless, as implicit exchange rate protection fell to about 30 percent in 1986, some industries obtained increases in tariff rates (above the previous maximum of 30 percent). Although liberalization and the absence of budgetary subsidies squeezed many public sector firms, the government has had difficulty following through on its commitment to consolidate or divest unviable enterprises. The rapid growth of beneficiary firms rather than the disappearance of inefficient firms has characterized the transition to a more efficient industrial structure.

A survey of thirty-two manufacturing firms in December 1987 revealed that 56 percent of the companies had increased output over 1986, and only 15 percent had lowered production. Industries that were able to expand despite competition from liberalized imports included those with a growing domestic market (plastics, furniture, and food processing), a specialized market niche (African prints and certain building materials), and monopoly power (matches and dry cell batteries). Some companies rejuvenated previous exports (wooden furniture, aluminium pots and pans, matches, African prints, and milk), while others sought new export markets (agricultural equipment, alcoholic beverages, and disposable syringes). Export growth was hampered, however, by financial constraints, obsolete equipment, poor-quality materials, and lack of marketing and design skills. Production cutbacks were attributed mainly to weak demand and competition from imports. The latter increased when certain consumer goods (mainly textiles) were made eligible for the foreign exchange auction in May 1987.

The foreign exchange auction system opened up access to raw materials, leaving low technical efficiency of obsolete machinery as the principal supply-side constraint. But firms that sought to remain competitive by investing in new machinery faced financial barriers. Their short-term liquidity position was strained by prior deposits required to make a foreign exchange bid, high interest rates, and the increased cost in cedis (the Ghanaian currency) of debt denominated in foreign exchange. The banking system was not channeling long-term finance effectively to bankable projects, and no formal money market existed to inject equity capital. Despite short-term responses in production, therefore, adjustments in cost structure and competitiveness proceeded more slowly.

The political acceptability of Ghana's reform program was initially aided by rising public expenditures and the dramatic shift from a shortage economy to overflowing markets. (Zambia had experienced neither the severe scarcities nor the significant increases in both imported and local supplies.) The positive effect of rising real wages, however, was partly offset by public sector layoffs and by the loss of scarcity rents from distribution of price-controlled goods. Furthermore, the market-oriented emphasis of the reforms elicited some criticism within the socialist-oriented government. As debt and worker dissatisfaction rise in Ghana, skillful political management is needed to avoid the kind of setbacks experienced by Zambia. In both countries, implementation was hampered by the strain on political will, decisionmaking capacity, and managerial resources.

Lessons

Comparison of the experiences of Zambia and Ghana shows the importance of debt and political considerations in the design and success of major reform programs. Zambia's already precarious debt situation made it imperative to accelerate reform in hopes of generating sufficient additional resources to sustain the process. These hopes proved false when copper prices prevented export earnings from rising, even though manufacturing for both export and domestic markets responded quickly. Economic decline had not gone as far in Zambia as in Ghana. The reform program was not widely seen as inevitable or as necessary to increase supplies. In retrospect, the pace of reforms exceeded what could be politically sustained, since resource constraints prevented imports and domestic production from increasing fast enough to forestall expansionary pressures and rising inflation.

Tight controls, highly distorted prices, and drought had devastated Ghana's economy. Ghana's reform program—aided by good rains—was able to achieve a visible turnaround in imports, domestic supplies, and inflation. The magnitude of corrections required in Ghana dictated a slower pace of reform than in Zambia, but the influx of new resources permitted a faster supply response. So far Ghana's success in improving fiscal and monetary stability has prevented an inflation-fueled acceleration of the auction-determined exchange rate, as occurred in Zambia. Although agricultural growth is central to successful implementation of the reform program in Ghana, rapid industrial recovery has played an important role in leading growth and maintaining it when agriculture slackened. The two countries' experiences suggest that visible economic improvements and astute political management are essential to sustain public support for reform.

Part III

Institutional Issues

Whereas part II emphasizes the importance of establishing appropriate incentives, part III reflects the view that simply "getting the prices right" is not sufficient in Africa. Institutional constraints can dampen the response to changed incentives and inhibit long-term industrial development.

Chapter 7, "The Business Environment," covers the principal determinants of the short-term response by entrepreneurs and managers. Since most manufacturing employment and entrepreneurial initiatives take place in small-scale activities, institutional and policy issues affecting the responsiveness of this sector are examined in chapter 8. Even when managers wish to respond appropriately, they may not be able to because of limited access to finance and technology, two components of long-term industrial development that are briefly mentioned in chapter 9. (Human resources and infractructure are two other important components that are not discussed in the limited space available.) Finally, chapter 10 addresses the critical issue of improving the performance of the public sector. It controls a large share of most countries' industrial capacity, and its decisions do not necessarily change in response to policy reforms.

The climate for private business has been adversely affected in Africa in two principal ways: through the public sector's direct ownership of industrial capacity, especially through nationalization, and through restrictive interventions in resource allocation and business decisions (section 7.1). Even in countries where a noninterventionist approach prevails, the small size of the market and the scarcity of resources make it difficult to avoid a certain degree of regulation (section 7.6). Price controls are commonly used and have consistently adverse consequences for industrial performance (sections 7.5 and 7.6). The inhibiting effect of these policies on competitive behavior is one reason for high-cost production (section 7.2). Efficiency and the consistency between policies and objectives could be improved through reform of the tax system and special investment incentives (sections 7.3 and 7.4).

The regulatory environment has been particularly biased against small-scale enterprises (SSEs), partly because offsetting incentives have been available only to large-scale firms (sections 8.1 and 8.2). Although a consensus exists that biases against SSEs should be removed, it is not so clear whether special promotional efforts are warranted or effective. Stabilization and liberalization policies may improve the relative attractiveness of SSEs by reducing the advantages and marginal wages of larger firms (section 8.4). SSEs have been largely excluded from formal sources of finance, but channeling additional finance to them could undermine their savings effort and choice of efficient techniques (sections 8.2 and 8.3). Similarly, there is general agreement that improving entrepreneurial and managerial skills in SSEs would facilitate industrial development in Africa, but the appropriate institutional means of doing so remains to be demonstrated (sections 8.5 and 8.6).

Lack of financial development constrains both the short-term response to policy change and long-run industrial development in Africa (section 9.1). Important issues include how to reduce crowding out of the private sector because of the need for public sector borrowing and how to link up formal and informal credit institutions (section 8.6). Regarding technology, a key issue is whether the problem is lack of development of appropriate technologies or a policy environment that leads to improper choices among available technologies (sections 9.2 and 9.3).

Public industries have been established (or taken over) to serve a wide variety of objectives, some of them contradictory (sections 10.1 and 10.2). The finding that performance has, on the whole, been unsatisfactory from a financial perspective is in large part a consequence of investment, operating, and pricing decisions made on the basis of other criteria. This does not mean that all public enterprises are unprofitable nor that they cannot be operated effectively (section 10.3). But in most cases, improving public sector performance will require clarifying objectives and the criteria for measuring performance, restructuring public holdings to what can be operated effectively with the resources available, and establishing a performance-oriented environment at the firm level (sections 10.4 and 10.5).

7

The Business Environment

7.1 *Impact of Regulations and Taxation on Private Industry*
Keith Marsden and Therese Belot

It is now generally accepted that over time the majority of public sector
enterprises or entities have not performed efficiently. Instead of accumulating surpluses or supplying services efficiently, a good number of these
enterprises have become a drain on the national treasuries. Due to this poor
performance, coupled with the growing recognition of the costs of ineffective public enterprises in terms of forgone economic development and the
scarcity of domestic and external resources for public sector expenditure, reappraisal of the strategy of heavy reliance on the public sector has become
imperative. From this reappraisal, a view has emerged—the need for
enhancement of the role of the private sector in development. . . . We in
Africa are facing a great challenge. We believe that the creation of a conducive environment for the growth of the private sector, an important agent of
economic growth, is essential.[1]

Similar declarations promoting the private sector as an engine of economic
growth have become common in many African countries. This section discusses weaknesses and constraints in the policy areas affecting private enterprise development and reviews actions being taken to overcome them.

Barriers to Entry in the Private Sector

In many African countries a variety of policies restricts private participation in
mining, manufacturing, and public utilities. Activities reserved for state
enterprises (or joint ventures with majority government ownership) are

Excerpted and edited from Keith Marsden and Therese Belot, *Private Enterprise in Africa: Creating a
Better Environment.* World Bank Discussion paper 17 (Washington, D.C., 1987).
    1. From a statement by Babacar N'Diaye, president of the African Development Bank, at the
International Conference on Privatization, February 17, 1986, Washington, D.C.

sometimes specified in investment codes or other legislation. In other cases, privately owned enterprises have come under public control through nationalization. More frequently, selective use of industrial licensing authority preserves state monopolies in sectors which are considered to be politically sensitive or in which the pursuit of social goals is paramount.

In Sudan extensive nationalization of private industrial enterprises during the 1970s was accompanied by high public investment in projects with low returns. In 1983 the government announced a private sector action program. Some parastatals have been converted to private companies, but policy decisions have worsened the environment for private investment. Private activities are threatened by high costs, lack of credit, rigid price regulations, disruptions in utility services and imported inputs, and uncertainty about the business climate.

Indigenization decrees in 1972 and 1977 required divestiture of foreign equity holdings in Nigeria. Public investment in manufacturing then grew more rapidly than private investment. The public sector has been responsible for two-thirds of total manufacturing investment since 1975. The Nigerian government indicated recently, however, that the private sector was expected to be the prime agent for industrial growth in the future; the government will invest in infrastructure and establish an appropriate legal and regulatory environment. Priority is being given to facilitating private sector activity by simplifying or eliminating government regulations.

Zaire is another country that has swung from hostility to private investment to active wooing of foreign investors. In 1971 a new policy of economic nationalism was launched. With few exceptions, foreign businesses were either nationalized or passed to private Zairean control. The government assumed the task of converting Zaire into a major industrial power through centralized controls and selective public investment. Although the goal was to produce a stable economic environment, the reverse happened; government intervention hindered rather than helped modernization. The Zairenization of the economy was no more a success than was centralized planning. The private sector suffered from nonreplacement of stocks and machinery and the withdrawal of working capital.

These policies of government intervention were ended in the late 1970s and early 1980s. Many companies were denationalized, and their former owners were invited to return to Zaire. This met with only limited success, however. The task of attracting fresh investment has also proved to be extremely difficult, despite liberalization measures that included the floating of the zaire (currency unit), an end to interest rate restrictions, the guaranteed right to repatriate profits, the abolition of certain monopolies, and the narrowing of budget deficits.

Three conclusions can be drawn from this examination of barriers to entry. First, these barriers deprived African economies of the benefits of private investment (both indigenous and foreign) and the skills and initiative that would have accompanied such investment. Second, they removed the competitive stimulus to efficiency that public monopolies have so obviously lacked. Third, governments would achieve their goals more effectively if they eliminated these barriers and used broader economic policies and market incentives to guide private decisions in the desired directions.

Obstacles to Foreign Investment

The level of foreign private investment in Africa is affected by the potential investor's perception of the business environment. A survey of 233 industrial firms in the Federal Republic of Germany found that the most important constraint was difficulty in dealing with government authorities. Other factors of particular importance related to ownership and return (transfer) of capital, the regulations governing local participation, financing conditions, and transfer of profits.[2]

Similar attitudes were encountered in a study sponsored by the European Economic Community. It concluded that "Africa is, overall, a zone which is far less sought after by investors in the developed countries."[3] The various reasons cited by European firms included:

Internal political pressure. A classic example of this is price approval. This problem occurs frequently in Africa, where the domestic prices of everyday goods have to be approved by the authorities.

Corruption. Many decisions and authorizations cannot be obtained without "compensation."

Excessive legalism. Because they often lack technical knowledge, authorities in developing countries may hide behind laws and regulations designed to protect the host country from any abuses by the foreign firms.

The attitudes of foreign investors may be unfair, but they are often critical in determining the level of direct investment flows from abroad. African governments that want to promote investment may need to take more vigorous action to change these perceptions or change the underlying reality. A continuing dialogue between private sector and government is desirable. The Chamber of Commerce and Industry is performing this role in several African countries. Such mechanisms can lead to a better understanding of needs and attitudes and a broader consensus on the reforms needed to promote development.

Taxation

All countries must seek a balance in their fiscal policies between the need to raise revenue and the need to create adequate incentives to work, save, and invest. They must also aim for equitable sharing of the tax burden and avoid undue distortion in the after-tax returns to different economic activities. In many African countries it has proved to be difficult to reconcile these objectives. The tax rates on corporate income are frequently high by international standards. For example, they are 60 percent in Ghana, Sudan, and Zaire, compared with 30 percent in Taiwan and Korea and 18.5 percent in Hong Kong. Rates of personal income tax also tend to be high in Africa. The top marginal rate is 80 percent in Rwanda and Zambia, 70 percent in Sudan, and

2. See Jurgen Riedel, "Attitudes in the Federal Republic of Germany to the Policies of Developing Countries Regarding Foreign Investors," *Industry and Development* 13 (1984): 1–38.

3. See *The Constraints on Industrial Cooperation Between Firms in the EEC and ACP Countries,* European Economic Community, Directorate-General for Development, February 1985.

60 percent in Zaire and Ghana. These rates are reached at relatively low income thresholds.

High corporate and personal income taxes have had four negative effects. First, they have reduced the private sector's capacity to accumulate reserves to finance expansion, modernization, and diversification. Second, they have deterred foreign investors (especially in labor-intensive industries that are easily moved, like textiles, clothing, and electronics), who have found more hospitable fiscal environments in East Asia. Third, entrepreneurial efforts have been diverted from formal productive activities, where financial transactions are more readily audited, to real estate speculation, trading, and "underground" activities where earnings can be easily hidden from the tax authorities. Fourth, high tax rates have increased the incentive to bribe low-paid tax officials.

In some countries the net result has been a contraction of the tax base and lower tax revenues. Government attempts to stem the fall in revenues by raising tax rates still further have only accelerated the decline. Ghana, for example, introduced a special sales tax on imports, excise taxes, advance tax payments for selected manufacturing sectors, and a substantially higher registration fee for retailers. Moreover, Ghana postponed or kept to a minimum crucial adjustments in the tax system, such as the level of personal income exemptions, depreciation allowances for corporations, and personal income tax brackets. Consequently, the tax burden on individuals and private enterprises that abided by the law increased sharply while actual tax revenues dropped from 13.8 percent of GDP in 1975 to 6.5 percent in 1984. In Sudan, the maximum tax rate on personal income was raised from 60 to 70 percent and new development and defense taxes were imposed, but the tax revenue/GDP ratio declined from 15.2 percent in 1976 to 12.5 percent in 1984.

Mauritius, on the other hand, used fiscal incentives to diversify its economy and create employment. Its Export Processing Zone (EPZ) Act of 1970 granted (1) tax holidays on corporate profits for ten years (extended up to twenty years on a declining basis since 1980); (2) tax holidays on dividends for any five-year period during the first ten years; (3) free repatriation of capital and dividends; and (4) duty-free entry of capital goods and inputs. These incentives were available only to firms exporting all of their output. Further measures introduced in 1984 included a reduction in the corporate tax rate on non-EPZ firms from 65 to 35 percent and a system of corporate tax benefits to non-EPZ exporters in which the rate is reduced 2 percentage points for each 10 percent of output exported. Against this background, the share of manufacturing in GDP rose from 8.0 percent in 1970 to 15.9 percent in 1983, and its share of total employment went from 6.4 percent to 19.0 percent over the same period. Manufacturing, which contributed only 2.2 percent of Mauritian exports in 1970, accounted for 38.6 percent in 1983. Export firms created 22,300 additional jobs in 1983–84.

Labor Regulations

Overregulated labor markets have generally resulted in bloated work forces and hampered the profitability of enterprises in Africa. In particular, pressures upon employers to expand or maintain employment for social welfare reasons have proved to be counterproductive. Only economic growth can produce long-term expansion of employment.

Botswana's labor legislation has tried to find a balance between protection of the rights, safety, and welfare of workers, the needs of employers, and the need for labor market flexibility. Minimum wages, the length of the work week, annual and maternity leave, and hiring and termination procedures are laid down. There is no provision for sick leave, although it is given in practice. Dismissal of workers is allowed if there is misconduct, willful disobedience, lack of skill, substantial neglect of duties, or unexcused absence from work. While government does not set wages in the private sector, it does attempt to restrain wage inequality and ensure that private and public sector wages are comparable.

In Mauritius, basic wage rates, working hours, sick leave, annual leave, absence from work, and compensation on termination of service are all regulated by legislation. A compulsory national pension plan is also in force, with contributions required from employers and employees. Labor-management relations are relatively stable, and strikes are uncommon. The government continues to view wage restraint as vital to the country's export competitiveness.

In Burkina Faso, on the other hand, it is extremely difficult for modern sector employers to cut back on staff or even to reduce working hours. According to some managers, approval by CDR (Revolutionary Defense Committee) representatives is required. Hiring new people generally involves using the government's labor exchange. Smaller and totally private firms have fewer problems.

The general conclusion that can be drawn from African experience is that labor policies should allow firms more flexibility in negotiating wages, including the possibility of linking wages to employee productivity. Restrictions on laying off excess or unproductive workers should be relaxed so that employers may take on new workers without excessive risk.

Price Controls

Most African governments control the prices of some agricultural and industrial products and of such services as electricity, transport, and telecommunications. The rationale for price controls is twofold: (1) to ensure that people with low incomes can buy basic necessities; (2) to contain inflationary pressures fueled by rapid monetary growth.

But price controls are a major disincentive to private firms. There are often long delays between an enterprise's request for a price increase and the government's ruling on the request. In Burkina Faso, a bicycle manufacturer had to wait eighteen months to increase prices; the prices of imported spare parts increased substantially in the meantime.

Price control enforcement requires large staffs, thereby adding pressure to already strained budgets. In Ethiopia, the price control administration employs 800 persons, but it is recognized that 800 is insufficient to perform this task effectively.

Price liberalization is a politically sensitive issue. Although many governments in the region recognize the many adverse effects of price controls, liberalization usually takes place in a gradual manner. In order to allow market forces to play a more important role in the economy, the Zambian government in 1982 abolished controls in all wholesale and retail prices except for wheat flour, maize flour, and candles. Since then the prices for a wide range of commodities have increased, thereby helping to restrain domestic demand while increasing the profitability of firms.

Price controls in Ghana have been substantially liberalized since 1985. Except for textile products, tobacco, beverages, and some less important items, manufacturers are required only to report price changes. The liberalization of price controls has been welcomed by private businesses, while the combination of higher prices and larger production volumes is beginning to turn former sellers' markets to buyers' markets.

In the 1970s the government of Malawi maintained a system of formal and informal price controls on a variety of items that were considered essential, either as consumer products or production inputs. By the early 1980s, with increased inflationary pressures, the system was creating serious disincentives for producers. It failed to signal shortages and surpluses and imposed a financial burden on firms that were experiencing large increases in input prices. In 1983 the government implemented a price liberalization program, reducing the number of items on the price control list from fifty-six to nine by August 1985.

These examples indicate the path that could be followed by other African countries where price controls cause market rigidities and hamper resource mobilization.

7.2 *Shelter from Domestic Competition*
Robert H. Bates

Public policies to promote domestic manufacturing often inhibit domestic competition. In some cases, restrictions on competition at home are a by-product of measures taken to restrict competition from abroad. In both Ghana and Kenya, for example, the tariff laws are written so that the incidence of protection is designated at the six-digit level of industrial classification.

In effect, then, protection is extended to the individual firm. In Kenya local firms lobby strenuously to place their products on schedule D. They do so because they can then "object" to imports of their product or of material which could be used for its manufacture. The trade law thus shelters them from domestic as well as foreign competition. Most trade programs involve the allocation of quotas or licenses; these permits to import are often distributed in accordance with historical market shares. Use of this criterion has been recorded for the Sudan, Ghana, and Nigeria. The effect, of course, is to freeze existing patterns of competition, thereby preventing the growth of more efficient and lower-cost firms.

Excerpted by permission from Robert H. Bates, *Markets and States in Tropical Africa: The Political Basis of Agricultural Policies* (Berkeley: University of California Press, 1981).

Bureaucratic procedures for extending protection from foreign competition tend to give an advantage to larger firms, and this too promotes market concentration. Larger and better staffed firms have a systematic advantage in preparing justifications for demands for protection, or for rations of foreign exchange.

The restriction of competition in the domestic economy is not merely an unintended consequence of the procedures used to govern relations with the international market, however. The consolidation of industries is sometimes done on purpose. As Leith noted for Ghana: "The import-license system, since it has virtual life and death powers over most industries, came to be used as an industrial licensing system as well. The Ministry of Industries saw a conflict between the need for competition among domestic producers and the wasteful expenditure involved in duplicating underutilized domestic facilities, but generally resolved it . . . in favor of 'rationalization' of industries and against new entrants."[4]

In other instances, the rights to import capital goods and inputs necessary for manufacturing a particular product have been purposefully restricted to particular enterprises. To secure the erection of an automotive assembly plant, the government of Kenya gave British Leyland the sole right to import particular parts and machinery. Similar privileges were extended to Firestone to secure its investment in a domestic tire plant. The effect was the promotion of a virtual monopoly for both firms. The extension of exclusive rights to import has been used to promote investments in Zambia as well. There, too, it has resulted in the creation of domestic monopolies in several industries: cement, food processing, matches, sugar, building materials, petroleum, and textiles.

It should also be noted that other policies have promoted industrial concentration: among these are tax credits, accelerated depreciation allowances, subsidized interest rates, and preferential duties on capital equipment. All these have been used by governments to promote the importation of capital and thereby lay the foundations for industrial development. Moreover, in negotiations with foreign investors, governments tend to favor those who promise larger investments. The result has been the adoption of capital-intensive technologies which are most efficient at high levels of output. But, by and large, the domestic markets of the African countries are small; there are few people and they are poor. Given the capital-intensive nature of the new firms and the small domestic markets, there tends to be idle capacity in many industries, and the incentives are thus strong to secure a reduction in the number of firms.

It is clear that this idle capacity is perceived as excess capacity. Such beliefs furnish incentives to restrict competition. [Firms] in the Kenyan cement industry repeatedly merged until only two companies remained; these firms then negotiated a division of the market, one producing 80 percent of its output for export and the other 90 percent of its output for internal use. And with this agreement there came a major rise in price. The East African paint

4. J. Clark Leith, *Foreign Trade Regimes and Economic Development: Ghana* (New York: Columbia University Press, 1974), p. 32.

industry was similarly characterized by initial overexpansion and vigorous price competition. Eventually, the four remaining firms agreed to form a cartel, called the East African Paint Industries Association. This cartel then secured tariff protection to restrict foreign price competition while implementing an internal price agreement within the East African market.

[Available data] suggest that the policies designed to promote industrial formation in Africa have produced a highly concentrated industrial structure. The total number of firms is small. Moreover, within particular industries there exist few firms, and a small number appear to produce a high proportion of the total output.

Consequences of Reduced Domestic Competition

We have explored some of the basic features of policies affecting the growth of the industrial and manufacturing sector in Africa. These policies shelter firms not only from foreign but also from domestic competition. One result is that many inefficient firms survive in the African market.

Evidence of this is contained in the figures on excess industrial capacity, which suggest that many firms fail to operate at the cost-minimizing levels of output. Further evidence is contained in qualitative description of the difficulties of operating modern plants under conditions prevailing in Africa. In describing the problems bedeviling new enterprises in Nigeria, [one author] reports that equipment was ordered at a long distance from its place of design and manufacture; the result was economic losses from inappropriate equipment and from delays while awaiting corrections in deliveries. Often the equipment could not employ local inputs. A furnace might be unable to work local silicons, or a textile plant might be unable to secure fibers of appropriate length from local producers. Problems such as these repeatedly plagued efforts to establish new firms. The obvious corollary is that the firms are inefficient and incur high costs, and that without substantial protection from meaningful economic competition, many of them could not survive.

The survival of such firms entails substantial costs, and it is consumers who pay. When protection is offered against lower-cost foreign goods, the result is an increase in domestic prices. And when domestic competition is restricted, firms can secure prices that give them higher profit margins. The result in both cases is a rise in consumer prices.

An Inherent Conflict

We have argued [elsewhere] that pressures from the urban sector generate demands for policies to secure lower consumer prices. We have now stressed the role of urban interests in securing policies that increase prices to consumers. The contrast is significant and important, and the apparent conflict can be resolved in a way that gives insight into the interplay of economic interests in the policy-making process.

We can begin with a single industry. It is reasonable for those who derive their incomes from the production of a product to seek a higher price for it. This is true of workers as well as the owners of firms, for both derive their incomes from the production of a particular good. But they spend their incomes widely, devoting but a small fraction, in most cases, to the purchase of the good they produce. Thus they benefit from an increase in its price.

Insofar as governments respond more readily to business combinations than to individuals, it is also reasonable for those who derive their incomes from making a particular product to combine with persons from other industries in seeking protection for their products.

There is a limit to this logic, however. Not all industries are equally attractive partners in this price-setting game. In particular, if one industry's product requires the expenditure of a very high portion of a person's budget, then persons will look for other industries when seeking partners with whom to combine in petitions for higher prices. In Africa, as in other poor areas, food is such a product; as much as 60 percent of the average urban dweller's budget is spent on food purchases. In the formation of combinations to secure price increases, food producers are therefore unattractive partners, and tend to be excluded from price-setting coalitions.

Other factors also help to resolve the apparent contradictory behavior of urban interests. By offering high levels of effective protection to an industry, the government can secure higher returns to all factors operating in that industry; this provides an incentive for capital to move into that industry, but it also enhances the value of labor. Labor and capital can both share in the gains generated by protection. The demands of labor are thus, ironically, assuaged by policies that try to provide incentives for capital investment by conferring higher prices on manufactured products.

Conclusions

Many would argue that the burden of higher prices represents a cost of the transition to an industrialized economy. Bergsman, for example, reappraised the economic growth of Korea, the Republic of China, Brazil, Singapore, and other semi-industrialized countries and stressed that their development involved passage through an initial stage that closely resembles that characteristic of contemporary Africa. Nonetheless, while these conditions may be a necessary prelude to later industrialization, they clearly are not a sufficient condition for it. This argument is supported by Bergsman's analysis, which notes the failure of other economies, and it should give pause to those who would see in the experience of these countries a promise of successful industrialization in Africa.[5]

Several characteristics distinguish the now semi-industrial states from their less successful counterparts. One, Bergsman contends, is their policies toward agriculture. In addition to the protected conditions afforded their industries, many of the governments of these states also provided a strong stimulus to farm production: "favorable prices plus heavy investment plus good access to inputs," in Bergsman's words.[6] Such policies contrast sharply

---

5. Joel Bergsman, *Growth and Equity in Semi-Industrialized Countries*, World Bank Staff Working Paper 351 (Washington, D.C., 1979).

6. Ibid., p. 80.

with those found in most of Africa. Another distinctive characteristic of successful cases is the existence of large markets for manufactured products. Either because of their exceptional size (as in the case of Brazil) or because they specialized in the manufacture of exports (as in the case of Korea, Hong Kong, or Singapore), the successful countries tended to have access to larger markets. In the first case, they had little incentive to maintain few firms; in the second, they lacked the power to exclude competitors. Large markets therefore promoted conditions under which efficient operations became an established part of the economic order.

In Africa, few nations attempt to export manufactured products. Most have small populations and the majority of their citizens are poor. Of all the nations in this study, only Nigeria offers a market of sufficient size and wealth to engender competitive struggles among a large number of firms. For most others, the present industrial order could be not a prelude to growth but a framework for economic stagnation.

7.3 *Improving Tax Structures*
Lyn Squire

Much of the literature on taxation and economic development has been concerned with "explaining" the level or composition of taxation in terms of GDP per capita and alternative structural variables. In a recent application to Sub-Saharan Africa, for example, Tanzi finds that "the share of mining in GDP and the export ratio, excluding mineral exports, are the most significant determinants of the tax ratio. Per capita income plays no role." Tanzi then proceeds to compare actual tax-GDP ratios with those predicted by his estimated equation to determine whether or not countries "have a relatively light tax burden."[7]

These exercises may be useful for descriptive purposes, but they have no normative content. In fact, if taxation is viewed as one of the major policy instruments available to governments, it seems more appropriate to reverse the direction of causality and examine the extent to which GDP is determined by the level and structure of taxation. Accordingly, this paper commences with a brief review of the development of tax structures in Sub-Saharan Africa through the 1970s and then explores the elements of an approach that may allow normative statements.

Taxation in Sub-Saharan Africa

Table 7.3.1 displays the development of tax structures in Sub-Saharan Africa from about 1970 to about 1980. By 1980, 17 percent of GDP was being channeled to the public sector through taxation, compared with about 14 percent in 1970. Despite this increase, the fiscal deficit increased from 3 percent of GDP to almost 8 percent during the same period in the sixteen countries for which

---

Excerpted from Lyn Squire, "Taxation and Economic Development in Sub-Saharan Africa," World Bank Country Policy Department, 1984 (restricted circulation).
    7. See Vito Tanzi, *Taxation in Sub-Saharan Africa,* IMF Occasional Paper 8 (Washington, D.C., 1981), pt. II, p. 46.

Table 7.3.1 *Taxation in Sub-Saharan Africa*

Country	GNP per capita, 1982[a] (dollars)	Tax revenue/GDP (percent)		Fiscal deficit[b]		Trade tax/ tax revenue	
		1970[c]	1980[d]	1970[c]	1980[d]	1970[c]	1980[d]
Chad	80	0.15	0.12	n.a.	−0.06	0.52	0.57
Ethiopia	140	0.09	0.15	−0.01	−0.04	0.39	0.42
Mali	180	0.01	0.12	n.a.	−0.09	0.38	0.23
Zaire	190	0.29	0.18	−0.06	−0.09	0.66	0.41
Malawi	210	0.12	0.16	−0.07	−0.14	0.34	0.25
Upper Volta	210	0.11	0.13	n.a.	−0.02	0.55	0.51
Uganda	230	0.01	0.01	−0.08	−0.02	0.41	0.45
Rwanda	260	0.07	0.11	n.a.	−0.02	0.50	0.50
Burundi	280	0.09	0.12	n.a.	−0.08	0.42	0.39
Tanzania	280	0.13	0.17	−0.06	−0.14	0.35	0.18
Somalia	290	0.12	0.15	n.a.	n.a.	0.53	0.65
Benin	310	0.11	0.15	n.a.	−0.08	0.60	0.69
Guinea	310	0.12	0.20	−0.04	−0.09	0.51	0.70
Niger	310	0.09	0.15	n.a.	−0.04	0.40	0.40
Madagascar	320	0.15	0.13	n.a.	n.a.	0.40	0.44
Togo	340	0.12	0.29	n.a.	−0.05	0.74	0.35
Gambia	360	0.13	0.16	n.a.	−0.10	0.83	0.77
Ghana	360	0.15	0.06	−0.03	−0.05	0.50	0.48
Kenya	390	0.13	0.19	−0.01	−0.04	0.32	0.24
Sierra Leone	390	0.15	0.15	0.01	−0.10	0.55	0.52
Sudan	440	0.16	0.11	n.a.	−0.06	0.47	0.54
Mauritania	470	0.08	0.17	n.a.	−0.16	0.37	0.39
Liberia	490	0.14	0.18	−0.01	−0.10	0.34	0.38
Senegal	490	0.16	0.18	0.00	−0.02	0.47	0.38
Lesotho	510	0.15	0.23	−0.09	−0.21	0.68	0.73
Zambia	640	0.27	0.23	−0.01	−0.12	0.10	0.09
Zimbabwe	850	0.13	0.19	n.a.	−0.10	0.12	0.07
Nigeria	860	0.10	0.19	n.a.	0.02	0.44	0.15
Cameroon	890	0.13	0.15	n.a.	0.00	0.58	0.40
Botswana	900	0.15	0.27	n.a.	−0.01	0.66	0.55
Swaziland	940	0.14	0.27	−0.02	0.03	0.57	0.68
Ivory Coast	950	0.20	0.22	n.a.	−0.07	0.56	0.47
People's Republic of the Congo	1,180	0.20	0.19	−0.02	−0.05	0.42	0.34
Mauritius	1,240	0.15	0.17	−0.03	−0.08	0.44	0.54
Gabon	4,000	0.19	0.21	n.a.	−0.10	0.65	0.36
Average		0.14	0.17	−0.03	−0.07	0.48	0.43
Number of observations		35	35	16	33	35	35

n.a. Not available.

a. World Bank, *Toward Sustained Development in Sub-Saharan Africa: A Joint Program of Action* (Washington, D.C., 1984), table 1.

b. Tax revenue minus total expenditure expressed as a percentage of GDP.

c. Average for 1969, 1970, and 1971 except Guinea (1974, 1975, 1976) and Uganda (1972, 1973, 1974).

d. Average for 1979, 1980, and 1981 except Chad (1974, 1975, 1976), Congo (1976, 1977, 1978), Gabon (1974, 1975, 1976), Gambia (1977, 1978, 1979), Ivory Coast (1978, 1979, 1980), Mauritania (1977, 1978, 1979), Niger (1978, 1979, 1980), Nigeria (1978, 1979, 1980), and Togo (1978, 1979, 1980).

data are available. Increased revenues and an increased deficit imply a very rapid increase in public expeditures.

Almost half of all revenue is generated from taxation of international trade, which accounted for 48 percent of revenue in 1970 and 43 percent in 1980. Not all countries reduced their reliance on trade tariffs. In thirteen countries the share increased from 48 percent in 1970 to 55 percent in 1980. In another twenty countries it decreased from 48 percent to 36 percent over the same period.

Most countries rely heavily on import duties. Of the thirty-five countries studied, twenty-one generated more than 80 percent of their tax revenues on trade from import tariffs. Only three countries—Ghana, Guinea, and Uganda—obtained less than 50 percent of tariff revenue from imports. These figures, however, omit both the surpluses of agricultural marketing boards and the nonroyalty revenues generated from oil and minerals, which are usually classified as income taxation. They therefore understate the importance of export activities as a source of revenue.

Analyzing Tax Structures

Sub-Saharan countries have increased their expenditures more rapidly than their tax revenues and have remained highly reliant on taxation of international transactions. Clearly, many countries will have to redress this imbalance between expenditures and revenue, probably by cutting the former rather than increasing the latter. Dependence on trade taxes suggests that countries should also examine the structure of taxation. One strategy would be to examine the proposition that any given level of revenue can be achieved at lower cost by less reliance on the taxation of trade than is observed in many Sub-Saharan countries. In this context, costs would include both the deadweight loss associated with distortions and the costs of administration and evasion. The presumption underlying this proposition is that the distortionary costs of trade taxes are, at the margin, higher than those of other taxes. To investigate the proposition further, it is necessary to examine these various costs in more detail.

Efficiency

Partial equilibrium analysis reveals that the deadweight loss per unit of revenue is an increasing function of the tax rate and of the responsiveness of demand and supply to price, and a decreasing function of the tax base. Given the difficulty of obtaining information on response coefficients, a complete analysis may not always be feasible. Information on revenue, and on the size of the tax base by instrument, however, can still be of value. For example, if the ratio of import taxation to imports exceeds the ratio of excise taxes to domestic sales, there is a presumption that the rate of taxation on imports should be reduced.

The evidence suggests that imports in many countries are taxed more heavily than either nonagricultural value added or domestic sales. For example, the realized rate of taxation on imports in Sudan exceeds 25 percent, compared with rates of less than 4 percent on both nonagricultural value added and domestic sales of consumer goods and services. Kenya, on the other hand, has a much more balanced tax structure, with realized rate of taxation of roughly 12 percent on both imports and nonagricultural value added, and 10 percent on domestic sales.

Apart from static efficiency, it may also be important to examine the effects of taxation on aggregate savings. The notion that transferring resources through taxation increases economywide savings may not always be correct. For example, a recent study revealed that a one-unit increase in tax revenue resulted in an increase in total (public and private) consumption of 1.13 in Malawi, 0.83 in Sudan, and 0.63 in Senegal. Increased taxation may therefore result in lower rates of savings.

Administration

The evidence suggests that a restructuring of taxation away from heavy reliance on import tariffs may yield improvements in efficiency. It is usually claimed, however, that trade taxes are preferred because countries do not have the administrative capacity to generate compensating revenues from taxation of domestic activities. To test this argument, table 7.3.2 reports the

Table 7.3.2 *A Decomposition of Changes in Tax Effort, 1970–80*

Countries reducing reliance on trade taxes	Percentage increase in tax effort, 1970–80[a]	Percentage increase in nontrade tax- ation, 1970–80[b]	Increase in nontrade taxation attributable to	
			Changes in tax bases[c]	Changes in realized tax rates
Togo	141.7	469.7	1.5	468.2
Nigeria	95.9	369.4	−0.8	370.2
Botswana	80.0	155.1	−18.8	173.9
Zimbabwe	46.2	37.4	11.5	25.9
Malawi	33.3	63.0	32.2	30.8
Tanzania	30.8	60.2	−3.1	63.3
Kenya	30.8	85.8	9.7	76.1
Burundi	27.7	43.2	15.4	27.8
Mali	25.0	57.2	5.5	51.7
Gambia	23.1	115.5	9.4	106.1
Upper Volta	18.2	31.2	5.2	26.0
Cameroon	15.4	103.3	−1.3	104.6
Senegal	12.5	55.3	8.9	46.4
Gabon	10.5	94.9	−21.1	116.0
Ivory Coast	10.0	18.9	1.2	17.7
Sierra Leone	0.0	0.3	5.7	−5.4
Congo	−5.0	−64.8	−2.5	−62.3
Zambia	−14.8	−60.9	49.0	−109.9
Zaire	−37.9	4.0	0.6	3.4
Ghana	−57.3	−53.7	−12.6	−41.1

a. Tax effort is defined as the ratio of revenue to GDP.

b. Nontrade taxation includes direct taxes and all nontrade indirect taxes. It is measured relative to GDP.

c. The tax bases are nonagricultural GDP for direct taxes and total consumption for nontrade indirect taxes.

change in tax effort—the ratio of total revenue to GDP—achieved during the 1970s by countries that reduced the share of taxation generated by trade taxes. The difficulties of collecting nontrade taxes nonwithstanding, these countries increased their tax effort by about the same number of percentage points— three—as did countries whose reliance on trade taxation increased (not shown).

These data suggest that countries can reduce trade taxes and simultaneously improve their tax effort. The improvement in tax effort, however, may have been the result of a coincidental expansion of the relevant tax bases rather than a predetermined effort to increase realized tax rates through higher nominal rates or improvements in collection. To explore this issue, table 7.3.2 also reports the results of a decomposition exercise. A change in revenue from nontrade taxation can be decomposed into changes in realized tax rates and changes in tax bases—nonagricultural GDP and total consumption. The table reveals clearly that, whether nontrade taxation increased or not, changes in realized tax rates were the main factor explaining changes in revenue. This suggests that countries have increased their revenue from domestic activities either by increasing tax rates or by improving collection efforts. But more convincing analysis would require the use of country-specific tax instruments and tax bases rather than the broad-brush approach adopted here.

Evasion

The empirical literature on evasion is primarily concerned with estimating the amount of evasion. This is obviously important if interest centers mainly on the consequences of changes in tax rates or tax administration on revenue. The extent of evasion, however, may not be the most relevant information if our primary interest is the real costs associated with evasion. These costs comprise transactions costs and costs associated with the possibility of discovery and punishment. Transaction costs involve the use of real resources and are therefore a cost to society. However, had evasion not taken place, certain transaction costs would have been incurred anyway. The *net* transaction costs associated with evasion are therefore the difference between the costs of, say, smuggling, and the costs of importing or exporting through normal channels. It is these net costs that enter the private calculation and that are relevant to society's assessment of costs, and not the total cost associated with an illegal activity.

7.4 Investment Incentives
   Alice Galenson

Once a decision is made to use incentives, a wide choice of options is available. The more direct the incentive, the less likely it is to create costly side effects and vice versa. For example, tariffs that restrict imports to encourage

Excerpted and edited from Alice Galenson, *Investment Incentives for Industry,* World Bank Staff Working Paper 669 (Washington, D.C., 1984).

local production raise the price of the protected product, thus discouraging consumption and creating a welfare loss for society. A more direct production subsidy (financed by a neutral tax) will cause fewer distortions in the economy. If the goal is employment creation, a direct subsidy for labor can be used. One of the incentives most frequently used to attract capital (that is, tariff exemption) tends to encourage its use in relatively capital-intensive activities and thus has little effect on employment. Similarly, some methods used to promote import substitution, save foreign exchange, and improve the balance of payments tend to promote an industrial structure that is heavily dependent on imports and unable to export. This section will discuss the criteria for granting incentives, the probable impact of the benefits found in most investment codes, as well as a broad range of interventions that affect investment decisions. More important than any of these, however, are the assurances and guarantees offered to reduce the risks faced by investors.

Measures to Enhance Investor Confidence

Surveys show that among the most decisive factors for foreign investors are political stability, favorable terms for the transfer of profits and the repatriation of capital, absence of discrimination against foreign ownership and control, and freedom from burdensome regulations. Predictability may be the most important assurance that can be offered to investors, who seem able to adapt to practically any conditions as long as the rules are clearly established and then followed carefully. Provision for compensation in the event of nationalization also falls into the category of necessary assurances. The presence of such factors reduces the risk associated with investing abroad, thereby reducing the rate of return demanded by the investor.

Investment Codes

African investment codes generally provide tariff and fiscal concessions to firms that meet certain conditions related to size, choice of sector, employment creation, location, and use of domestic raw materials. Although investment codes usually apply equally to domestic and foreign investment, they are aimed primarily at the latter. Investment codes signal the government's interest in creating a stable environment for investors, and many of them spell out guarantees to investors in areas such as repatriation of profits and equality of treatment for foreign firms. At the same time, investment codes, by establishing fixed rules, can relieve pressure on the government to make ad hoc concessions.

Tariff concessions are an integral part of many investment incentive packages. Material and equipment inputs to production are frequently exempt from import duties for a period of five to ten years but sometimes as long as fifteen to twenty-five years. Mauritania extends an exemption on raw materials and spare parts for twelve years to firms located outside main cities, and Niger gives exemptions of up to fifteen years to small enterprises. The exemptions often apply only to goods not produced domestically.

This benefit may be costly not only in terms of government revenue forgone but also in terms of productive efficiency because of distortions in the allocation of resources. Exemption from duties on capital equipment favors the use of capital over labor, since labor is usually taxed and is often paid a minimum wage greater than its opportunity cost. Thus, this exemption will tend to increase the capital-intensity of the production process. Highly sophisticated imported technology may also increase dependence on expensive expatriate technical staff. Furthermore, the duty exemption increases the rate of effective protection, thereby sheltering inefficient firms from competition and discouraging domestic production of the exempt goods. Thus, while protection fosters import substitution in final goods, it may actually increase the country's dependence on imports.

Tax holidays offer full or partial exemption from income and other taxes for a period generally ranging from five to ten years. Most African countries fall into this range, but Ivory Coast and Niger grant up to fifteen years. In some cases the length of the period of exemption varies directly with the size of the investment, while in others (mainly outside of Africa) it varies with the number of jobs created. Other criteria may also be used, including location, production of priority goods, and use of local raw materials.

Tax holidays allow firms to recover their capital more quickly and maintain greater liquidity in their early years. However, they also have limitations. A tax exemption is worthless if there is no tax liability, and many firms (particularly in infant industries) earn little profit in their early years. Some countries solve this problem by beginning the period of exemption not in the first year of operation but in the first year that profits are earned. Others, including Nigeria and Malawi, allow losses incurred during the holiday period to be written off against profits earned later.

As with tariff exemptions, the most obvious cost of a tax holiday is the revenue forgone by the government, although this is not a cost if the investment would not have been undertaken without the tax holiday. Another possible cost is the impact on resource allocation. Depending upon the tax system and how the tax holiday is applied, it may encourage short-term investments that cease when the holiday period ends. One way to ensure against excessive revenue loss if firms become profitable quickly is to set a ceiling on their benefits. Senegal restricts exempt earnings to 100 percent of the original investment, Liberia to 150 percent.

The attractiveness of tax concessions to foreign investors depends on the tax systems in their home countries. If the tax rate is at least as high in the home as in the host country, and if the two countries have no agreement preventing double taxation, tax holidays will have no effect on a firm's tax liability and will in fact merely transfer revenue from the host to the home country. For this reason, some countries have "tax-sparing" agreements whereby the investor's home country gives credit for taxes that would have been paid in the host country if no tax exemption had been given.

Employment Incentives

Employment creation is an objective of most industrialization programs. The instruments used to reach this goal range from general incentives for increased investment to subsidies for the use of labor. Many incentives seek to attract capital, which is scarce, in order to employ more labor. However, since many manufacturing processes can be carried out using various combinations of capital and labor, an incentive that reduces the price of capital may actually increase the ratio of capital to labor.

In a labor surplus economy, wage rates should be low enough to encourage labor-intensive industries with no further incentives. Neutral incentives to promote investment and growth generally, while leaving the relative costs of capital and labor unchanged, would be preferable from the point of view of productive efficiency. Distortions in the market, however, are frequently caused when minimum wages fix the cost of labor above its opportunity cost, thereby discouraging its use. Guaranteed employment or high severance pay have the same effect. Removal of the distortions is thus desirable. In Mauritius, for example, firms that specialize in production for export are exempt from indemnifying laid-off workers.

Incentives are sometimes awarded on the basis of the number of jobs created or the ratio of labor to capital. In Senegal, for example, enterprises can qualify for investment code benefits by investing two hundred million CFA francs and creating at least fifty jobs for Senegalese, or simply by creating one hundred jobs. The problem with this approach is that a firm may temporarily employ more labor than it really needs or use part-time labor to qualify for the concessions. Monitoring such practices is difficult.

Business Climate

Perhaps the main determinants of investment are those beyond the direct control of the government, such as political and economic stability, adequate markets, and availability of inputs. But the government does control other determinants—whether private investment is discriminated against, whether the terms for repatriation of profits are favorable, whether businesses are free of burdensome controls. These factors establish the basic investment climate, and without them all other incentives are likely to prove fruitless. Although tariff protection may be an important investment incentive in some cases, the evidence suggests that other incentives are not a significant factor in investment decisions.

A recent paper by Balassa analyzes the policies adopted in nineteen low- and middle-income Sub-Saharan African countries. Balassa distinguishes between market-oriented and interventionist countries, the former placing greater reliance on the price mechanism and market forces than the latter. The market-oriented economies include Botswana, Cameroon, the Ivory Coast, and Mauritius, while economies exhibiting the greatest degree of public intervention include Benin, Ethiopia, Ghana, Madagascar, Mali, Tanzania, and Zambia. An intermediate group consists of Burkina Faso, Kenya, Malawi, Niger, Senegal, Sudan, and Togo.[8]

8. Bela Balassa, "Adjustment Policies and Development Strategies in Sub-Saharan Africa," World Bank, Development Research Department, Discussion Paper DRD41, Washington, D.C., 1982.

During the 1973–79 period, the first group experienced average annual GNP growth rates of 6.8 percent, while the intermediate group averaged 3.5 percent and the interventionist group only 1.5 percent. In the same period, incremental capital-output ratios (ICORs) were lower in the market-oriented countries, while domestic savings rates were higher.[9]

Impact of Incentives in Ghana

Another study examined in a limited way the impact of investment incentives in Ghana.[10] The study estimated the effect of various interventions on the profitability in a single year (1972) of seven firms. It found that only two of the seven would have been profitable without the concessions, whereas the incentives allowed all but two to generate profits. Four of the firms earned excess profits, with actual rates of return ranging from 23 percent to nearly 600 percent. On the other hand, six of the seven firms generated large economic losses, which totaled nearly 60 percent of their gross output in economic prices. Protection of output provided the greatest incentive, contributing about 20 percent more than the investment concessions. Access to subsidized credit was also important.

Ghana's concessions were intended to promote efficient use of the country's resources, to earn foreign exchange, to promote interindustry linkages, to employ Ghanaians, and to promote investment in rural areas. The first two objectives were clearly not met by the firms in the sample, since only one was economically profitable to the country and, taken as a whole, the firms lost foreign exchange. There was little evidence of better linkages between the seven firms and other Ghanaian firms (most of the seven imported their inputs), the firms were mostly capital-intensive, and only one of them was located in a rural area. Thus, the concessions, while presumably costly to the government, did not help Ghana meet any of its objectives.

7.5 Removing Price Controls in Ghana
World Bank Staff

Ghana has used assorted price controls since 1962 for several purposes: to limit rents accruing to sellers in times of scarcity, to combat inflation, and to keep down prices of key items in the cost of living. But price controls have proven ineffective in times of extreme scarcity and rapid inflation and have often exacerbated the problems brought about by currency overvaluation and expansionary fiscal and monetary policies.

By 1970 nearly 6,000 prices relating to more than 700 product groups were controlled. Efforts to liberalize the system were reversed following a change

---

Reprinted from World Bank, *World Development Report 1987* (New York: Oxford University Press, 1987).

9. The higher the ICOR, the more capital is required to generate the same output; that is, the lower the efficiency rate of its use.

10. William D. Ingram and Scott R. Pearson, "The Impact of Investment Concessions on the Profitability of Selected Firms in Ghana," *Economic Development and Cultural Change* 29, no. 4 (July 1981): 831–39.

of government, and a Prices and Incomes Board was given authority over all price and wage changes. But with inflation reaching 100 percent a year during the 1970s, frequent requests for price adjustments greatly exceeded its administrative capacity. Delays of up to six months forced firms to choose between accumulating stocks, losing money by selling at the old price, or evading the controls altogether.

Rapid inflation increased the gap between market prices and official prices. Failure to adjust the exchange rate meant that imports through official channels cost as little as a tenth of their market value. Price controls prevented producers from realizing this scarcity rent, which would have given them extra incentive to produce more. But the inability to enforce controls at the retail level made trading an increasingly lucrative activity. Obtaining access to goods at the official price for resale—a practice known as *kalabule*—became an important source of income. By the early 1980s the market value of civil servants' monthly allocation of rice, milk, soap, and so forth (though not received regularly) could equal their monthly take-home pay.

Controls over distribution of scarce goods became increasingly important. During the 1970s, military trucks transported canned milk to the north for sale at the same price as in the southern cities of origin. But this greatly increased the profits from smuggling it to neighboring countries. Similarly, northern rice was smuggled out because price controls made it impossible to cover transport costs to the south. The tighter the controls on a commodity, the scarcer it became. The markets of Togo became well stocked with soap, milk, textiles, and other products that were made in Ghana and then smuggled out, while liquor and other luxuries with high scarcity premiums and less stringent controls were brought in. During the 1980s, land borders were closed for some time in an effort to stem smuggling, and storekeepers were forced to sell their stocks at controlled prices (often below what they had paid). But this worsened the scarcity of goods on the market and drove up prices further.

Price and distribution controls became interwoven with political power in 1982, as the new government attempted to broaden and decentralize political participation. Many of those who joined village and workers' committees were more concerned with obtaining access to goods at controlled prices than with the government's difficulty in subsequently moving away from controls.

As the economy worsened, the government recognized that price controls were not working and that economic recovery required shifting profits from black marketeers to producers. It reduced underlying distortions and inflationary pressures through a reform program introduced in April 1983 that featured devaluation and restrained fiscal and monetary management. The government also wished to lessen its direct responsibility for prices and distribution, which entailed high administrative costs as well as political pressures. Yet it could not totally abandon such controls while monopolies and excess profits were seen to exist and while it was also trying to restrain wage increases. It therefore adopted a strategy of gradually softening the enforcement of controls.

The first step was to shift most commodities to a system whereby most producers simply notified the Prices and Incomes Board of price changes; the board retained its right to intervene. The list of goods requiring prior approval was reduced first to twenty-three and gradually (over sixteen months) to eight, which greatly reduced the board's workload and turnaround time. Firms were permitted to charge a provisional price approved quickly by the board, and the review of its recommendations was shifted from the Ministry of Finance and Economic Planning to a tripartite commission with representatives from government, labor, and business. This public review process maintained the principle of intervening whenever changes were out of line, while eliminating the need to publish official prices.

The consumer price index rose by only 10 percent in 1985, the year after price controls were eased; inflation had fallen from 122 percent in 1983 to 40 percent in 1984 following the introduction of the reform program. The inflationary impact of massive devaluations and price liberalization during 1983–85 was limited because market prices already reflected scarcities and because various measures operated to reduce the gap between supply and demand. On the supply side, the incentive effects of price liberalization helped in four ways: hoarded consumer goods were released, scarcity rents were shifted from distributors to producers, agricultural producers responded to favorable rainfalls by greatly increasing food availability, and industrial producers sought additional foreign exchange through a newly opened auction window for foreign exchange. On the demand side, the ability of consumers to absorb price increases was limited through fiscal and monetary restraint.

These policies generally improved the market situation. Increased local supplies of some commodities such as milk, bread, soap, and beer brought market prices down, sometimes below the previous official prices, while increased imports eliminated scarcity rents for other goods (for example, tires and vegetable oil).

Three main factors contributed to the success of Ghana's liberalization of price controls, First, market prices already reflected scarcities, so that liberalization mainly shifted scarcity rents from distributors to producers. Second, complementary policies helped raise marketed supplies and restrain inflationary pressures, so that consumer resistance was minimized. Third, price control enforcement was depoliticized by permitting provisional price changes while retaining the right of review and by including representatives of interested groups in the review process.

7.6 *Investment Promotion and Policies in Malawi*
World Bank Staff

Industrial development in Malawi faces four major constraints. The domestic market is small in absolute size and particularly in purchasing power. The geographical location results in both extremely high transport costs for overseas trade and a continuing threat of serious disruption of flows. Access to markets in neighboring countries is irregular because of a variety of foreign

---

Excerpted, edited, and updated from "Malawi: The Development of Manufacturing," World Bank Eastern Africa Regional Office, May 1981 (restricted circulation).

exchange problems and import controls. Finally, technical, professional, and managerial skills and experience are scarce.

The broad objectives of Malawi's industrial policy are

- A conducive environment for private foreign and domestic investment
- Selective promotion of import substitution, and more general support for export-oriented industry, to exploit Malawi's low labor costs and primary raw materials
- Integration within and between industries, especially those involving primary raw materials
- Promotion of small-scale industry and technologies appropriate to Malawi's economic conditions
- Development of an indigenous Malawian entrepreneurial class and continued training of Malawians in technical and managerial skills
- More balanced regional distribution of economic activity
- Limitation of licensing and controls to areas in which social costs exceed private costs or competition is inadequate
- Parastatal investment where an economically viable opportunity has been identified but adequate private investment is not forthcoming.

But Malawian policymakers, particularly in the industrial field, are faced with a dilemma. The Malawian economy, and even more so the industrial sector, is very small, indeed so small that the economies of scale for production of many goods, particularly manufactured goods, justify few plants or only one to satisfy demand in the local market. One way to avoid monopolistic pricing practices in such a situation is to expose local producers to competition from imports. Since 1985, however, import competition has been limited by restrictive trade policies (which are slated for liberalization by 1989), and the government has regulated investment and pricing to minimize uneconomic decisions in the protected, monopolistic environment.

Allocation of Investment

Investment is regulated mainly through licensing of new investments. Otherwise, central government institutions exercise little direct influence on industrial development except through overall industrial policy formulation and through a process of subtle persuasion.

Several facts support the view that policies have been implemented fairly well. First, manufacturing output has grown quite satisfactorily since independence. Second, there has not yet been a large industrial investment that turned out to be a white elephant. Third, even at the level of medium-size investment projects, real failures have been rare, although some projects have needed prolonged special support. The government is well aware that many industries remain "infants" longer than expected, more because of unreasonable expectations about what can be achieved within a few years than because of mistakes in investment decisions or inefficient project implementation.

The system has been implemented in a reasonably nonrestrictive way, at least for indigenous investors, because its managers and technicians share a strong basic commitment to a free enterprise system in which the government keeps a low profile even while exercising regulatory functions. The present system could easily be misused by people with different objectives or could be mishandled by less competent people. This dependence on a relatively limited number of highly competent and motivated individuals might be considered its major weakness. Technically, the most difficult decisions involve new industrial projects with substantial economies of scale. The Malawian economy is so small that a major mistake on a large project could have very serious consequences. The approach is to rely on investors (including parastatal management) to make the basic decisions, with the government playing an oversight role.

Malawian authorities have tried to counter the sociopolitical problem of potentially excessive concentration of economic power through the creation of parastatals. Although fairly autonomous, these institutions in the last analysis remain responsible to the government, and therefore the government should be in a position to prevent abuse of their power. Nevertheless, the emphasis on parastatals tends to introduce a bias against small-scale industrial enterprises since large-scale enterprises can attract better management, have greater access to credit, and tend to be favored by administrative decisions. As a result, plant sizes are larger than required in some industries, such as bakeries, seed processing, and fish processing.

On the other hand, the potential for small-scale industrial enterprises (excluding artisans and craftsmen) is limited since Malawi's industry in general is not yet large enough to farm out production of parts and components to small-scale firms. In principle, the government wishes to promote small-scale enterprises owned and run by Malawians, but while there are substantial numbers of artisans and craftsmen, there are few Malawians capable of financing, starting up, and running a small industrial enterprise. Whatever talent exists is rapidly absorbed into larger industrial enterprises, which are eager to increase the number of Malawians in middle- and upper-management positions. In spite of the government's commitment to the development of small-scale enterprise (of all types, that is, not only industrial), it has not succeeded so far in preparing a comprehensive plan to implement this policy.

Pricing

Price controls apply only to relatively few, although important, commodities. Therefore, control has been supplemented with an informal system of price administration that enables the Ministry of Trade, Industry, and Tourism to intervene whenever it feels that price increases are higher than what is needed to keep enterprises financially sound. Informal pressures are sometimes applied to delay politically sensitive price increases.

Delays in formal or informal price approvals constitute the principal private sector criticism of the government's industrial policy. Such delays—as long as twelve months—weaken companies' financial positions and may affect product mix. Reportedly, firms that originally manufactured essentials (which are subject to particularly stringent price controls) are diversifying into nonessentials (which are usually more profitable and less subject to price restraint) to cross-subsidize their output of essentials. The danger is that eventually the firms might reduce or drop production of essentials. The government thus needs to find a workable balance between its desire to keep down inflation and the need to provide sufficient incentives for producers to continue, or expand, their production of essential goods.

Compared with the wealth of laws, decrees, and regulations in many developed and developing countries, industrial policy in Malawi appears to be surprisingly lean. This moderation in formal policymaking is, of course, made possible by the informal influence the government has exerted on industrial developments. In Malawi's special situation, this has proven to be an effective way to provide some protection in a monopolistic market situation. As long as the system is handled with reasonable restraint, it is likely to produce reasonably good results.

The Small-Scale Sector and Entrepreneurship

8.1 Magnitude and Importance of Small-Scale Industry
Carl Liedholm and Donald C. Mead

The role of small-scale industries in African development has recently emerged as an important concern. The Lagos Plan of Action, for example, argues that as part of their industrial strategies, countries should aim at creating "a network of small- and medium-scale industries as well as actively promoting and encouraging the informal sector." Even today, however, relatively little is known about these activities in Africa. Consequently, policymakers and planners charged with formulating programs to assist small-scale industry are frequently forced to make decisions "unencumbered by evidence."

[Here we set] forth what is known about small-scale industries in Sub-Saharan Africa and the implications of these findings for policies and programs. "Small-scale" is defined as those establishments with fewer than 50 workers. Although somewhat arbitrary, such a limitation excludes most foreign-owned firms and those with more modern and sophisticated management skills, more capital-intensive production techniques, and greater access to capital, technical assistance, and government incentive schemes.

Overall Magnitude and Importance

The available evidence indicates that small-scale firms are a significant if not dominant component of the industrial sectors of most African countries. Not only are the overwhelming majority of industrial establishments small, but they account for the vast bulk of industrial employment. Small-scale firms in countries with the required data generally account for two-thirds or more of

Excerpted by permission from Carl Liedholm and Donald C. Mead, "Small-Scale Industry in Sub-Saharan Africa: Empirical Evidence and Strategic Implications," in Bob Berg and Jennifer Whitaker, eds., *Strategies for African Development* (Berkeley: University of California Press, 1986).

186

total industrial employment; indeed, for one country, Sierra Leone, with quite complete and accurate data, the figure is 95 percent. Moreover, most of the employment is concentrated at the smallest end of the size spectrum, with relatively less employment found in firms in the 10 to 49 worker size range. Small-scale firms also generate an important portion of the value-added of Africa's industrial sectors, although their share of value-added is not as great as their employment contribution.

COMPOSITION. An examination of available data indicates that clothing production—primarily tailoring—predominates in most countries, ranging from 25 percent of all establishments in rural Burkina Faso to 52 percent in Nigeria. Wood production—primarily furniture-making—follows, with metal-working (usually blacksmithing), food production (primarily baking), and vehicle, shoe, electrical, and bicycle repairs also found with some frequency. In the rural areas of several countries, such as Burkina Faso and Botswana, beer brewing is a dominant activity, usually undertaken by women. In general, small-scale firms are involved in the production of "light" consumer goods—clothing, furniture, simple tools, food, and drink.

LOCATION. A surprising yet significant finding is that, in most countries, the vast majority of small industries are located in rural areas. Moreover, employment in small rural manufacturing industries often exceeds that generated by all urban manufacturing firms. In Sierra Leone, for example, 86 percent of total industrial sector employment and 95 percent of industrial establishments were located in rural areas. Similar findings have been reported elsewhere in Africa. These figures may actually understate the true magnitude of rural industry because country censuses often fail to register the smallest of the rural industries.

SIZE. The overwhelming majority of these firms are very small, with most employing fewer than five persons. Studies in Nigeria, Sierra Leone, and Ghana have found that 95 percent or more of the small-scale firms employ fewer than five individuals. Many are simply one-person enterprises. In rural Burkina Faso, for example, 52 percent of the small-scale firms were one-person activities, while in Sierra Leone the figure was 42 percent. Such findings indicate that most small-scale industrial firms in Sub-Saharan Africa are [small indeed].

OWNERSHIP. The available evidence indicates that the overwhelming majority of small firms are organized as sole proprietorships. In Nigeria, Sierra Leone, and Burkina Faso, for example, over 97 percent of the small firms are set up in this fashion. Female sole proprietors dominate certain small industries in a number of countries, such as beer brewing in Burkina Faso, Botswana, and Ghana, gara dyeing in Sierra Leone, and clothing production in Ghana. There are a few limited liability companies, partnerships, and cooperatives, but almost no small enterprises in the public sector.

LABOR AND CAPITAL. A review of the available data indicates that hired labor is generally a minor component of the labor force in small enterprises. Apprentices play a dominant role in parts of West Africa (Nigeria, Ghana, and Sierra Leone), but are quite minor elements of the labor force in East Africa, where the tradition of an organized, indigenous apprenticeship system is lacking. Proprietors and family workers play a key role in small-scale industries. Most entrepreneurs have little formal education, have learned their technical skills as apprentices in other small-scale enterprises, and lack extensive training in marketing, financing, or management.

The overwhelming source of capital, either for establishing or expanding firms, is personal savings, relatives, or retained earnings. In these countries, less than 4 percent of the funds come from formal sources such as the commercial banking system or the government.

GROWTH. Although systematic information on industrial growth is limited, available evidence indicates that small-scale industrial activity in Africa has been increasing. Small-industry employment, for example, grew at a 6 percent annual rate during the 1960s in Ghana and at the same rate over the 1974–80 period in Sierra Leone. Whether small-scale industry has been increasing at a faster rate than large-scale is not clear. In Sierra Leone, small-scale employment grew at a faster rate than large-scale, but in Ghana, the opposite pattern occurred. Nevertheless, since small-scale industries account for such a large portion of industrial employment, even if small producers were to grow at slower rates than the large, the absolute increases in small-scale employment could still be substantial. In Ghana during the 1960s, for example, small-scale industries absorbed five times as many workers as the large-scale firms, although the latter grew at a faster rate.

Limited evidence from Sierra Leone and from other developing countries outside of Africa indicates that one-person firms are increasing the least rapidly (indeed, in Sierra Leone they were declining), while those in the 10 to 49 worker size group are growing the fastest. The number of and employment in small firms appear to be growing the most rapidly in the urban areas. In Sierra Leone, for example, small-industry employment grew at a 6 percent annual rate from 1974 to 1980 in urban areas, but at less than half that rate in rural areas.

By enterprise types, food-related activities (such as baking and milling), tailoring and dressmaking, furniture-making, and metal-working have generally grown rapidly, even after large-scale domestic factory production in these sub-sectors has begun. Moreover, several newer activities, such as bicycle, auto, and electrical repair, have grown especially rapidly. On the other hand, activities such as spinning and weaving, shoe and leather goods production, and pottery generally appear to have been declining in importance.

Determinants of the Role of Small-Scale Industry

DEMAND PROSPECTS. The overwhelming bulk of products made in small firms are simple consumer goods that cater primarily to the needs of relatively low-income urban and rural households. Consequently, a key issue is whether the demand for these products increases as local incomes increase. Most entrepreneurial surveys in Africa indicate that lack of demand is an important constraint facing most small firms. Although some have argued that these types of products are inferior (i.e., demand for them would decline as incomes increase), the few empirical studies indicate that there is a strong, positive relationship between local income and demand for small-scale industry products.

In Sierra Leone, for example, [it is] reported that an income increase of 10 percent would increase the demand for the products of small-scale firms by almost 9 percent. Consequently, the growth of demand for small-scale industry products would appear to be closely linked to corresponding increases in household income, particularly among the rural and low-income segments of the population.

Are there important sources of demand for small-industry products that stem from their backward and forward production linkages with other segments of the economy? In general, these sources of demand appear to be less developed in Sub-Saharan Africa than in other parts of the developing world. The strongest of these production linkages in Sub-Saharan Africa, however, are found in the agricultural sector, where the processing of several crops, such as rice and oil palm in West Africa, and the production of implements for traditional agriculture are frequently undertaken by small-scale firms. Production linkages with large-scale industry appear particularly weak in Sub-Saharan Africa.

Further, foreign demand for small-industry products is relatively small, limited to a few specialty products such as gara-dyed cloth from Sierra Leone and baskets from Botswana.

SUPPLY FACTORS. Small-scale industries are generally more labor-intensive than their larger-scale counterparts. Since capital and foreign exchange are relatively scarce in Sub-Saharan Africa, and labor, particularly unskilled, is relatively abundant, those firms that generate more employment per unit of capital would appear to represent activities or techniques most appropriate to the country's factor endowments. Both aggregate and industry-specific data consistently show that small firms in Sub-Saharan Africa generate more employment per unit of scarce capital than their large-scale counterparts.

A key related issue is whether these same labor-intensive small-scale firms use the scarce factor of capital more effectively than their larger-scale counterparts. Aggregate data are limited and do not show consistent results. A few industry-specific studies have been completed in which firms in the same industry are grouped together. The findings from these studies indicate that small-scale firms in these industries generate more output per unit of scarce capital than their larger-scale counterparts.

Do these same small enterprises also generate a higher rate of "economic profit" than their larger-scale counterparts? The economic rate of return to capital, a measure that reflects profit when all inputs including family labor and capital are valued at their opportunity cost, may be a better measure of economic efficiency or total factor productivity than the output-capital ratio, which assumes that labor and other factor inputs have a "shadow price" of zero. Although economic profitability data are limited, the available results are consistent with the previous capital productivity findings: small-scale firms generated higher "economic" rates of return to capital than did their larger-scale industrial counterparts. While not conclusive, these findings do indicate that in several lines of activity, small-scale industries are economically efficient.

8.2 *The Policy Environment for Small-Scale Enterprises*
John M. Page, Jr., and William F. Steel

Two elements of the economic environment result in insufficient investment in small-scale enterprises (SSEs). The first is trade, investment, and other policies that implicitly favor large-scale industry. The second is capital market failures, which may preclude adequate investment in small-scale industry even where lending policies are neutral with respect to size.

Policy Biases

A common problem of small-scale enterprises in less developed countries is inadequate access to imported capital goods, intermediate inputs, and spare parts. Foreign trade regimes that employ rationing systems for imports, coupled with overvaluation of the exchange rate, tend to favor large-scale, modern enterprises that can exercise substantial political and economic power. Direct allocations of import licenses to large-scale firms provide an implicit subsidy. Small firms that are excluded from direct access to import licenses are subject to both higher prices of imported inputs and greater uncertainty of supply. Even where foreign exchange allocations are potentially available to small firms, they remain at a disadvantage because of their limited administrative resources and their consequent inability to undertake the bureaucratic procedures required to obtain an import license. Even in economies where direct controls are not employed, the structure of protection that has evolved in support of an import-substitution strategy frequently discriminates against small firms. In Cameroon, Kenya, and Sierra Leone, for example, small firms producing manufactured goods were not entitled to duty drawbacks on imported intermediates of the same scope and magnitude as large firms during the 1970s.

Capital Market Failures

Government policy in many African countries has acted to suppress the real rate of interest for both deposits and loans. Faced with demands in excess of the funds available, the banking system has generally responded by rationing credit and by holding low-risk portfolios. Venture capital for industrialization has been provided to large-scale firms via public sector loan windows, often

Excerpted and edited from John M. Page, Jr., and William F. Steel, *Small Enterprise Development: Economic Issues from African Experience*, World Bank Technical Paper 26 (Washington, D.C., 1984).

at highly subsidized rates of interest, while small-scale enterprises have been excluded from the commercial credit market both by their higher level of risk and because of the greater unit costs of administering small loans. Government regulations concerning quality standards, technical specifications, and procurement also are biased against the output of small enterprises.

Current policy initiatives in several countries appear intended to redress this bias against small enterprises by creating additional public lending institutions, by providing guarantees for a portion of commercial bank loans to small enterprises, or by setting aside a specific portion of commercial bank funds for the exclusive use of small-scale borrowers. In very few cases, however, have these programs achieved significant results. Where public lending institutions have been created to channel credit to the small enterprise sector, rates of interest have generally been lower than or similar to those charged to large-scale enterprises. Requirements that a portion of the loan portfolio of the commercial banks be reserved for the use of small enterprises have resulted in slow disbursement and have not greatly increased loans to the intended recipients.

Thus, in most countries, interventions by the state in the markets for foreign exchange and capital have tended to discriminate against small firms. Small enterprises therefore represent a smaller proportion of industrial firms than would be the case under more neutral policies on protection and interest rates.

Program Design

In designing programs and policies, it is essential to know the ultimate development objective. Is it increased employment per se or higher and more equitably distributed incomes? Since in African countries there is very little open unemployment in the sense of workers unable to find any source of income, it may be argued that it is the nature and productivity of employment that is important, not the number of jobs as such. Although employment and productivity ideally grow together, measures to promote employment simply by favoring increased labor intensity may reduce the average level of output per worker. Investments that use labor unproductively do not promote development, whereas investment that raises output by improving productivity or efficiency may be beneficial even if it does not increase employment. In other words, the object of expanding the SSE sector should be not simply to provide employment but to increase *productive employment* in a way that improves the utilization of resources and the distribution of income.

The next question is whether it is supply or demand constraints that cause employment and productivity in SSEs to be less than what is wanted. Analysis of these constraints in particular situations is necessary to determine the appropriate measures to take. Otherwise, the measures may introduce new distortions instead of correcting existing ones. Supply constraints that are commonly found include lack of access to investment and working capital, problems of raw material supply, lack of skilled labor, insufficient training and knowledge, inadequate infrastructure, and inappropriate equipment. Demand side constraints include weak aggregate demand, unequal distribution of income, and competition from subsidized large-scale industries and imports. Government regulations also may discourage investment or growth in SSES.

Supply-Oriented Measures

FINANCIAL ASSISTANCE. Programs to channel more credit to SSES are probably the commonest approach used to assist them. Such programs are intended to overcome the lack of access to institutionalized credit that characterizes SSES. The risk of this approach is that if lack of access is the reason for relatively high labor intensity and capital productivity in SSES, making capital available on favorable terms may encourage small firms to use capital more intensively and less productively. Subsidized credit programs also risk replacing the personal savings that typically are the source of investment in SSES. Inadequate attention is often given to financing working capital in established SSES, which can make existing investment and workers more productive. When the credit for special finance programs comes from outside the country, there is a risk of substituting foreign for domestic capital, contrary to the intended objective. Hence, programs financed by outside donors must be designed to ensure that they complement rather than replace domestic savings.

TECHNICAL ASSISTANCE AND TRAINING. Assistance and training in managerial, financial, and technical skills are essential components of any program to develop SSES. Especially for smaller firms, whose owners tend to be trades people rather than experienced entrepreneurs, such assistance may be more important than credit. For SSES with machinery, assistance in its utilization, maintenance, and repair can raise the productivity of capital. There is insufficient knowledge, however, about how to provide technical services and training effectively. Past efforts to provide technical assistance have had difficulty in identifying and reaching recipients. These services must be provided through extension programs that reach managers and workers in their establishments, a process that is at least as difficult as agricultural extension. A nominal charge may be useful to make potential users appreciate the value of the services offered.

TECHNOLOGY. Lack of appropriate technology is rarely cited by SSE entrepreneurs as a problem. Nevertheless, development of techniques that can be used efficiently in small-scale units is a potentially dynamic approach to stimulating both employment and productivity growth. Public as well as private funds for research and development have been concentrated almost exclusively on techniques suitable for large, capital-intensive undertakings. In this context, greater support for intermediate technology development may be justified, although it must be accompanied by measures to ensure marketing, proper utilization, and servicing of new techniques.

INFRASTRUCTURE. Direct provision of infrastructure, usually in the form of industrial estates, has been used in some countries (especially in Asia) to help

SSEs get established. This approach, however, does not seem suited to Africa, except where the principal objective is to help medium-scale domestic enterprises compete with foreign firms. Industrial estates would not be attractive to entrepreneurs wishing to remain outside the formal sector, and in any case the total investment per worker is likely to be so high as to contradict the labor-intensity argument for promoting SSEs. Part of the rationale for a SSE strategy in Africa is that it does not require substantial prior investment in infrastructure.

INPUT SUPPLIES. Although SSEs are much less dependent on imported inputs than are larger firms, their ability to produce is often constrained by the lack of certain critical materials (for example, baking powder and yeast), spare parts (for example, grinding wheels for small corn mills), or capital goods (for example, carpenter's tools). SSEs in Africa encounter two types of input supply problems: obtaining imported materials and spare parts when imports are licensed or otherwise restricted, and obtaining supplies that are controlled by a state marketing agency. SSEs are too small to be able to deal effectively with government administrative mechanisms and so have difficulties obtaining these supplies directly. A government that is serious about assisting SSEs must consider their needs in allocating foreign exchange and domestic materials. Where cooperatives and manufacturers' associations already exist, governments can encourage them to act as agents for their members in obtaining materials.

Demand-Oriented Measures and Policy Environment

INCOME LEVEL AND DISTRIBUTION. Demand-side measures are a less obvious way of assisting SSEs than supply-oriented interventions, but they may well be more important. SSEs have consistently been found to be very responsive to market opportunities. Since the income elasticity of demand for SSE products is thought to be relatively high among the lower-income population, measures that promote rapid growth of this population's income would tend to stimulate the SSE sector. SSEs have a definite advantage over large-scale firms in being able to locate closer to dispersed rural sources of increased demand for nonagricultural goods and services.

PROTECTION. Large-scale firms are often subsidized through low interest rates, incentive schemes, tax rebates, and allocation of scarce foreign exchange while being protected from foreign competition by tariffs and import restrictions. Such measures may give them an advantage over more economically efficient SSEs. Restoring competitive conditions by reducing subsidies and protection may be politically difficult, especially if the government wishes to take visible measures to promote private investment and industrialization. Devaluation can be used to reduce the need for tariff protection and quantitative restrictions; a higher cost of imported goods protects all producers (including agriculture as well as industry) and provides incentives to export and to utilize local inputs. A second-best solution is to provide corresponding protection to SSEs. Efforts to include SSEs under incentive-tax rebate schemes, however, are likely to benefit only the larger SSE firms that can deal effectively with formal requirements, to the worsening disadvantage of the smaller (and more labor-intensive) enterprises. A more suitable approach is to avoid giving special benefits to large-scale investments in goods that are already supplied by SSEs.

REGULATIONS. The environment created by public laws, regulations, and policies often has a negative effect on SSEs even when the government's official policy is to help SSEs. Enterprises that are too small to comply readily with registration and tax laws are forced to remain clandestine or to submit to policy harassment. On the other hand, exemption of SSEs would sharpen the line between formal and informal sectors and discourage firms from expanding to the size covered by the laws. Local governments can maintain a conducive environment through zoning regulations that allow small enterprises to operate.

8.3 Factor Markets
John M. Page, Jr.

Evidence that small enterprises are largely excluded from access to commercial and public banks is ubiquitous in Africa. Table 8.3.1 summarizes data from studies in several countries regarding the sources of funds for initial capital investments by small- and very small-scale firms. Personal savings supplemented by loans or gifts from relatives dwarf all other sources of funds, consistently representing more than 80 percent of initial investment capital.

Availability of Capital

The paucity of funds obtained from commercial banks or public development agencies is striking. Only in Ghana and Kenya do combined borrowings from public and private lending institutions approach 10 percent of initial investment. In most of the surveys, less than 1 percent of the respondents reported success in obtaining a public or private sector loan.

The causes of such exclusion are difficult to pinpoint and vary to some extent with the institutional characteristics of individual countries. Public agencies, including development banks, have until quite recently ignored small enterprise lending. Lack of administrative capacity to screen loans, as well as failure of initiative on the part of lending agencies, have reduced the effectiveness of public agencies even where loan windows for small-scale enterprise (SSE) promotion have been created. In Ghana, experience with a SSE loan scheme was characterized by progressive increases in the size of disbursements and discrimination against small borrowers. Reports on public lending agencies in Kenya provide similar anecdotal evidence of lack of initiative and favoritism toward large-scale established applicants. Studies of

Excerpted and edited from John M. Page, Jr., *Small Enterprises in African Development: A Survey,* World Bank Staff Working Paper 363 (Washington, D.C., 1979).

Table 8.3.1 *Sources of Finance for Initial Investment by Small Enterprises in Some African Countries*
(percentage of initial investment by source)

Source of finance	Nigeria Western region	Nigeria Ibadan	Ghana	Tanzania	Sierra Leone	Uganda
Own savings	97.7	59.0	90.8	78.0	60.2	77.5
Relatives	1.9	35.0		15.0	19.5	—
Banks	0.02	2.0	10.8	1.0	0.9	0.8
Government	—			1.0	—	—
Moneylenders	0.03	—	—	—	0.9	—
Other	—	4.0	—	6.0	18.3	21.7

—Not included.

Sources: S. A. Aluko, O. A. Oguntoye, and Y. A. O. Afoja, *Small-Scale Industries: Western State of Nigeria* (Ile-Ife, Nigeria: University of Ife, 1972); George R. Bosa, *The Financing of Small-Scale Enterprises in Uganda* (New York: Oxford University Press, 1972); Carl Liedholm and E. Chuta, "The Economics of Rural and Urban Small-Scale Industries in Sierra Leone," Michigan State University, African Rural Economy Paper 14, 1976; Karl Schadler, *Crafts, Small-Scale Industries and Industrial Education in Tanzania* (Munich: Weltforum Verlag, 1968); and William F. Steel, *Small-Scale Employment and Production in Developing Countries* (New York: Praeger, 1977).

financial institutions in Cameroon, Nigeria, Sierra Leone, Uganda, and Zambia similarly indicate that government credit schemes have been ineffective in meeting the needs of small-scale borrowers.

Private bank lending to small firms is limited by the high administrative cost of loans to smaller firms and by the greater perceived risk of default. A direct solution to this problem would be to allow lenders to charge differential rates by category of borrower, but that is frequently prohibited by government banking regulations. In addition to the higher real costs of small-scale lending, some evidence exists that small enterprises are the victims of extralegal charges on the part of bank officials.

Despite the SSE sector's isolation from the institutional market for credit, neither suppliers' credits nor the curb market appear to be significant sources of initial capital funds. Small-scale, informal credit markets are well established in Africa, and two surveys reveal that moneylenders provide a small portion of the initial capital for intermediate sector activities. They are not, however, a major source of investment funds to small manufacturing activities.

The predominance of self-finance for small-scale firms suggests that a major contribution of the SSE sector may be in generating new savings. Little evidence exists, however, concerning the savings behavior of small entrepreneurs. Savings out of wage income or profits from trading predominate as sources of investment capital. In addition, savings from agriculture represent approximately one-third of initial small-scale investments.

A similar pattern of limited access to institutional credit emerges when data on the sources of funds for expansion and working capital are examined. Investments for the expansion of existing enterprises are overwhelmingly financed out of retained earnings. Commercial banks and public institutions provide a greater proportion of the funds for expansion than for new investment, but in no survey did the proportion of firms receiving credit from public or private banks exceed 25 percent.

Lack of access to commercial credit is perhaps most acute as a problem for small firms in obtaining adequate working capital. Respondents to several surveys identified insufficient working capital as a major constraint on their ability to maintain adequate stocks of finished goods and raw materials. The credit squeeze is exacerbated by business practices that require firms to extend credit to purchasers but to pay cash for inputs. Contracts with the government in particular have been identified as a major problem for small-scale suppliers, owing to excessive delays in payments.

An estimate of the opportunity cost of capital to small enterprises is of crucial importance to an understanding of the question of relative factor intensities. High rental costs of capital to small-scale firms relative to those for modern industry would support the contention that the observed labor intensity of small-scale firms represents an efficient adaptation to relative factor prices.

One analyst reported rates of interest on commercial and development bank loans to small enterprises in Kenya in the range of 8.5 to 9.5 percent. Computation of the implicit interest rate from repayment schedules provided by loan recipients indicated that the effective interest rates on such loans were in the range of 12 to 20 percent. Another study reports that the rate of interest on Ghanaian commercial bank loans to small enterprises was approximately 13 percent in 1973. Other studies report similar magnitudes for commercial and development bank loans to small borrowers.

Evidence on the interest rates charged by noninstitutional lenders is severely limited, but rates in excess of 100 percent per annum have been documented. In large measure, these high rates of interest reflect the real costs of providing credit in small amounts. The unit costs associated with gathering information and transacting loans, each of which is small, are substantial.

The major unanswered question regarding the opportunity cost of capital to small enterprise is the magnitude of the alternative returns to funds provided out of personal and family savings. Opportunity costs for self-finance may lie below those for borrowed-in funds by an amount equal to the real costs of providing credit. Given extreme capital market segmentation, it has been said that the interest rate premium is approximately 10 percent. This suggests that the opportunity cost of funds provided from retained earnings may lie in the range of 15 to 25 percent.

Overall, the pattern that emerges is one of an intermediate sector with limited access to institutional credit markets and principally financed by individual entrepreneurs. These capital funds are generated in agriculture, in the sse and informal sectors, and in wage employment in modern industry or services. Rates of interest on borrowed funds and the opportunity cost of self-financed investments exceed 20 percent and may be as high as 35 to 50 percent. Rates of return to small-scale enterprises are similarly high, although they exhibit great variability.

It is apparent that a significant difference exists between the rates of interest paid by modern large-scale enterprises and the sse sector. Capital is relatively scarce for small firms and they therefore have greater incentives to conserve its use. The observed labor intensity of small enterprises is undoubtedly in part a reflection of this fact.

Labor Markets

Differences in the wages for labor between the modern formal sector and small-scale enterprise are relevant both to the choice of production technique and to the ability of small firms to compete with larger enterprises. If labor markets are imperfect, small firms may be able to match the unit costs of technically superior enterprises because their wage costs are substantially lower. Thus, inferences concerning the relative efficiency of small enterprises based upon their survival or profitability are irrelevant.

There appears to be general agreement that wages in the formal sectors of most African economies are relatively unresponsive to labor market conditions and are downwardly rigid. Among the sources of this rigidity are the apparent propensity of foreign firms to pay wages in excess of the competitive wage, the predominance of public sector enterprises paying high wages to unskilled labor, union pressures that cause productivity gains to be translated into wage increases, and minimum wage legislation. Evidence from East Africa supports the hypothesis that urban wages did not decline in response to the pressure of an excess supply of labor in the 1960s. In fact, wages in the urban formal sector increased in the period between 1960 and 1970, resulting in a substantial rural-urban income differential.[1]

In contrast, lack of barriers to entry in the unprotected sectors of the urban economy should make the urban wage outside the formal sector responsive to changes in the supply of labor. In those activities characterized by very low barriers to entry—personal services and petty commerce, for example—it has been argued that disguised employment may exist since the marginal product of labor can be driven to zero if the supply of labor is sufficiently large. Additions to employment become a means of sharing income, and the wage depends on the supply of workers available to the sector.

The SSE sector, characterized by some form of barriers to entry due to the presence of physical or human capital requirements, lie between these two extremes. Because they are largely unregistered, small enterprises escape paying the minimum wage commonly found in the formal sector of most African economies and usually avoid employers' contributions to social insurance schemes. Moreover, there is reason to believe that the wage in the SSE sector is responsive to changes in the labor supply. Because apprentice labor is overwhelmingly the primary source of labor input to artisanal firms, increases in the number of individuals seeking apprentice training should reduce the net cost to employers.

---

1. In the mid-1980s, however, a combination of declining per capita incomes and reform programs that include devaluation and higher agricultural producer prices ''have helped to raise the terms of trade between the countryside and the city'' (World Bank, *Financing Adjustment with Growth in Sub-Saharan Africa, 1986–90*. Washington, D.C., 1986, p. 21). Furthermore, aggregate data may mask changes for new workers, as shown in section 8.4.

That a wage gap exists between small and large firms is clear. The magnitude of the gap, however, is variable and difficult to identify. Various studies report differentials for unskilled labor in Senegal and Upper Volta on the order of 50 percent. Evidence from Zaire and Egypt indicates that although SSE sector wages equal or exceed the legal minimum wage, they fall short of the actual wages paid to unskilled workers in the modern private or public sector. All of the studies concur that wages for labor in small-scale industry exceed annual incomes in the agricultural sector, but no comparisons exist between incomes in urban casual employment and small enterprises. Differences in the wage rates between the large-scale and SSE sectors partly reflect divergences in skill levels and labor turnover. In sum, a wage gap exists, but the real differential is probably not as large as the nominal difference in wage rates for unskilled labor.

8.4 *Labor Market Adjustment in Côte d'Ivoire*
   Victor Lavy and John Newman

The case of Côte d'Ivoire demonstrates that reliance on aggregate data can lead to erroneous conclusions concerning the role of real wages in labor market adjustment during a recession. Using data from the 1979 and 1984 censuses of firms and employees in the private and semipublic sectors, we find that the aggregate data indicate countercyclical movement in real wages, whereas the micro data indicate a procyclical movement and an employment loss nearly twice as great as that perceived using the aggregate data. The micro data also reveal that roughly as many firms entered as exited during the recession, but the new entrants were much smaller and therefore did not compensate for the employment loss.

In 1981, the government initiated a drastic financial recovery and structural adjustment program that called for a reduction in the public sector deficit, a decline in the current account deficit, restoration of overall balance of payments equilibrium, removal of price distortions, and incentives to improve resource allocation. The government instituted a 24 percent cut in real public investment that year, followed in 1983 by a further 20 percent decline in public expenditures. The contractionary measures contributed to a deepening recession between 1981 and 1984.

Modern sector employment decreased from 248,350 employees in 1979 to 207,793 in 1984, while the number of firms rose from 3,243 to 4,231 (table 8.4.1). Of these firms, however, 1,106 were established before 1979 but were not included in the 1979 survey. Roughly two out of every three firms in the 1979 survey had gone out of business by 1984, accounting for 66 percent of all job losses. Although the number of exiting firms exceeded new entrants by only 127, the 25,853 jobs contributed by entering firms were far from sufficient to compensate for the 67,511 jobs lost through the closure of firms.

Excerpted and edited from Victor Lavy and John Newman, ''Labor Market Adjustment during a Recession: The Micro and Macro Evidence,'' World Bank, Welfare and Human Resources Division, Living Standards Measurement Study Working Paper, February 1988.

Table 8.4.1 *Number of Firms and Employees and Weighted Average Real Wage in Côte d'Ivoire, 1979 and 1984*

	1979			1984			
Item	Firms	Employees	*Average real wage per month (thousands of* CFA *francs)*	Firms	Employees	*Average real wage per month (thousands of* CFA *francs)*	*Percentage change*
Survivors	1,079	180,839	951	1,088	145,741	1,103	16
Exits	2,164	67,511	929	—	—	—	—
Entries	—	—	—	2,037	25,853	1,114	—
Expanded coverage	—	—	—	1,106	36,199	832	—
Total Including expanded coverage	—	—	—	4,231	207,793	1,057	12
Excluding expanded coverage	3,243	248,350	945	3,125	171,594	1,104	17

—Not applicable.

Source: Calculated from Côte d'Ivoire, Office National de Formation Professionelle, *Enquête de Main d'Oeuvre,* 1979 and 1984.

Apparent Increase in Aggregate Real Wage

Although restoration of equilibrium in the labor market in recessions would appear to call for a fall in real wages, one widely held view is that this either has not taken place or has taken place very slowly; the result is prolonged unemployment. Strong labor unions and institutional forces such as minimum wage laws in developing countries are viewed as the impediments to real wage adjustment. Studies supporting this view, however, have been based mainly on analysis of aggregate wage changes and implicitly assume that the composition of the work force remains the same over the business cycle.

Table 8.4.1 presents average real wages for surviving, exiting, and new firms, weighted by the number of employees in the firm relative to the total employees in the category. New firms had an average mean wage that was 20 percent higher in real terms than the firms that went out of business. Although new entrants did not differ from those that survived the recession, firms that were included in the 1984 survey as a result of expanded coverage had 25 percent lower wages. These tended to be smaller, more service-oriented firms.

Excluding expanded coverage, the aggregate data indicate that real wages increased by 17 percent, while employment fell by 31 percent. This strong countercyclical movement of wages suggests that slow adjustment or rigidity of real wages may have been an important cause of employment loss in the modern sector. In contrast to these aggregate data, however, the distribution of the change in mean real wages across surviving firms provides evidence of real wage flexibility: 51 percent of the firms witnessed a real decrease in their mean wage. The reductions were greatest among small firms and agricultural firms and lowest among large firms and firms in the manufacturing sector.

Evidence of Real Wage Decline

An alternative explanation for the loss in employment in the modern sector is that wages were flexible and fell below earnings in the informal sector; many workers therefore shifted to the informal sector. Over the five-year period, those who retained their jobs experienced a mean 7 percent increase in real wages, despite the severe recession. The distribution of real wage changes shows, however, that this did not apply to all workers: 44 percent of the males and 42 percent of the females suffered real wage decreases. Over 55 percent of uneducated workers suffered a real wage decline.

To examine the extent of real wage flexibility, we used individual data to estimate the real wage profiles for 1979 and 1984. For workers who retained their jobs, comparison of the actual wage in 1984 with the wage predicted on the basis of 1979 coefficients indicates that the return on vocational and technical training and on specific experience decreased. In 1979 and especially in 1984, in industries where entry of new workers over the previous five years was relatively high, workers who retained their jobs received relatively low wages. The real wage profile moved downward slightly because of decreases in the returns on the characteristics of workers and firms. But since the profiles are upward sloping, an individual employed in 1979 received a higher real wage five years later in 1984.

The coefficients changed more between the two years for newly hired workers than for retained workers. Wages for the newly hired in public firms went from 8 percent less than in private firms in 1979 to over 28 percent less in 1984, but the public-private wage differential among retained workers did not change. Thus, the effort to reduce the size of the public sector led to lower nominal wages for the newly hired without reducing the wages of those who remained employed. At the mean of the sample for surviving and new firms, the real wages of the newly hired fell by 22 percent during the five-year period. Real wages of the newly hired in firms included as part of the expanded coverage were even lower; thus there was an average decline of 34 percent in real wages for all the newly hired in the aggregate 1984 sample. These differences point out the importance of using micro data to control for compositional changes.

Smaller Size of New Firms

The 2,037 new firms that were formed successfully between 1979 and 1984 accounted for almost half of the firms in the modern sector in 1984 but provided only 12 percent of total employment. Most of the entering firms were very small: 80 percent employed fewer than 10 people, and 11 percent employed from 10 to 19 people. Their average size was 13 employees, compared with 135 in the surviving firms and 37 in new firms created between 1974 and 1979.

The decline in the real wage of the newly hired was not sufficient to keep the number of new jobs created from falling by over 40 percent between 1979 and 1984. What accounts for this disappointing rate? Part of the explanation is found in the decline of employment in public sector enterprises. The public sector share in new employment fell from 30 percent between 1974 and 1979 to 16 percent between 1979 and 1984. The percentage of jobs created by the nontraded goods sector, however, went from 24 percent to 51 percent—at a time when the real exchange rate was declining thanks to inflation of 48 percent and the fixed nominal exchange rate. The unfavorable real exchange rate may have inhibited new firms from investing in the traded goods sector. Apparently, firms do respond to relative prices, and raising the real exchange rate can be expected to increase employment.

8.5 *Weaknesses in Small Enterprise Management*
Enyinna Chuta

In this paper, some weaknesses in the managerial processes of small enterprises will be indicated. Specifically, problems relating to conceptualization and problems of goal-setting, keeping of adequate records for accounting purposes, organization of business, and inventory control will be discussed. This will be followed by a comparative appraisal of channels for providing management training for small enterprises in West Africa.

The Nature of the Problem

Empirical evidence about the managerial processes used by small entrepreneurs in West Africa is patchy. Surveys undertaken do, however, indicate certain general shortcomings. First there is the question of the motives of entrepreneurs. A survey conducted in Sierra Leone in 1974 showed that 58 percent of 226 small entrepreneurs studied became active with the declared aim of making profits. What is significant here is the 42 percent who gave other reasons. Among these, a goal related to security was ranked next in importance to profits in the response of 16 percent of sample respondents. Other reasons for entering business included having a family enterprise, following a father's occupation, and acquiring prestige. Supporting evidence comes from Upper Volta where a survey showed that 55 percent of entrepreneurs interviewed said that their principal motivation was financial gain, whereas 27 percent were motivated by the desire to help family members. If long-run viability of small enterprises is of any importance in the development process, entrepreneurs must be profit motivated. Promotional efforts will have either to seek ways of identifying and encouraging those entrepreneurs with proper goals or to use appropriate procedures to develop well-motivated entrepreneurs.

The misperception of problems is suggested by various data. In West Africa such surveys as have been made show that between 60 and 70 percent of

Excerpted by permission from Enyinna Chuta, "Upgrading the Managerial Process of Small Entrepreneurs in West Africa," *Public Administration and Development* 3 (1983): 245–83.

small-scale industrial proprietors believe that the greatest problem facing their business is—or was—shortage of capital, whereas observers suggest that other problems such as poor management, lack of demand or poor-quality products may, in fact, be more important. Although small entrepreneurs should be the best determinants of their special needs, the emphasis on capital needs cannot be reconciled with frequently observed excess capacities of 35 and 49 percent on the average for Sierra Leone and Ghana, respectively, and also of accumulated inventories.

A major information gathering process available to small entrepreneurs is the keeping of simple records of their daily operations. However, enquiries show that record keeping is not widely practiced in small enterprises in Nigeria, Mauritania (Nouakchott) and Togo (Lomé).

One obvious hypothesis is that the capacity to define one's problems, gather information and process it is related to literacy and educational attainment. Actual evidence on the relationship between level of education and successful management of small-scale enterprise is mixed. Some studies have indicated no precise correlation between formal schooling and business success. However, [another study] emphasized the basic fact that "without some competence in reading, writing, and simple arithmetic, it is hard to practice business at all," i.e., understand such important management functions as reading bank statements, sending or receiving purchase orders.

Data from the 1970s have shown the low level of formal education of most small-scale entrepreneurs in West Africa. In Western Nigeria, for instance, about 90 percent of rural small-scale entrepreneurs had less than primary VI education and 44 percent were virtually illiterate. In Sierra Leone, 75 percent of the small-scale proprietors did not have any formal schooling at all. Similar findings on inadequate schooling of small proprietors come from francophone West African countries.

Increasing the number of literate small entrepreneurs could facilitate the upgrading of their managerial processes in general and could obviously facilitate improved record keeping.

Besides the lack of record keeping, the owners of most small enterprises in West Africa do not know how to calculate profits. During field interviews in Sierra Leone in 1974–75, a small entrepreneur indicated that he could recognize lack of profitability in his business only when he ran out of "pocket-money." Attempts to ascertain from other entrepreneurs how frequently they tried to figure up their profits or losses did not show that this was an important aspect of their operation. Needless to mention, gifts made from regular enterprise production were considered necessary acts of charity which did not jeopardize the profitability of the business. [One] study showed that only 14.5 percent of sample entrepreneurs could break down their production costs correctly. A crucial dimension of management upgrading among West African entrepreneurs is to develop the awareness of the need to evaluate the performance of the business from existing records on a regular basis.

The efficiency of small enterprises in West Africa could be greatly enhanced either individually or collectively, if they were better organized. In Sierra Leone, over three-quarters of small enterprises are unregistered and unincorporated sole proprietor enterprises. Entrepreneurs may not even be aware of procedures for business registration or incorporation.

Small enterprises frequently overbuy their inventories without due consideration to adverse seasonal conditions such as high humidity, heavy rainfall or dry conditions. Consequently, a large inventory is stored while the enterprise is acutely short of working capital. A further adverse effect of such a practice is heavy inventory loss owing to deterioration resulting from bad weather conditions. Some of these losses are due to lack of knowledge of price trends over time, nature of the inventory items and poor estimation of future market demands. Compounding their problems are lack of knowledge of locational price differentials, and transportation problems due to poor road conditions.

Management of risk through the purchase of insurance is often unthought of in small-scale enterprises in West Africa. Although these industries are more exposed to fire and theft than large corporations, they are not protected by any form of insurance. Because of their limited capital and size, diversification in order to spread out risk is not practiced. As most of the small firms are one-product enterprises, seasonal fluctuations hurt them most. However, in both Sierra Leone and Nigeria where diversification of investment was attempted, that effort was often marked by lack of business viability arising from limited management capacity.

Delivery of Management Training

In West Africa, both formal and informal channels are used for delivering different kinds of services to small enterprises. The informal channel is essentially the apprenticeship system whereby on-the-job training is undertaken within the firm over a stipulated period of time. The formal channel includes various methods through which governments, local promotional institutions and aid donors deliver various kinds of essential services (including management training) to small enterprises.

With apprenticeship training, skills of each trade are learnt informally as trainees continue to receive instructions from their masters on various aspects of the job. The period of training ranges from three to ten years depending on the trade. Although most apprentices pay fees to learn their trade, they sometimes are paid small allowances to defray the cost of midday meals, transportation, etc. A major weakness of the apprenticeship system, however, is that it is devoid of management training.

Throughout West Africa, governments have established trade and vocational centres for technical training in the fields of carpentry, metalwork, mechanical and electrical work, etc. Although one major objective of establishing these facilities has been to nurture future small entrepreneurs, most of the ex-trainees have consistently sought wage employment in the modern sector. For example, out of 45 trainees interviewed at the Vocational Improvement Centre, Maiduguri, Nigeria, in 1970, only three were self-employed.

Fortunately, all systems of industrial extension services in West Africa deliver management information. In Nigeria, the Industrial Development Centres (IDCs) established at state levels combine the individual (firm level), group (seminars and courses) and mass (radio, films, etc.) approaches in delivering technical and management training and other services to small enterprises. The IDCs rely more on the individual approach for reaching their clients since this can be more fully adapted to the skills, educational level and scale of operation of the entrepreneur. However, the IDCs are not decentralized enough (beyond the state capitals) to have effective outreach in small towns and villages.

The Technology Consultancy Centre in Ghana (based at the Kumasi University of Science and Technology) provides technical and, to a limited extent, management training to small enterprises. The Centre establishes new on-campus production units to demonstrate the use of new appropriate technology and advises off-campus units when approached on production and management skills. However, the Centre's on-campus location, about four miles away from industrial areas, creates a barrier between itself and small enterprises. A decentralization of the Centre's facilities to enable it to establish a physical presence in rural towns and villages would enhance its contribution to the development of small enterprises.

Sierra Leone has planned to embark on a rural industrial extension programme. Under the new decentralized extension programme fifty extension officers have just been trained for posting in six different provincial locations to introduce new projects, improved production methods, better management and marketing techniques, etc. Although it would be premature to speculate on the performance of the Sierra Leone extension programme, success will depend among other things on the availability of funds for requisite staff. Nevertheless, the Sierra Leone programme, when implemented, will constitute the most decentralized extension services network for promoting small enterprises in West Africa.

In The Gambia, management and other essential services are delivered to small enterprises through the extension mechanism provided by the Indigenous Business Advisory Service. [It] provides advisory services relating to marketing products, setting up new enterprises and book-keeping systems, obtaining loans from banks, etc. The effectiveness of the Service has been limited, however, due to an overconcentration of effort in Banjul and to what up to now has been a lack of autonomy from the Ministry. Unlike Ghana and Sierra Leone, availability of funds has not been a serious constraint.

8.6 *Developing Entrepreneurship in West Africa*
Sri-ram Aiyer

Hundreds of new small-scale enterprises (SSEs) have been created in West Africa with the help of lines of credit and other assistance projects, many by people new to entrepreneurial roles. Some of them have prospered and paid back their start-up loans, but surely not the majority. The relative cost-effectiveness of the lending effort has not been high. The credit projects have not always reached the target groups. Almost all the projects have funded fewer and larger beneficiaries than hoped for. Investment costs per job have thus been higher than projected—well over what they are in Asia—especially if project overheads (for example, technical assistance) are counted.

Excerpted and edited from Sri-ram Aiyer, "A Strategy for SSE Development in Western Africa," World Bank, Western Africa Projects Department, 1985 (restricted circulation).

The quality and relevance of technical assistance have left much to be desired. The programs have often been staffed with overly sophisticated persons in terms of expertise, able to relate mainly to modern medium and large enterprises, often highly oriented toward development of particular subsectors, excessively optimistic about markets, and placing undue emphasis on the preparation of feasibility studies (invariably for new investments). The cost of this technical assistance has proved to be extremely high. In some countries the cost of operating the promotion and technical assistance organizations has exceeded the total cost of all the subprojects assisted. Furthermore, lack of coordination between the technical assistance and credit delivery systems has reduced the effectiveness of both. Although women have traditionally played an important role in entrepreneurial activity in Africa, their participation in SSE projects seems to have been very limited, not only as investors but even as employees, with the notable exception of carpet weavers in Mauritania.

Over time, the functioning of the credit delivery system has deteriorated. The causes include government ownership and intervention in management and lending policies, appointment of chief executives subject to government patronage, and intervention in day-to-day operations by government functionaries. This has led to lending decisions biased toward larger, higher-cost, and less viable projects. The credit programs have also been afflicted by high arrears and overhead costs, reflecting the overall weakness of the financial institutions and of the enterprises financed. Inadequate working capital can be a problem even if demand is sufficient since SSEs often must extend credit to their clients but their access to normal banking facilities is limited. This problem does not seem to have received adequate attention.

The commercial banks have remained averse to lending to SSEs, perceiving them as high risk—and with some reason, judging from actual results. Guarantee funds have usually been rapidly depleted and then not replenished, thus losing credibility, and this in turn has also deterred commercial banks from lending. Sometimes the procedures for invoking a guarantee have been excessive, including liquidation of the enterprise and takeover of its assets by the bank, thus defeating the objective of loan guarantee programs.

In sum, government-controlled promotional organizations, development finance corporations (DFCs), and commercial banks have all had trouble performing their assigned tasks. For small- and even medium-scale enterprises the pace of development has been far slower than was anticipated.

Small-Enterprise Issues

Should SSE projects experiment with entrepreneurial identification and development efforts? The Entrepreneurship Development Institute of India (EDII) uses techniques drawn from behavioral science to select entrepreneurs with high potential, reinforces their entrepreneurial orientation, and then assists them in starting and running enterprises. The success rate averages over 75 percent, compared with 50 percent in other countries (including developed countries). India has been surprisingly successful in extremely backward areas, where entrepreneurs have traditionally been hard to find. Difficulties with entrepreneurship in Africa lead us to argue that a similar approach should be tried there. Existing "entrepreneurial development programs" in Africa have been directed solely at management and technical training.

There is some skepticism about the transferability of these techniques because of the differences between Indian and African economies. The Indian techniques, however, have been tried in backward areas with problems similar to those in Africa. African visitors have expressed interest and support for trying these techniques in Africa. A systematic process to identify and develop entrepreneurial talents would build up the seedbed of African entrepreneurs needed as a base of sustained industrial expansion.

Should the focus for the near term be placed on existing enterprises rather than on new enterprises? The consensus is that it should, both because of a general need for rehabilitation of existing assets in Africa and because such a focus is likely to yield high returns. This does not mean focusing on "sick" enterprises, but rather on providing resources to enterprises on the basis of performance and potential.

Should credit lines be provided directly to DFCS, commercial banks, or voluntary organizations as credit intermediaries for SSES, or through an apex financing institution? There seems to be an emerging consensus that an apex approach should be used because this allows credit to be passed on to other institutions in accordance with their relative ability to reach clients in each country. Since the difference between DFCS and the others has been progressively reduced, particularly in the francophone countries of West Africa, the apex approach offers the flexibility of building on the strengths of each institution and overcoming weaknesses through technical assistance.

Commercial banks commend themselves as credit intermediaries for SSES because of their branch networks, their quick appraisals, and their experience in providing working capital. They typically have more domestically generated resources than DFCS. On the other hand, they often have a very conservative orientation, and greater institutional development may be required to enable them to move into term lending.

The "mutualiste" and "Banque Populaire" models[2] seem generally to be better able to work with the smaller indigenous enterprise and also need to be included in a comprehensive approach to making credit available to SSES.

Should credit be handled separately from other inputs, especially with micro enterprises? Failures with entirely separate structures lead to the conclusion that integration of credit and extension efforts is essential for successful promotion of SSES. This does not necessarily mean that they must be provided by the same institution as long as there is regular consultation and coordination between those providing credit and those providing extension services.

What kinds of subsidy are rationally defensible, and what are their impacts on the viability of intermediaries? Credit programs should be designed to increase subborrowers' access to term financing or foreign exchange but should not provide a subsidy in the form of below-market interest rates, since it is access rather than cost that is the problem. Any subsidies should go to institutions to

2. Informal credit associations common in West Africa that give members periodic access to relatively large sums of pooled contributions.

compensate them for the initial costs. In general, projects seem to work best with rates that are not overly subsidized; market-determined higher rates signal seriousness on the part of lenders, apportion money to better clients, and give better incentives to lenders. In addition, higher rates avoid subsidizing capital use and increase the viability of financial institutions and their capacity to mobilize savings for onlending. In francophone West Africa, however, lending rates and credit terms generally are mandated, often at the regional level, and are difficult to change.

What level of technical assistance should be mounted? Effective preinvestment technical assistance is a much more important element to successful SSE development than the provision of credit. More successful assistance efforts require a focus on generic areas affecting small enterprise, such as accounting and inventory control (as in some Partnership for Productivity projects in Kenya and Burkina Faso), or provision of lower-level vocational skills, as in the Servulart program in Mali, where French weavers and machinists help their Malien counterparts.

What institutional vehicles should be chosen—government units, chambers of commerce, voluntary agencies, or some eclectic mix? Within the West African region's projects, nongovernmental organizations (NGOs) have been associated with the government promotion offices in Cameroon and, somewhat less successfully, in Liberia. At least one project attempted at the outset to involve the chamber of commerce. The NGOs, which include privately funded foundations, voluntary services, religious organizations, and so on, have the flexibility that the public sector often lacks to operate personnel systems that will attract the right level of technically skilled people. The technical assistance institutions should obtain some assistance from the public budget but closely follow the patterns of private institutions in their management and staffing. All the experience suggests that a decentralized institutional structure contributes best to effective outreach. The importance of integration and complementarity between all the actions at the level of entrepreneurial development, technical assistance, and credit delivery cannot be emphasized enough. The success of any approach, however, requires a liberal regulatory environment vis-à-vis SSEs and a satisfactory macroeconomic policy framework.

An Operational Strategy

A systems approach is required that comprises four critical subsystems in SSE development and does so in an integrated fashion. These four subsystems are entrepreneurial identification and development, preinvestment work and technical assistance, credit delivery, and technical assistance and extension services to operating enterprises. In each country, the strategy must be to try to identify gaps in each of the subsystems and suggest steps to bridge the gaps. In all countries, the strategy must be to ensure integration of and complementarity between the subsystems.

This systems approach represents a departure from past SSE assistance in several respects, including greater attention to the smallest enterprises within a sector; explicit programs for entrepreneurial and human development; development of a variety of institutions, especially under nongovernmental auspices, for technical assistance; reorientation of technical assistance to the precise needs of clients; and efforts to help SSEs choose the most economically appropriate technologies. Sometimes it may not be possible to tackle simultaneously the gaps in all four subsystems without undue delays in a lending operation, in which case one or more problems may have to be dealt with at a later time.

A critical assumption of this approach is that the macroeconomic and regulatory framework affecting SSE development is satisfactory. Where this is not the case, attention should be focused on the policy framework. Sometimes, the best assistance for SSEs is simply to reduce the licensing and controls required of them and to eliminate taxes, subsidies, and special investment incentives that discriminate against them. Where a low interest rate policy discourages lenders from dealing with SSEs, moving toward market-determined rates that are adequate to cover lending costs and risks may be the most effective means of increasing the availability of credit to SSEs.

This does not mean that direct assistance efforts must be postponed until an optimum policy environment has been achieved. Rather, the systems approach should be preceded by an assessment of how the macroeconomic and regulatory framework is likely to influence the effectiveness of direct assistance efforts and be complemented by steps to alter policies that would have a significant negative impact. Whether these steps should be prior to or parallel with the assistance effort will depend on the circumstances in each country.

9

Financial and Technological Issues

9.1 Regulation of the Financial Sector
Keith Marsden and Therese Belot

Shortages of investment funds and working capital in Africa are in part the reflection of low income levels and large subsistence (nonmonetized) segments of economies. But they also spring from weaknesses in policies and institutions that hamper resource mobilization and restrict the private sector's access to finance. Four constraints are examined here: first, financial market regulations that reduce savings deposits and discourage banks from lending to SSES; second, the absence of stock markets and merchant banks able to mobilize equity capital; third, crowding out of the private sector from financial markets because of excessive borrowing by government and public enterprises; and fourth, public investment programs that monopolize the use of foreign loans and grants.[1]

Financial Market Regulations

An analysis of interest rate policies in a number of developing countries from 1970 to 1982 revealed that, by and large, nominal interest rates were set by the government, rates changed little over time, and real rates were primarily determined by variations in the rate of inflation. Real deposit rates over the period were negative. In many countries they were 3 to 6 percentage points below the real rates that prevailed in the developed countries, thus encouraging the outflow of funds. In countries with very high inflation, deposit rates were substantially negative, sometimes below minus 20 percent. The variability of real rates affected resource mobilization. As a result, total domestic

Excerpted and edited from Keith Marsden and Therese Belot, *Private Enterprise in Africa: Creating a Better Environment,* World Bank Discussion Paper 17 (Washington, D.C., 1987).

1. In addition, heavy taxation (see section 7.1) squeezes corporate profits and entrepreneurial incomes and therefore limits their ability to generate internal investment funds.

credit that could be made available to borrowers (public and private) by the monetary authorities and by banks expanded only slowly in real terms over the past decade. In some countries the level actually declined in relation to GDP.

Although Kenya's financial depth as measured by the ratio of money and quasi-money (M_2) to GDP compared favorably with other countries in the same income category, its financial depth seriously eroded during the period 1978 to 1983. The ratio of M_2 to GDP fell from 32 percent to 25 percent. The resurgence of inflation and ceilings on loan rates, along with the substantial reserves the government required the banking system to hold, kept deposit rates low and weakened the ability of the banks to mobilize deposits. The decline in financial depth was accompanied by a slide in domestic saving rates. The ratio of gross private saving to GDP deteriorated from a peak of nearly 27 percent of GDP in 1977 to a low of 11 percent in 1983.

Similarly, in Ghana the M_2/GDP ratio declined from 29 percent in 1977 to 12 percent in 1984. At the same time, there was an increasing preference for holding liquid funds outside the banking system and an increasing velocity in money circulation as firms and individuals traded financial assets for fixed assets as a hedge against inflation. These trends were aggravated in 1982–83 by a substantial drop in public confidence in the financial system following the demonetization of 50-cedi notes and the freezing of all bank accounts in amounts above 50,000 cedis ($18,000 at the official exchange rate). Although the government has taken steps to address these problems, the task of reversing past trends is still at an early stage and public confidence in the banking system has yet to be restored.

Low loan-rate ceilings fixed by governments have also restricted the operating spreads of financial institutions and discouraged lending to smaller, riskier businesses. Much of the subsidized credit went to wealthy individuals or those with political influence, while smaller borrowers had to pay higher interest rates in the informal credit markets. This directed credit often induced recipients to make capital-intensive investments.

Lack of Equity Funds

Very few African countries have active equity markets, either in the form of stock exchanges or in the form of merchant banks that can provide a full range of securities-related services. The financial policies of many countries have inadvertently had an anti-equity bias. Inflation with low interest rates deepened equity values through retained earnings in the 1970s but retarded the growth of equity markets external to firms. In addition, many government programs reduced the cost and risk of debt, but not of equity. These programs included explicit or implicit insurance that covered not only small depositors but also large, sophisticated investors; lender-of-last-resort facilities that guaranteed the liquidity of financial intermediaries; special institutions (development finance institutions, agricultural banks, etc.) that provided debt at subsidized rates; tax policies that made equity financing more expensive, particularly by treating interest as a cost before calculating profit taxes and the double taxation of dividends; and lastly, bail-outs of corporations that diminished the danger of excessive debt.

Equally important, controls on output prices often reduce corporate earnings and hence their ability to raise equity funds. However, nascent capital markets do exist in some countries. In Kenya, for example, secondary trading in long-term securities is carried out by six Nairobi-based stockbroking firms. The brokers act only as agents for clients and typically match the buy and sell orders in-house. New issues of long-term private sector securities are controlled by the government.

Crowding Out by Public Sector Borrowing

Private firms' access to bank credit has been restricted in many countries because governments and public enterprises have been given first claim on financial resources. The public sector's share of outstanding domestic credit exceeds 60 percent in fourteen out of thirty-five countries covered by the statistics. The private sector's share was less than 25 percent in six countries—Burundi, Ethiopia, Ghana, Sierra Leone, Tanzania, and Zaire. Only in Botswana and Cameroon were governments net lenders rather than borrowers of domestic financial resources.

Government demand for domestic credit increased for three reasons. First, the growth of expenditures on public investment and public services outpaced the growth of revenue and caused larger budgetary deficits. For example, deficits reached 10.6 percent of GDP in Kenya in 1980–81, 16.5 percent in Malawi in 1981, and 11.5 percent in Senegal in 1980–81. Second, the operating costs of public enterprises exceeded their income, and the gap was filled by additional loans provided by the banking system or by government subsidies. In Ghana, for example, the combined operating deficit of state-owned enterprises in 1982 amounted to 2,880 million cedis, equal to 3 percent of GDP and the same amount as total government expenditures on education, health, social security, and welfare that year. Third, although foreign aid grants and concessionary loans from abroad financed a significant proportion of their public investment programs, some African countries found it more difficult to borrow in international markets. They therefore drew more heavily on private domestic savings to meet their financing needs.

However, there is evidence that African countries are becoming increasingly aware of the negative effects on the private sector of budgetary deficits and heavy government borrowing. Measures being taken to curb the public sector's financial appetite include:

- Restraining the expansion of public sector employment and wages (for example, in Kenya and Senegal)
- Reducing recurrent expenditure by cost savings in education and housing (Côte d'Ivoire and Mauritius)
- Reducing losses of, and subsidies to, public enterprise by restructuring, stricter monitoring, and divestiture (Senegal and Togo)
- Subjecting public investment programs to more rigorous scrutiny (Côte d'Ivoire, Kenya, Malawi, Mauritius, Senegal, Togo).

Many African governments are also trying to eliminate budgetary deficits by raising tax revenues. This may be achieved without negative repercussions by broadening the tax base or improving tax collection. But there is a risk that imposing higher marginal tax rates on individuals and firms already heavily burdened by taxes may encourage tax evasion and corruption; reduce the willingness to work, save, and invest; and squeeze profits that could have been plowed back into business.

Public Investment Programs Monopolizing the Use of Foreign Loans

Private domestic savings are low in many African countries. Public savings have also declined because government expenditures have risen faster than government revenue. Thus, African countries (particularly low-income countries) have had to rely increasingly on foreign savings—that is, financial flows from abroad—to finance domestic investment. In 1970–74, gross investment in these countries averaged 17.9 percent of their GDP, and 84 percent of this investment was financed by domestic savings (public and private). By 1984, however, their investment-GDP ratio had dropped to 14.3 percent, and foreign savings accounted for 55 percent of investment.

Private enterprises have had very limited access to medium- and long-term funds from abroad. At the end of 1984, outstanding and disbursed medium- and long-term debt to Sub-Saharan African countries amounted to $56.5 billion. Only 0.6 percent of this total represented direct loans to private enterprises, whereas public enterprise received 13.9 percent and mixed public-private enterprises 1.6 percent. Loans to development banks in Africa accounted for 0.8 percent of outstanding foreign debt. The amount available for private enterprises was even less because state-owned enterprises were also beneficiaries of subloans from development finance institutions.

The responsibility for this neglect of the private sector may lie more with governments than with foreign lenders. Governments guarantee repayment of this debt and therefore have the final say in how the funds are used. African governments have preferred to use foreign loans for public investment programs and to cover deficits. Loans to central governments and central banks for these purposes accounted for three-quarters of total foreign debt. Foreign lenders have agreed to these priorities and perhaps even encouraged them. Some official sources of concessional loans may have shared the preference of governments for public investment because it allowed foreign donors more direct involvement in the selection of projects and in procurement.

There are signs of a reappraisal of investment strategies on the part of both foreign lenders and African governments. Guinea and Togo, for example, have requested foreign aid organizations to help finance privatization programs by providing loans to private enterprises willing to acquire the physical assets of state-owned enterprises.

9.2 Technological Change
Frederick T. Moore

Concern with technological progress as a source of economic growth in the developing world has taken second place in the literature to concern with

Excerpted and edited from Frederick T. Moore, *Technological Change and Industrial Development*, World Bank Staff Working Paper 613 (Washington, D.C., 1983).

choice of technology—or, more generally, efficiency in the allocation of resources—at the level of the firm, and the possibilities of substitution among factors, particularly the substitution of labor for capital. This stems from concern about providing employment to the growing populations of the developing countries. The greater the possibilities of substitution, the greater will be the ability of the industrial sector to absorb labor.

Some take the position that there are no substitution possibilities, that production uses factors and other inputs in fixed proportions. Hence, the isoquant for capital and labor is a right angle. This is the assumption in input-output models and in some (but not all) process models. Others, however, maintain that there are extensive substitution possibilities. The isoquant is relatively flat and only slightly convex to the axes. It is relatively easy to substitute small amounts of one factor for another if factor prices shift slightly.

Several points should be noted. First, the questions of substitution and choice of technology apply primarily to investment in a new plant. Once an investment has been made and the problem is one of additions or modifications to an existing plant, the possibilities for substitution are much more limited.

Second, choice of technology normally refers to the use of primary factors—that is, all varieties of capital equipment and all classes of labor. It may also refer to inputs of raw materials and intermediate products. Substitutions can occur—aluminum for steel or plastics for wood, for example—but it is assumed that the end products of alternative technologies that are being compared are close substitutes—in theory, perfect substitutes.

This conclusion gives rise to a number of difficulties and is the source of significant differences of opinion. What is a "close" substitute? Is handmade soap a close substitute for a manufactured detergent, or a hand saw for a circular power saw? Whether products are close substitutes depends on the cross-elasticity of demand. There is little agreement as to what constitutes a close, as opposed to a distant, substitute. From the point of view of the consumer or user, the question is whether the products provide equal satisfaction or have equal capabilities. But even when the technical characteristics and prices of two products are the same, one may be preferred because after-sales service is better.

Third, discussions of technological choice should be neutral with respect to the issues of technological progress and contribution to growth. The analyses reviewed below do not discuss whether one type of technology is apt to have greater potential for future adaptation and acceleration of growth than another type. Whether capital-intensive or labor-intensive configurations are more conducive to later adaptation, innovation, and growth is an issue that does not appear to have been addressed. Yet it is clearly an issue of importance to a developing country that is concerned not only with the efficiency of its industrial structure but also with its potential for growth. To understand the process of innovation and growth, it is appropriate to take a different starting point, namely, that of the activities of research, development, and engineering of new products and processes.

Whether different types of technology are apt to be more or less conducive to growth depends on the extent of their linkages—both backward linkages to suppliers and forward linkages to markets. Different industries exhibit different degrees of linkages. One hypothesis asserts that capital-intensive firms or industries tend to have stronger linkages than labor-intensive ones; the direct effects are greater. One study calculated the direct and indirect effects on output and employment,[2] and the results seem to indicate that the indirect effects of capital-intensive industries are extensive. But the aggregation of data in the input-output models used, where both capital-intensive and labor-intensive firms are included in the same aggregated "industry," may limit the applicability of these conclusions.

Finally, it is important to note that in analyses of limitations on choice of technology, only occasionally is the minimum efficient size of plant considered. Comparisons are made of the production costs of specific technologies to arrive at judgments as to their relative efficiencies, and size of plant is implicit or explicit in the calculations. But the analyses do not consider whether the long-run average cost curve is "flat bottomed"—that is, whether plants of different sizes and different technologies are about equally efficient throughout a range of output. For investment decisions, however, it is important to know the minimum efficient size of plant.

Continued concern with technological choices and the prospects of substituting labor for capital are based on the necessity of providing employment for a growing labor force and of increasing incomes through increases in productivity. If substitution possibilities are widespread throughout industry, as has been assumed, the microeconomic effects of the substitution of labor-intensive technologies for ones that are more capital-intensive might be substantial.

The questions that naturally come to mind then are: If this is so, what prevents even greater shifts to these simpler technologies? Why is there a current belief that these shifts are being frustrated? Several answers have been offered.

First, and perhaps most important, government policies in developing countries often have created a bias toward capital-intensive investment. Through low customs duties and excise taxes on capital goods imports, tax holidays, preferential access to credit, and similar policies, an environment favorable to capital-intensive investment has been created. This is reinforced by policies and laws designed primarily to improve the general welfare but that may inhibit labor-intensive choices—for example, minimum wages set higher than productivity prices, restrictions on firing, large fringe benefits, and so on. There is general agreement that, whatever the intentions were, the actual effect of many industrial policies in the developing countries is to favor capital-intensive choices. They have altered the structure of industry, but that does not necessarily mean that they have brought about the dominance of capital intensity in all industries.

Second, the blame for the favoritism toward capital intensity is sometimes laid at the door of transnational corporations (TNCs). They are presumed to transfer, without change, the capital-intensive techniques of industrial countries to the developing countries because they are familiar with these tech-

2. J. J. Stern and J. D. Lewis, *Employment Patterns and Income Growth,* World Bank Staff Working Paper 419 (Washington, D.C., 1980).

niques, and redesigning plants in developing countries would be costly. Some studies seem to support this argument. One study compared the investment behavior of TNCs in Ghana, plants owned by expatriates resident in Ghana, and indigenous firms. The results indicated that the first two groups reacted similarly and differently from the indigenous firms, which had lower capital-labor ratios. But other analysts have come to opposite conclusions. One survey found no strong evidence that TNCs adapt either better or worse than local firms to changes in factor prices, and a study of the behavior of subsidiaries of Unilever found that the capital per employee in developing countries was less than half that found in industrial countries. Another study found evidence that TNCs did adapt to local factor prices in metalworking industries in Brazil. In short, these studies do not demonstrate the presumed culpability of the TNCs.

Third, the argument is sometimes made that the concentration of income and wealth in developing countries leads both to a distortion of market demand in favor of modern goods and to limitations on the growth of demand for simpler products. But this position would take us beyond the bounds of this study.

Finally, the absence of a shift to simpler techniques may be attributable to a lack of information about technological choices and an inability to use existing technologies efficiently. This is an aspect of X-inefficiency.

Thus, no general judgments can be made, based on the existing studies. Some of the evidence holds forth promise of greater labor absorption, but the coverage of industries is limited, and the existing studies of the macro effects have a number of defects. In individual cases, however, it should be possible to determine the economic prospects for substitution and, if they exist, to take advantage of them in the interests of expanding employment opportunities.

9.3 *Inappropriate Technology Choice*
F. C. Perkins

Tanzania's industrialization programme has, in general, promoted the establishment of enterprises using large-scale capital-intensive, often technically, and almost invariably economically inefficient techniques. Its technological choice policy in industry has in most instances failed to promote the achievement of major national development objectives, such as employment creation, economic self-reliance, decentralization of development, rapid growth of output, conservation of scarce development capital and efficient allocation of resources.

Similar, apparently irrational technological choices have been observed in developing countries as diverse as Indonesia, Ethiopia, Ghana, Thailand and Kenya, to mention only a few. This may indicate that there are persuasive reasons, beyond questions of economic efficiency and profitability, for the selection of such capital-intensive and inefficient technologies in unskilled labour abundant, capital and skilled labour scarce developing countries. Sev-

Excerpted by permission from F. C. Perkins, "Technology Choice, Industrialization and Development Experiences in Tanzania," *Journal of Development Studies* 19, no. 2 (January 1983): 213–43.

eral possible explanations for this phenomenon, in Tanzania and other developing countries, are discussed below.

Factor Prices

There is a large body of neo-classical economic literature which maintains that inappropriate technological choices are made in many developing countries because production factors, particularly labour and capital, are incorrectly priced. Minimum wages, job security legislation and payroll taxes keep labour costs above the level at which all labour could be employed. Cheap credit from the formal banking sector and investment incentives based on capital employed (rather than capacity) encourage entrepreneurs to value capital at less than its social opportunity cost and hence to select more capital-intensive techniques.

However, though factor price distortions of this type certainly do exist in Tanzania, even at these distorted market prices the more capital-intensive techniques in each industry had higher unit production costs (and were presumably less profitable) than more labour-intensive techniques. Hence, one would still expect entrepreneurs to choose more labour-intensive techniques than those actually selected.

Other Factors of Production

In the ten industries studied it was invariably found that the small-scale and labour-intensive techniques required fewer skilled production, technical and managerial personnel than did the capital-intensive, advanced technology units. Hence, the use of the latter technologies cannot be explained by the serious skilled labour shortages in Tanzania, and is in fact likely to exacerbate such shortages.

Products and Income Distribution

Virtually all of the small-scale and labour-intensive techniques examined were found to be capable of producing goods which consumers considered to be of comparable quality to items produced by alternative, more capital-intensive techniques. The only possible exceptions to this finding were jaggery and pit-sawn timber. Hence, it is unlikely that the skewed distribution of income in Tanzania (and other developing countries), favouring higher income consumers of superior quality goods, would explain the use of capital-intensive techniques in those industries examined.

Organizational Factors

Tanzania has many hundred small, informal sector units, about 350 small- and medium-sized formal sector firms, with between 10 and 100 employees, and about 150 large-scale parastatals, local firms and transnational corporation subsidiaries. The varying access of these types of enterprise to credit facilities, factor and final goods market and technological knowledge greatly influences the type of technology which they employ and probably largely explains the spread of technologies found operating in each industry. However, it does not explain why large-scale, capital-intensive firms, with favoured access to markets and technical knowledge, often choose inefficient, high cost technologies.

Risk and Lack of Information

It may be that, due to inadequate information, such firms overestimate the risk of using more labour-intensive technologies, or may not even know of their existence. This was found to be the case in a study of several large tin can producers in Thailand. However, in a number of industries in Tanzania, parastatals operated both capital- and labour-intensive techniques. (These included the textiles, grain, sugar, and timber milling, garment-making, printing and farm implement-making industries.) Hence, in these industries, a lack of knowledge could not explain the technological choices made by the parastatal sector.

Monopoly and Oligopoly

Several large Tanzanian firms, including a number of parastatals, have an element of monopolistic and oligopolistic power, which may provide a permissive factor, enabling them to use less efficient, capital-intensive technologies and still remain in business. High tariffs provide protection against import competition for virtually all domestic industries. The price-fixing methods of the National Price Commission, which guarantee firms in many industries a fixed rate of profit above costs, similarly insulate firms which are using inefficient technologies from market competition.

Technical Factors

None of the more capital-intensive technologies examined was found to use raw materials more efficiently than alternative, labour-intensive techniques, so technical characteristics of this kind cannot explain the use of capital-intensive techniques.

However, once a few large, technically advanced industries are established in a country, they are likely to require further investment in supporting infrastructure and new enterprises to supply power, water and technically specified intermediate goods and packaging, etc. Technical linkages of this sort may partially explain the government's continued investment in economically inefficient, advanced technology industries.

Technological Determinism

One school of thought on this subject claims that advanced capital-intensive technologies are used in developing countries because no efficient, labour-intensive or small-scale alternatives exist. However, the findings clearly indicate that, at least in Tanzania, this is not the case.

Engineering Criteria

Analyses in Ethiopia, Ghana and Indonesia conclude that capital-intensive, inefficient technologies are probably not selected by economists on the basis of cost efficiency, but by engineers, who largely staff project appraisal teams in developing countries. [One argument is] that because of their educational background in industrialized countries (or in institutions using similar curricula), engineers usually consider installing only the most technically advanced technologies available, which optimize engineering criteria such as output per minute, etc. Because projects are forced through rapidly in many developing countries, once it is "established" that a project will generate a reasonable rate of return, it simply goes ahead. Such studies often assume that proposed units will achieve a rate of capacity utilization which is unrealistically high in developing country conditions. They rarely if ever bother to compare the production costs of the proposed technology with those of available labour-intensive techniques.

Bureaucratic Objectives and Selection Criteria

In the industries examined virtually all newly established parastatals were very capital-intensive while most private and co-operative firms employed more labor-intensive techniques. It is therefore likely that an important explanation for the employment of economically inferior, capital-intensive techniques will be provided by the nature of the decision-making process in the public sector.

Conclusions

In general, the bias in the programmes of SIDO (Small Industries Development Organization) and the large-scale parastatal sector as a whole towards advanced, imported technologies can probably be adequately explained by several of the factors discussed above. The parastatals' technological choices also reflect their financial and technological dependence on foreign aid and transnational corporation partners. This is at least partially a result of failures in the budgetary planning and foreign aid management processes, caused by shortages of experienced and skilled personnel, the lack of coherent project selection criteria which reflect national development priorities, and inadequate co-ordination between Ministries and parastatals.

10

Public Enterprise Management and Restructuring

10.1 *Performance of African Public Enterprises*
John Nellis

This study deals with public enterprises (PEs) that are supposed to "earn most of their revenue from the sales of goods and services, are self-accounting, and have a separate legal identity."[1] These economically important and quasi-independent entities have been created by African governments to do what private sectors and bureaucracies are believed to be unable to do.

The greatest difficulty in dealing with African PEs is obtaining accurate facts and figures. Different sources give different figures, consistent time series data are not available, and data on performance are particularly unreliable. Countries in the region do not use a standard definition of PEs, much less the definition employed here. In some countries profits are not adjusted for government transfers or for special tax incentives or hidden subsidies, such as privileged access to inputs at special prices or unofficial permission to incur large arrears without penalty. All of this makes cross-country comparisons difficult.

Worldwide, PEs are responsible for about 10 percent of gross domestic product (GDP) on average in both developed and developing countries. In contrast, the figure is much higher in some African countries, as table 10.1.1 shows. Moreover, these figures understate the importance of PEs in the modern sector of many Sub-Saharan African economies. For example, PEs account for over 90 percent of manufacturing value added in Ethiopia, almost 80 percent in Somalia, over 50 percent in Zambia, and 40 percent in Cameroon. Furthermore, PEs make up a large part of investment in several countries.

State enterprises are typically capital-intensive and hence are usually not a

---

Excerpted and edited from John R. Nellis, *Public Enterprises in Sub-Saharan Africa*, World Bank Discussion Paper 1 (Washington, D.C., 1986).

1. Mary M. Shirley, *Managing State-Owned Enterprises*, World Bank Staff Working Paper 577 (Washington, D.C., 1983), p. 2.

Table 10.1.1 *Public Enterprise Share in* GDP *and Gross Fixed*
Capital Formation
(percent)

Country	Year	Public enterprise share in GDP[a]	Gross fixed capital formation
Sudan	1975	40.0	n.a.
Zambia	1979–80	37.8	61.2
Guinea	1979	25.0	n.a.
Mauritania	1984	25.0	37.2[b]
Senegal	1974	19.9	17.9
Tanzania	1974–77	12.3	32.7[c]
Togo	1980	11.8	n.a.
Côte d'Ivoire	1979	10.5	39.5
Niger	1984	10.0	n.a.
Kenya	1970–73	8.1	17.3[b]
Sierra Leone	1979	7.6	19.6
Botswana	1978–79	7.3	7.7
Liberia	1977	6.8	14.1
Gambia	1978–80	n.a.	37.9
Ethiopia	1978–80	n.a.	36.5
Malawi	1978	n.a.	21.6
Mauritius	1977–79	n.a.	14.4

n.a. Not available.

a. At factor cost, except at market price for Guinea, Senegal, and Botswana.

b. 1978–79.

c. 1970–80.

major source of employment. Nevertheless, they are relatively more important employers in Sub-Saharan African countries than elsewhere. And in
some Sub-Saharan African countries the PE contribution to formal sector
employment is very high. For example, PEs were responsible for 75 percent of
modern sector employment in Guinea in 1981, 58 percent in Niger in 1981,
and 40 percent in Burundi in 1980.

Performance of Public Enterprises

The general view is that African PEs have yielded a very low rate of return on
the large amount of resources invested in them. While no aggregate figures
on PE performance are available for the region as a whole, limited data for
individual countries and subregional groupings show reason for concern. Of
the PEs in a sample drawn from twelve West African countries, 62 percent
showed net losses, while 36 percent had negative net worth. By Kenyan
government estimates, more than US$1.4 billion had been invested in all
Kenyan PEs by the early 1980s, yielding an annual average rate of return of 0.2
percent. The overall performance of PEs is so poor that even those African
governments most committed to socialist principles are openly voicing concern. For example, the Tanzanian commissioner for public investment said in
late 1984 that the "public enterprise sector in Tanzania has been in existence
for almost 19 years, but the performance has been disappointing."[2]

2. M. A. M. Mkulo, "Interview," *Public Enterprise*, February 1985, p. 189.

In Niger, the cumulative total of deficits for twenty-three loss-making enterprises, as of 1983, had surpassed CFAF40 billion—close to $90 million at present exchange rates and considerably more at 1983 rates. Even after deducting the surpluses of some fifteen nondeficit PES, the net deficits of the PES surpass CFAF29 billion, or roughly 4 percent of Niger's 1982 GDP. In Tanzania, between 1976 and 1979 one-third of all PES ran losses. In Benin, more than 60 percent of all PES show net losses; more than three-quarters have debt-equity ratios greater than 5 to 1, close to half have negative net worth, and more than half show negative net working capital.

PE performance is equally distressing in many other countries. Cumulative PE losses in Mali reached 6 percent of GDP by the end of the 1970s. A 1980 study of eight Togolese PES revealed that their losses equaled 4 percent of GDP. Half of a sample of thirty-nine industrial PES in Madagascar ran substantial losses in the period of 1981–83. Reports from Senegal, Sierra Leone, Sudan, Mauritania, Nigeria, and Zaire reveal, at best, heavy losses in many PES in the periods studied and suggest, at worst, permanent loss-making PE sectors.

In some countries the bulk of the losses in PE sectors can be traced back to one or a small number of grossly inefficient firms. This means that many individual African PES (although few PE sectors) are running at a profit. Data are not sufficient to establish a regional or much of a sectoral pattern, but some information is available. In Sierra Leone, production and financial enterprises have shown much higher returns to capital than service enterprises, and it seems reasonable to think that this is the pattern elsewhere. In Ethiopia, the industrial PE subsector showed sustained and substantial net profits from 1979 to 1982.

With the proper mix of macroeconomic policies and internal management arrangements, African PES can produce significant benefits for the country. Malawi's Agriculture Development and Marketing Corporation, the Tanzania Investment Bank, and the Palmindustrie Corporation in the Côte d'Ivoire are all examples of PES that were in great difficulties prior to successful restructuring efforts.

Of course, judging PE performance on the basis of profits and losses is questionable. PES in a monopoly position can be extremely inefficient but very profitable, while an efficient firm may show losses if its output prices are kept artificially low by government decree or if it is obliged to fulfill noncommercial objectives. Price controls, subsidies, and overt or hidden transfers all distort the incentive structure and make precise evaluation of performance difficult.

Investment Decisions

Inappropriate investment decisions are another major contributor to poor PE performance. In Somalia in 1976 a plant where banana exports were boxed had a break-even production level greater than national banana production. By 1982 the factory was operating at 25 percent of capacity.

The problem of underutilized capacity is extremely common in African PES; it is difficult to find firms working at anything close to originally planned output. This is an obvious misallocation of resources. Another common problem is that public enterprise plants in just about every African country have been located because of political and regional considerations despite the added costs and distorted allocations such sitings caused.

In several instances, PE investment decisions have been predicated on the continuation of historically high prices for the commodity to be produced or have relied excessively on uncontrollable external factors. Nevertheless, this does not prevent one from perceiving some general trends.

Pricing Policies

It is clear that pricing policies have had a generally negative effect on African PE performance. Many Sub-Saharan countries have a regime of controlled prices that have seldom been adjusted to keep pace with rising costs. Indeed, market and profit calculations have taken second place to sociopolitical considerations in most countries. Controlled prices for both the materials bought by PES and the products or services sold by them has led to inefficiencies in resource allocation, contributed to large operating losses, reduced financial accountability, and increased the dependence of PES on government subsidies.

Aggregate data to illustrate these generalizations are not readily available, but numerous individual examples can be cited. In Benin, for example, the government kept the retail price of cement low while the prices of essential imported production materials rose rapidly. The result was an annual loss of CFAF1 billion by two cement factories up to the end of 1982. In Niger and Madagascar, PES in grain marketing and foodstuff trading were required to sell commodities well below the efficiency price and often below the cost of production. In Niger, these losses were not subsidized. In Madagascar, the PES were supposed to receive compensation for loss-making socially priced items but rarely did. In Sierra Leone, a transport PE sought to raise fares in 1974; government approval of the request came only after five years. A second request in 1981 was approved in 1983. The two increases, however, did not match the inflation rate.

Overstaffing

Almost every Sub-Saharan African country has overstaffed its PES. Official reports from the People's Republic of the Congo, Ghana, Guinea, Liberia, Nigeria, Somalia, and Tanzania (among others) have all emphasized the seriousness of this problem. In country after country, PE officials complain of being unable to suspend, fire, or discipline their employees in any meaningful way. Nor do they possess discretionary power on salaries and benefits. They have neither sticks nor carrots.

Acute and costly problems of overstaffing at the lower levels coexist with scarcities of skilled labor and experienced managerial personnel. PES in Nigeria and Zimbabwe suffer from shortages of technicians and middle management even in the most overstaffed organizations. Unified salary systems equalized the salaries and benefits of the PES and the regular civil service and may have slowed the flow from the civil service to the PE sector, but they seem to have increased the flow of competent managers from the PE to the private sector.

A significant number of African countries have admitted the overstaffing problem, however, and have begun to take steps to correct it. Lay-offs in PES have been reported recently in Niger, Nigeria, Senegal, Sierra Leone, Tanzania, and Togo. Authorities in Benin, Guinea, Mali, and Mauritius are also working along the same lines.

Liquidity and Debt Ratios

In case after case one finds African PES that are undercapitalized. Government transfers to PES have ceased because of budgetary restrictions, while the amounts of accounts receivable have increased. This has led PES to rely increasingly on commercial borrowing to finance new investments and even to pay for daily operations. Historically high interest in U.S. dollar exchange rates has caused severe financial problems for these PES. In Somalia, for instance, interest charges amount to close to 50 percent of the losses of manufacturing PES. Because most African governments guarantee PE debts and because management is not held accountable for these loans, many enterprises have overborrowed. This has led to high debt-equity ratios, increased arrears to banks and suppliers, and virtual paralysis of operations.

In Benin, for example, the majority of PES have a debt-equity ratio exceeding 5 to 1. Out of a sample of thirty PES, only 20 percent have debt-equity ratios below 2 to 1, and 50 percent have ratios that are above 10 to 1. In Togo, data on six key public enterprises indicate that in 1980 they were seriously undercapitalized, with a debt-equity ratio of 8 to 3. Furthermore, four PES had indefinite ratios because of negative net capital positions.

In Sudan, a huge amount of net working capital is tied up in receivables and inventories. The equity of many corporations has shrunk because of large operating losses. Fixed assets have increased only slightly because most of the increases in resources have gone to finance current assets. High debt-equity ratios are also true of enterprises in Madagascar, Nigeria, Sierra Leone, and Zambia.

PES in most of Sub-Saharan Africa are desperately short of liquidity because they are often not paid or paid very late for their products or services. Partly as a result of the fact that few government bills are paid on time, many African PES have in turn stopped paying taxes and have stopped paying each other. PES in Togo, for example, have been saddled with large accounts receivable. For eight enterprises these amounted to nearly five months of sales in 1980, while liquid assets covered only two weeks of operating costs.

High rates of taxation on profits, and government requirements to transfer a large portion of post-tax profits to its budget, have often cut into funds for reinvestment, forced additional borrowings, and caused cash-flow problems. In Mali, 90 percent of post-tax profits must be transferred to the government budget. In Niger, any accumulated surplus of the major development bank has often been reallocated at the discretion of the government.

General Problems

Several determinants of poor performance are general and apply to almost all PES, whatever the culture, region, or economic system in which they are found. These general problems include unclear and contradictory objectives, excessive political interference in decisions that should be made by managers or boards of directors, overly frequent rotation of managers, incompatibility of civil service procedures with commercial operations, and lack of competition.

Africa PEs exhibit all of these problems, but the intensity of at least some of them is greater in Sub-Saharan Africa than elsewhere. For example, the scarcity of experienced managers is absolutely greater in Africa than in the Middle East, Asia, or Latin America. This reflects both the poor human resource base inherited at independence and the appointment policies of a number of governments, which have stressed political loyalty over operational skills. Poor pay for managers is frequently cited as an impediment to recruitment and performance.

The degree of supervisory concentration in Africa on issues unrelated to productivity seems to be extraordinary. In Senegal and elsewhere, the PE sector is subject to the supervision and control of a large number of imperfectly coordinated bodies, with different types of PEs being supervised by different bodies and with different agencies having as their responsibility only a part of the supervisory process. The result is a lack of coherence and continuity in policymaking and supervision. At the very least, much time and effort are wasted in attempts to inform ministerial and interministerial committees about what is taking place.

Centralization and Management

The high degree of government centralization in Sub-Saharan African countries has a decided impact on PE performance. Ministers and high administrative officials interfere often in management decisions. Even though there are many rules designed to limit such interference, at least in theory, most of the time they are simply ignored. Since ministers and high officials often encounter interference from above, they see it as normal behavior toward their own subordinates.

The dominance of centralized governments and the absence of a substantial private sector in most African countries mean that PEs have no "role model" to follow other than government. Thus, there is no substantial sector of obviously more efficient performance against which PE activities can be compared. Moreover, African educational systems are still geared to producing mostly bureaucrats, technocrats, and professionals. Schools of commerce and business administration are few, and training in them is limited to postgraduate studies. Training institutions turn out people who think in terms of applying regulations, not seizing opportunities. In industrialized countries there is frequently an interchange of executives from the private to the public sector and back, often to the benefit of both. In Africa there is little revitalizing interchange of this sort.

Conclusion

The cumulative nature of African PE problems should be apparent by now. Weak accounting results in feeble information and evaluation systems. Inexperienced management is sometimes not fully aware of the inadequate data base on which it bases decisions. Boards of directors do not fulfill the needed policy-setting and decisionmaking roles because of deficiencies in their composition (mainly civil servants representing ministries), and functioning. Civil servants in supervising agencies and ministries—and the fact that there is almost always more than one of each is a part of the problem—are usually good at the meticulous and time-consuming application of regulations, while ministers frequently ignore them with impunity, especially with regard to personnel issues. All of these institutional and managerial difficulties typically take place in a macroeconomic environment of distorted prices, subsidies, and overvalued exchange rates.

10.2 Problems of Public Enterprises in Sierra Leone
World Bank Staff

Public enterprises may be established for ideological reasons, for reasons of national interest, or because private markets have failed to provide certain goods and services. In Sierra Leone, ideology appears to have played little role in government ownership. The reasons that government officials and public enterprise managers give for total or partial public ownership are similar to those found in many other countries: to generate revenue for the government, to prevent the creation of private monopolies, to influence prices, to improve access to foreign equity or loans, to provide commercially unprofitable but socially necessary services, and to start new commercial activities.

Not all of the stated rationales are based on identifiable market failure. Sometimes public enterprises are seen as additional policy tools, mainly to influence prices or to channel subsidies. In certain cases the stated objectives are contradictory (see table 10.2.1). For example, the Sierra Leone Petroleum Refining Company is expected to contribute to government revenues; at the same time, its prices are controlled to keep petroleum prices down.

Most of the objectives are not being realized. Sometimes this is because they are contradictory, sometimes because of inappropriate policies, or sometimes because there is too much interference from the government. Factors external to Sierra Leone's economy have also prevented the realization of objectives. Occasionally it is because the objectives are not specified quantitatively.

The twenty-six public enterprises in Sierra Leone account for between 10 and 12 percent of value added in GDP, about 15 percent of gross capital formation, and 4 percent of total employment in the formal sector. Most public enterprises are currently facing serious financial problems, and the government has underlined the need for major structural adjustment in the sector. Poor financial performance is in part the result of, as well as a contributor to, the weak economy.

Excerpted from "Review of Public Enterprises in Sierra Leone," World Bank Western Africa Region, 1985 (restricted circulation).

Table 10.2.1 *Interrelationships among Public Enterprise Objectives in Sierra Leone*

Objectives	Control prices	Improve access to foreign finance	Provide nonprofitable service	Control monopolies	Encourage new commercial activities
Government revenue	− −	+	− −	+/−	−
Control prices		−	+	+	+/−
Access foreign finance			+	−/+	−
Nonprofit services				+	0
Control monopolies					+

+ + = Strong positive association, + = positive association, − = negative association, − − = strong negative association, 0 = neutral association

Internal Management

The unprofitability of most of the public enterprises has been largely the result of factors outside the control of management and staff: government interference (particularly price controls), depressed world trading conditions, lack of foreign exchange, and domestic credit restrictions.

Management problems, however, have contributed to the current difficulties of some public enterprises. Very few enterprises set annual targets, work out operational plans, or review activities on a systematic basis. Some enterprises have begun setting up management information systems, a step in the right direction. A prerequisite to sound target-setting and operations analysis is for the government itself to clarify each enterprise's financial and social objectives.

Unsound investment decisions have affected financial viability in some enterprises. The present insolvent position of the National Development Bank is largely the result of several loan decisions that were made without adequate analysis. Several factors have contributed to this situation. Many investments lacked feasibility studies and market analysis. There is no detailed operations planning even in the larger organizations, and monitoring is unsystematic and inadequate. The quality of management information is generally poor. Above all, the governing boards, which are the appropriate bodies for review and scrutiny of management performance, have not been active. Their task has remained all the more difficult in the absence of well-defined criteria for evaluation of performance.

A strong positive factor is the experience and loyalty of senior management. The general managers and chairmen of many public enterprises have been serving their companies for many years. It is common practice to fill management positions from within public enterprises, and some have worked their way up from very junior to the most senior positions. This policy is in favorable contrast to that found in state-owned enterprises in some other countries.

There is no evidence of large-scale overstaffing in public enterprises. The National Diamond Mining Company has been successful in adjusting its work force to current operational needs, and the Sierra Leone Port Authority is gradually reducing its work force through attrition and early retirement. In each case, careful negotiation with staff and unions has been required.

The current wage policy is conducive to attracting qualified people to the public enterprise sector. Although there is some variation between the enterprises, salaries and benefits are usually better in public enterprises than in the government and in many cases are comparable to the private sector. The government's attempts to influence public enterprise wages have had limited impact. Enterprise chairmen and general managers have managed to bypass some official controls in order to attract and motivate key staff.

Some public enterprises have tried to promote efficiency through incentives for better performance at the working level. The Sierra Leone Petroleum Refining Company offers merit increases for good performance and a no-accident bonus to drivers. Sierra Leone External Communications has an incentive-bonus scheme.

The current problems with motivation often originate from a lack of clarity about corporate objectives, either in the enabling acts or in the implementation of those acts. There is an apparent reluctance on the part of enterprise management and the government to agree upon financial targets for each planning period.

Financial Control

Financial management skills are in short supply in several public enterprises. Accounting, budgeting, and cost accounting systems are in some instances inadequate. Billing control is almost invariably poor, contributing to large build-ups of overdue accounts. Accounting systems for inventory are often deficient. A further problem is the almost total lack of internal auditing.

The payment of debts by the government and by the enterprises themselves is considerably in arrears. Many enterprises reported that the government and other public enterprises were their main debtors. The National Power Authority has adopted the practice of offsetting the amounts owed to the government (in the form of foreign loan repayments and interest and subsidies) against its charges to the government for the supply of electricity. In times of high inflation, unpaid bills are an especially heavy burden. This problem of arrears should be resolved through a reconciliation of receivables and payables among the enterprises and by instituting procedures to avoid a recurrence of the problem.

Relations between Government and Public Enterprises

Despite the variety of relationships and lack of uniform control by the government, there is a high degree of centralized decisionmaking. Most major domestic pricing decisions are made at the cabinet level, which sometimes causes long delays in the establishment of new prices. Investment decisions are often made at the cabinet level as well. A 1977 cabinet order states that the cabinet must review all investment proposals in excess of 20,000 leones (the Sierra Leone currency unit). This centralized decisionmaking is often caused in part by ineffective department-enterprise relationships.

Those people in the public sector with scarce management and engineering skills tend to be given jobs with the public enterprises themselves, rather than with the supervising ministry. This tendency gives the public enterprises a certain authority over the sponsoring ministries that is augmented by access to the resources that public enterprise managers are able to give to ministerial staff. This elitism reinforces the strong linkages of the general manager with the cabinet and the state house. In addition, many public enterprise managers gain strength from having held their jobs for many years, often longer than their supervising ministers or permanent secretaries.

Informality also characterizes the relationships between government and public enterprises. Sometime the cabinet and ministers override or ignore the legal powers of public enterprise. In general, the informality in Sierra Leone's government-enterprise relationships was effective in the 1960s and 1970s, when the economy was on an upward trend. More clearly defined objectives and procedures are required now to overcome many of these enterprises' current difficulties.

The Impact of External Conditions

Many managers feel they have little control over the efficiency of their operations. Key input prices are determined by world market conditions. Examples include crude oil, spare parts, and rice. Major product prices are also determined by world market conditions: diamonds, coffee, cocoa, and shrimp. The government's inability to deliver resources to its public enterprises weakens the relationships. The scarcity of foreign exchange is perhaps the most critical problem.

The improvement of government-enterprise relations and of the performance of the enterprises themselves is thus closely tied to pursuing appropriate pricing and foreign exchange policies. In turn, it is likely that foreign donor assistance in structural adjustment will require an effective formal government relationship with public enterprises.

Recommendations

Setting clear objectives for public enterprises is the first order of business. As a former minister of finance said in his 1979 budget speech, "what now needs to be done, as a matter of urgency, is to move on from statements of general principles to prescriptions of norms and targets which could serve as a concrete guide in the conduct of their complex and multifarious operations." If the government wants the enterprise to pursue goals that will result in a deterioration in its financial performance, the financial costs to the enterprise should be calculated and compensation set aside as part of the annual budget.

A clear formulation of public enterprise objectives would show that some of the commercially oriented public enterprises are good candidates for privatization. Certain economic and social aspects, however, also need to be recognized in the sale of public enterprises. The financial market in Sierra Leone is very small and highly segmented. Domestic private savings are low, and the banking system is not geared to providing medium-term financing. The current economic situation of tight money, high inflation, and stagnant private demand for investments would also make any large sale of public enterprises and assets difficult. In view of the limited number of potential buyers and stagnant economic conditions in Sierra Leone, a rapid privatization program may cause financial loss to the government. The government, therefore, should phase the program, promote competition among potential buyers, and identify potential foreign buyers.

One problem in government–public enterprise relations is that, despite the de facto centralization of decisionmaking, no single government department has overall responsibility either for defining efficiency and objectives or for monitoring and comparing the performance of enterprises. A public enterprise commission such as that suggested by the minister of finance would provide a more appropriate forum for guiding overall policy, setting standards, and giving advice on performance.

10.3 *State Ownership in Ethiopia*
World Bank Staff

Before the 1974 revolution, the only public enterprises (PES) in Ethiopia were a few publicly owned entities, mainly in the utilities sector and in transportation. The government also had minority holdings in a few industrial enterprises, notably in sugar and textiles. Following the Declaration of Socialist Economic Policy in 1975, the government nationalized seventy-two foreign and locally owned companies, most of them engaged in manufacturing, and acquired majority ownership of twenty-nine others. Public enterprises in Ethiopia have become an important instrument for the structural transformation of the economy. They account for almost all employment, output, exports, and value added in medium- and large-scale enterprises. They are seen as instruments to promote economic growth, to contribute to domestic resource mobilization, to control inflation, and, in more general terms, to help establish a socialist order.

On the whole, Ethiopia's public enterprises are reasonably well managed and their operations have been profitable, although at modest levels. However, a slowdown in the rate of growth of production and profits is expected in the near future, particularly in the manufacturing sector, on account of difficulties in further increasing capacity utilization, anticipated production bottlenecks resulting from the aging of plant and equipment, and low levels of investment.

The Ministry of Industry, which controls the majority of public enterprises,

Excerpted and edited from "Ethiopia: Recent Economic Developments and Future Prospects," vol. 2, May 31, 1984; and "Ethiopia: Industrial Sector Review," December 1985, World Bank Eastern and Southern Africa Region (restricted circulation).

is organized according to the "corporation model." Under this ministry there are twelve corporations with 153 enterprises in the areas of food, meat, sugar, beverages, tobacco and matches, textiles, leather and shoes, woodworking, building materials, printing, chemicals, and metalworking. Textiles, food, and beverages are the largest corporations both in terms of their contribution to output and employment and the number of plants they control. The corporations are headed by general managers selected by the minister and appointed by the government; enterprises are headed by managers selected by the corporations and appointed by the minister.

The Ministry of Industry, in coordinating the activities of its corporations and public enterprises, issues policies with respect to planning and budgeting, plant rehabilitation, investments, and personnel management. Through the corporations it also controls enterprise performance by setting and guiding reporting procedures and coordinating plant programs.

The structure allows for close monitoring of all aspects of PE operations, particularly in the areas of investment, personnel (hiring, firing, promotions, and transfers), finance (availability of funds for continued operations), and operations (sales, production, and export). A gradual decentralization of some of these activities is now taking place.

Control of Public Enterprise Operations

The operations and expenditures of public enterprises are closely monitored and controlled at both corporation and ministry levels. Enterprises send monthly and quarterly reports to the corporation and the ministry on the implementation of their budgets and work programs. Corporations may receive weekly or even daily information from the plants if a problem requires close attention. Corporations also audit the accounts of the enterprises. In addition to this internal audit, public enterprises are audited externally once a year. Corporations are not holding companies in the technical or legal sense, since each enterprise manages its own finances. To make an expenditure above a certain level, an enterprise has to receive the approval of the corporation.

The ministries perform a control function, mainly through the corporations. The Ministry of Industry, for example, has four coordinators who meet regularly with corporation managers to review the progress made on the annual work programs and budgets and who visit plants at least twice a year. An audit committee within the Ministry reviews the reports of the internal and external auditors. The Central Planning Supreme Council (CPSC) receives quarterly and monthly reports from the public enterprises through the relevant corporations and ministries. The CPSC acts only if there is a need for coordination among different ministries and agencies.

As the foregoing suggests, corporations, ministries, and the CPSC are routinely informed about the implementation of annual programs and budgets. The system is also organized in such a way that early action can be taken if serious problems are encountered. However, unless care is taken to avoid duplication and excessive detail, such monitoring can take up considerable management time.

System of Incentives and Managerial Autonomy

At higher and middle management levels, incentives consist essentially of prospects of promotion or transfer to higher-paying positions. Since 1974, salaries have been frozen at all levels of management, along with civil service salaries. In the manufacturing sector, if output goes up in a given plant from one year to another, the total wage bill for workers receiving 650 birr (US$315) or less is increased by 5 percent. The distribution of these additional funds is based on monthly wages, giving a larger increase to lower-wage earners.

While these measures are useful in keeping up workers' morale, their effectiveness is questionable. For one thing, none of the incentives is related to individual or small-group performance. Increased production could result from a variety of factors, including improvements in management, and may or may not have a great deal to do with increased efforts by lower-paid workers. Moreover, changes in output and profitability of an enterprise are not entirely the product of workers' efforts. Changes in average output are affected by the capital and input mix, while the profitability of a plant varies according to the prices it pays for its inputs and the prices it is allowed to charge for its output.

The authorities are aware of these shortcomings and are in the process of introducing other incentives. Already some textile factories pay wages on a piece rate. However, a widespread application of such a system is not always practical.

The autonomy of managers is circumscribed by several factors. Managers do not usually have a choice in procuring inputs. Sometimes the corporations purchase selected inputs for all plants. For example, all ginned cotton is procured through the textiles corporation. Plant expansion plans are usually conceived by managers and approved by higher authorities. Plant requirements for skilled personnel are determined in the annual plans, and the personnel is allocated by the ministry; managers are allowed to select employees only below a certain wage level. The employment of personnel who are accountable to the manager has to be approved by the corporation.

The only real pressure for good performance is in terms of fulfilling production targets and financial plans. Although enterprises are required at least to break even, there is no real managerial incentive to lower costs. Profits or losses are, more than anything else, a function of input and output prices. Under such circumstances, managers cannot be held responsible for the financial performance of their enterprises.

Performance

The output of PES has increased substantially in recent years. The index of production shows that from 1979–80, the year in which production targets were first set, to 1982–83, the volume of output for all PES grew by 32 percent.

Industrial public enterprises in Ethiopia have been profitable, particularly compared with many African countries. Gross profit margins for industrial sector PES have slightly exceeded those for the public enterprise sector as a whole. Both return on sales and return on total net assets were consistently higher in food, tobacco and matches, chemicals, metalworks, and woodworking than for public enterprises as a whole. Returns have been relatively low in textiles, leather and shoes, and printing. The building materials subsector is the only one that recorded losses throughout the period.

Debt-equity ratios vary significantly among enterprises in different sectors and have worsened over time for all sectors. This indicates a weakening of the financial structure of PEs, partly because of transfers of residual surpluses to the Treasury, which limits equity growth.

PEs have contributed substantially to government revenue over the past four years. The contributions have taken three forms: capital changes, corporate taxation, and residual surpluses. PEs are allowed to keep 10 percent of after-tax profits as an addition to general reserves until such reserves reach 30 percent of equity capital. The other 90 percent of profits, called residual surplus, is payable to the national Treasury within seven months after the end of the fiscal year. The effect of these levies, coupled with delay in some price adjustments by the authorities, is that some PEs appear to be experiencing substantial cash-flow problems.

The mandate given to PEs to accomplish social and economic objectives simultaneously has led in some instances to inefficient ways of achieving certain goals and to a situation in which the financial profitability of the firms is not a good indicator of their economic efficiency. The structure of incentives, price controls, and protection is such that many inefficient producers have a good chance of being financially profitable. The inverse relationship between financial profitability and economic profitability suggests that, in more than half of the cases in the sample, firms that are net contributors to the Treasury were utilizing scarce resources inefficiently.

One major cause of the financial difficulties encountered by public enterprises is delay in price adjustments by the authorities, partly because of delays in submission of data and subsequent analysis. In many cases, price increases are not sufficient to permit enterprises to offset cost increases. The problem is not as serious in those enterprises where input prices are also controlled by the government. Some enterprises that have experienced a decline in their output prices because of changed international prices are facing financial strains that are unrelated to government policy. The leather and shoe industry is in this latter category.

Using price controls to pursue social objectives, such as helping those who are relatively poor or curbing inflation, is not usually an effective method. Among other potentially undesirable consequences, the administration of price controls has become a major factor in weakening public enterprises.

Financial Performance of Public Enterprises

Compared with similar operations in many African countries, public enterprises in Ethiopia are relatively well managed and profitable. The ratio of before-tax profits to sales (profit margin) for 1980–82 was between 6.2 percent and 9.2 percent.

Data are not available to make separate estimates of profitability in different sectors. However, there is sufficiently detailed information on manufacturing enterprises for a period of five years between 1976–77 and 1980–81. A number of coefficients estimated from these data reveal the financial performance and strength of manufacturing enterprises in different subsectors. These are presented in table 10.3.1. According to the ratios given in this table, profit margins (before tax) for the manufacturing sector were slightly higher than the average for the public enterprise sector as a whole, and they fluctuated throughout the period. On the other hand, profit margins have been consistently higher than the sector's average in tobacco and matches, sugar, chemicals, metalworks, and woodworking. Profit margins have been relatively low in textiles and fiber, and leather and shoes, while the building materials subsector has recorded losses throughout the period.

Two other ratios shown in table 10.3.1 shed further light on the profitability of manufacturing enterprises. The *return on total net assets* is an indicator of financial performance in relation to total net assets. It is the ratio of profits before tax (that is, including taxes) to net assets (which includes net fixed assets, other long-term assets, and current assets). In recent years, returns on total net assets have been relatively high in most sectors, even though there was a pronounced decline in 1980–81, the last year estimates were available. The sectors that have consistently recorded high returns on total net assets are tobacco and matches, food and beverages, chemicals, metalworking, and woodworking.

Estimates of *return on net worth*, which is the ratio between profits before tax and net worth, are also given in table 10.3.1. Return on net worth measures the return on the enterprise's own assets and eliminates the impact of both long- and short-term borrowing. The pattern of returns on net worth is not

Table 10.3.1 *Financial Ratios for Public Manufacturing Enterprises in Ethiopia, 1980–81*
(percent)

Industry	Profit/ sales	Return on total net assets	Return on net worth	Debt/ equity	Net worth/ total net assets
Food and beverages	6.0	7.4	30.7	3.2	0.2
Sugar	22.0	9.5	18.8	1.0	0.5
Tobacco and matches	11.6	11.0	22.6	1.1	0.5
Textiles and fiber	9.4	9.2	26.9	1.9	3.4
Leather and shoes	1.2	1.2	500.0	414.3	—
Printing	26.8	24.0	75.6	2.2	0.3
Chemicals	14.3	14.2	51.6	2.6	0.3
Metalworks	10.1	10.4	40.4	2.9	0.3
Building materials	−33.1	−22.8	−132.3	4.8	0.2
Woodworking	11.5	12.3	50.9	3.1	0.2
All industry	8.9	8.2	26.0	2.2	0.3

significantly different from that of returns on total net assets, indicating that the composition of liabilities is rather uniform among different groups of enterprises. Those subsectors that experienced relatively high returns on total net assets also recorded high returns on net worth. One notable difference was in leather and shoes, where the returns on net worth were much higher than the return on total net assets.

Also shown in table 10.3.1 is the *debt-equity ratio,* which is the ratio between total liabilities and the net worth of enterprises. Debt-equity ratios vary significantly among enterprises in different sectors. In almost all sectors, the ratio has increased dramatically over time, indicating a weakening of the financial strength of enterprises. Not surprisingly, the ratio is lower in sectors where financial rates of return are higher. For the ratio between *net worth and total net assets* the variations are not as pronounced. If anything, a declining trend is observable, pointing out the weakening of the financial position of public enterprises in the manufacturing sector.

Technical Efficiency of PES

PES have been rated according to suitability of technology, standard of production management and operational skills, standard of maintenance and condition of fixed assets, and external factors, such as availability of materials and markets for the product. From a technical standpoint, the technology employed was regarded as relatively satisfactory. Although the condition of plants and the caliber of management and operational skills were regarded as adequate in many firms, particularly in view of the upheaval that followed the 1973 revolution, the standard of production management and operational skills and the standard of maintenance and conditions of fixed assets are below par in some firms. Technical experience in many firms is not yet adequate for reasonable productive efficiency. Firms afflicted with these problems are present in all subsectors. However, there is a high variance within each subsector.

Conclusions

On the whole, public enterprises in Ethiopia are reasonably well managed and, with the exception of the state farms, their operations have been profitable, even though at modest levels. However, there are signs of impending difficulties. In the manufacturing enterprises, existing capacity is nearly fully utilized, and many factories, including those in textiles, food, and cement, are working on three shifts. Moreover, machinery and equipment in many plants appear to be old, and the need for frequent repairs and alterations will affect productivity adversely in the coming years. Many enterprises are facing serious shortages of working capital. Transfers made to the government in various forms leave some public enterprises with limited liquidity to finance their own operations. The tardiness of the authorities to approve sufficient price increases for products and services has caused further deterioration in the financial position of enterprises, particularly those that face increased input prices.

10.4 Agenda for Reform
John Nellis

Although every African country has a firm or sector that performs comparatively well, the aggregate level of performance of African public enterprises
(PES) has been so modest that just about every observer recognizes the need
for fundamental reform. For the majority of African leaders and administrators, the hope is that many if not most PES can be retained under state ownership and that methods can be found to make them more efficient and
productive. Steps to achieve such rehabilitation of PES are discussed in detail
below.

But for a growing number of persons concerned with PE performance, rehabilitation is not enough. Increasingly, one hears recommendations for divestiture, for the sale or liquidation of PES.

Divestiture

The arguments for divestiture are simple and straightforward. First, many
African PES should never have been created in the first place and do not have
the slightest comparative advantage. In many cases the assessment of the
economic prospects of an enterprise was made by a private sector agent
attempting to sell a plant and equipment or by representatives of a donor
agency that took an optimistic view in order to advance a politically advantageous project. The result was the many PE "white elephants" that litter the
African landscape. Proponents of divestiture argue that internal reforms are
insufficient. They argue that a more enduring solution is to sell to the private
sector those that can be sold. Those for which no buyer can be found should
be closed and their assets liquidated.

Second is the argument that the state is a poor entrepreneur. That is, even
where PES may be covering their costs or making a return on capital, African
states are paying a high opportunity cost because the resources producing a
modest return in PES could produce a higher return elsewhere. If African
entrepreneurs have neither the skills nor the resources to purchase PES, then
foreign private sectors should be encouraged to undertake the risks. But most
governments—African or otherwise—are nervous at the prospect of introducing or reintroducing a large foreign private sector.

An African counterargument to divestiture occurs at this point. In most
African countries the internal markets are so small that large manufacturing
firms frequently acquire a monopolistic or oligopolistic position. There is no
reason to believe that the replacement of an inefficient public monopoly by a
poorly regulated or unregulated private monopoly would add greatly to a
country's socioeconomic welfare unless it could be shown that the new private sector monopolies would invest their earnings in the economy in a more
productive manner than government monopolies. Indeed, it is apparent that
the factors that contribute to poor PE performance (a poor macroeconomic

Excerpted and edited from John R. Nellis, *Public Enterprises in Sub-Saharan Africa*, World Bank
Discussion Paper 1 (Washington, D.C., 1986).

policy environment, poor managers, poor information systems, pervasive corruption) are the same factors that weaken the African states' capacity to regulate large private sector firms.

There is a growing sense that even unproven measures such as privatization, which at least hold some promise for improvement, must be tried, since the current situation cannot be tolerated. Although privatization receives the bulk of attention and is the subject of intense debate within Africa, closures and liquidations of PEs appear to have been far more frequent. In a 1985 sample of fifteen Sub-Saharan countries, a preliminary reading of the data indicates that about eighty-eight closures and liquidations of PEs took place in the period 1979–84. In roughly the same time period, there were about twenty-three sales of assets or equity, mainly the former. It appears that there were equity sales in only four countries—Kenya, Mali, Senegal, and Zaire.

Many of the closures (in Cameroon, Guinea, Liberia, Madagascar, Mali, Senegal, and Togo) have been partial. That is, an enterprise loses its market, or never produces at a rate sufficient to cover variable costs, or exhausts all available avenues of credit, or suffers some technical reversal that causes it to reduce production to a trickle or stop it altogether.

The reluctance to liquidate is mainly due to political sensitivities. A PES withering away in piecemeal fashion is not likely to provide political opponents with a provocative issue. Informal closure keeps open the option of a revival of the enterprise, under public management, at some future date. It also allows postponement of the final settlement of debts. In short, it is an example of following the path of least resistance.

Divestiture, admittedly, is a very new activity in Africa, and no reliable patterns have yet emerged. What one can say now is that few African entrepreneurs have overcome the combined lack of local capital markets and lack of willingness of local representatives of international banks to support purchase efforts. Some international entrepreneurs are willing to take the high risk of investing in African PEs, but they often demand high rates of protection and mechanisms to allow them to recoup their investment in an extremely short period. For example, a portion of a near-defunct Togolese PE steelmill was leased to a private foreign entrepreneur. The arrangements have been criticized, however, because the new firm was assured a protection rate of 41 percent and tax-free importation of all raw materials, and because the leasor pays Togo a modest annual lease fee of $175,000, a fraction of the interest charges the government of Togo must continue to pay on the original large investment. Togo could have shut, dismantled, or sold the steel mill and then imported the high-priced products now made locally. Although the Togolese may hope that this arrangement will attract other leasors and buyers, they run the risk that new entrants will demand the same uneconomic terms.

The Togolese case illustrates that more is at stake than privatization. African governments must be strengthened in their capacity to select PE candidates for divestiture, to market these enterprises, and to negotiate mutually beneficial sales, lease, or management contracts with private sector parties. Innovative actions—such as leveraged buyouts, where the manager or managers of a firm purchase the enterprise from its owners by raising capital from a third party that takes some equity in the firm—are needed. In the Côte d'Ivoire, a leveraged buyout of an agroindustry PE was arranged with the participation of the International Finance Corporation. Donors should also be prepared to provide African governments with the technical—and in some cases the financial—assistance that is necessary if divestiture is to be a success.

Rehabilitation

A basic fact must be faced: even if every conceivable candidate for divestiture were sold or liquidated in the near future, a substantial PE sector would still exist in every Sub-Saharan country. It is within the realm of possibility that traditional PE activities, such as utilities, might be transferred to private own-ership in the long run, but it is not at all likely. African governments regard the provision of many services as "strategic" natural monopolies. They do not contemplate selling these organizations to private owners, although the private sector has shown some interest in purchasing them. The PES in ques-tion are the largest public enterprises in terms of assets, employees, and financial losses. The only remaining alternative is to attempt to improve per-formance under present ownership.

Markets and Competition

The key to internal reform of African PES is to devise a system of incentives that will reward improvements in efficiency. The most direct way to do this is for African governments to allow private firms to compete with PES where possible, while at the same time instructing PES to operate on commercial market lines and to maximize their profits.

A number of African governments are considering ways to push their PES into a more competitive, market-oriented position. In Benin, Kenya, Mali, Niger, and Togo, for example, macroeconomic policy changes have been planned—and in some cases are being implemented—that would end the regulated monopoly position of some PES and impel others to adopt pricing, investment, and credit policies more in line with those used by private firms.

The Reform Process

The reform process proceeds in two main phases, each of which is divided into three stages, as follows:

Phase One. Preparation
Stage 1. Diagnosis
Stage 2. Devising an improvement plan
Stage 3. Drawing up a contract-plan (or its equivalent)

Phase Two. Execution
Stage 1. Implementing and monitoring the improvement plan
Stage 2. Evaluating performance
Stage 3. Revision of contract-plan on basis of lessons learned

This approach is derived from Senegal, which in 1978 became the first African country to commence reform of the PE sector. The terminology may differ in other countries, of course, and neat division into stages doubtless imposes too much order on what is everywhere a fluid and experimental process. Nonetheless, the principal steps are (1) diagnostic studies to gain basic information and to alert relevant parties to the nature and scope of the problem; (2) the drawing up of an improvement plan for PEs that must be salvaged; and (3) the drawing up of a contract-plan or some similar mechanism specifying the obligations and expectations of the government and the enterprise. The first phase must be seen as tentative. The process must be closely watched and guided, achievements and problems must be clearly analyzed, and the contract-plan must periodically be revised, since the changing economic environment will necessitate periodic revisions.

In Senegal, the rehabilitated PEs submit reports to their boards twice a year. The boards discuss them and then pass them on to the supervising ministry and eventually to central PE regulating bodies. The government uses these reports to allocate rewards or sanctions and to launch stage 2, performance evaluation. When performance evaluation shows that achievements are out of line with objectives as presented in the contract-plan, a revision of the contract-plan is called for. In Senegal, the process calls for an annual revision of contract-plans to redraw objectives and government obligations. Elsewhere the intervals between formal revisions are longer, though the high degree of uncertainty in Africa makes it unlikely that the many assumptions and predictions necessarily contained within a contract-plan will hold up over time. This means that frequent revision, as in Senegal, will probably be the norm.

The reform actions called for are administrative-intensive operations that would demand much of weak and already overstrained administrative systems. It must also be stressed that even if the African countries successfully attack their institutional-managerial obstacles to good PE performance, they must at the same time take steps to improve the macroeconomic setting in which the PEs operate.

10.5 *Establishing a Performance-Oriented Environment*
Mahmood A. Ayub and Sven O. Hegstad

Attempts to achieve a more efficient public enterprise sector must begin with an understanding of the factors inhibiting adequate performance. Are they purely inherent, arising from public ownership per se? Or are there other important determinants of performance, separate and apart from ownership, that can be influenced by governments?

To some extent, the poor performance of public industrial enterprises relative to their private counterparts can be explained by some inherent differences relating to ownership. These include lack of a significant financial stake

---

Excerpted and edited from Mahmood A. Ayub and Sven O. Hegstad, *Public Industrial Enterprises: Determinants of Performance*, World Bank Industry and Finance Series 17 (Washington, D.C., 1986). The background materials for this study comprise thirteen country studies of public industrial enterprise sectors. These studies were complemented by interviews with senior managers of successful and not-so-successful public enterprises. The countries included were Austria, Brazil, France, Ghana, India, Israel, Italy, Norway, Pakistan, Portugal, Sweden, Tunisia, and Zambia.

on the part of the government officials representing the state, the limited threat of bankruptcy and reorganization, the circuitous chain of decisionmaking, and the generally close political ties between trade unions and government officials and board members. Although these inherent factors are important, evidence from our study indicates that factors not strictly related to ownership per se are equally important.

Foremost among these factors are the degree of competition that public enterprises are exposed to, the degree of financial autonomy and accountability of public enterprises, and the extent to which and manner in which the ownership, strategic, and operational roles of the government are kept separate. If these factors can be managed appropriately, the performance gap between public and private enterprises can be reduced significantly, and to levels that in many cases can be justified by the infrastructural, strategic, or social reasons that motivated the creation of many public enterprises in the first place.

Fostering a Competitive Environment

Inappropriate macroeconomic, trade, and industrial policies are the most potent constraints on competition for both public and private firms. These policies include the maintenance of an overvalued exchange rate, reliance on quantitative restrictions and bans, high tariff protection, price controls, domestic content legislation (especially in the automobiles and electronics subsectors), investment licensing, regulations on entry and exit, and other regulatory constraints.

The rationalization of these policies can improve the competitive environment considerably, but there are other ways as well. First, governments can make explicit attempts to nurture competition among public industrial enterprises and between public and private firms. Evidence indicates that such competition can occur even among public enterprises that are considered strategic. Central monitoring agencies should therefore make information on comparative performance widely available. In countries where performance targets are reviewed by such agencies, at least some of the meetings should be devoted to a comparative analysis of performance with public managers under the same roof.

Another way to subject public enterprises to competitive pressures is to encourage them to seek export markets. A small shift of the products to export markets can have a sizable impact on the quality of management and competitiveness, even if the impact on the balance of payments is minimal.

In industries in which economies of scale are not important, competition can also be enhanced by breaking up overly centralized and monolithic holding companies or even large industrial enterprises. Occasionally, the break-up of large enterprises may be necessary but not sufficient for better performance (for example, if the regulatory environment that hampered operations remains unchanged).

In short, public enterprises, to the largest extent possible, should be subjected to competitive pressures. Toward this end, consideration should be given to introducing public enterprises on stock exchanges, establishing joint ventures with the private sector, stimulating export initiatives, breaking up monopoly firms, allowing competition among public enterprises, and breaking up or reorganizing rigid conglomerates into more flexible and dynamic bodies.

Financial Autonomy and Accountability

The success of government officials in managing public enterprises depends crucially on a number of financial issues. These include the extent to which the enterprises are exposed to financial discipline; the importance of financial objectives, including payment of dividends; the clarity of social objectives; and the degree of restriction on access to subsidies from the state.

Subjecting public enterprises to *financial discipline* can be a potent way of improving financial performance. A combination of more autonomy in financial matters and greater exposure to, and control by, markets normally creates among public enterprise managers a stronger sense of responsibility and a more genuine interest in the financial viability of the enterprise.

Access of public enterprises to capital markets is an important way of institutionalizing financial discipline. Independent bankers scrutinize investment and financing decisions before they extend funds. The use of bond markets, equity markets, and joint ventures opens the public enterprise to the public and to special audits and reporting requirements.

Public enterprises should be encouraged to raise, to the extent possible, all their debt financing outside the government and the central bank. Whenever government debt financing is used, market interest rates should be charged, and joint ventures and floating of minority equity positions on stock exchanges should be encouraged.

Sound financial management entails specifying *financial objectives*, establishing a mechanism to monitor these indicators, and holding managers accountable for the outcome. The main measures to be used include return on assets or capital employed, return on equity, dividend pay-out ratio, maximum debt-equity ratio, and prespecified level of internal financing of large investment projects. The establishment of broad financial objectives and enforcement of a clear dividend policy are even more important in state-owned enterprises than in private firms because of the former's inherent bias toward giving excessive priority to nonfinancial objectives. Even though the dividends in many cases may be small, the principle of paying them is more important than the amount. The enforcement of dividend policy is a highly visible and substantive action demonstrating that the government gives high priority to financial management and that state equity is not considered a free good. It also forces management to rethink its growth strategies and, ideally, to focus on improving productivity and profitability in order to finance the "new" financial obligations created by the dividend requirement.

Public enterprises are frequently expected to pursue a variety of *social objectives*, which can include such diverse goals as redistributing income, subsidizing particular regions of a country, and creating or maintaining employment. The fulfillment of at least some social objectives by public enterprises may be necessary and, in some cases, even advisable.

The problem is not the fulfillment of these objectives. But the multiplicity of objectives and the absence of priorities among them lead to a situation in which social objectives become an excuse for poor financial performance, or become so predominant that they overwhelm the main objective of the public enterprise as a productive unit. In using public industrial enterprises for social purposes, governments need to address two relevant issues. First, are the social objectives truly being fulfilled? Second, are there no better ways to achieve them?

There is evidence that the pursuit of social objectives by public enterprises can lead to inadvertent and perverse results. The case of Zambia's publicly owned agro-based industries (largely producing vegetable oil products, detergents, and soap) is illustrative. Stringent price controls on refined oils and fats have led not only to large financial losses but also to low morale and a shift in the product mix away from the production of oils and fats. This result was precisely the opposite of the government's social priorities. Price controls are intended to benefit the poor, but they often end up subsidizing large industrial users, wholesalers, or the upper-middle class in urban areas.

In many instances there may be preferred alternatives to the use of public enterprises as agents of social change. The objective of regionally balanced economic growth is better achieved by a scheme that encourages investment through not only income and corporate tax credits but also direct cash grants from the treasury.

In a number of countries, especially France, Italy, and Sweden, public enterprises are compensated explicitly through the budget for undertaking social objectives. This approach prevents public enterprises from being saddled with excessive social burdens and, at the same time, avoids random departures from efficiency criteria. However, such compensatory payments for undertaking noncommercial objectives should be viewed as second-best or even third-best solutions and should be used sparingly. In principle, public enterprises should receive government funds only under the following circumstances: (1) increases in equity capital to finance viable expansion; (2) increases in equity capital as part of restructuring to create viable operations; and (3) subsidies for performing noneconomic social functions. The latter type of agreement should be used only in those rare cases in which the economic impact of the social function is substantial. Elimination of subsidies is one of the strongest actions that a government can take to effect a reorientation in financial policies and to force more economically oriented behavior on public managers.

A review of the accounts of the major public enterprises in our sample indicated a complicated maze of transfers between central budgetary authorities and a public enterprises. To improve *financial discipline and transparency* in financial relations, and to be able to record "true" financial results, governments should demand tax, duty, interest, dividend, and amortization payments from public enterprises the same way they do from private enterprises. Losses and negative cash flow would then have to be financed explicitly in a more transparent way through new equity, loans, and so on. It is important that the "true" financial situation of enterprises be reflected in the dialogue between public enterprise managers and the government about the enterprises' future development.

Managerial Autonomy and Accountability

The role of the owner(s) of a private enterprise involves defining the business charter, setting the overall objectives of the enterprise, appointing and dismissing the board of directors, and approving annual accounts and dividend payments. These powers are formally executed through an annual shareholders' meeting. The board of directors performs a strategic role. Its major functions are to decide upon strategic plans, monitor performance against targets, and appoint, advise, and dismiss the chief executive officer (CEO). Typically the board meets four to eight times a year and is composed of persons with high stature and professional experience relevant to the business of the firm. The CEO and top management perform an operating role. Their major responsibility is to manage and develop the enterprise in accordance with agreed objectives (table 10.5.1).

How do public enterprise structures differ from this? The relatively short experience of governments with the management of public enterprises, the multitudinous (and occasionally conflicting) objectives they are assigned, and the lack of adequate information flows between public enterprises and government invariably lead to encroachment by government (as owners) on the strategic and even operational functions of public enterprises. This breakdown in the demarcation of the major functions is the source of much of the poor performance of public enterprises.

In a private enterprise, the power to undertake investments is almost always delegated to the CEO by the shareholders and the board of directors. The logic is that the manager will be judged on the basis of the financial outcome of his decision. The board can, therefore, exercise its control function by examining outcomes (profit) rather than the processes by which the

Table 10.5.1 *Conventional Roles in Corporate Management*

Roles and functions	Basic characteristics
Ownership role (owners)	
Define enterprise charter	Long-term view
Appoint and dismiss the board of directors	Broad objectives
	Broad, noninvolved monitoring of performance
Approve annual accounts	
Strategic role (board of directors)	
Provide strategic guidance	Medium-term view
Control performance	Specific strategies and operational targets
Appoint and dismiss the chief executive officer	Close monitoring of performance
Operating role (management)	
Develop and manage the enterprise according to agreed upon objectives	Shorter-term view
	Development of alternative strategies, plans, and programs
	Management of resources
	Detailed control of operational performance

outcome are generated. In the case of public enterprises, on the other hand the government may get involved in the investment decision because of its macroeconomic impact on the overall fiscal deficit and concern about the quality of projects. As a result, high government officials in countries such as Ghana, India, Pakistan, and Zambia are involved in detailed investment decisions. There are several problems with this process. It is time consuming for an already overstretched bureaucracy, the ministries lack the information and the business acumen to make the correct decisions, and, most important, it absolves management of its responsibility and accountability for enterprise performance.

The preceding is just one example of an oft-repeated phenomenon. It is also evident in detailed ministerial involvement in the hiring and firing of staff, wage setting, working-capital decisionmaking, procurement policies, foreign travel, and much else. When outcomes cannot be quantified and when the incentives structure does not affect managers' decisions, it is difficult to control what happens. When governments cannot control outcomes, they attempt to control processes. And ineffective control frequently leads to excessive interference.

Recognition of the inefficiency of large centrally planned bureaucracies and increased understanding of the importance of the individual manager are complementary forces. They are currently moving many governments toward more decentralization, and in many cases to the most decentralized organizational mode of managing public enterprises, the transfer of ownership to the private sector.

As countries move from industrial infancy through growth and maturity into the postindustrial era, there is a pattern as to which organizational structures dominate in different periods. At the risk of oversimplification, figure 10.5.1 illustrates how public enterprises have tended to move through five increasingly decentralized stages as the economy grows and matures. This evolution toward increasingly decentralized management models can be explained by some of the characteristics of the process of industrialization. As industrialization increases, the complexities and competitiveness of the marketplace as well as the speed of change accelerate. Rigid and bureaucratic management models that are appropriate at earlier stages become obsolete, and more decentralized management structures become a necessity for survival.

How can governments avoid, or at least ameliorate, problems arising from excessive centralization? The experience of public industrial enterprises, as well as of large private enterprises, indicates that the worst repercussions of a poor organizational structure can be avoided through scrupulous adherence to the following principles: (1) clear demarcation of major roles and responsibilities, as indicated earlier; (2) full delegation of authority in line with delegated responsibility; (3) the appointment of professional directors and managing directors with experience directly relevant to their tasks; and (4) placement of controls closer to the action and under people knowledgeable about the issues at hand. Adequate decentralization may not by itself be sufficient for satisfactory performance. However, its absence can confound the most meticulously worked out organizational structure.

Figure 10.5.1 *Life Cycle of Public Enterprise* (PE) *Organizations*

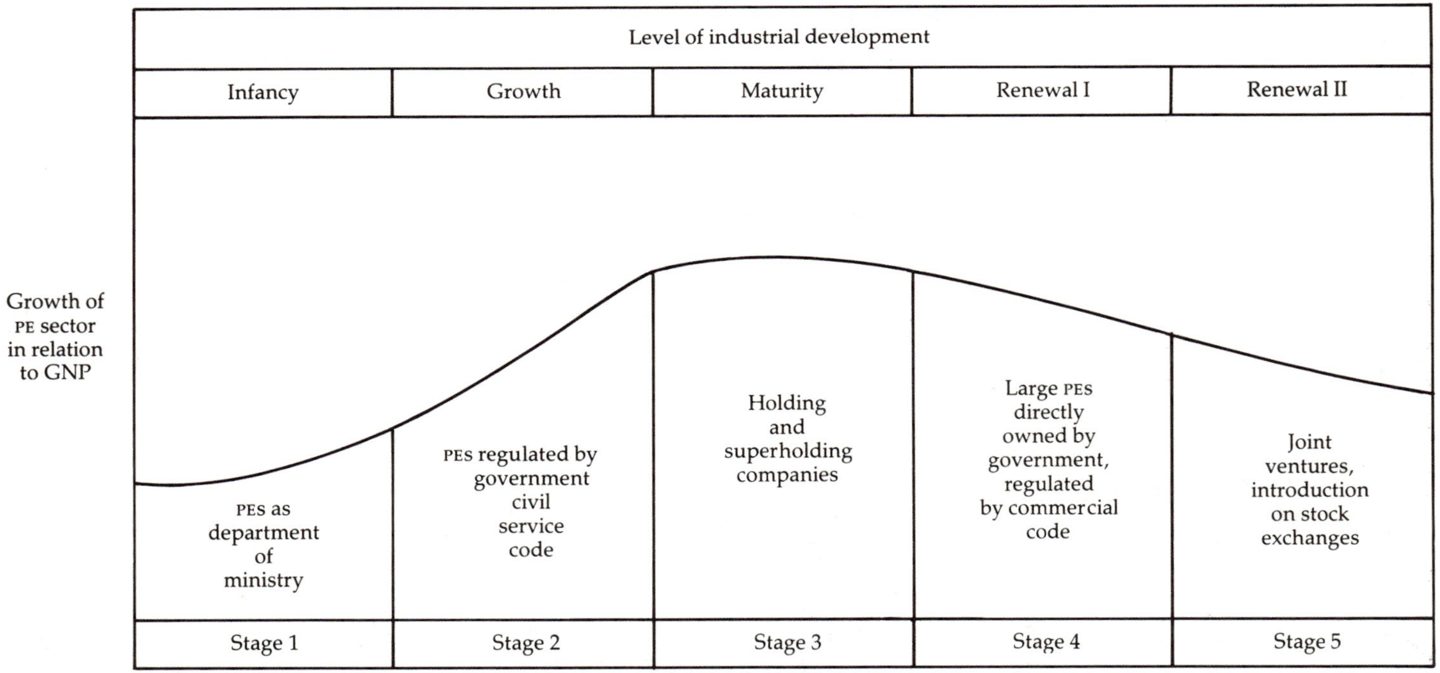

Level of industrial development
Infancy
Growth
Maturity
Renewal I
Renewal II
Growth of PE sector in relation to GNP
PES as department of ministry
PES regulated by government civil service code
Holding and superholding companies
Large PES directly owned by government, regulated by commercial code
Joint ventures, introduction on stock exchanges
Stage 1
Stage 2
Stage 3
Stage 4
Stage 5

	Division of powers in organizational model				
Ownership role Strategic role Operating role	Government Government Government	Government Government/management Management/government	Government Holding company Management	Government Board Management	Government/private Board Management

Managerial Skills

The quality of the managerial staffs of public enterprises in developing countries varies considerably across countries and even across enterprises in the same country. At one extreme are Brazil and Israel, where public enterprise managers are generally well educated in their fields, are disdainful of government bureaucracy, and are knowledgeable about private enterprise methods. At the other extreme are Ghana, India, Pakistan, and Zambia, where many public managers are closer in their attitudes to bureaucrats than to private entrepreneurs.

A number of factors explain the variations in the quantity and quality of managerial skills in developing countries. First, public enterprise managers are generally paid substantially less than their counterparts in the private sector. For example, in Zambia, public enterprise salary ceilings are still set with reference to civil service levels. Second, public enterprises in developing countries typically experience high rates of turnover of managerial staff, either because of political changes or because of civil service rotation. Third, public enterprises are frequently thought of as dumping grounds for retired politicians and generals. Their lack of technical and managerial know-how becomes a formidable handicap and a source of poor performance. Fourth, there have been severe shortages of managerial skills in some sample countries, particularly Ghana and Zambia. This problem has not only created bottlenecks but also caused excessive dependence on chief executive officers and a few managers. To some extent the problem has become even more acute in countries such as Zambia, which encourage the increasing participation of nationals in place of expatriates.

How can governments reduce these constraints? One of the most effective ways of nurturing more dynamic public enterprise management is to depoliticize hiring and firing. Sufficient managerial autonomy and accountability would ensure a less bureaucratic response. One solution is to employ senior management staff under special contracts with no tenure and subject to dismissal at any time, but at higher salaries than employees in other public enterprises.

Holding Companies

The rationale for setting up a holding or multisector holding company is that it can act as an effective buffer against excessive political interference; provide effective coordination of decisionmaking, clear strategic guidance, and improved financial discipline; assist in pooling scarce managerial talents, thereby infusing industrial and enterprise-level experience into the enterprises; and lead to benefits of synergy, such as economies of scale in large procurement contracts, establishment of foreign marketing outlets, lower-cost financing, and so on.

These arguments are all very valid, and some state-owned holding companies have indeed performed adequately. However, the overall experience with large state-owned multisectoral holding companies has been negative. Instead of being buffers against excessive political interference, they can become powerful tools for political domination and interference. In some cases the sheer size of the multisectoral companies creates unnecessary layers of management and results in slow and bureaucratic decisionmaking. A somewhat more attractive organizational arrangement, though still a second-best solution, is a well-focused sectoral holding company.

Another form, prevalent in some of the sample countries, consists of public enterprise oversight agencies and specialized government bureaus. Broadly speaking, these entities, also called focal points, are of two types: those that perform the ownership role, and those that are supervisory or advisory.

Strong political support and real operational powers are the cornerstones of a successful supervisory focal point. The case of the State Enterprises Commission (SEC) in Ghana is instructive. The precise role of SEC has never been very clear, and its political support has wavered. The agency's work is frustrated by delayed reporting by public enterprises. On the other hand, public enterprise managers interviewed consider the agency an unnecessary bottleneck in their operations.

Evidence from the sample countries also indicates that, particularly in the case of developing countries, there are strong reasons for elevating the ownership role of oversight agencies beyond the realm of one individual ministry. They can report to an intersectoral committee, be organized as a quasi-governmental unit, or be attached to the prime minister's or president's office. This type of solution has several advantages: it increases the status and importance of the unit and enables it to attract high-caliber managers and staff; it will be easier to create a less political and more enterprise- and industry-oriented culture in a unit operating half outside the normal ministries; it may, in certain situations, be a more politically acceptable solution, since no existing functional ministry will gain power over the others; and it avoids undue concentration of power in one functional ministry.

Technical Notes

A. Comparative Advantage
Gerald M. Meier

A country with a comparative advantage in an exportable commodity can produce the exportable at a comparatively lower cost than another commodity. In a free-trade situation, comparative advantage would determine the composition of a country's exports and imports and also the gains from the trade. In a positive sum game, each country's specialization in its comparative advantage commodities would allow all trading countries to enjoy mutual benefits from trade whenever there are international differences in relative costs of production.

The sources of comparative advantage are to be found in the technological differences among countries or differences in relative factor supplies that create cross-country differences in relative prices. *Relative price* is the quantity of one commodity that must be given up in exchange for one unit of the other commodity.

The Ricardo Theory

In the oldest and simplest demonstration of comparative advantage, David Ricardo proved that even if a country has an *absolute* advantage in every commodity (that is, can produce every commodity at an absolutely lower real cost than another country), the country would still gain if it specialized in its *comparative* advantage commodity and exported it in exchange for an importable. Under conditions of free trade, a country will specialize in the production and export of those commodities that it can produce with greatest comparative advantage (that is, those for which its costs are *comparatively lowest*) and will import commodities in which it has a comparative disadvantage (that is, those that it can produce only at high relative cost).[1]

---

1. David Ricardo, *On the Principles of Political Economy and Taxation* (1817; Cambridge, England: Sraffa ed., 1951), p. 135.

Table A.1 *Ricardo's Labor Theory of Value*

	Commodity (one unit)	
Country	Wine	Cloth
Portugal	80	90
England	120	100

To illustrate the meaning of comparative costs, Ricardo focused on a simple example of two countries, two commodities, and one factor of production— labor (see table A.1). In Portugal (*P*), one unit of wine (*W*) costs 80 units of labor, and one unit of cloth (*C*) costs 90 units of labor, while in England (*E*), 1W costs 120 units of labor, and 1C costs 100 units of labor. Even though Portugal has an absolute advantage in both commodities, Ricardo concludes that it is to the advantage of Portugal to export wine in exchange for cloth. Portugal has a comparative advantage where its absolute advantage is largest. Portugal has a comparatively greater advantage in *W* since 80/120 is less than 90/100. England in turn exports cloth, a commodity in which its disadvantage is relatively less. If labor is perfectly mobile within each country and price equals labor costs, then in the pretrade situation the domestic exchange ratio between the two commodities would be 1W:0.88C in *P* and 1W:1.2C in *E*. Thus, *W* is comparatively cheap in *P*, whereas *C* is comparatively cheap in *E*. In *P*, 1W can be transformed into the production of 0.88C by sacrificing the production of 1W. In *E*, 1.2C can be transformed into the production of 1W by sacrificing the production of 1.2C. Costs of production are assumed constant in Ricardo's labor theory of value.

When the countries are opened up to trade, a basis for trade arises from the relative productivity differentials or differences in the countries' comparative cost ratios. After *E* and *P* are opened to foreign trade, some exchange ratio on world markets will be established. This international exchange ratio must lie within the range of the domestic exchange ratios, between Portugal's 1W:0.88C ratio and England's 1W:1.2C. Otherwise, one country would not trade. Exactly where the rate will be established between the domestic exchange ratios will depend on world conditions of demand and supply.

Consider, for example, that demand and supply conditions determine the equilibrium international ratio as 1W:1C. Then *E* would specialize in the pro- duction of *C*, its comparative advantage commodity, and export 1C for 1W, thereby gaining 0.17 unit of wine for each unit of cloth exported (the pretrade exchange ratio is 1C:0.83W). Alternatively, *E* would acquire 1W at a lower real cost than in the pretrade situation, a saving of 0.2 unit of *C* because the pretrade exchange ratio is 1W:1.2C. And *P* would specialize in *W*, its compara- tive advantage commodity, thereby gaining 0.12 unit of cloth for each unit of wine exported (the pretrade exchange ratio is 1W:0.88C). Alternatively, *P* would acquire the same quantity of *W* and *C* as produced before trade at a lower total real cost after trade by following its comparative advantage.

The gains from trade stem from the fact that the cost of each country's importable in terms of its exportable is lower on international markets than on domestic markets. The cost of "indirectly producing" the importable commodity *W* through specialization in the export of commodity *C* is less than if *E* produced the importable *W* directly at home. Similarly, the cost of indirectly producing the importable commodity *C* through the specialization in its export commodity *W* is less than if *P* produced the importable *C* directly at home.

Each country specializes in producing the commodity that uses fewer resources than would be needed to produce domestically the commodity it imports. It exports the commodity in which it has a comparative advantage and imports the commodity in which it has a comparative disadvantage. Exports can be viewed as the intermediate goods used for the "production" of imports. Foreign trade is like an industry that uses exports as inputs to produce imports as output. Indeed, in a centrally planned economy in which the foreign trade sector is treated as an industry, the principle of comparative advantage should be adopted as the efficiency rule for determining what to export and what to import. In following its comparative advantage, each country maximizes output (imports) per unit of input (exports).

If the number of commodities and the number of countries are increased, the model becomes more complicated, but the logic of the analysis remains the same. Commodities will be ranked by their comparative factor-productivity ratio such that each of a country's exports will have a higher factor-productivity ratio than each of its imports. Any number of commodities and any number of countries can be arranged in a chain of declining comparative advantage. In this chain the position of the dividing line between exports and imports will depend on demand conditions for each country's products and on the equilibrium conditions that world demand equals world supply and that value of export equals value of imports for each country.

Ricardo's comparative differences in real costs will translate into absolute differences in money prices provided the relative wage differentials are within the relative productivity differentials in the countries. If, for example, labor is three times more productive in country I than in country II, the absolute money price of the exports from I will be less than the absolute money price of the substitute commodity in II, provided the minimum wage rate is not more than three times higher in I than in II. Under competitive conditions, the wage differences must be within the productivity differences (real costs) or else only one country would be able to export, and its wage rates would be bid up to compensate for this. Or the exchange rate would have to be altered to preserve the condition of balanced trade.

The Heckscher-Olin Theory

Removing the restrictive assumptions of the Ricardian model—one factor of production and constant costs of production—the Swedish economists Eli Heckscher and Bertil Ohlin formulated a more modern theory of comparative advantage.[2] The starting point for this model is the very opposite of Ricardo's. Instead of one factor being assumed, it is recognized that countries are endowed with many factors but in different proportions. As long as there are international differences in relative factor supplies, this alone is sufficient to explain differences in comparative costs and the basis for international specialization.

Assume the same identity of factor qualities and production functions among all countries, no economies to scale, and the same pattern of demand in every country. Even with the strong assumption that all these variables are identical in every country, there is still a sufficient source of trade as long as the relative factor endowments differ among the countries. Relative factor abundance accounts for comparative advantage: a country will export commodities that use intensively in their production the country's relatively abundant factor.

Consider the quantities of two factors, labor (L) and capital (K). If the ratio of L to K in country I is greater than the ratio of L to K in country II, country I is abundant in L and II in K. The relatively abundant factor will also have the relatively low factor price. (Wage will be relatively low in I, and the return to capital relatively low in II.) Commodities embodying intensively the relatively abundant factor will therefore have a relatively low marginal cost and, in turn, a relatively low money price. The labor-abundant country will be able to sell on world markets labor-intensive commodities at a low price, while the capital-abundant country will export capital-intensive commodities. Thus, the minimum difference between countries that is a sufficient condition to explain the pattern of trade is variation in relative factor endowments. If an economy's factor endowment is relatively abundant in unskilled labor, then it will tend to specialize in exports using comparatively large amounts of unskilled labor. Or if an economy's relatively abundant factor is land, it will specialize in land-intensive exports. On the other hand, if the factor endowment is relatively abundant in capital, technology, or skilled labor, the country will export capital-intensive, technology-intensive, or skilled-labor-intensive commodities.

From the Heckscher-Ohlin (H-O) theory of comparative advantage, it follows that when factors of production are not mobile internationally, trade in commodities will be a substitute for the international mobility of factors. The theory also allows for increasing costs of production. Consider three factors of production: labor, land, and capital. Assume that labor is used to produce both food and clothing; land is used only in food; and capital is specific to the clothing sector. These assumptions rule out Ricardo's condition that an industry would expand by hiring more labor without driving up unit costs. Instead, production possibilities would reflect increasing costs. If, for example, extra labor is moved to the clothing sector, diminishing returns will decrease labor's productivity at the margin because capital is specific to the clothing sector. The departure of labor from the food industry will at the same time raise the

---

2. Bertil Ohlin, *Interregional and International Trade* (Cambridge, Mass.: Harvard University Press, 1933).

productivity of the remaining workers in food. On both counts, the relative costs of producing clothing rise. When there are increasing costs, the country will not specialize completely in its comparative advantage as under the Ricardian constant-costs case, but instead a small amount of domestic production may still prove competitive with imports even though the country relies on imports to provide the bulk of its consumption of the importable.

The H-O theory of comparative advantage also concludes that as long as there are international differences in relative costs of production—as will arise through differences in relative factor endowments—there will be mutual gains from trade; each trading country will be better off than without trade.

If the "givens" in the H-O model were relaxed, additional sources of trade could be readily identified. When production functions are not identical in each country, a country may import a commodity because it simply does not have the technical knowledge or skills to produce it. If economies of scale are realized in the production of a commodity, this commodity at some scale of output may become lower in price than in other countries and hence may become exportable. When consumption patterns differ, a country may export a commodity for which it has relatively low demand, whereas the importing country has a relatively high demand for the product. Differences in the production functions, presence of economies of scale, and different demand patterns account for much of the world trade in manufactures. In addition, differences in the availability of skilled labor (human capital), research and development (R&D) expenditure (technological change), and product cycle promote trade.

These differences also account for dynamic changes in comparative advantage. One can envision various stages of comparative advantage through which a country moves over time, beginning with a resource-intensive export, then an unskilled-labor-intensive export, skilled-labor-intensive export, capital-intensive export, and finally R&D- and knowledge-intensive export.

As the intensities of different inputs change over a product's life cycle, so too does the comparative advantage of producing the product in one country or another. In its early phase, a new product is research-intensive and high-skill-intensive. The suppliers concentrate on the home market where any technical difficulties in production can be most readily solved and where demand is less elastic. In the second, or growth, phase, mass production and distribution become possible. Costs and prices fall and the commodity is exported. In the third, or mature, phase, the product and manufacturing operations have become standardized and routine, sales then level off, price elasticity of demand is high, and exports diminish. In the first two phases the innovating country had advantages from introducing and producing the newest products, but these advantages are lost by the third phase. The trading partner, which formerly imported the product, may now be able to duplicate the routine type of production. Overseas producers may gain a comparative advantage in the "old" product and actually begin to export it to third countries and to the first country that has lost its initial comparative advantage. As the comparative advantage in input requirements changes over the product's life cycle, so does the comparative advantage of producing the product in one country rather than in another. Through technical change, there is continually changing international division of labor.

On the basis of the theory of comparative advantage, it can be concluded that free trade is superior to no trade and that, with only few exceptions, free trade is also superior to protected trade. A possible exception is based on the infant-industry argument discussed in technical note B.

B. *The Infant Industry Argument*
   W. M. Corden

The infant industry argument has been the main growth-related argument for protection. The argument was endorsed by John Stuart Mill in a famous and oft-quoted passage in his *Principles.*

> The only case in which, on mere principles of political economy, protecting duties can be defensible, is when they are imposed temporarily (especially in a young and rising nation) in hopes of naturalizing a foreign industry, in itself perfectly suitable to the circumstances of the country. . . . There may be no inherent advantage on one part, or disadvantage on the other, but only a present superiority of acquired skill and experience. A country which has this skill and experience yet to acquire, may in other respects be better adapted to the production than those which were earlier in the field. . . . But it cannot be expected that individuals should, at their own risk, or rather to their certain loss, introduce a new manufacture, and bear the burden of carrying it on until the producers have been educated up to the level of those with whom the processes are traditional. A protecting duty, continued for a reasonable time, might sometimes be the least inconvenient mode in which the nation can tax itself for the support of such an experiment.[3]

It is undoubtedly now one of the most widely accepted arguments for protection in less-developed countries, just as it has in the past been used to justify protection in the United States, Germany, Canada and Australia.

In order to analyse this argument clearly, two distinctions must here be stressed. The first is between *economies of scale*—essentially a static concept—and *economies of time.* The former result in falling costs as the scale of output at any point in time increases (with given factor prices), while the latter result in falling costs as the length of time over which output has proceeded increases, and are sometime called *dynamic* economies. The second distinction is between *internal* and *external* economies, the question being whether the economies, whether of scale or of time, are internal or external to the decision-making unit, namely *the firm.*

The essence of the infant industry argument is that it is an argument for temporary protection. Hence (a) *time* must enter the argument in some essential way; it cannot rest solely on static economies of scale, whether internal or external. Furthermore, (b) it is an argument for intervention to alter the pat-

---

Excerpted by permission from W. M. Corden, *Trade Policy and Economic Welfare* (Oxford: Clarendon Press, 1974).

3. John Stuart Mill, *Principles of Political Economy,* book V, chap. 10, in *Collected Works of John Stuart Mill,* vol. 3 (Toronto: University of Toronto Press, 1965), pp. 918–19.

tern of production, and so will require some kind of distortion, imperfection or externality in the system somewhere.

It will be shown that an argument for temporary protection can be built in two main ways: one resting on dynamic internal economies and the other on dynamic external economies. But some other approaches, concerned in turn with investment coordination and with static economies of scale, will also be mentioned.

Dynamic Internal Economies

We shall now see whether an infant industry argument for protection can be built with dynamic internal economies as the main ingredient. The average costs of a firm are assumed to fall the longer its output has continued; it learns from experience. This is to be distinguished not only from costs falling with scale of output in the static sense but also from costs falling over time for exogenous reasons. Sometimes these dynamic economies are called *irreversible* economies, since experience of production in one year causes costs to fall once and for all for later years.

But there is a preferable way of looking at this. When factors of production are engaged in producing output in a particular year, two products really result, *visible* current output, saleable currently on the market, and the *invisible* accumulation of experience and knowledge, in fact the creation of human capital. The learning may be on the part of the management of the firm or of its workers. If the firm's employees gain in experience and so become more valuable to it, then for the analysis here to apply their wages and salaries must not rise so much that the firm does not profit at all. The suppliers of inputs to the firm may be the learners; if this is to lead to internal economies to the firm concerned, the prices of the products of the suppliers must fall (or the quality of the products must improve).

The learning of the firm concerned may lead to improved quality of product, including improved consistency of the product (an important effect in less-developed countries). It may consist in part of *market familiarization*—learning to give the customers the type of product and the service they really want—hence becoming more efficient at product differentiation. And the improved efficiency may be as much in distribution as in production. The quality improvement that results from continued production and sale may be only in the minds of customers; as they become more familiar with the product they may be prepared to pay more for it, or, alternatively, less advertising is needed to sustain sales at a given price and given physical quality.

An infant industry argument can be constructed from dynamic internal economies in three possible ways. In all cases the first-best argument is for some form of direct subsidization.

IMPERFECTION OF PRIVATE INFORMATION. The first approach rests on an imperfection of private information or of private ability to assess information. Investment in learning capital may be very long-term investment. One may have to produce for many years before significant fruits emerge. It could be argued that private enterprise simply does not look so far ahead, and that the state, in the form of its civil servants or planners, has a longer view and sees a more favorable learning curve than the firm's owners or managers do.

But the case is not really very strong. First-best policy is for the state to spread more information. If private entrepreneurs are not aware of the prospects for expansion of demand that will result from planning or other developments, there are well-known ways of making them aware. "Indicative planning" is a possible method of spreading information about market prospects. But do government, planning authority, or tariff board really have better information?

Why should the private firm (or state enterprise) concerned have less information about the prospects for its own cost curves than a central state authority? The planners or civil servants may be more optimistic than private firms and more ready to speculate about the future because they will not personally have to meet the losses if the risks do not come off. A private firm, if small, might go bankrupt if its investments are misplaced and so have more at stake.

IMPERFECTION OF CAPITAL MARKET. The second approach depends on imperfection of the capital market. The potential infant may be unable to obtain finance to cover initial losses at a rate of interest which correctly indicates the social discount rate. There will then be underinvestment, or failure to invest at all, in the creation of long-term learning capital. (We assume now that there is no divergence between the private firm's information or expectations and the government's.)

PECUNIARY EXTERNAL ECONOMIES. A third approach to getting an infant industry argument out of dynamic internal economies rests on the so-called pecuniary external economies which result from indivisibilities. Any indivisible lump of investment will generate pecuniary external economies (producers' and consumers' surpluses) outside the investing firm: the extra investment is likely to lead to an increase in the wages of the workers employed in the industry concerned, to higher incomes in industries supplying non-traded inputs and to extra output and so a lower product price, unless the latter is set by a fixed import price. Thus the gains from the investment will not stay completely within the firm making it.

The weakness in the argument is that all investment, if it is indivisible, gives rise to pecuniary external economies; investment in learning is not unusual. One would have to show that the indivisibilities in learning are in some sense greater than in alternative investment, whether within the same firm or other firms. There appears to be no logical reason derived from pecuniary external economies for subsidizing this particular form of investment in preference to others.

Dynamic External Economies

When the process of production by firm X creates an invisible capital asset the benefits of which go in later years to other firms, and other firms are not charged for it, there are dynamic external economies or external economies of time. These provide some basis for an infant industry argument since they contain both the externality and the time element, the two requirements for an argument for temporary protection. But in addition it is necessary that the dynamic external economies be *reciprocal.*

If firm X's production creates a capital asset the product of which goes to firm Y, and Y does not pay X for it, then X should be subsidized to encourage it to produce an amount of the asset that takes into account the latter's marginal product to Y. But it is not an argument for temporary subsidization since production by X may add to this asset at all times. One might then introduce the assumption that production by X adds to this asset only for a limited period; then we have an argument for temporary subsidization, but not an "infant industry" argument since it cannot be said that firm X "grows up" in any sense.

So we must assume *reciprocal* dynamic external economies. Production by X creates an asset the benefits of which go in later years at least partly to Y, while at the same time production by Y creates an asset the benefits of which go partly to X. Now there is a case for subsidizing both firms to encourage them to produce these assets. The result of the accumulation of the two assets will be that in later years the costs of both firms fall. Initial subsidization of the two firms will expand their production, perhaps getting both going for the first time, and eventually the subsidies can be removed without their outputs falling as a result.

If the group of firms which generate the reciprocal external economies for each other is called an "industry," the external dynamic economies are then internal to the industry. As time passes the costs of the firms in the industry fall. Alternatively we might call the group of firms the "manufacturing sector." The economies are then internal to the manufacturing sector—an argument widely used today since it [supports] general protection of the whole manufacturing sector. Since protection means favoring one sector of the economy at the expense of others, one cannot protect the whole economy; hence there can only be an argument for protection if the external economies are limited to some groups of firms within the economy or if they differ between groups.

What might give rise to dynamic external economies? Most commonly the training of labour is cited, the accumulation of human skills through "on-the-job" training being the "K" of our story. If a firm trains labour specifically for use only in that firm, no external benefits will accrue to other firms. We are here concerned with more general training, whether in technical skills appropriate to an industry or perhaps in the habits of working regularly in a factory environment, a skill required for all manufacturing industry. Firm X trains labour in this way, and this experienced or trained labour may then go off to other firms. An essential element in the argument is the inability to tie the workers to the firms where they obtained their training.

The argument is that there is an externality because firms are creating assets from which other firms benefit even though the other firms do not pay for them. The assets in this case are not "public goods" because the more labour one firm takes out of the common pool of skilled labour the less is available for others. The asset K—the Human Capital—is being embodied in specific workers and they will reap the rewards once they are trained by being able to obtain appropriate higher wages.

The crucial question is who pays for the training. Here we come to a possible argument for intervention or protection. Capital markets are not usually well organized for such purposes. First-best policy is to improve the capital market (if that is feasible) and second-best policy is to provide finance or subsidization specifically for labour training. A reasonable third-best policy might be to subsidize the employment of labour by those firms or industries that contribute in a significant way—more than average—to the pool of trained labour available to firms other than themselves. Subsidizing their output might be a convenient fourth-best and tariffs a fifth-best policy.

Wide Application of the Infant Industry Argument

The infant industry argument is usually applied to import-competing industries. But it can also apply to export industries or to industries producing non-traded goods. There is no strong reason why import-competing industries should have higher learning rates and, more specifically, why they should have more difficulty in foreseeing or financing internal dynamic economies or generate more external economies.

Many industries and countries have experimented in exporting new products. Indeed, there is a special learning problem in breaking for the first time into foreign markets, so that there could be an *infant marketing argument* additional to the usual infant industry argument concerned with production. Here again, an argument for *protection* must rest additionally on capital market imperfection, inadequacy of private information or judgment, or externalities.

The infant industry argument is also usually associated with manufacturing. This may be because historically many countries have deliberately sought to shift the output pattern from agriculture to manufacturing, and inevitably there is more scope for learning in any new field of activity. Perhaps manufacturing is more difficult, requires a higher stage of techniques and knowledge, and so inevitably generates more learning economies.

But one must remember that a protection argument requires not just learning, but in addition either capital market or information imperfection, or otherwise externalities. In less-developed countries private agriculture usually finds capital harder to obtain and more costly than industry. Furthermore, the scope for learning in agriculture is often immense. Governments usually deal with this directly by providing free agricultural extension services, but it is doubtful whether in any country the subsidization implicit in this matches the subsidy equivalent of manufacturing protection.

Finally, learning can potentially take place in many activities. If it is desired to foster the learning process either because of information or capital market imperfections believed to be associated with the process, or because it has external effects, then one must protect the industries where learning is relatively higher. In a general equilibrium framework all externalities and arguments for protection must be seen in relative terms. If one fosters industries where there is learning but does this by reducing the output of, or perhaps completely ending, other industries where there are much greater potentialities for learning (measuring learning in terms of its later fruits), then total learning for the whole economy may actually decline as a result of protection.

C. *Domestic Resource Cost and Effective Protection*
William F. Steel

The impact of incentives on efficiency can be analyzed using the effective protection rate (EPR) and the domestic resource cost (DRC) of foreign exchange. Both measures use as an efficiency criterion the concept of value added at world prices (VAWP), or the world price of the product minus the cost of tradable inputs, also valued at their world (or border) prices. And both measures indicate the impact of protection on value added at domestic prices. The EPR measures the percentage differential of domestic value added over VAWP that is permitted by the structure of protection (including quantitative restrictions as well as tariff duties and other taxes). The DRC measures the ratio of the economic cost of the resources actually used in an activity to the net value of foreign exchange saved or earned in that activity. This technical note explains the derivation and use of these measures, and how they are related to economic profitability and international competitiveness.

Economic Efficiency

An industrial activity is competitive at economic prices if the economic value of its output exceeds the opportunity costs of the commodities and factors of production employed in producing it. If the full-time profile of inputs and outputs is known and a suitable time discount rate is applied to costs and benefits occurring at different points in time, the net present value of any project (actual or proposed) at economic prices provides the correct measure of its net contribution to economic welfare. In that sense, economic activities with positive net present values are efficient.

Available data, however, are not always well adapted to the application of the present value criterion. In these circumstances it is possible to employ a single-period efficiency measure based on the *annual* economic profitability of an industrial activity:

$$(C.1) \quad B_j = P_j - \sum_i^n a_{ij}P_i - \sum_s^m f_{sj}P_s$$

$$\begin{bmatrix} \text{Unit} \\ \text{economic} \\ \text{profit} \end{bmatrix} = \begin{bmatrix} \text{Economic} \\ \text{price per} \\ \text{unit of} \\ \text{output} \end{bmatrix} - \begin{bmatrix} \text{Economic} \\ \text{value of} \\ \text{intermediate} \\ \text{inputs} \end{bmatrix} - \begin{bmatrix} \text{Economic} \\ \text{value of} \\ \text{factor} \\ \text{inputs} \end{bmatrix}$$

P_j, P_i, and P_s are the shadow prices of output, material inputs, and factor inputs, respectively, used in the production of j, and a_{ij} and f_{sj} are the number of units of material inputs and factors of production, respectively, required per unit of output.[4] The activity is judged efficient if the economic value of the output is at least as great as the economic value of the intermediate and factor inputs required to produce it ($B_j > 0$).

If all produced inputs and outputs are assumed to be tradable, the first two terms on the right-hand side of equation (C.1) give the annual VAWP, which represents the annual net addition to national income evaluated at world prices. The third term represents the opportunity cost of factor inputs evaluated at economic prices. When the opportunity cost of factor inputs exceeds the net addition to national income, unit economic profits are negative, and the resources employed could be more efficiently employed in their best alternative use.

Domestic Resource Cost Criterion

Criteria for choosing among projects generally compare the net benefits per unit of a scarce, budgeted factor. Foreign exchange is an important constraint on African industries, which depend heavily on imported inputs and equipment. VAWP is the difference between the world values of output and tradable inputs and can be taken to represent the net addition to foreign exchange availability as a result of the project. If domestically supplied factors of production are evaluated at their opportunity costs, equation C.1 may be rewritten as the ratio of domestic factor costs evaluated at economic prices to value added at world prices:

$$(\text{C.2}) \qquad \text{DRC}_j = \frac{\sum\limits_{s}^{m} f_{sj} P_s}{P_j - \sum\limits_{i}^{n} a_{ij} P_i} = \frac{\text{Economic value of primary factors}}{\text{Value added at world prices}}$$

The resulting domestic resource cost ratio measures the amount of "net" foreign exchange that domestic resources can generate for the firm in question. If this rate of transformation exceeds one, the opportunity cost of domestic factors of production (in terms of foreign exchange) exceeds the addition to value added at world prices by these factors, and the net benefit criterion would turn negative.[5]

Minimizing the domestic resource cost ratio in activities producing tradable goods is equivalent to maximizing value added at world prices per unit of domestic resources employed. Thus, evaluating firms in terms of their resource cost ratio provides a measure of relative economic efficiency. Firms

---

4. For tradable commodities, the shadow price is represented by the world (border) price—free on board (f.o.b.) for exportables; cost, insurance, freight (c.i.f.) for importables.

5. The DRC criterion can also be written as the ratio of domestic resource costs in terms of domestic currency to value added at world prices in terms of foreign currency. There is no difference in substance between the latter measure of the DRC and that used here, which expresses the opportunity cost of domestic factors in terms of border prices and compares the resulting ratio with one (or with the ratio of the estimated shadow exchange rate to the official exchange rate).

with DRCs less than or equal to one may be classified as *efficient* in the sense that the domestic resources that they employ produce as much or more value added at world prices as they would in the activities from which they are drawn. Activities with resource cost ratios greater than unity are termed *inefficient* in the sense that the resources they use would be more productive in alternative activities.

Ranking of firms by the domestic resource cost ratio provides an index of efficiency among activities that produce tradable goods. Unlike the unit social profit criterion, the DRC ratio may be used either to compare the performance of firms within a single industry or to compare the performance of several different industries. Within industries, the intramarginal ranking of firms provides substantial information concerning the relative levels of economic costs of production across firms.

Considerable attention has been focused on the DRC as a measure of comparative advantage. Comparative advantage exists if the economic opportunity cost of producing a commodity is less than its border price. Hence, activities with positive unit economic profits, or DRCs less than one, are those activities in which the economy has a comparative advantage. In addition, the smaller the DRC of an individual activity within an economy, the greater the scope for efficient expansion of exports or import substitutes. Nevertheless, some care should be exercised in the interpretation of static DRC ratios as indicators of comparative advantage; they provide a snapshot of potential lines for export expansion or efficient import substitution, but the picture may change with the passage of time and with increases in output.

Effective Protection Rate

Variations in economic efficiency tend to reflect the structure of incentives to producers, which can be analyzed by using the concept of effective protection. The effective protection coefficient (EPC) measures the ratio of domestic value added that is permitted by the structure of protection (determined by tariffs, other taxes on trade, import bans, and quantitative restrictions) to VAWP. The latter represents the level of value added implied by the absence of trade restrictions. If all commodities are traded, the effective protection coefficient is given by:

(C.3)
$$\frac{P_j' - \sum_{i}^{m} a_{ij} P_i'}{P_j - \sum_{i}^{m} a_{ij} P_i} = \frac{\text{Value added at domestic prices}}{\text{Value added at world prices}}$$

where P_j' and P_i' are the domestic market prices of output and inputs, respectively. Thus, the effective protection coefficient is the ratio of value added in domestic prices to value added at world prices. For comparability with nominal tariffs, an equivalent measure is the effective protection rate (EPR), or the percentage increase above VAWP that is permitted by the structure of protection:

(C.4)
$$\text{EPR} = 100 \, (\text{EPC} - 1)$$

Table C.1 *Domestic Resource Cost and Effective Protection*

Steps in calculation	Import substitution			Export production		
	Output	*Traded inputs*	*Value added*[a]	*Output*	*Traded inputs*	*Value added*[a]
1. World (border) price	100 (c.i.f.)	50 (c.i.f.)	—	90 (f.o.b.)	30 (c.i.f.)	—
2. Domestic value at shadow exchange rate (5:1)	500	250	250 (VAWP)	450	150	300 (VAWP)
3. Rate of protection (tariff rate, or impact of QRs)	50	30	—	0	30	—
4. Domestic value at market prices (from lines 2 and 3)	750	325	425	450	195	255
5. Protection (taxation) to producer (line 4 − line 2)	250	(−75)	175	0	(−45)	(−45)
6. Ratio of value at domestic prices to VAWP (line 4/line 2)	1.50	1.30	1.70 (EPC)	1.00	1.30	0.85 (EPC)
7. Effective protection rate (100% × line 5/line 2)	—	—	70	—	—	−15
8. Domestic labor and capital actually used, valued at shadow prices						
a. Shadow price = 1.0	—	—	425	—	—	255
b. Shadow price = 0.8	—	—	340	—	—	204
9. DRC ratio of domestic resource costs to VAWP (line 8/line 2)						
a. Shadow price = 1.0	—	—	1.70	—	—	0.85
b. Shadow price = 0.8	—	—	1.36	—	—	0.68

—Not applicable.

a. Value added equals output minus inputs (assumed to be all tradable).

The effective protection coefficient and the domestic resource cost ratio are closely related. Both have as their denominator the value added at international prices, and so the only difference is in their numerators. The EPC's numerator shows how high the level of domestic resources costs, profits, and rents can be in a particular economic activity. This level is determined by domestic prices. The DRC includes in its numerator only domestic resources actually used and values them at shadow rather than market prices. The EPC thus indicates the potential for resource costs and transfers arising from the existing structure of protection; the DRC indicates the extent to which these potential costs are realized. The difference between the two depends on the structure of domestic taxes and subsidies, on the supply functions for domestic primary factors, and on the effectiveness of regulatory measures such as price controls.[6]

Example

Table C.1 presents the calculation of DRC and effective protection for an import substitution activity and an export activity that produce comparable products. The export product has a lower border price (line 1) because it is valued f.o.b. instead of c.i.f., but its VAWP is higher because its raw material input content is less (line 2). Both activities use tradable inputs subject to duties of 30 percent (line 3). For the import substitution product, these duties are more than offset by the addition to its domestic output price permitted by the 50 percent duty on competing imports (line 5). No such protection is available to the export producer, who ends up paying a net tax with no compensation in terms of a higher output price. The result is that the exporter must use fewer domestic resources than is implied by VAWP in order to stay competitive on world markets, whereas the import substitution industry can use excess resources and still compete with imports (line 4). In other words, the exporter faces negative effective protection of 15 percent (line 7), while effective protection to value added in import substitution is 70 percent (well above the 50 percent nominal protection). If the domestic resources actually used correspond to what is permitted by the system of protection and if shadow prices equal market prices, then the EPC and DRC are equivalent (lines 6 and 9a). Shadow prices different from market prices are one reason why the DRC may, in practice, differ (line 9b).

D. Total Factor Productivity
Mieko Nishimizu and John M. Page, Jr.

The most familiar concept of productivity is that of partial productivity—for example, the average productivity of a single input, such as labor. This is generally measured by the value of output per unit of input—bushels of wheat per worker or tons of steel per machine-hour. Judgments regarding changes in the efficiency of production are frequently based on changes in three partial productivity measures. Rising labor productivity is viewed as an improvement in productive efficiency. Deterioration in the capital-output ratio is taken to imply declining investment efficiency.

The world is more complicated than this, however, and all sorts of changes

6. Calculation and comparison of these measures is complicated in practice by the presence of nontraded goods, whose prices are established by the working of domestic markets and may fall above their exportable value (f.o.b.) but below the price of an equivalent import (c.i.f.). Certain commodities and services such as construction, transport, and utilities are almost universally not traded. One method to incorporate nontraded inputs into the cost and incentives measures is to break down their cost of production into tradable inputs and domestic factors. They can then be entered directly in the numerator or denominator of the ratio, as appropriate. Different methods for treating nontraded goods can affect rankings if firms vary significantly in their use of nontraded inputs.

can occur simultaneously in production. The productivity of equipment may increase because of better maintenance or because workers become more skilled in its operation. The productivity of material inputs may increase because of better quality, changes in equipment, or improved inventory management. Labor productivity growth may be observed because of the increased productivity of other inputs rather than greater efficiency on the part of labor itself. This is the main shortcoming of partial productivity measures.

Total factor productivity (TFP) can be thought of as an index that sums up the partial productivities of all inputs in a production process, so that the efficiency with which all inputs are utilized and combined in production can be captured jointly. In this way the interaction between changes in the level and quality of one factor and the partial productivities of all other factors can be captured and related to changes in cost performance and production efficiency.

Production Functions

In economic analysis, the interactions between inputs and outputs are normally summarized by specifying a production function, which gives the maximum amount of output that can be produced with a given amount of inputs. The production function for a given level of technology provides a series of such maximum output levels, each corresponding to a given level of inputs. Figure D.1 depicts two such production functions, each corresponding to a different level of technology: $t = 0$ and $t = 1$. At a given level of technology, more output can be produced only by adding more inputs. To raise output from $q(0)$ at production point a to $q'(1)$ with technology $t = 0$, inputs would have to be increased to the level $z'(0)$ corresponding to production point b'.

The economic concept of TFP change is simply the notion that greater output can be produced over time with a given level of inputs. Figure D.1 shows the production function to have shifted upward from $t = 0$ to $t = 1$. This shift represents a technical change, resulting in a larger amount of maximum output that can be produced at every level of inputs. It is now possible, for example, to produce the amount of output $q'(1)$ at production point b using the same input level of $z(0)$ as was used at production point a to produce only $q(0)$. Thus, the technical change represented by the shift in the production function means that the efficiency with which all inputs are combined in production increases. This is the definition of TFP change. Thus, the term "TFP change" is often synonymous with "technical change."

The Measurement of TFP Change

The basic analytical framework for TFP measurement assumes that the behavioral objective of a producer is to minimize costs and that production is constrained only by the technological limits of production possibilities. Within these limits, the producer is presumed to exercise direct control over production efficiency by changing the configuration of products and inputs. The basic framework also assumes that markets for the producer's products and

Figure D.1 *Effect of Technical Change on Production Function and Productivity*

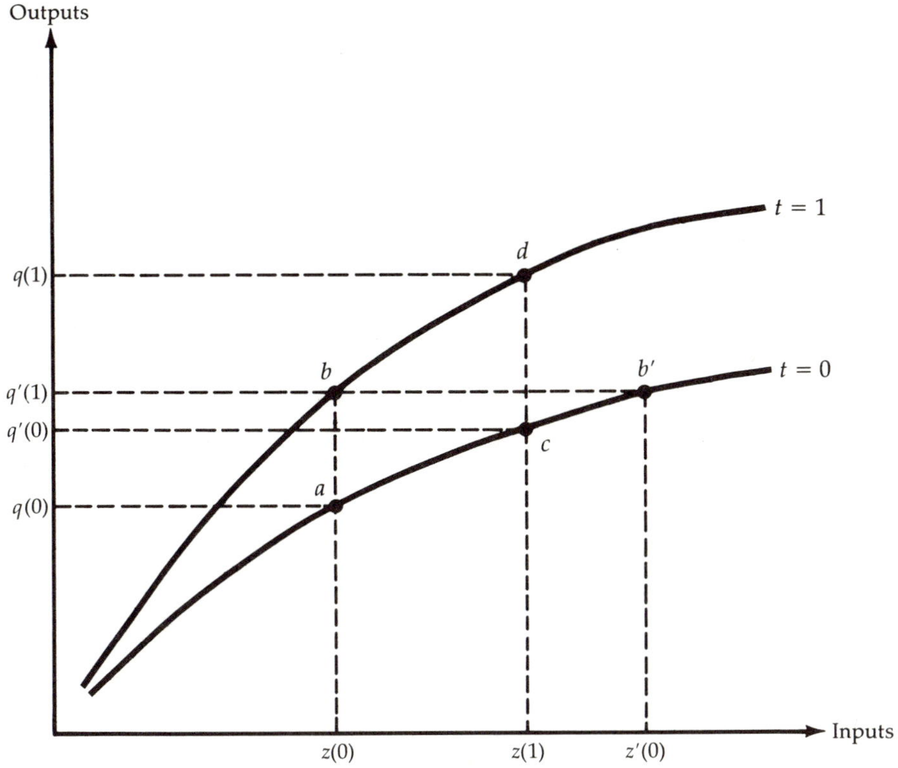

inputs are competitive. Therefore the producer cannot influence prices directly, and price of products and inputs are given as parameters to the producer.

In order to minimize costs, the producer should always choose a production point at the maximum feasible limit on the production function. Had no change in input level occurred between the two periods, measuring TFP change would be trivial: it would equal the growth in output at the given input level. In reality, however, both input growth and TFP growth contribute to output growth simultaneously. The thrust of TFP measurement, therefore, is to separate these two forces contributing to growth.

Given a set of output and input prices, suppose that the producer has chosen the cost-minimizing production points at $a = [z(0), q(0)]$ for $t = 0$, and $d = [z(1), q(1)]$ for $t = 1$. The contribution of input growth to output can be measured as the movement from a to c along the old production function, or as $q'(0)/q(0)$ at the TFP level of $t = 0$. In this case, TFP growth is captured as the shift in the production function at $z(1)$, the vertical distance cd or $q(1)/q'(0)$.

Statistically, however, only one point on each production function (a and d) is observed, since the two forces contributing to growth—input growth and TFP change—are at work simultaneously. The measurement of TFP therefore requires that the hypothetical production point $c = [z(1), q'(0)]$ be measured, so that the contribution of input growth to output growth can be estimated. This contribution can be captured by using the output elasticity of each input—a production function parameter indicating the percentage of growth in output that can be derived from a 1 percent growth in input. The output elasticities of different inputs can be obtained by estimating production functions econometrically. Alternatively, they can be estimated by using the following convenient condition attached to producers' equilibrium in competitive markets: that cost shares of each input in total cost of production are equal to output elasticities of each input.

Thus, the rates of change in TFP (the distance c to d in figure D.1) can be estimated as the growth rate in output (the movement from a to d) net of the contribution of input growth (the movement from a to d) net of the contribution of input growth (the movement from a to c), as follows:

% change in TFP = % change in output
     − [output elasticities − % change in inputs]

= % change in output
     − [cost shares × % change in inputs]

The same framework can be applied to capture TFP differences between two production units by letting the two production functions represent different producers with different levels of technology or efficiency.

Improvement or deterioration in the efficiency of production will also be reflected in changes in the unit cost of production. It is important to remember that a TFP increase (decrease) implies that a decrease (increase) in unit cost of production has accounted for all input price changes. A 3 percent increase in TFP implies a 3 percent decrease in the real unit cost of production.

Factors Affecting TFP Change

Conceptually, the factors affecting the efficiency of an economic unit of production such as a firm can be classified into two broad categories: those within a firm's sphere of direct influence and those outside a firm's direct control. The distinction between these two categories is useful in understanding some of the limitations of the analytical framework for measuring TFP, as well as in understanding what TFP indices represent, their uses, and application.

Factors within a firm's sphere of direct control are those that we called *technology* earlier. These factors can be further divided into two groups. One group has to do with the efficiency of each input, which can change quite independently of the input's quantity in production and also independently of the amount and efficiency of any other inputs combined in production. This group includes factors such as the influence of training and education on labor productivity, new technology embodied in machinery and equipment, and higher grades of primary inputs. The other group of factors affects the efficiency of performance of different inputs simultaneously and the efficiency of interaction among different inputs in a production process. It includes management of a firm layout of physical plant, economies of scale, efficiency in the management of product portfolio, and any other factors that take advantage of what is called *economies of scope* (for example, shared overhead costs among different production lines).

Factors beyond a firm's direct control have to do with the production environment. They include availability of infrastructure (for example, roads or telecommunication) and demand conditions that affect the performance of a firm through fluctuations in capacity utilization. They include government policies and regulations that affect prices or allocation of products and inputs (for example, tariffs, taxes, subsidies, foreign exchange allocation system, pricing policy), the degree of competition in the market place (for example, investment, licensing, state monopoly), and the management autonomy of firms themselves.

Measured TFP change captures the impact on production efficiency of all of these factors. Changes in technological levels—that is, shifts in the production function—are difficult to distinguish empirically from changes in TFP that occur within the given level of technology. Both changes, however, respond to decisions at the enterprise level. These decisions in turn are motivated and constrained by changes in the production environment. One objective of TFP analysis is to measure the impact of changes in the production environment on cost performance.

Productivity Change and Structural Adjustment in Industry

On the supply side, the growth of an economy, an industry, or a firm is determined by the rate of expansion of its productive resources and by improvements in their efficiency—that is, the rate of growth of TFP. Perhaps one of the most significant stylized facts that has emerged from the empirical literature is the importance of TFP's contribution to growth. As much as one-third to one-half of growth in output can be attributed to TFP growth. Where the growth of employable resources is constrained, high rates of TFP growth are critical to growth of production.

A relevant example today is the case of many developing countries that face balance of payments problems. To achieve stabilization, many of these countries have reduced government expenditures. This results in little or no growth, with adverse political consequences in many countries. A more sustainable alternative would be a program to reduce expenditures and increase income simultaneously. Given the balance of payments constraints on growth, the supply response for such an alternative must come from greater efficiency in resource use and allocation—that is, improvement in TFP performance.

In recent years structural adjustment has become an explicit goal of many developing countries. One objective of structural adjustment is to improve the competitive performance of industry. Whether at the enterprise level or the industry level, structural adjustment in industry can be thought of as the process of reallocating resources according to changing conditions and improving cost competitiveness through total factor productivity change.

Differential rates of TFP growth among economic activities have a major impact on resource allocation and on the economic structure in the medium to long run. An important part of the structural adjustment process involves exploiting changes in comparative advantage. To achieve more competitive industrial structures by shifting comparative advantage in their favor, Sub-Saharan African countries need to improve their rates of industrial TFP growth relative to those in the rest of the world.

E. Equilibrium Real Exchange Rate
Sebastian Edwards

The type of exchange problems that developing countries face are related, among other things, to issues such as the promotion of nontraditional exports, economic instability, imported inflation, capital flight, and foreign investment. One of the most important of these exchange rate–related problems has to do with defining whether a country's real exchange rate is overvalued or out of line with respect to its long-run equilibrium value. There is general agreement that maintaining the real exchange rate at the "wrong" level results in significant welfare costs. On the one hand, it generates incorrect signals to economic agents; on the other, it results in greater economic instability.

The long-run external (that is, current account) equilibrium position of a country will be affected by the real exchange rate as opposed to the nominal exchange rate. It is indeed the *real exchange rate* that determines (among other variables) the trade and current accounts behavior. In the literature, however, there has been some disagreement about the definition of the real exchange rate. In this note, the concept of "equilibrium" real exchange rate is introduced, and a distinction between the concepts of long-run sustainable equilibrium real exchange rate and short-run equilibrium real exchange rate is made. Then some of the alternative definitions offered in the literature are reviewed and discussed.

Equilibrium

The equilibrium real exchange rate is used to determine whether the actual real exchange rate is misaligned (that is, whether the currency is overvalued or undervalued) and the magnitude of those misalignments.[7] Robert Mundell provided an early formal analysis of the determination of the equilibrium real exchange rate. Assuming the case of a small economy that faces given terms of trade, Mundell defines the equilibrium real exchange rate as the relative price of international to domestic goods that simultaneously equilibrates the money market, the domestic goods market, and the international goods market.[8]

Excerpted and edited from Sebastian Edwards, "Real Exchange Rate Misalignment in Developing Countries: Analytical Issues and Empirical Evidence," and "Trends in Real Exchange Rate Behavior in Selected Developing Countries," World Bank, Country Policy Department, Discussion Papers 1985–43 and 1985–16, 1985.

7. Although the term "overvalued" is often applied to the exchange rate, it is actually the national currency whose value is set too high; that is, the amount of local currency required to buy a unit of foreign exchange (the usual measure of the exchange rate) is too low.

8. Robert Mundell, *Monetary Theory* (Santa Monica, Calif.: Goodyear Publishing, 1971).

More recently, Rudiger Dornbusch has developed a model of an open dependent economy to analyze the determination of the equilibrium real exchange rate.[9] In its simpler version the model considers a two-goods economy with a tradables and a nontradables sector. It is assumed that the production of tradables depends positively on the real exchange rate, while the production of nontradables depends negatively on the real exchange rate. On the other hand, the demand functions for tradables and nontradables are assumed to depend on the real exchange rate and real expenditure. The equilibrium real exchange rate is defined as the relative price of tradables to nontradables at which income equates expenditure and the markets for both tradable and nontradable goods are in equilibrium.

A problem with a number of models on the equilibrium real exchange rate is that they do not distinguish between the effects of temporary and permanent changes in the real exchange rate determinants. Once this distinction is made, it is then possible to define both a short- and a long-run equilibrium real exchange rate. This distinction can be crucial in some policy discussions. For example, it is possible that although a particular value of the real exchange rate can reflect a short-run equilibrium situation, it may be way out of line with respect to long-run equilibrium. This case will arise whenever the determinants of the equilibrium real exchange rate experience temporary changes. For example, if there is a *temporary* transfer from abroad, the real exchange rate that equilibrates the external and internal sectors will appreciate. Although this new real exchange rate will be a short-run equilibrium rate—in the sense that it accommodates the transfer—it will be out of line with respect to its equilibrium long-run value (that is, once the transfer has disappeared).

The important distinction between the short-run equilibrium and long-run sustainable equilibrium real exchange rate has been introduced explicitly in some recent analyses of the determination of the equilibrium real exchange rate. In most of these studies the long-run equilibrium real exchange rate has been associated with a situation in which there is equilibrium in the internal and external sectors *and* foreign assets are being accumulated or decumulated at the desired rate. For example, John Williamson writes: "The fundamental equilibrium exchange rate is that which is expected to generate a current account surplus or deficit equal to the underlying capital flow over the cycle, given that the country is pursuing international balance as best it can and not restricting trade for balance of payments reasons."[10]

The long-run equilibrium real exchange rate is defined, then, as the relative price of tradables to nontradables that is consistent with *long-run sustainable* external equilibrium. This long-run equilibrium real exchange rate should also be compatible with internal (that is, full employment) equilibrium and with the long-run desired levels of protection.

Definition of the Real Exchange Rate

The real exchange rate has been loosely defined as a measure of the degree of competitiveness of domestically produced goods relative to goods produced

9. Rudiger Dornbusch, *Open Economy Macroeconomics* (New York: Basic Books, 1980).
10. John Williamson, *The Exchange Rate System* (Washington, D.C.: Institute for International Economics, 1983).

in the rest of the world. Unfortunately, at a more formal level there is no agreement on the exact definition of the real exchange rate. Although this is not serious, it does generate some communication problems; it is not always clear what a particular author means when he or she refers to "the" real exchange rate. Some experts have defined the real exchange rate as the nominal exchange rate times the ratio of the foreign to domestic price level. Recently, however, most authors have defined the real exchange rate as the domestic relative price of tradable goods. Still other experts define the real exchange rate as the ratio of foreign to domestic unit labor costs.

According to earlier views, the real exchange rate was defined as the nominal exchange rate corrected (that is, multiplied) by the ratio of a foreign to a domestic price level. The main idea was that in an inflationary world changes in the nominal exchange rate would have no clear meaning and that explicit consideration should be given to changing values in the domestic and foreign currencies, as measured by the respective rates of inflation. In this context a number of writers also refer to the real exchange rate as the purchasing power parity (PPP) exchange rate. This approach is subject to the well-known criticisms and problems of the PPP theory, including those related to the selection of appropriate price indexes and of an adequate reference time period.[11]

Today most authors define the real exchange rate in the context of a dependent-economy type of model, with tradable and nontradable goods. In this setting the real exchange rate has been defined as the (domestic) relative price of tradable to nontradable goods. If E is the nominal exchange rate defined as units of domestic currency per unit of foreign currency, P_t^* is the world price of tradables in terms of foreign currency, P_n is the price of nontradable goods, and no taxes on trade are assumed, the real exchange rate (e) is then defined as:

$$(E.1) \qquad\qquad e = \frac{E\,P_t^*}{P_n}$$

The reason for defining the real exchange rate in this way is that in the context of a tradable and nontradable goods model, the trade and current accounts will depend on the (domestic) relative price of tradables to nontradables. Assuming that the supply of tradables depends positively on the relative price of tradables (EP_t^*/P_n) and that the demand depends negatively on this relative price and positively on real income, the current account—defined as the excess supply of tradables—will be a positive function of real income and of the relative price of tradables to nontradables. In this setting a higher relative price of tradables will result in a higher supply of and lower demand for these goods and, normally, in an improved current account. The real exchange rate, defined as the relative price of tradables to nontradables, then captures the degree of competitiveness (or profitability) of the tradable goods sector in the domestic country. Other things being equal, a higher e means a

11. See Arnold C. Harberger, "Balance of Payments Crises: Lessons of Experience," paper presented at the National Bureau of Economic Research/World Bank Conference on Exchange Rates, November–December, 1984.

higher degree of competitiveness (and production) of the domestic tradables sector.

To have a clear understanding of the concepts involved, compare the tradable-nontradables relative price definition with the (older) PPP definition of the real exchange rate. The PPP real exchange rate is defined as:

(E.2)
$$\frac{e}{PPP} = \frac{EP^*}{P}$$

where P and P^* are domestic and foreign price indexes. Assuming that these indexes are weighted averages of tradable and nontradable prices, it is possible to find the relation between percentage changes in the real exchange rate as defined in equation E.1 and the PPP real exchange rate. In general, changes in the two definitions of the real exchange rate will differ. Moreover, changes in these two definitions can even go in the opposite direction, depending on the behavior of foreign relative prices (P_t^*/P_n).

A common confusion that sometimes appears in the literature is to use the concepts of the real exchange rate and the terms of trade interchangeably. Of course, since the terms of trade are defined as the relative price of exportables to importables and the real exchange rate is defined as in equation E.1, there is no reason for them to be equivalent.

Measurement

From an empirical point of view, the problem of choosing real world counterparts of P^*_t and P_n in equation (E.1) has to be tackled. Similar problems have to be faced if a PPP definition is used or even if the real exchange rate is defined as a broad index of competitiveness of the domestic economy. Ideally, one would want to have data on tradable and nontradable prices. In almost every country, however, these prices are not available. For this reason, some proxy for this analytical concept of e should be found. Much of the discussion on the appropriate measurement of the real exchange rate has been closely related to the PPP literature on selecting price indexes to deflate the nominal rate.

Traditionally, four alternative price indexes have been suggested as possible candidates for the construction of real exchange rate indexes: (1) the consumer price indexes (CPI) at home and abroad, (2) the wholesale price indexes (WPI), (3) the GDP deflators (GD), and (4) wage rate indexes. It has also been suggested that two of these indexes should be combined or that some specific components of the CPI or WPI should be used as proxies for the prices of tradables and nontradables. In practice, however, this last procedure has the same problems as those arising from the use of more standard price indexes.

The most commonly used index of the real exchange rate in empirical and policy discussions is that constructed using CPIs as the relevant price indexes. A CPI-based exchange rate index provides a comprehensive measure of changes in competitiveness since the CPIs include a broad group of goods, including services. Another advantage is that almost every country periodically (that is, monthly) publishes data on CPI behavior. A problem with this measure, however, is that since the CPIs includes a large number of nontradable goods, it does not accurately indicate changes in the degree of competitiveness of the tradable goods sector. Also, in a number of developing countries, CPI figures can be seriously distorted by the existence of price controls on some of the goods with relatively high weights in the index.

Some authors have suggested that these problems would be solved if WPI indexes, which contain mainly tradable goods, are used in the computation of the real exchange rate. On the other hand, it has been argued that since these indexes contain highly homogeneous tradable goods whose prices tend to be equated across countries when expressed in a common currency, use of WPIs will yield real exchange rates that vary little and do not really measure actual changes in the degree of competitiveness.

One way of surmounting some of these difficulties is to use the GDP deflator in the construction of real exchange rate indexes. The GD is a genuine price index of aggregate *production* and is not subject to distortions stemming from price controls, so that a real exchange rate index computed using GDs provides a good indicator of changes in the degree of competitiveness in production. However, a crucial drawback of the GD is that for most developing countries it is available only on a yearly basis and with considerable delays. Also, as in the case of the CPI, the GD has a large component of nontradable goods.

Some authors prefer to compute the real exchange rate as a ratio of unit labor costs. This index is, in some sense, a direct measure of relative competitiveness across countries; it gives an idea of how many hours of a worker in country A can be bought with the average wage of a worker in country B. It has also been argued that relative labor costs are more stable than relative goods prices. But again, a number of analytical problems arise. An indicator based on wage rate behavior is highly sensitive to cyclical productivity changes. For this reason the IMF has constructed the so-called normalized unit labor costs indexes that correct the competitiveness measure by these productivity changes. Unfortunately, adequate data are available only for the industrial countries. Another shortcoming is that it takes into account only one factor of production; differences in the capital-labor ratio across countries may bias the index.

A problem with the traditional measures of the real exchange rate is that by using the same price indexes in the numerator and denominator—CPIs, WPIs, wage rates, or GDP deflators—they are not proxies in any clear sense for the domestic relative price of tradables to nontradables. Some authors have recently suggested constructing a real exchange rate index that has the domestic country's CPI in the denominator and the foreign country's WPI (or a weighted average of the relevant foreign WPIs) in the numerator: $e = (E\ WPI^*)/CPI$. It has been argued that since foreign (that is, U.S.) WPIs contain mainly tradable goods, they are a good proxy for the nominal price of tradables abroad. On the other hand, since the CPI has a substantial proportion of nontradables, it is an appropriate proxy for P_n.

F. *Effective Exchange Rates*
Richard J. Carroll and William F. Steel

The nominal exchange rate is an important policy tool that affects both the balance of payments and production incentives. Correct policy formulation depends on accurate evaluation of the exchange rate and its trends over time. Two such measures are both known as the *effective exchange rate* (EER), although they are quite different in concept and purpose. The traditional approach attempts to take into account the net effect of fiscal measures on the prices of imports and exports, while the multilateral version represents the exchange rate in terms of a weighted basket of currencies instead of a single currency. Both these measures, as well as the nominal (unadjusted) exchange rate, can be adjusted for relative rates of inflation in the country and abroad to convert them to real terms (see technical note E).

Tax/Subsidy Version

The traditional version of the EER measures the amount of local currency required for a given type of foreign exchange transaction, taking into account the net impact of all the measures that directly affect the prices of traded goods. These measures include tariffs, other taxes, surcharges, subsidies, and special incentives that apply to traded goods. Their net effect in lowering the cost of foreign exchange (or raising it, if taxes predominate) is termed the *effective subsidy* (S). The effective exchange rate indicates the net addition to the nominal exchange rate (E_0) resulting from the effective subsidy:

$$(F.1) \qquad\qquad EER = E_o (1 + S)$$

Taxes and subsidies often differ substantially for imports and exports, and the EER can be used to represent the true exchange rates that apply to each category or even to specific goods. (One problem is that there may be as many EERS as goods.) In most African countries, taxes on exports result in a lower effective than nominal exchange rate, while tariffs and other charges on imports raise the effective amount of local currency required above the nominal rate. The net impact of these differences can be substantial. For example, Egypt's 1962 devaluation of 23 percent in the official exchange rate resulted in depreciation of the EER by only 3 percent because import surcharges and export subsidies were simultaneously removed.

If there are no quantitative restrictions (QRS), price controls, or other measures that affect domestic prices of tradables without directly entering into the cost of imports or exports, then the EER equals the ratio of the domestic to the foreign price of whatever category of goods is being measured. When QRS on imports do exist, the excess of the actual market price over the world price multiplied by the EER for imports gives a measure of the additional scarcity premium resulting from the QRS.

Real Effective (Basket) Exchange Rate

The multilateral basket approach is the one most commonly referred to by economists as the *effective exchange rate* (EER'). It represents an average of a currency's bilateral nominal rates of exchange with other currencies, weighted by their importance in trade. It does not take into account policies that affect the domestic cost of traded goods. It is used mainly to track net movements in the exchange rate over time, adjusting for relative changes in value among foreign currencies. It therefore can most readily be calculated by using an index (E_i^*) of each nominal bilateral exchange rate (E_i) in the period (t) relative to a base period (0) and weighting each currency by its proportionate share in trade (w_i, where $\sum_i^n w_i = 1$) as follows:

(F.2)

$$E_i^* = E_{i,t}/E_{i,0}$$

$$EER'_t = w_1 E_1^* + w_2 E_2^* + \ldots + w_n E_n^* = \sum_i^n w_i E_i^*$$

The multilateral exchange rate can also be calculated separately for imports (using import weights for the w_i) and exports (using export weights).

The real effective exchange rate (REER) is used to determine whether the real value of a currency has changed relative to other currencies after adjusting for differential rates of inflation. Changes in the price index (PW_i^*) of each foreign partner from the base period to year t are weighted by the same trade shares used to calculate the EER to obtain the foreign price index, as follows:

(F.3)

$$PW_t = \sum_i^n W_i PW_{i,t}^*$$

The REER in the year t is then calculated by adjusting the nominal EER'_t for the ratio of the foreign to the domestic price index (P_t), as follows:

(F.4)

$$REER_t = EER'_t \frac{PW}{P_t}$$

A recent study of thirty-four developing countries shows that the REER and a bilateral exchange index (such as that against the U.S. dollar) can move in significantly different ways, at least since major currencies began floating in 1971.[12] With appreciation of the U.S. dollar in the 1980s, the effective and bilateral exchange rate indexes have even moved in opposite directions for many countries. Within a particular type of index, however, use of a consumer price index as against a wholesale price index made relatively little difference.

G. Direct Controls and Rent Seeking
Gerald M. Meier

When a government intervenes with physical quantitative controls over imports or the licensing of investment in capacity creation and expansion, these restrictions give rise to rents in various forms, and people often compete for these unearned profits. The imposition of a quantitative restriction on imports, for example, raises the price of imports and gives a rent to the importer who is able to secure a license for the limited quantity of imports. The importable goods can be sold at a premium as the market price becomes

---

12. Sebastian Edwards, "Trends in Real Exchange Rate Behavior in Selected Developing Countries," World Bank, Country Policy Department, Discussion Paper 1985–16, April 1985.

greater than the world price. There is a redistribution of income from consumers of the importable to the importer. The rent seekers compete in various
ways, some perfectly legal, but others involve bribery, corruption, smuggling, and black markets.

The rent-seeking activity—the use of time and resources to secure the
import license—has no social value. In the importer's attempt to capture the
restriction-created rents, there is an opportunity cost as real resources are
used in lobbying or other rent-seeking activities. As importers engage in
activities to receive the favor of government, resources that go into the rent-
seeking activities are diverted from other productive activities. Although the
rent-seeking activity is rational in terms of self-interest, it is socially wasteful.
The marginal social product of the rent-seeking activity is less than the private
marginal product and the activity should be limited.

Consider figure G.1. In the free trade situation, the price of the importable
would be P_f, and the supply of imports from abroad would be given by the
perfectly elastic supply curve S_f (a small-country case in which the country
cannot influence its terms of trade). In the free trade situation, OH would be
produced at home and HM—the excess demand—imported from abroad at
the price of P_f. If the government imposes a quantitative restriction on
imports equal to a quota in the amount HQ, then the total supply available to
the economy is composed of $S + S'_f$ where the distance between S and $S + S'_f$
is equivalent to the quota HQ at all price levels. As a result of the quota, the
price of the importable rises to P_q. Domestic producers of the competing
importable gain. The government may gain revenue if it sells import licenses

Figure G.1 *Impact of Quota on the Price of Importables*

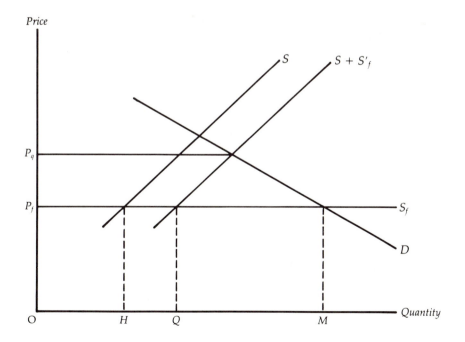

equivalent to the quota. But consumers lose through the higher price and smaller amount of consumption of the importable. It can be shown that there is a net welfare loss insofar as the decrease in consumer surplus is greater than any increase in producer surplus plus government revenue.

In addition to this net welfare loss, there is an additional loss if rent-seeking activity occurs in order to gain the import licenses and earn the premium on imports. The rent seeking entails costs in addition to the production and consumption costs of the quota. The additional production cost of the rent seeking itself may be estimated as equal to the value of the rents. Because a tariff can always be found that is equivalent to a quota in bringing about the same increase in price from P_f to P_q, the rents can be calculated as the rent per unit of imports—that is, the tariff equivalent—times the amount imported. Empirical evidence for a number of countries indicates that the value of rents associated with import licenses can be relatively large. Prevention of loss from rent seeking can be achieved only by restricting entry into the activity for which a rent has been created. But enforcement of laws against illicit forms of rent seeking itself involves costs.

Beyond rent seeking, Jagdish Bhagwati has considered directly unproductive, profit-seeking activities as a general concept that embraces a wide range of economic activities, including the subset of rent-seeking activities.[13] Other such activities include tariff evasion and tariff seeking, where lobbies seek protectionist trade tariffs. All these activities hold out the hope of making a profit but are directly unproductive—that is, they yield pecuniary returns but do not produce goods or services directly or indirectly via increased production or availability to the economy of goods that enter a utility function. These activities, however, use real resources, and as such they result in a contraction of the goods and services available to the economy.

13. Jagdish N. Bhagwati, "Directly Unproductive, Profit Seeking (DUP) Activities," *Journal of Political Economy* (October 1982).

Appendix Tables

Appendix Table A. Country Economic Indicators and Production Structure, 1986

| Country ranked by GNP per capita | Basic indicators | | | | | Structure of GDP (percent) at current factor cost | | | | | | | Trade share (percent of GDP) | |
| | | | | | | Agriculture | | Industry | | Manufacturing | Services | | | | |
	Population (millions)	GDP (millions of U.S. dollars)	GNP per capita (U.S. dollars)	Land area (thousands of square kilometers)	Life expectancy at birth	GDP	Labor force (1980)	GDP	Labor force (1980)	GDP	GDP	Labor force (1980)	Exports	Imports
1. Ethiopia	43.5	4,960	120	1,222	46	48	80	15	8	10	36	12	13	22
2. Burkina Faso	8.1	930	150	274	47	45	87	22	4	14*	33	9	16	35
3. Malawi	7.4	1,100	160	119	45	37	83	18	7	12	45	9	22	24
4. Zaire	31.7	6,020	160	2,345	52	29	72	36	13	1*	35	16	33	25
5. Guinea-Bissau	0.9	150*	170	36	39	51*	82	6*	4	1*	43*	14	6*	33*
6. Chad	5.1	910*	180*	1,284	45	46*	83	11*	5	9*	43*	12	13*	22
7. Mali	7.6	1,650	180	1,240	47	50	86	13	2	7	37	13	15	27
8. Mozambique	14.2	4,300	210	802	48	35	85	12	7	24*	53	8	3	11
9. Madagascar	10.6	2,670	230	587	53	43	81	16	6	12*	41	13	14	15
10. Uganda	15.2	3,310	230	236	48	76	86	6	4	5	18	10	12	10
11. Gambia, The	0.8	180*	230	11	43	28*	84	16*	7	9*	57*	9	19*	56*
12. Burundi	4.8	1,090	240	28	48	58	93	17	2	10	25	5	12	19
13. Tanzania	23.0	4,020	250	945	53	59	86	10	5	6	31	10	10	26
14. Togo	3.1	980	250	57	53	32	73	20	10	7	48	17	33	39
15. Niger	6.6	2,080	260	1,267	44	46	91	16	2	4	39	7	18	21
16. Guinea	6.3	1,980	270*	246	42	40	81	22	9	2	38	10	25	18
17. Benin	4.2	1,320	270	113	50	49	70	13	7	4	37	23	14	29
18. Somalia	5.5	2,320	280	638	47	58	76	9	8	6	34	16	7	19
19. Equatorial Guinea	0.4	120*	280*	28	45	45*	12	11*	6	5*	44*	22	19*	36*
20. Central African Rep.	2.7	900	290	623	50	41	72	12	6	4	47	21	20	24
21. Rwanda	6.2	1,850	290	26	48	40	93	23	3	16	37	4	12	19
22. Kenya	21.2	5,960	300	583	57	30	81	20	7	12	50	12	27	28
23. Zambia	6.9	1,660	300	753	53	11	73	48	10	20	41	17	46	43

24. Sierra Leone	3.8	1,180	310	72	41	45	70	22	14	4	33	16	13	13
25. Sudan	22.6	7,470	320	2,506	49	35	71	15	8	7	50	21	9	15
26. Comoros	0.4	160*	320	2	56	42*	85	14*	6	4*	44*	11	10*	29*
27. São Tomé and Principe	0.1	50*	340	1	65	27*	56	20*	8	9*	52*	36	41*	51*
28. Lesotho	1.6	230	370	30	55	21	86	27	4	13	52	10	12	127*
29. Ghana	13.2	5,720	390	239	54	45	56	17	18	12	39	26	10	14
30. Mauritania	1.8	750	420	1,031	47	34	69	24	9	5*	42	22	56	48
31. Senegal	6.8	3,740	420	196	47	22	81	27	6	17	51	13	28	27
32. Cape Verde	0.3	120*	460	4	65	20*	52	29*	23	5*	50*	25	3*	69*
33. Liberia	2.3	990	460	111	54	37	74	28	9	5	35	16	43	24
34. Angola	9.0	5,290*	590*	1,247	44	49*	74	17*	10	3*	33*	17	38*	20*
35. Zimbabwe	8.7	4,940	620	391	58	11	73	46	11	30	43	17	26	23
36. Nigeria	103.1	49,110	640	924	51	41	68	29	12	8	30	20	14	9
37. Swaziland	0.7	430*	690	17	55	22*	n.a.	34*	n.a.	25*	44*	n.a.	55*	81*
38. Côte d'Ivoire	10.7	7,320	730	323	52	36	65	24	8	16	40	27	40	28
39. Botswana	1.1	1,150	840	600	59	4	70	58	13	6	38	17	63	90*
40. Cameroon	10.5	11,280	910	475	56	22	70	35	8	12*	43	22	23	13
41. Djibouti	0.4	360*	970*	22	49	6*	n.a.	23*	n.a.	10*	71*	n.a.	4*	62*
42. Congo, People's Rep.	2.0	2,000	990	342	58	8	62	54	12	6	38	26	47	31
43. Mauritius	1.0	1,160	1,200	2	66	15	28	32	24	23	53	48	63	59
44. Seychelles	0.1	190*	2,730*	0.3	70	9*	n.a.	18*	n.a.	11*	73*	n.a.	11*	56*
45. Gabon	1.0	3,190	3,080	268	52	10	75	35	11	7*	55	14	37	30
Sub-Saharan Africa	424.1	165,990	370	20,895	50	36	75	25	9	10	36	16	19	18
All low-income economies	2,493.0	621,260	270	33,608	61	32	72	35	13	24	32	15	10	14
All middle-income economies	1,268.4	1,740,010	1,270	37,278	63	15	43	36	23	22	48	34	22	21

n.a. Not available.

Sources: World Bank, *World Development Report 1988* (New York: Oxford University Press). Asterisk (*) indicates data from African Development Bank, *Selected Statistics on Regional Member Countries, 1988* (data base not consistent with other figures).

Appendix Table B. *Manufacturing Value Added in Sub-Saharan Africa, 1973–85*

Group and country ranked by GNP per capita	1985 manufacturing value added		Annual growth in 1980 prices (percent)		Share in GDP at current prices (percent)		
	Per capita (U.S. dollars)	Total (millions of U.S. dollars)	1973–79	1979–85	1973	1979	1985
Low-income economies[a]	20	4,836	1.4	0.8	9.2	8.5	8.7
Ethiopia	15	639	0.6	4.4	10.0	10.7	13.5
Burkina Faso	9	69	4.2	2.5	8.9	8.1	7.0
Malawi	11	76	5.7	1.1	8.9	8.1	7.0
Zaire	2	59	−5.1	−1.0	7.6	3.8	1.2
Chad	9	46	−1.6	3.3	8.9	8.1	7.0
Mali	10	77	5.8	−0.8	8.9	8.1	7.0
Mozambique	17	240	1.9	−8.0	n.a.	n.a.	7.0
Madagascar	28	282	0.6	−0.2	13.4	12.6	12.0
Burundi	21	97	3.0	9.4	10.0	10.5	9.0
Tanzania	15	323	3.1	−3.6	11.0	12.0	5.2
Togo	16	49	0.7	0.7	8.7	7.1	7.0
Niger	9	60	5.1	−1.4	6.3	4.2	3.8
Guinea	7	44	−2.7	1.8	2.4	2.1	2.1
Benin	11	45	0.8	6.1	6.3	6.4	4.4
Somalia	27	145	5.9	−0.3	7.5	8.4	5.9
Central African Rep.	19	49	2.7	−3.0	7.8	8.3	7.6
Rwanda	53	319	5.1	10.1	4.1	12.8	18.6
Kenya	36	728	6.6	4.1	12.0	12.7	12.6
Sierra Leone	13	47	5.2	3.0	6.0	5.8	6.4
Sudan	21	469	7.3	1.6	6.9	7.0	7.2
Ghana	58	737	−3.3	−4.2	11.7	8.7	10.7
Senegal	72	474	3.9	3.4	13.9	15.4	18.5
Middle-income oil importers	110	3,691	2.6	5.9	14.7	14.2	19.9
Zambia	93	621	1.8	2.1	12.3	18.3	27.7
Lesotho	18	28	6.6	8.3	5.1	5.4	10.7
Mauritania	41	69	10.4	10.9	4.8	7.0	10.0
Liberia	24	54	9.7	−8.0	5.0	8.6	4.9
Zimbabwe	173	1,456	−1.0	4.4	23.7	23.6	29.0
Swaziland	35	27	3.8	6.0	8.9	8.1	7.0
Côte d'Ivoire	118	1,189	7.3	12.1	12.7	10.6	17.0
Botswana	46	49	19.0	0.9	5.9	8.3	6.1
Mauritius	194	198	7.3	4.5	15.0	14.9	18.7
Middle-income oil exporters	103	11,559	16.3	6.9	5.3	9.5	12.7
Nigeria	100	9,927	17.5	5.6	4.5	9.5	13.0
Cameroon	98	998	8.0	17.4	10.8	8.6	11.8
Congo, People's Rep.	68	128	6.0	9.0	7.1	8.4	5.9
Gabon	508	506	15.4	9.8	8.3	10.6	13.8
Sub-Saharan Africa	53	20,086	7.2	4.8	8.7	9.7	12.2
Selected other countries	133	138,314	7.2	2.7	21.9	24.0	23.0
India	43	32,760	4.7	4.9	14.1	17.8	16.6
Philippines	148	8,089	5.6	−0.5	25.2	24.0	24.7
Colombia	224	6,364	0.5	4.6	19.6	16.9	18.6
Brazil	451	61,171	7.0	0.4	29.3	27.4	27.8
Malaysia	370	5,757	10.4	5.9	15.0	19.4	18.4
Korea, Rep. of	589	24,172	16.4	6.7	25.7	28.8	28.0

n.a. Not available.   a. Mozambique is not included in the group average.
Source: World Bank, Industry Development Division, industry data base.

Selected Bibliography

General Economic Environment

Four World Bank reports on the need for domestic policy reforms to accelerate growth have been particularly influential: *Accelerated Development in Sub-Saharan Africa: An Agenda for Action* (1981); *Sub-Saharan Africa: Progress Report on Development Prospects and Programs* (1983); *Toward Sustained Development in Sub-Saharan Africa: A Joint Program of Action* (1984); and *Financing Adjustment with Growth in Sub-Saharan Africa, 1986–1990* (1986). Washington, D.C.: World Bank.

Acharya, Shankar N. "Perspectives and Problems of Development in Sub-Saharan Africa." *World Development,* vol. 9 (1981): 134–37.

Adedeji, Adebayo, and Timothy M. Shaw. *Economic Crisis in Africa: African Perspectives on Development Problems and Potentials.* Boulder, Colo.: Lynne Rienner, 1986.

Bates, Robert H. *Rural Responses to Industrialization: A Study of Village Zambia.* New Haven, Conn.: Yale University Press, 1976.

Bienefeld, Manfred. "The Lessons of Africa's Industrial Failure." *IDS Bulletin 16, 3* (July 1985): 69–77.

Browne, Robert S., and Robert Cummings. *The Lagos Plan of Action vs. the Berg Report: Contemporary Issues in African Economic Development.* Lawrenceville, Va.: Brunswick, 1984.

Chuta, Enyinna, and Carl Liedholm. "Rural Small-Scale Industry: Empirical Evidence and Policy Issues." In Carl K. Eicher and John M. Staatz, eds., *Agricultural Development in the Third World.* Baltimore, Md.: Johns Hopkins University Press, 1984.

Cook, Gillian Patricia. *Development in Africa South of the Sahara, 1970–1980.* Capetown: University of Capetown Libraries, 1984.

DeVries, Barend A. "Industrial Policy in Small Developing Countries." *Finance & Development,* vol. 21, no. 2 (1984).

Economic Commission for Africa. *ECA and Africa's Development 1983–2000.* Addis Ababa, April 1983.

———. *Industrial Growth in Africa.* New York: United Nations, 1963.

Ewing, A. F. *Industry in Africa.* London: Oxford University Press, 1968.

Fransman, Martin, ed. *Industry and Accumulation in Africa.* London: Heinemann, 1982.

Helleiner, Gerald K. "The IMF and Africa in the 1980s." *Princeton Essays in International Finance*, no. 152 (July 1983).

Hyden, Goran. *No Short Cuts to Progress: African Development Management in Perspective.* Berkeley: University of California Press, 1983.

Kamarck, Andrew M. *The Economics of African Development.* London: Pall Mall, 1967.

Khane, Abd-El Rahman. "The Importance of the External Environment for Industrial Development in Developing Countries." *Industry and Development*, vol. 12 (1984): 1–7.

Killick, Tony. "Trends in Development Economics and their Relevance to Africa." *Journal of Modern African Studies*, vol. 18, no. 3 (1980): 367–86.

Lancaster, Carol, and John Williamson, eds. *African Debt and Financing.* Washington, D.C.: Institute for International Economics, 1986.

Lubeck, Paul M., ed. *The African Bourgeoisie: Capitalist Development in Nigeria, Kenya, and the Ivory Coast.* Boulder, Colo.: Lynne Rienner, 1987.

Luke, David F., and Timothy Shaw, eds. *Continental Crisis: The Lagos Plan of Action and Africa's Future.* Lanham, Md.: University Press of America, 1984.

Onwuka, Ralph, O. Abesunrin, and D. N. Shista. *African Development: The OAU/ECA Lagos Plan of Action and Beyond.* Lawrenceville, Va.: Brunswick, 1985.

Organisation of African Unity. *Lagos Plan of Action for the Economic Development of Africa, 1980–2000.* Geneva: International Institute for Labour Studies, 1982.

Poor Countries of Africa: Structural Problems and Development Crisis. Occasional Papers of the German Development Institute, no. 71. Berlin, 1982.

Rajana, Cecil. "Third World Industrialisation: Industrial Cooperation under the Lomé Convention." *Journal of African Studies*, vol. 10, no. 2 (Summer 1983): 30–49.

Ravenhill, John, ed. *Africa in Economic Crisis.* New York: Columbia University Press, 1986.

Roemer, Michael. "Economic Development in Africa: Performance since Independence and a Strategy for the Future." *Daedalus*, vol. 3, no. 2 (Spring 1982): 125–48.

Rose, Tore, ed. *Crisis and Recovery in Sub-Saharan Africa.* Paris: Organisation for Economic Co-operation and Development, 1987.

United Nations Industrial Development Organisation. "The Changing Role of Manufacturing in African Economic Development: Trends, Prospects and Issues." *Industry Development*, vol. 8 (1983): 1–15.

Wheeler, David. "Sources of Stagnation in Sub-Saharan Africa." *World Development*, vol. 12, no. 1 (January 1984): 1–23.

Country Experience

Adeboye, T. O. "Nigeria's Industrialization: A Reconsideration of Strategy and Policy Options." *Research for Development*, vol. 1, no. 1 (January 1981): 53–68.

Andrea, Gunilla. *Industry in Ghana.* Uppsala: Scandinavian Institute of African Studies, 1981.

Burrows, John. *Kenya: Into the Second Decade: Report of a Mission Sent to Kenya by the World Bank.* Baltimore, Md.: Johns Hopkins University Press, 1975.

Esseks, John D. "Government and Indigenous Private Enterpise in Ghana." *Journal of Modern African Studies*, vol. 9, no. 1 (1971): 11–25.

Ewusi, Kodwo. *Industrialization, Employment Generation and Income Distribution in Ghana, 1950–1980.* Accra: Adwensa, 1986.

Frank, Charles R. *Employment Objectives and Economic Development in Africa with Special Reference to Nigeria.* New Haven, Conn.: Economic Growth Center, Yale University, 1967.

Fransman, Martin. *The Capital Goods Industry in Sub-Saharan Africa.* Edinburgh: Centre of African Studies, Edinburgh University, 1985.

Kilby, Peter. *Industrialization in an Open Economy: Nigeria, 1945–66.* Cambridge: Cambridge University Press, 1969.

Lewis, Arthur W. "Reports on Industrialization and the Gold Coast." Accra: Government Printing Office, 1953.

Odufalu, J. O. "Indigenous Enterprise in Nigerian Manufacturing." *Journal of Modern African Studies,* vol. 9, no. 4 (1971): 593–607.

Onyenelukwe, J. O. C. *Industrialization in West Africa.* London: Croom Helm, 1984.

Page, John M. Jr. "Technical Efficiency and Economic Performance: Some Evidence from Ghana." *Oxford Economic Papers,* vol. 23, no. 2 (July 1980): 319–39.

Pearson, D. S. *Industrial Development in East Africa.* Nairobi: Oxford University Press, 1969.

Roemer, Michael. "Ghana, 1950–1980: Missed Opportunities." In Arnold C. Harberger, ed., *World Economic Growth.* San Francisco: ICS Press, 1984.

Rweyemamu, Justinian F. "The Historical and Institutional Setting of Tanzanian Industry." In Kwan Kim and others, eds., *Papers on the Political Economy of Tanzania.* London: Heinemann, 1979.

Schätzl, Ludwig H. *Industrialization in Nigeria.* Munich: Weltforum Verlag, 1973.

Teriba, O. *The Structure of Manufacturing Industry in Nigeria.* Ibadan, Nigeria: Ibadan University Press, 1981.

Teriba, O., and M. O. Kayode, eds. *Industrial Development in Nigeria: Patterns, Problems, and Prospects.* Ibadan, Nigeria: Ibadan University Press, 1981.

Wangwe, Samuel M. "Excess Capacity in Manufacturing Industry: A Case Study of Selected Firms in Tanzania." In Kwan Kim and others, eds., *Papers on the Political Economy of Tanzania.* London: Heinemann, 1979.

———. "Industrialization and Resource Allocation in a Developing Country: The Case of Recent Experiences in Tanzania." *World Development* vol. 11, no. 6 (1983): 483–92.

Young, Alistair. *Industrial Diversification in Zambia.* New York: Praeger, 1973.

Critique of Neoclassical Theory

Addo, Herb, A. Samir, and United Nations University. *Transforming the World Economy: Nine Critical Essays on the New International Economic Order.* London: Hodder and Stoughton, 1984.

Amin, Samir. *Class and Nation, Historically and in the Current Crisis.* New York: Monthly Review Press, 1980.

———. *Dynamics of Global Crisis.* New York: Monthly Review Press, 1982.

———. *Neo-colonialism in West Africa.* Harmondsworth, Eng.: Penguin, 1973.

———. *Unequal Development: An Essay on the Social Formations of Peripheral Capitalism.* New York: Monthly Review Press, 1976.

Arrighi, Giovanni, and John S. Saul. *Essays on the Political Economy of Africa.* New York: Monthly Review Press, 1973.

Braud, Oscar, R. Brown, and P. Wright. *International Trade and Imperialism*. Atlantic Highlands, N.J.: Humanities Press, 1984.

Cruise O'Brien, Rita. *Political Economy of Underdevelopment Dependence in Senegal*. Beverly Hills, Calif.: Sage, 1979.

Emmanuel, Arghiri. *Unequal Exchange: A Study of the Imperialism of Trade*. New York: Monthly Review Press, 1972.

Griffin, Keith, and John Gurley. "Radical Analyses of Imperialism, the Third World, and the Transition to Socialism: A Survey Article." *Journal of Economic Literature*, vol. 23, no. 3 (1985): 1089–1143.

Rodney, Walter. *How Europe Underdeveloped Africa*. Harare: Zimbabwe Publishing House, 1972.

Roemer, Michael. "Dependence and Industrialization Strategies." *World Development*, vol. 9, no. 5 (May 1981): 429–34.

Thomas, Clive Y. *Dependence and Transformation: The Economics of the Transition to Socialism*. New York: Monthly Review Press, 1974.

Entrepreneurship

Adamu, So. "A Statistical Analysis of Some Determinants of Entrepreneurial Success: A Nigerian Case Study." *Nigerian Journal of Economics and Social Sciences*, vol. 11, no. 1 (1969): 29–41.

Bennell, P. "Industrial Class Formation in Ghana: Some Empirical Observations." *Development and Change*, vol. 15, no. 4 (1984): 593–612.

Harris, John R. "Nigerian Entrepreneurship in Industry." In Carl Eicher and Carl Liedholm, eds., *Growth and Development of the Nigerian Economy*. Lansing: Michigan State University, 1970.

Hart, Keith. "Small-Scale Entrepreneurs in Ghana and Development Planning." *Journal of Development Studies*, vol. 6, no. 2 (1970): 104–20.

Kilby, Peter, ed. *Entrepreneurship and Economic Development*. New York: Free Press, 1971.

Lawson, Rowena M. *African Entrepreneurship and Economic Growth*. Accra: Ghana University Press, 1974.

McClelland, D. C., and O. G. Winter. *Motivating Economic Achievement*. New York: Free Press, 1969.

Marris, Peter, and Anthony Somerset. *The African Entrepreneur*. New York: Africana, 1971.

Nafziger, E. Wayne, "The Relationship between Education and Entrepreneurship in Nigeria." *Journal of Developing Areas*. vol. 4, no. 4 (1970): 349–60.

Omal, W. J. "Entrepreneurship in Economic Theory." *American Economic Review, Papers and Proceedings*, vol. 58 (1968): 64–71.

Papanek, G. "The Development of Entrepreneurship." *American Economic Review*, vol. 52, no. 1 (1962): 46–58.

Foreign Investment and Multinationals

Dunning, John, ed. *International Investment*. New York: Penguin, 1972.

Kaplinsky, Raphael, ed. *Readings on the Multinational Corporation in Kenya*. Nairobi: Oxford University Press, 1978.

Schatz, Sayre P. *Nigerian Capitalism.* Berkeley: University of California Press, 1977.

Solomon, Robert F., and David J. C. Forsyth. "Restrictions on Foreign Ownership of Manufacturing Industry in a Less Developed Country: The Case of Ghana." *Journal of Developing Areas,* vol. 12, no. 3 (April 1978): 281–96.

Industrial Incentives and Controls

Choksi, Armeane M. *State Intervention in the Industrialization of Developing Countries: Selected Issues.* World Bank Staff Working Paper 341. Washington, D.C., 1979.

Guisinger, Stephen E. "Direct Controls on the Private Sector." In John Cody, Helen Hughes, David Wall, eds., *Policies for Industrial Progress in Developing Countries.* New York: Oxford University Press, 1980.

Ingram, William D., and Scott R. Pearson. "The Impact of Investment Concessions on the Profitability of Selected Firms in Ghana." *Economic Development and Cultural Change,* vol. 29, no. 4 (July 1981): 831–39.

Martin, John P., and John M. Page, Jr. "The Impact of Subsidies on X-Efficiency in LDC Industry: Theory and an Empirical Test." *Review of Economics and Statistics,* vol. 65, no. 4 (1983): 608–17.

Usher, Dan. "The Economics of Tax Incentives to Encourage Investment in Less Developed Countries." *Journal of Development Economics,* vol. 4, no. 2 (June 1977): 119–40.

Labor

Alfthan, Torkel. "Industrialization in the Ivory Coast: Impact on Employment and Basic Needs Satisfaction." *International Labour Review,* vol. 126, no. 6 (1982): 761–74.

Bloch, Peter C. "Wage Policy, Wage Structure and Employment in the Public Sector of Senegal." Discussion Paper 1985–41. World Bank, Country Policy Department, Washington, D.C., May 1985.

Boagye, A. A. "Pattern of Industrialization and Impact on Employment and Incomes in Ghana." *Jobs and Skills Program for Africa (JASPA) Working Paper.* Addis Ababa: International Labour Organization, 1983.

Fallon, Peter R. "The Labor Market in Kenya: Recent Evidence." Report ORD-156. World Bank, Development Research Department, Labor Market Division, Washington, D.C., October 1985.

International Labour Organisation. *Employment, Incomes and Equality: A Strategy for Increasing Productive Employment in Kenya.* Geneva, 1972.

Meesook, Oey A., and others. "Wage Policy and the Structure of Wages and Employment in Zambia." Discussion Paper 1986-1. World Bank, Country Policy Department, Washington, D.C., January 1986.

Small-Scale Industry

Anderson, Dennis. "Small Industry in Developing Countries: A Discussion of Issues." *World Development,* vol. 10, no. 11 (November 1982): 913–48.

Bosa, George R. *The Financing of Small-Scale Enterprises in Uganda.* Nairobi: Oxford University Press, 1969.

Child, Frank C. *Small-Scale Rural Industry in Kenya.* African Studies Center Occasional Paper 17. Los Angeles: University of California, 1977.

Chuta, Enyinna, and Carl Liedholm. "The Economics of Rural and Urban Small-Scale Industries in Sierra Leone." African Rural Economy Paper 14. East Lansing: Department of Agricultural Economics, Michigan State University, 1976.

———. "Rural Small-Scale Industry: Empirical Evidence and Policy Issues." In Carl K. Eicher and John M. Staatz, eds., *Agricultural Development in the Third World*. Baltimore, Md.: Johns Hopkins University Press, 1984.

Ettema, Wim. "Small-Scale Industry in Malawi." *Journal of Modern African Studies*, vol. 22, no. 3 (1984): 487–510.

Harper, Malcolm. *Small Business in the Third World*. New York: Wiley, 1984.

Hawbaker, George, and Howard H. Turner. *Developing Small Industries: A Case Study of AID Assistance in Nigeria, 1962–71*. Washington, D.C.: U.S. Agency for International Development, 1972.

Kilby, Peter. *The Development of Small Industry in Eastern Nigeria*. Washington, D.C.: U.S. Agency for International Development, March 1962.

———. "Small-Scale Industry in Kenya." Employment and Rural Development Study 69. World Bank, Development Economics Department, Washington, D.C., 1981.

Little, I. M. D. "Small Manufacturing Enterprises in Developing Countries." *World Bank Economic Review*, vol. 1, no. 2 (January 1987): 203–35.

Marsden, Keith. "Creating the Right Environment for Small Firms." *Finance & Development*, vol. 18, no. 4 (December 1981): 33–36.

Phillips, D. A. "Industrialization in Tanzania: The Case of Small-Scale Production." In Kwan Kim and others, eds., *Papers on the Political Economy of Tanzania*. London: Heinemann, 1979.

Staley, Eugene, and Richard Morse. *Modern Small Industry for Developing Countries*. New York: McGraw-Hill, 1965.

Steel, William F. *Small-Scale Employment and Production in Developing Countries: Evidence from Ghana*. New York: Praeger, 1977.

United Nations. Economic Commission for Africa/UNIDO *Bulletin of Small-Scale Industry in Africa*, January 1, 1976.

State-Owned Enterprises

Ayub, Mahmood A., and Sven O. Hegstad. "Management of Public Industrial Enterprises." *World Bank Research Observer*, vol. 2, no. 1 (January 1987): 79–101.

Bhatt, V. V. "Institutional Framework and Public Enterprise Performance." *World Development*, vol. 12, no. 7 (July 1984): 713–21.

Gantt, A., and G. Dutto. "Financial Performance of Government-Owned Corporations in Less Developed Countries." *International Monetary Fund Staff Papers*, vol. 25 (1968): 102–42.

Gordon, David. *Development Finance Companies, State and Privately Owned: A Review*. World Bank Staff Working Paper 578. Washington, D.C., 1983.

Jones, Leroy P. "Definition and Taxonomy of Public Enterprise." In F. Fernandes, ed., *Seeking the Personality of the Public Enterprise*. Vienna: United Nations Industrial Development Organisation, 1981.

Killick, Tony. "The Role of the Public Sector in the Industrialization of African Developing Countries." *Industry and Development*, vol. 7 (April 1983): 47–88.

Sheahan, John. *Differences in the Roles and Consequences of Public Enterprise in Developing Countries.* Research Memorandum Series. Williamstown, Mass.: Williams College, 1981.

————. "Public Enterprise in Developing Countries." In William G. Shepherd, ed., *Public Enterprise.* Lexington, Mass.: Lexington Books, 1976.

Shirley, Mary M. *Managing State-Owned Enterprises.* World Bank Staff Working Paper 577. Washington, D.C., 1983.

United Nations Industrial Development Organisation. *The Changing Role of the Public Industrial Sector in Development.* Vienna, 1983.

Technology

Bhalla, A. S., ed. *Technology and Employment in Industry: A Case Study Approach.* Geneva: International Labour Office, 1975.

Byerlee, Derek, and others. "Employment-Output Conflicts, Factor Price Distortions and Choice of Technique: Empirical Results from Sierra Leone." *Economic Development and Cultural Change,* vol. 31, no. 2 (1983): 315–36.

Eckaus, Richard S. *Appropriate Technology for Developing Countries.* Washington, D.C.: National Academy of Sciences, 1978.

Fransman, Martin. "Conceptualising Technical Change in the Third World in the 1980s: An Interpretive Survey." *Journal of Development Studies,* vol. 21, no. 4 (July 1985): 572–652.

Marsden, Keith. "Progressive Technologies for Developing Countries." *International Labour Review,* vol. 101, no. 5 (May 1970): 475–502.

Moore, Frederick T. *Technological Change and Industrial Development.* World Bank Staff Working Paper 613. Washington, D.C., 1983.

Pack, Howard. "The Employment-Output Tradeoff in LDCs: A Microeconomic Approach." *Oxford Economic Papers,* vol. 26, no. 3 (1974): 388–404.

Pack, Howard, and Larry E. Westphal. "Industrial Strategy and Technological Change: Theory versus Reality." *Journal of Development Economics,* vol. 22 (1986): 87–128.

Roemer, Michael, Gene M. Tidrick, and David Williams. "The Range of Strategic Choice in Tanzanian Industry." *Journal of Development Economics,* vol. 3, no. 3 (September 1976): 257–75.

Stewart, Frances. "Choice of Technique in Developing Countries." *Journal of Development Studies,* vol. 9 (1972): 99–121.

————. "Manufacture of Cement Blocks in Kenya." In A. S. Bhalla, ed., *Technology and Employment in Industry.* Geneva: International Labour Office, 1975.

————. *Technology and Underdevelopment.* Boulder, Colo.: Westview, 1977.

Svejnar, E. "Technology and Factor Proportions in Investment Decisions: African Aspects." *East African Economic Review,* vol. 7, no. 1 (1975): 1–24.

Symposium on Technological Change and Industrial Development. *Journal of Development Economics,* vol. 16, nos. 1–2 (September/October 1984).

United Nations Industrial Development Organisation. *Report on the Identification and Application of Relevant New Technologies for the Implementation of the Programme for the Industrial Development Decade for Africa.* Vienna, 1984.

White, Lawrence J. "Appropriate Factor Proportions for Manufacturing in Less Developed Countries: A Survey of the Evidence." *Economic Development and Cultural Change,* vol. 27, no. 1 (1978): 27–59.

Trade Strategy

Balassa, Bela. "Policy Responses to External Shocks in Sub-Saharan African Countries." *Journal of Policy Modeling*, vol. 5, no. 1 (March 1983): 75–105.

———. *The Structure of Protection in Developing Countries*. Baltimore, Md.: Johns Hopkins University Press, 1971.

Bell, Martin, and others. "Assessing the Performance of Infant Industries." *Journal of Development Economics*, vol. 16, nos. 1–2 (1984): 101–28.

Bhagwati, Jagdish N. "Directly Unproductive, Profit-Seeking (DUP) Activities." *Journal of Political Economy*, vol. 90, no. 5 (October 1982): 988–1002.

———. *Foreign Trade Regimes and Economic Development*. Vol. 11, *Anatomy and Consequences of Exchange Control Regimes*. Cambridge, Mass.: Ballinger, 1978.

Corden, W. M. "Trade Policies." In John Cody, Helen Hughes, David Wall, eds., *Policies for Industrial Progress in Developing Countries*. New York: Oxford University Press, 1980.

Helleiner, Gerald K. "Outward Orientation, Import Instability and African Economic Growth: An Empirical Investigation." In Sanjaya Lall and Frances Stewart, eds., *Theory and Reality in Development: Essays in Honor of Paul Streeten*. New York: St. Martin's Press, 1985.

Krueger, Anne O. *Foreign Trade Regimes and Economic Development*. Vol. 10, *Liberalization Attempts and Consequences*. Cambridge, Mass.: Ballinger, 1977.

———. *Liberalization Attempts and Consequences*. Studies in International Economic Relations. Cambridge, Mass.: Ballinger, 1978.

———. The Political Economy of the Rent-Seeking Society." *American Economic Review*, vol. 64, no. 3 (June 1974): 291–303.

Leith, J. Clark. *Foreign Trade Regimes and Economic Development: Ghana*. New York: Columbia University Press, 1974.

Lewis, Stephen R., Jr. "Africa's Development and the World Economy." *Research Memorandum Series*, Memorandum 103. Williamstown, Mass.: Center for Development Economics, Williams College, 1985.

Little, Ian, Tibor Scitovsky, and Maurice Scott. *Industry and Trade in Some Developing Countries*. Paris: Oxford University Press, 1970.

Oyejide, T. Ademola. *Tariff Policy and Industrialization in Nigeria*. Ibadan: Ibadan University Press, 1973.

Ridler, Neil B. "Comparative Advantage as a Development Model: The Ivory Coast." *Journal of Modern African Studies*, vol. 23, no. 3 (1985): 407–17.

Rwegasira, Delphin G. *Exchange Rates and the Management of the External Sector in Sub-Saharan Africa*. African Development Bank, Research Paper 3. Abidjan, April 1984.

Semboja, Joseph. "Effective Rate of Protection and Industrialization in Tanzania." University of Dar es Salaam Economic Research Bureau Paper 78.4, Dar es Salaam, 1978.

Steel, William F. "Import Substitution and Excess Capacity in Ghana." *Oxford Economic Papers*, vol. 24, no. 2 (July 1972): 212–40.

Index

African Common Market, 35
African Economic Community, 35
"Africa's Priority Programme for Economic Recovery, 1986–90" (OAU), 3, 123
Africa (Sub-Saharan). *See names of specific African countries*
Agricultural equipment, 35–36
Agriculture: development strategy and, 30, 31; in Ghana, 11, 75; incentives and, 127–28; industrial development and, 11; industrial restructing and, 12; labor force in, 6; performance of, 87; policies on, 10, 14, 85, 135; price adjustments in, 133; protection and, 15; in Zambia, 157
Agroprocessing, 12, 115–17
Amin, Samir, 106
Angola, 83, 85
Arusha Declaration, 55

Balance of payments, 14, 44, 112, 121; correcting overvalued currencies and, 125; in Côte d'Ivoire, 198; in Ghana, 71; in Zambia, 152, 153
Balassa, Bela, 41, 179
Barriers to entry, 39, 44; private sector and, 163–64
Benin, 10, 179, 221, 223, 237
Bergsman, Joel, 171–72
Bhagwati, Jagdish, 274
Black market, 17, 157; for foreign currency, 114
Borrowing. *See* Loans
Botswana, 81, 109, 111, 167, 179, 187, 211
Brazil, 171, 172
British Leyland, 169
Burkina Faso, 95, 167, 179, 187, 198, 201, 207
Burundi, 211
Business environment: domestic competition and, 168–72; industrial reform and, 19–21; investment incentives and, 176–80; investment promotion in Malawi and, 182–85; price control removal in Ghana and, 180–82; regulation and, 163–68; taxation and, 165–66, 172–76

Cameroon, 8, 26, 179, 211, 219, 236
Canada, 252
Capacity: excess, 12, 86–90; protection for investment in industrial, 7; underutilization of, 3
Capacity utilization: in Africa, 87–88; foreign exchange allocation and, 95; manufacturing in Ghana and, 72; in Nigeria and, 142; Zambian manufacturing and, 63
Capital: accumulation, 7; industrialization constraints and, 27–28; intensity, 88; liberalization and, 122; markets, 190–91, 254; perceived lack of, 8; Senegalese manufacturing and, 67; small-scale industry and, 188, 194–97; Zambia and deepening of, 64
Capital goods, 34, 44, 49, 169; Zambia and, 61; Zimbabwe and, 51
Capital Investment Act (Ghana), 74
Capital-labor ratios, 215
Capital-output ratio, 58, 63
Central planning, 37, 108
Chad, 95
Colonialism, 6–7, 20, 32; economic dualism and, 77
Comparative advantage, 247–52
Competition, 12, 37, 94, 103, 112, 193; business environment and domestic, 168–72; in Ethiopia, 237; in Ivorian industry, 152; public sector and, 239–40; restructuring and, 99; in Senegal, 70; technology and, 24

South Korea. *See* Korea, Republic of
Spare parts, 51, 71, 141
Specialization, 97
Subregional markets, agroprocessing and, 117
Subsectoral shifts: adjustment policy and, 14; restructuring and, 12–13
Subsidies, 3, 91, 241; in Côte d'Ivoire, 150–51, 152; credit and, 192, 210; effective exchange rate and, 271; entrepreneurship and, 206–07; interest rates and, 191; manufactured exports and, 111; price, 116; protection and, 16; public sector and, 90, 211; in Zambia, 157
Sudan, 53, 83, 84, 86, 179, 221, 223; corporate taxation in, 165; domestic competition in, 168; private sector in, 164
Supply: demand linkages and, 4; small-scale industry and, 189–90, 192–93
Supply-side policies (small-scale enterprises), 96
Szereszewski, Robert, 73

Taiwan, 109
Tanzania, 7, 9, 10, 83, 84, 86, 108, 179, 222; entitlement schemes in, 111; import substitution in, 28; manufacturing in, 53–60; productivity in, 88; public sector in, 89, 211, 220; technological choice in, 215, 216, 217
Tariff adjustment in Côte d'Ivoire, 16
Tariff barriers, 9; excessive protection and, 113
Tariffs, 217, 274; in Côte d'Ivoire, 150–51, 152; investment codes and, 177–78; liberalization and, 119; in Mauritius, 146; in Nigeria, 139; in Senegal, 68; in Zambia, 153, 154
Tax: evasion, 176; holidays, 178; incentives, 31, 32, 79
Taxation, 135, 194; business environment and, 165–66, 172–76; deficits and, 211; effective exchange rate and, 271; exports and, 36, 85, 105, 145–46; imports and, 113
Technical assistance, 192, 205
Technological change, 212–15
Technological choice, 214; inappropriate, 215–18
Technology, 7, 55, 93; industrialization and, 24; self-reliance analysis and, 33, 34; small-scale industry and, 192; transfer, 96
Thailand, 215
Thomas, Clive, 107
Togo, 14, 123, 179, 181, 202, 211, 221, 236, 237
Total factor production (TFP), 64, 261–66
Trade liberalization. *See* Liberalization (trade)
Trade policies: ideal view of industrialization and, 95; in Senegal, 68
Training, 96; on-the-job, 203; small-scale industry and, 192
Transnationals, 44, 59, 80, 214, 215
Transport, 39, 88, 91, 94, 112; African industri-

alization and, 6; cost information and, 41; equipment, 158; of food crops, 42

Uganda, 84, 86
Unemployment, 118, 121
United Kingdom, 144, 145
United States, protection in, 252
Upper Volta (Burkina Faso), 95, 167, 179, 187, 198, 201, 207
Urban-rural bias, 127–28
Urban sector: migration into, 81; price-setting games and, 171; wages in, 128, 198

Value added, 12, 87, 174; Africa and, 80; in Côte d'Ivoire, 150; efficiency concept and, 257; in Mauritius, 143; productivity and, 88; public sector and, 89; resource-based industrialization and, 39; small-scale sector and, 187; Zambian manufacturing and, 63

Wages, 21, 29, 114, 115, 167, 211; African (compared with Asian), 59; employment incentives and, 179; industrialization constraints and, 27; small-scale sector and, 197–98, 199–201; urban, 128, 198; Zambian manufacturing, 63
West African Economic Community, 68, 147
West African Monetary Union (UMOA), 149
Williamson, John, 267
Worker layoffs, 4, 21, 167; public sector overstaffing and, 18, 223. *See also* Employment
World Bank, 31, 99, 155; adjustment lending, 128–38; Special Facility for Africa, 132

Zaire, 10, 14, 15, 83, 86, 123, 198, 236; copper production and restructuring in, 102; corporate taxation in, 165, 166; exchange rate in, 125; private firm takeover in, 20; private sector in, 164; public sector in, 211, 221
Zambia, 7, 10, 14, 18, 20, 23, 24, 25, 26, 83, 84, 86, 88, 109, 123, 179, 219, 223; adjustment program in, 152–57, 159; agriculture in, 157; balance of payments and, 152, 153; capacity utilization and, 87; capital in, 64, 195; capital goods in, 61; credit in, 155–57; corporate taxation in, 165; dependence and, 107; employment in, 61–63; entitlement schemes and, 111; exchange rate in, 125–26, 152, 153, 159; exports and, 65–66; government interference and, 13; GDP in, 60, 61; imports and, 65, 154, 155, 158; incentives in, 152, 154; intermediate goods in, 61; manufacturing in, 53–66, 153; productivity and, 88; public sector and, 89, 241, 243, 245; resource allocation and, 17; subsidies in, 157; tariffs in, 153, 154
Zimbabwe, 6, 83, 84, 86, 96, 222; capital goods in, 51; credit and, 112; export subsidies and, 111